D1452730

THE AUDIENCIA
IN THE
SPANISH COLONIES

AS ILLUSTRATED BY THE
AUDIENCIA OF MANILLA

BY

CHARLES HENRY CUNNINGHAM, Ph.D.

GORDIAN PRESS

NEW YORK

1971

Originally Published 1919
Reprinted 1971

Library of Congress Catalog Card Number 72-131250
SBN 87752-130-1

CONTENTS

PREFACE

It seems proper to say at the outset that a general study of the Spanish colonial system convinced me of the need of an extended investigation of the audiencia, which was the central institution in the colonies. It was, however, the circumstance of my being situated in Manila for some years and thus having at my disposal the original documents bearing upon the history of the audiencia which was situated there that led me to study this particular tribunal. At first sight it may appear that something of direct applicability to Spanish-American conditions, which would have been gained by the study of the Audiencia of Mexico, or Guadalajara, or Lima, has thus been lost. Nevertheless, if it is borne in mind that the audiencia system was common to all the Spanish colonies, and that the laws by which it was constituted and regulated applied to the different political divisions of America as to the Philippines, the assumption will not seem wholly unjustified that the Audiencia of Manila may be taken as a typical legal and political institution.

A large part of the time expended in collecting the materials upon which this book is based was spent in the various depositories in Manila. The most notable group of documents there is to be found in the Philippines Library, and it is with pleasure that I express here my obligations to Dr. James Alexander Robertson, the librarian; for not only did Dr. Robertson place at my disposal all the resources of the library, but he contributed generously from his adequate knowledge of Philippine history and afforded continual inspiration during the course of my labors in Manila. I am also deeply conscious of the assistance so kindly rendered by Don Manuel Artigas, chief of the Division of Filipiniana, and by Don Manuel Yriarte of the Philippine Archive.

Preface

In addition to research in the Philippines Library, the Philippine Archive, and the Audiencia Records in Manila approximately three years have been spent in the archives of Spain. The main centre of my work, of course, has been the Archive of the Indies at Seville, where I was given free access to all the available materials, and every facility was extended to me by the chief of the archive, Don Pedro Torres Lanzas, and by his obliging assistants. I am also indebted for many courtesies to Don Miguel Gómez de Campillo of the National Historical Archive at Madrid, and to Don Juan Montero, chief of the archive at Simancas.

The object of this prefatory note would not be achieved if I failed to express adequately my acknowledgment to my teacher and friend Professor Frederick J. Teggart, of the University of California. His inspiration led me to appreciate the importance of institutional studies; his continued encouragement has helped me over the hard places in the work; and I am conscious now of the extent to which he has sought, by vigilant criticism, to guard me against precipitateness. I am indebted to Professor Herbert Bolton for valuable aid and for advice in the final presentation of the manuscript; to Dr. Charles Wilson Hackett for a systematic revision of the Bibliography and of the footnotes; to Professor E. C. Barker for advice and assistance; to Professor W. R. Shepherd and Professor Francis S. Philbrick for their criticism of portions of this book; and to Messrs. A. H. Allen and Morse A. Cartwright of the University of California Press for their many manifestations of courtesy and patience in the supervision of its publication. To Professor H. Morse Stephens of the University of California and to the generous order of the Native Sons of the Golden West I am indebted for the rare opportunity of two years of foreign residence and research in the various archives of Spain.

Finally, my greatest indebtedness is to my wife, who has

cheerfully given up the pleasures and conveniences of life among friends in home surroundings to accompany me to less pleasant places, in order that I might succeed in the work which I have undertaken.

CHARLES H. CUNNINGHAM.

INTRODUCTION

The audiencia was primarily a judicial tribunal. It has been considered almost entirely as such by these modern historical writers who have referred to it in passing. Its legislative, administrative, executive, and ecclesiastical functions have received little attention. This may be owing to the fact that little or no documentary study of the audiencia has heretofore been made. A great deal of attention has been devoted in this book to the non-judicial functions of the audiencia. A chapter has been given, indeed, to its purely judicial activities, but the chief purpose of this investigation has been to show that the audiencia was more than a court of justice, and to bring out its governmental and ecclesiastical functions.

This study will be confined, chronologically, to the period extending from the time of the creation of the audiencia, at the close of the sixteenth century, to the end of the eighteenth. This limitation is advisable, first, because the vastness of the subject requires it, and second, because the audiencia became more concerned with judicial and less with administrative, political, and economic affairs through the constitutional changes which were made at the close of the eighteenth and at the beginning of the nineteenth centuries. The audiencia thus loses its interest, from our present viewpoint, after the eighteenth century. Again, it may be said that owing to the loss of colonies by Spain in the early nineteenth century, and the general anarchy that prevailed after 1810, a continuation of an intensive study beyond that period would be without value because its subject-matter would be no longer characteristic.

In assuming that the Audiencia of Manila was typical of all the audiencias in the Spanish colonial system, it is not claimed that the tribunal in the Philippines was identical in every function and detail with those of the other colonies of Spain. It is no doubt true that local conditions brought about pronounced differences and that each audiencia had its own local characteristics and powers, which differed from those of the others. The subject is so vast, however, and the research required for a comparative study of all these institutions would be so extensive that it would occupy more than a lifetime to complete it.

The main interest of this investigation does not lie in the organization, the scope, nature, or detailed powers of the audiencia as an institution of the Philippines, but in its larger relation to the general field of Spanish colonial history and government. It applies to the entire field of Spanish colonial administration. It is related to the government of Perú, New Spain, Cuba, and other colonies wherein there were audiencias, and where functions similar to those of the Manila tribunal were exercised. The establishment of all these audiencias was part of the same movement, and the act of their creation was the product of experience gained in Spain through efforts at centralization there. The audiencias of the colonies were alike dependent on the Council of the Indies; common institutions and departments of government existed in Spain for the control and regulation of the tribunals of the colonies. All were of equal judicial rank before the Council of the Indies, and cases appealed to the latter from the several audiencias were treated in the same manner and considered as having equal rank and importance. The general powers and attributes of these audiencias were prescribed in the same code, the *Recopilación*, and general laws and *cédulas* of reform were expedited from time to time and sent to the tribunals of all the colonies. Such is the basis, therefore, of the claim that this is in reality a study of the audiencia as an institution, illustrated particularly by the history of that of the Philippines.

A study of the audiencia of any colony is concerned with all of the problems that came up in its life—with legal, political, ecclesiastical, and social conditions. It will be seen that the audiencia was the one tribunal which regulated, checked, and often controlled both church and state in the colonies; it represented the king, and its duty was to see that the royal commands were obeyed; it was the royal audiencia. Isolated as were the officials of the Philippines, in those distant seas, removed from any but the most remote influence of the home government, beset on all sides by hostile forces, and dependent on themselves alone, conditions there present an especially favorable field wherein to note the ultimate possibilities of the authority of the audiencia. It is the design of this treatise to examine conditions in the Philippines under the aspects noted, and to assign them their place in the history of Spanish colonization. The investigation of what was, beyond doubt, the most important and many-sided institution in the Spanish administration of the Philippines provides a means of approach to that larger field of study.

A survey of the Spanish colonial system or a study of the government of any one colony will reveal the fact that political life and power there were vested chiefly in three institutions. Upon these the peace, prosperity and security of each colony largely depended. These institutions were the audiencia, the office of viceroy, or captain-general, and the church. By means of the two former the royal interests in the colony were represented, and through the latter one of the chief aims of Spain's colonial system was effected, namely, the conversion of infidels and the subsequent care of their souls. The church added to its own power in various ways. No study of Spanish colonial institutions would be complete which failed to consider the church as a political power. It is to a consideration of these three chief factors of colonial government, and their interrelation, that this study will be dedicated. After a review of the circumstances surrounding the establishment of the Audiencia of Manila, we

shall devote ourselves to a detailed study of the audiencia itself.
We shall first notice the audiencia's judicial functions as a court
of ordinary justice and secondarily as a court of *residencia*.
The second part of this section will be concerned with the semi-
judicial and administrative functions of the audiencia.

The title of captain-general was primarily of military significance, and it was exercised alike by viceroys and governors;
the official designation of the former being "my viceroy and
captain-general" and that of the latter being "my governor and
captain-general." Not all governors were captains-general.

The viceroys in the larger divisions and the captains-general
in the smaller ones represented the king as head of the church
and state in their several districts. Because these officials were so
powerful and their duties so multitudinous, they came into contact with every department of the government. The audiencias
came into relation with these officials most frequently. It is
therefore necessary to study the governor and captain-general
first from the viewpoint of his position as chief executive of the
colony and as representative of the king. The frequency of their
relations and the identity of their spheres of authority suggest
that we give attention to the conflicts of jurisdiction of the governor and audiencia; finally, we shall take note of the occasions
on which the audiencia assumed the government on the event of
a vacancy, noticing the laws authorizing such action and the
principles underlying them.

The importance of the church in the Spanish colonial system
has already been alluded to. The extent of its power and the
frequency and importance of its relations with the audiencia
demand considerable attention. After studying the general
phases of the relations of the audiencia and the church, we shall
see that the tribunal exercised ecclesiastical authority of a very
pronounced character. This power it derived from two sources:
first, from the authority that was entrusted to it by virtue of the
royal patronage; second, from its status as a court of justice

with jurisdiction in ecclesiastical affairs similar to that which
it had as an ordinary tribunal of justice. The above is an outline of the plan of this book.

That which impresses the modern student most with regard
to Spanish administrative machinery was its failure to effect
deliberately the division of powers which, with our traditions,
we consider essential to a well-balanced government. The terms
"executive" and "judicial" are employed in this book, as they
were in Spain's colonies, to designate functions rather than departments. The viceroy, as president of the audiencia, had cognizance of certain judicial matters, and more or less participation in them, though he was forbidden to act as judge, especially
over affairs in which he had already officiated as executive. The
audiencia likewise shared many executive functions, yet it was
not judge of its own acts, for when judgment was passed on
the administrative acts or judicial pronouncements of an *oidor,*
either on appeal or by review of sentence, that magistrate was
expected to retire, or to be occupied with some other case. So,
while there was no judicial department with solely judicial
functions, or a legislative or executive department, as they are
known in some modern states, there existed certain interrelations
which did not entirely result in confusion, as one might suppose.
On the contrary, it may be often noted that as a resultant of this
system, men and acts of an exceedingly well-balanced and statesmanlike character were produced. We shall see, moreover, that
they were far from meriting the disapprobation that is frequently heaped upon so-called Spanish governmental incapacity.

The defects which appear so conspicuous in Spanish administration were largely due to the extremely methodical turn of
the Spanish official mind, the vastness of the empire which was
to be governed, and the lack of facilities available for efficient
administration. It was a government of *expedientes,* literally a
government on paper. All acts, estimates, budgets, and plans
had to be drafted and written out, duplicates and triplicates of

each report had to be made, advice had to be taken, and opinions rendered, whether the matter went any further than the theoretical stage or not. We do much the same in our modern age, but inventions and labor-saving devices have fortunately spared us much of the time and effort which a few centuries ago had to be expended to accomplish proportionate results. The apparent unwieldiness of the Spanish colonial empire would have been materially reduced by the use of the telegraph, cable, steamship, typewriter and carbon-paper.

An effort has been made that this should be something more than a theoretical dissertation. A knowledge that certain laws were promulgated is only half of what is necessary in a study of this character. It is imperative to understand how these laws were applied, and whether they were efficiently and effectively carried out. Every phase of the audiencia's history has, therefore, been illustrated wherever possible with one or more concrete cases, taken from actual practice. Many of these illustrations are comparatively insignificant by themselves, involving persons of no historical importance and concerning matters of a seemingly trivial nature. Nevertheless, it has been necessary to consider these matters carefully because they were typical and true to actual conditions, and because they reveal better than anything else could the affairs which were the concern of the audiencia, showing the part played by the tribunal in the life of the colony.

In the preparation of this work due deference has been paid to the standard authorities usually cited by writers of Spanish-American history. So little attention has been given by students of Spanish colonial history to the audiencia as an institution, however, that the present writer has been obliged to depend almost entirely on the hitherto untouched documentary material in Spain and the Philippines, and to place almost his sole reliance upon it. This material consists of laws, *cédulas,* royal orders, ordinances, correspondence, and lastly, but most important, records of cases and actual happenings in the form of letters, memorials, reports, complaints and contemporary accounts. These latter convey, as nothing else can, an idea of how the laws were carried out, what was their effect, what part the audiencia played in the interpretation and execution of the law, and the relations of the tribunal to the other authorities and institutions of government. Of this sort of material there is much, and in its light the history of the Spanish colonies and of their institutions yet remains to be written.

CHAPTER I

THE AUDIENCIAS OF THE SPANISH COLONIES

The Spanish system of colonial administration was an adaptation beyond the seas of fundamental administrative, judicial and ecclesiastical institutions and principles which had grown up and had proved serviceable throughout a long period of successful use in Spain. As the audiencias and their allied officials had shown themselves to be efficient as agencies of centralization in the isolated provinces of Spain, so they were utilized, by the organization which they effected, to bring the colonies nearer the mother country. When Spain was confronted with the necessity of governing her vast empire, it was natural that she should profit by her former administrative experience, and make use of those institutions of government which had proved successful at home.

The purpose of the present chapter is to emphasize the fact that these institutions which had served in Spain, and were still in process of development there, were utilized in all of the colonies. The Philippine audiencia, which will be more particularly studied in subsequent chapters, was not a rare and isolated exception, but rather an integral part of a great administrative system.[1] This will more clearly appear from a sketch of the early development of colonial administration.

In accordance with the terms of the concession made by the Catholic Monarchs at Santa Fé on April 30, 1492, Columbus was given the title of "Admiral, Viceroy, and Governor of the Un-

---

[1] Vander Linden, in his *L'expansion coloniale de l'Espagne* (p. 360), states that the Philippine audiencia exercised fewer governmental functions than did the audiencias of New Spain and Perú. It is true that the jurisdiction of the Audiencia of Manila was confined to a territory which was politically and economically of less importance to Spain and to the world in general than New Spain and Perú. It is the

discovered Lands and Seas of the Indies."[2] He was likewise entrusted with the duty of proposing three candidates for the government of each colony, and from these three names the king was to select one. It was further provided that the *alcaldes* and *alguaciles* for the administration of justice should be named by Columbus, and that he should hear appeals from these minor judges in second instance. This is a brief outline of the first government and judiciary provided for the New World. It is improbable that this arrangement was the product of any great amount of study or reflection. It was formulated before the New World had even been discovered, and this scheme, as well as the conditions of commerce and tribute which went with it, were largely proposed by Columbus, and acceded to by the Catholic Monarchs without anticipation of the tremendous consequences which were to come from that voyage of discovery and those which were to follow it.

When Columbus undertook his second and later voyages the Catholic rulers began to modify the conditions of the original compact by sending royal representatives with him to take account of his expeditions. The difficulties which Columbus had in the government of his West Indian colony are too well known to be more than referred to here. Through the influence of Fonseca, and the gradual realization of the tremendous size and importance of the new dominions, the rulers of Spain began to feel that a mistake had been made in granting to this Genoese sailor and to his heirs the complete proprietorship and govern-

---

conviction of the writer that the distance and isolation of the Philippines, their proximity to Japan, China, and the hostile colonies of the Portuguese and the Dutch, the necessities of self-dependence and defense, the corruption of the governors and officials and the problem of dealing independently with the ecclesiastical organization within the colony, forced the Audiencia of Manila to take upon itself powers and responsibilities as extensive, at least, as were assumed by the Audiencia of Mexico.

2 "Título expedido por los Reyes Católicos, 30 de Abril, 1492," in Navarrete, *Colección de viages*, II, 9-11; also see Vander Linden, *op. cit.*, 277-283; 338.

ment of this distant empire. The abrogation of the contract was a natural consequence. It was the repudiation of a colonial system which had been created in the dark, and formulated without a knowledge of the conditions and problems to be met. Such an arrangement was foredoomed to failure, and if the colonies were to be administered successfully, reform was necessary.

In 1507, the towns of Española petitioned the king for the same privileges and forms of government as were possessed by the towns of Spain. The request was granted, and municipal rights were bestowed upon fourteen towns. These concessions included the privilege of electing their own *regidores* and *alcaldes ordinarios*[3] and the rights of local legislation and administration of justice. The principle was subsequently enunciated that,

inasmuch as the kingdoms of Castile and of the Indies are under one crown, the laws and the order of government of one should be as similar to and as much in agreement with the other as possible; our royal council, in the laws and establishments which are ordered, must strive to reduce the form and manner of their government to the style and order by which the kingdoms of Castile and León are governed and ruled, to the extent that the diversity and difference of the lands and nations permit.[4]

In 1511, a tribunal of independent royal judges was constituted in the colony of Española to try cases appealed from

---

[3] See Altamira, *Historia de la civilización española*, II, 477–480; Bancroft, *History of Central America*, I, 247–288; Helps, *Spanish conquest*, (1856), I, 187–227:

In the Spanish colonies an *alcalde* was usually an ordinary judge, not always trained in the law to the extent of being a *letrado* or *togado*. An *alcalde ordinario* or an *alcalde de ayuntamiento* tried cases in first instance. An *alcalde mayor* or an *alcalde de partido* might try cases on appeal from these. Generally speaking, *alcaldes ordinarios* were town judges, in contrast to *alcaldes mayores* who had provincial jurisdiction as well. *Alcaldes ordinarios* and *regidores* were members of the town *ayuntamientos* or *cabildos* (municipal councils). *Regidores* did not exercise judicial functions.

[4] *Recopilación de leyes de los reinos de las Indias* (hereinafter to be referred to as the *Recopilación*), lib. 2, tit. 2, ley 13. For an account of the *Recopilación*, see footnote 40, below.

the town magistrates and the governor.[5]   This judicial body
may be considered as the predecessor of the royal audiencia
which was established fifteen years later.   The organization and
purpose of the tribunal were exactly similar to those of the
courts existing in the frontier provinces of Spain before the
establishment of audiencias.   The chief reason for its creation
was the need of checking the abuses of an absolute governor.
This tribunal was composed of three magistrates, who were
possessed of the licentiate's degree, designated as *alcaldes
mayores,* and appointed by the king.   They were empowered to
hear and determine appeals from the governor and from his
tenientes and *alcaldes.*[6]   These magistrates, acting collectively,
became at once official organs for the expression of the needs
of the colony in non-judicial matters, frequently presenting
memorials to the Council of the Indies independently of the
governor.[7]   The crown had already assumed direction of the
administrative and executive affairs of the colony of Puerto
Rico, on August 15, 1509, by naming a special governor for that
island.   On July 25, 1511, Diego Colón, son of the dis-
coverer, was named governor of Española, and of the other
islands and of the mainland discovered by his father.   This

---

5 Bancroft, *History of Central America,* I, 269; see note 27 of this
chapter.

6 In some of the early Spanish colonies the *alcalde* was elected by his
fellow-townsmen. He exercised the functions of judge and chief executive, subject to the governor, or *adelantado,* and in the absence of the
latter assumed the government of the colony. *Alcaldes* in new settlements or on expeditions were different in character and exercised functions distinct from those of the *alcaldes* of the later periods.   This
earlier type probably existed in Española under Columbus (see Bancroft, *History of Central America,* I, 175, 330, note 7). That their duties
varied in different colonies may be deduced from the statement of
Bancroft that "the *alcaldes mayores* of New Spain under Cortés were
merely entrusted with judicial powers . . . later those of San Luís
Potosí and other places acted also as lieutenants for captains-general,
and exercised, in other respects, the duties and ceremonies of governors" (Bancroft, *History of Mexico,* III, 520).   The term, therefore,
does not always convey a clear impression of the exact nature of the
duties attached to the office.

7 Bancroft, *History of Central America,* I, 269.

latter act of royal intervention did not confirm, but rather abrogated in practice, the claims of this same Colón to the inheritance of the provinces which had been given formerly to his father. This act maintained the pre-eminence and authority of the Spanish monarchs in these territories.[5] The further growth and development of the West Indian colonies, and especially the increasing Spanish population, called for the establishment of a more efficient tribunal of administration and justice. This need was met in the creation of the first audiencia in America, that of Santo Domingo, which was established September 14, 1526.

The law, which has been cited already, providing that the administration of the Indies should be patterned in all ways after the governments of Castile and León, shows very clearly the natural influence of the early history and institutions of Spain. The audiencias established in the colonies were at first similar in jurisdiction and organization to those of Spain, which country had already succeeded in governing provinces that were, in effect, almost as isolated and as far from actual contact with the court as were the Indies. The audiencia of Spain had proved of immense value as an agency of direct control. It had been found satisfactory under conditions very similar to those in the Indies, which were not regarded as foreign possessions, but as integral parts of Castile, being the property of the monarchs of that kingdom, and under their personal direction.

Before proceeding with a description of the growth of the audiencia system, it is desirable, first, to note the establishment in Spain of two organs for the administration of colonial affairs. These may be examined here conveniently, because their creation antedated the institution of the audiencia in the colonies. The first, chronologically, as well as in importance, was the *Casa de*

---

[8] Altamira, *Historia*, II, 479.

Contratación, which was created January 10, 1503.[9] This essentially commercial body was intended at first to supervise the import and export trade of Spain with the colonies, and to arrange for the sale and distribution of imported articles, concessions of cargo to individuals, the lading and discharging of cargo, and the collection of duties. The functions of this body were soon amplified to the extent that it was given jurisdiction over emigration to the colonies. In 1509 it was granted further authority over certain criminal cases relating to trade, and in 1510, *letrados* were added to the tribunal of the *Casa* for the better determination of legal affairs.

As established in 1503, the *Casa de Contratación* consisted of a treasurer, auditor (comptroller), and factor.[10] That the institution flourished and increased in importance may be deduced from the reform of Philip II, on September 25, 1583, whereby the above mentioned officials were retained and a royal audiencia was created within the *Casa*. This was composed of three *jueces letrados* and a *fiscal*, besides the numerous subordinate officials who usually accompanied the judicial tribunal.[11] Though at first it exercised some of the functions which belonged later to the Council of the Indies, it came subsequently to be subordinate to that body.[12] It was transferred to Cádiz in 1717, and was suppressed by the royal decree of June 18, 1790,[13] its remaining attributions being assumed by the *Consulado* of Seville.[14]

---

9 Bourne, *Spain in America*, 222; Vander Linden, *L'expansion coloniale de l'Espagne*, 339; see note in Bancroft, *History of Central America*, I, 280–283.

10 Bourne, *Spain in America*, 222; Moses, *The Spanish dependencies in South America*, I, 250–1; see *Col. Doc. Ined.*, XXXI, 139–155.

11 *Recopilación*, 9–1–2, 5.

12 *Ibid.*, 2–2–82, *auto* 36; Desdevises du Dezert, *Espagne de l'ancien régime. Les institutions*, 100–101; see Veitia Linaje, *Norte de la contratación de las Indias Occidentales*, *passim*.

13 Zamora y Coronado, *Biblioteca de legislación ultramarina*, 1, 450–451; II, 374 *et seq.*; also *Recopilación*, 9–1–1, note 1; Vander Linden, *op. cit.*, 344.

14 Desdevises du Dezert, *op. cit.*, 100.

The beginnings of the Council of the Indies may be noted in the creation of a special committee of the Council of Castile for the supervision of administrative affairs in the colonies. This was eight years after the establishment of the *Casa de Contratación,* when another need than the purely commercial, for which the *Casa de Contratación* had served, began to be felt.[15] The inadequacy of the system devised by the Catholic Monarchs at Santa Fé had already become evident. The problems of administration in the colonies were making clear the need of a more effective system of regulation. Just as the number of suits to be tried before the old *tribunal de la cort del rey* had increased to such an extent that the king could no longer attend to them personally, so the problems of administration in the new colonies demanded more attention and regulation than could be provided by the administrative machinery at hand. The functions of this new tribunal, if it may be designated as such at this time, do not seem to have been clearly expressed at first, at least by any law or decree now at hand, but it appears that they were advisory rather than administrative. It soon became evident that a distinction had to be made between the prerogatives of this council and those of the *Casa de Contratación.* During the early history of these two tribunals there was considerable conflict of jurisdiction between them. It is probable that until the reform of August 4, 1524, was promulgated, active supervision of colonial affairs was maintained by the Council of Castile, both the *Casa de Contratación* and this new tribunal of the Indies acting under its direction. Charles V gave new life to the tribunal of the Indies on the above date by assigning to it definite legislative and administrative powers, putting at its head Loaysa, the general of the Dominican order and his own confessor. The Council was further modified by

---

[15] Escriche, *Diccionario,* I, 578; see Desdevises du Dezert, *Les institutions,* 95–102; Robertson, *History of America,* IV (Book VIII), 21.

Charles V in 1542, and by Philip II in 1571, in the following terms:

It is our royal will that the said council shall have the supreme jurisdiction in all our occidental Indies . . . and of the affairs which result from them, . . . and for the good government and administration of justice, it may order and make with our advice, the laws, pragmatics, ordinances and provisions, general and particlular, . . . which . . . may be required for the good of the provinces . . . and in the matters pertaining to the Indies, that the said our council be obeyed and respected, and that its provisions in all, and by all be fulfilled and obeyed in all particulars.[16]

The Council of the Indies, as established in 1524, consisted of a president, a high chancellor, eight members who were lawyers, a *fiscal*, two secretaries and a lieutenant chancellor.[17] All these were required to be of noble birth and qualified by experience and ability to carry to a successful issue the high responsibilities which they were called upon to discharge.[18] Besides there was a corps of accountants, auditors, copyists, reporters and clerks. The number of these last-mentioned functionaries was enormous, especially in subsequent years, when correspondence with twelve or thirteen different colonies was maintained.

The Council of the Indies was the high court of appeal to which all cases from the colonial audiencias came for final adjudication. It was, however, not only a court of appeal in judi-

---

[16] *Recopilación*, 2–2–2.

[17] By the royal decree of March 24, 1834, the *Consejo de Castilla* and the *Consejo de Indias* were amalgamated. In place of these was created the *Tribunal Supremo de España é Indias*, with judicial functions and a *Consejo Real de España é Indias* for governmental and administrative affairs. On September 28, 1836, the *Consejo Real de España é Indias* was suppressed. On July 6, 1845, the *Consejo de Estado* assumed charge of affairs pertaining to the Indies, with a separate *Ministerio de Ultramar*. This reform was re-enacted on September 24, 1853 (Martínez Alcubilla, *Diccionario*, III, 313–315; Escriche, *Diccionario*, I, 578–579).

[18] It became the practice in later years to reward successful colonial administrators, including viceroys, governors, and magistrates, with membership in this council. Among those so elevated were Juan Solórzano y Pereyra, magistrate of the Audiencia of Perú, José de Gálvez, visitor of New Spain, Governor Simón de Anda y Salazar, and the able *fiscal*, Francisco Leandro de Viana, of the Philippines. These men rendered very distinguished service in the colonies.

cial matters, but also a directive ministry for the supervision of the administrative acts of the colonial audiencias and executives.

The unqualified success of the Audiencia of Santo Domingo, both as a tribunal of justice and as an administrative organ, led to the general establishment of the institution throughout the Spanish colonial empire. The audiencias which were created in Spain's colonies from 1526 to 1893 follow in the order of their establishment.[19]

SANTO DOMINGO, created September 14, 1526, consisting of a president, four *oidores*,[20] and a *fiscal*.

MEXICO,[21] created November 29, 1527, consisting of two chambers or *salas*, a criminal and a civil, a president, eight *oidores*, four *alcaldes del crimen*, and two *fiscales* for civil and criminal cases respectively.

PANAMÁ, created February 30, 1535, with a president, four *oidores* and a *fiscal*.

LIMA, created November 20, 1542, with two chambers, a civil and

---

[19] *Recopilación*, 2–15–2 to 14; see Danvila y Collado, *Reinado de Carlos III*, III, 151–157. No attempt is made here to indicate all subsequent changes.

[20] *Oidor*, a *ministro togado* who heard and sentenced civil suits in an audiencia (Escriche, *Diccionario*, II, 661). In this treatise the Spanish term *oidor* will be retained throughout to designate a magistrate of that particular class. *Oidor* is sometimes incorrectly translated into "auditor", which in English means a reviewer of accounts (Spanish, *contador*). The Spanish term *auditor* has a special meaning, referring to a particular kind of magistrate, as *auditor de guerra, auditor de marina* or *auditor de rota* (Escriche, *Diccionario*, I, 369–371). Blair and Robertson, in their *Philippine Islands* (Cleveland, 1908), have used the terms *oidor* and "auditor" interchangeably, or rather, in almost all cases they have translated *oidor* as "auditor", but this usage will not be followed here for the reasons given.

The *oidor* is also to be distinguished from the *alcalde del crimen*. The latter existed only in the larger audiencias of Mexico and Perú, or in Manila, Havana or Puerto Rico in the later nineteenth century. *Alcaldes del crimen* in the sixteenth, seventeenth and eighteenth centuries were subordinate in rank to *oidores*, but by virtue of the reforms of 1812, 1836 and 1837, the latter were required to be *togados*, and the ministers of all the audiencias were placed in the same class. (Escriche, *Diccionario*, I, 154; I, 363–369; II, 661; Bancroft, *History of Central America*, I, 297; see also Pérez y López, *Teatro de la legislación*, XXI, 351–369; IV, 525–528; Martínez Alcubilla, *Diccionario*, I, 525–526.)

[21] The original *cédulas* refer to this audiencia as La Audiencia Real de la Nueva España—see Puga, *Provisiones, cédulas*, f. 7.

a criminal, a president, eight *oidores*, four criminal *alcaldes*, and two *fiscales*, as in Mexico.

SANTIAGO DE GUATEMALA, created September 13, 1543, with a president, five *oidores*, and a *fiscal*.

GUADALAJARA, created February 15, 1548, with a president, four *oidores*, and a *fiscal*.

SANTA FÉ (New Granada), created July 17, 1549, with a president, four *oidores*, and a *fiscal*.

LA PLATA (Charcas), created September 4, 1559, with a president, five *oidores*, and a *fiscal*.

SAN FRANCISCO DE QUITO, created November 29, 1563, with a president, four *oidores*, and a *fiscal*.

MANILA, created May 5, 1583, with a president, four *oidores*, and a *fiscal*.

SANTIAGO DE CHILE, created February 17, 1609, with a president, four *oidores*, and a *fiscal*.

BUENOS AYRES, created November 2, 1661, with a president, three *oidores*, and a *fiscal;* recreated July 2, 1778, when Buenos Ayres was made a viceroyalty.

CARACAS, created June 13, 1786, with a regent, three *oidores*, and a *fiscal*.

CUZCO, created February 26, 1787, with a regent, three *oidores*, and a *fiscal*.

PUERTO RICO, created June 19, 1831, to consist of a president, regent, three *oidores*, and a *fiscal*.

HAVANA, created September 26, 1835, reorganized June 16, 1838, to consist of a regent, four *oidores*, and two *fiscales*.[22]

PUERTO PRÍNCIPE, transferred in 1797 from Santo Domingo, reorganized September 26, 1835, to consist of a regent, four *oidores*, and a *fiscal*. This audiencia was suppressed and its territory added to that of Havana on October 21, 1853. It was recreated on February 22, 1878, and on May 23, 1879.

SANTIAGO DE CUBA, created September 26, 1835, to consist of a regent, four *oidores*, and a *fiscal*. This audiencia was later suppressed, and its territory was added to the Audiencia of Havana; it was again reformed and added to Puerto Príncipe on February 22, 1878.

CEBÚ (Philippines), created February 26, 1886, to consist of a president, four magistrates, a *fiscal*, and an assistant *fiscal*.

VIGÁN (Philippines) created on May 19, 1893, to consist of one

---

[22] Zamora y Coronado, *Biblioteca*, I, 452; I, 483–486; Martínez Alcubilla, *Diccionario*, VIII, under "Justicia". See also Danvila y Collado, *Reinado de Carlos III*, VI, 157–158.

chief justice, two associates, a prosecuting attorney, and an assistant prosecutor.

It will be noted that the audiencias of Mexico and Lima contained the greatest number of magistrates. They were divided into two *salas*, a civil and a criminal, with appropriate judges and *fiscales* for each.[23] The judges of the criminal branch were designated as *alcaldes* and not as *oidores*. These audiencias were at first conterminous in territorial jurisdiction with the respective captaincies-general of those names, but they enjoyed no greater power or pre-eminence before the Council of the Indies than the audiencias of the lesser captaincies-general. In the words of the royal decree of establishment,

there are founded twelve royal audiencias and chanceries . . . in order that our vassals may have persons to rule and govern them in peace and justice, and their districts have been divided into governments, *corregimientos* and *alcaldías mayores* who will be provided in accordance with our orders and laws and will be subordinate to our royal audiencias and to our Supreme Council of the Indies . . . and may no change be made without our express order or that of the Council.[24]

Many changes were made in the territorial jurisdiction of the various audiencias. The audiencias of Lima and Mexico, in addition to their jurisdiction over their respective viceroyalties, exercised governmental authority over the adjacent districts when the viceroys were absent; the Audiencia of Lima over Charcas, Quito and Tierra Firme (Panamá), and that of Mexico over what was later Guadalajara, the Philippines, and Yucatán. All of these, except the latter, came to have audiencias, with the usual powers and authority.[25]

The first seven audiencias were founded by Charles V. Three

---

[23] By the royal decree of May 23, 1879, the audiencias at Havana and Manila were each given a civil and criminal *sala* and a *fiscal* was provided for each *sala* as in the audiencias of Mexico and Lima. When it was necessary, *oidores* could be transferred from one *sala* to the other.—*Colección legislativa de España*, CXXII, 1093–1100.

[24] *Recopilación*, 2–15–1.

[25] See Professor Shepherd's brief description of the governmental machinery of Spain's colonies, in his *Guide to the materials for the*

were created by Philip II. The audiencias of Santiago de Chile and Buenos Ayres were established by Philip III and Philip IV, respectively. The greater number of these audiencias was created at the time of the most rapid extension of the tribunals in Spain; their establishment was part of the same general tendency; they were therefore closely related. When the audiencias of Santo Domingo and Mexico were formed, there had been already in existence in Spain the chanceries of Valladolid, and Granada. Thirteen audiencias were established in Spain after those of Santo Domingo and New Spain were created in the colonies. The two Spanish audiencias mentioned above were designated as models for the tribunals of the Indies, and the principle was laid down that if a necessary provision was omitted from the laws of establishment of the colonial audiencias, ''all the presidents and audiencias of those our realms are ordered to preserve the order and practices which are followed in the chanceries of Granada and Valladolid.''[26]

Territorially, the audiencias of Santo Domingo, Mexico, and Lima were the nucleii from which and around which most of the other audiencias were established. Being the first in their respective sections, they included more territory than they could govern with facility; thus it later became necessary to divide up their districts. Santo Domingo held sway at first over Española, Cuba, and Puerto Rico, with authority also over Venezuela and subsequently over Louisiana and Florida.[27] New Gra-

---

history of the United States in Spanish archives, 10–12; note also the articles recently published by Desdevises du Dezert in the *Revue historique* (CXXV, 225–264; CXXVI, 14–60, 225–270) under the title of "Vice-rois et capitaines gènèraux des Indes espagnoles a la fin du XVIII siècle."

26 *Recopilación*, 2–15–17.

27 *Ibid.*, 2–15–2. Although the *Recopilación* and Danvila y Collado (cited in note 19) give the date of the establishment of the Audiencia of Santo Domingo as 1526, the royal decree issued at Pamplona, October 22, 1523, is addressed to *nros oydores de la audiencia real de la Ysla Española* (A. I., 139–1–6, *tom.* 9, *fol.* 225). There are various references antedating 1526 in this and the following *legajo*.

nada was conceded an audiencia in 1549, and to this province were added the possessions of Panamá when the audiencia of that name were suppressed. The Audiencia of Mexico, created eight years before New Spain was made a viceroyalty, had territorial jurisdiction at first over a vast empire, which was later divided into smaller governments with audiencias. Its limits, as defined in the laws of the Indies, extended on both oceans from the Cape of Florida to the Cape of Honduras, and included Yucatán, and Tabasco.[28]

The audiencias of Guadalajara, Santiago de Guatemala, and Manila all set definite limits to the jurisdiction of the Audiencia of Mexico. The Audiencia of Lima had authority at first over most of Spanish South America, but its scope was in the same manner diminished from time to time by the establishment of the audiencias of Santa Fé, La Plata (Charcas), Quito, Santiago de Chile, and Buenos Ayres. Before the Audiencia of Cuzco was instituted in 1787, jurisdiction over that ancient city and district was divided between the audiencias of Lima and La Plata; Arica, although it belonged to the district of Lima, was not governed under that jurisdiction, but was administered by a *corregidor* directly responsible to the audiencia at Charcas.[29] Chile and Panamá were subordinate governmentally to the viceroy of Perú, but the audiencias were independent.[30]

Cuba was early divided into two districts under the rule of captains-general, those of Havana and Santiago de Cuba.[31] By *cédula* of February 24, 1784, Havana was made independent of the Audiencia of Santo Domingo in administrative matters. Aside from the one at Puerto Príncipe, audiencias were

---

28 *Ibid.*, 2–15–3. For the exact limits of this audiencia see Puga, *Provisiones, cédulas*, ff. 12–13; 47–48, and Hackett, "Delimitation of political jurisdictions in Spanish North America to 1535," in *Hispanic American Historical Review*, I, 60, note 102.

29 *Ibid.*, 2–15–13, 14, 15.

30 *Ibid.*, 5–1–2, 3; 2–15–4, 12.

31 *Ibid.*, 5–1–16.

not created in Cuba, however, until 1835 and 1838, respectively. Prior to this, Cuba was subject to the Audiencia of Puerto Príncipe, the successor of Santo Domingo, in judicial matters, as the governments in Cuba were military. However, military cases were carried before the captains-general of Havana and of Santiago de Cuba, respectively.[32]

Although all the audiencias had the same rank before the Council of the Indies, both as political and judicial tribunals, those of Lima and Mexico may be said to have been tribunals of the first class, for reasons which we have noted. Indeed, it must be remembered that it was the individual captaincy-general that had an audiencia, whether the captaincy-general happened to be a viceroyalty or not. Judged by the amount of power they exercised, there were three classes of audiencias: those of the viceroyalties, of the captaincies-general, and of the presidencies. On this basis of classification, it may be said that the first-mentioned were the superior institutions. In matters of military administration, the captains-general had the same power as the viceroys, while the audiencias exercised less intervention in the government than in the presidencies.

---

[32] Zamora y Coronado, *Biblioteca*, I, 486–487. The following will give some idea of the size and rank of the respective audiencias of the Spanish colonies in the later eighteenth century. This table was compiled from the *Reglamento de 4 de Mayo, 1788* (Pérez y López, *Teatro*, IV, 522–524).

Audiencia.	No. of Salas.	No. of fiscales.	Magis-trates.	Salary of regent, pesos.	Total budget, pesos.
Lima	2	2	15	10,000	95,000
Mexico	2	2	15	9,000	85,500
Charcas	1	2	5	9,725	43,745
Chile	1	2	5	9,720	43,740
Buenos Ayres	1	2	5	6,000	36,726
Manila	1	2	5	7,000	31,500
Guadalajara	1	2	5	6,600	29,700
Guatemala	1	2	5	6,600	29,700
Santo Domingo	1	2	5	6,600	29,700
Santa Fé	1	2	5	6,600	29,700
Quito	1	2	5	6,600	29,700
Cuzco	1	1	3	9,000	27,000
Caracas	1	1	3	5,000	18,200

In the latter, the audiencias (and presidents) exercised governmental functions as well as judicial, with appeal to the viceroy. Though they had no military power, and their scope was strictly limited in financial affairs, these audiencias actually governed their districts. This the audiencias of the viceroyalties never did, except when they governed *ad interim*.

Before proceeding with a study of the powers and duties of the colonial audiencias, it would be well to compare them, as to extent of jurisdiction and authority, with those which were in operation in Spain. Were they equal? Did the colonial institutions, on account of their isolation, exercise prerogatives which were unknown to the tribunals of the Peninsula, or vice versa? These questions were answered by Juan de Solórzano y Pereyra, a distinguished Spanish jurist, *oidor* of the Audiencia of Lima in 1610, and subsequently councillor of the Indies.[33] Solórzano y Pereyra illustrates fourteen points of difference wherein the audiencias of the colonies exceeded those of the Peninsula in power and authority, in these matters exercising jurisdiction equal to the Council of Castile. This, he said, was "on account of the great distance intervening between them and the king or his royal Council of the Indies, and the dangers which delay may occasion." Therefore, he said, the audiencias had

---

[33] Solórzano y Pereyra, *Política Indiana* (Madrid, 1647). This was the first great general work on the political institutions of the Indies, and probably the most valuable and comprehensive of its kind ever published, barring possibly the *Recopilación*. It comprises history, description, law, discussions of suits and cases, litigation and legal citations. Its ample title-page states that it is "divided into six books, in which, with great distinction and study, are treated and resolved all matters relating to the discovery, description, acquisition and retention of the Indies, and their peculiar government, as well as concerning the persons of the Indians and their services, tributes, tithes and *encomiendas*, as concerning spiritual and ecclesiastical affairs and doctrine, inquisitors, commissaries of crusade and of the religious. And in regard to temporal affairs, concerning the secular magistrates, viceroys, presidents, audiencias, the Supreme Council and its *junta de guerra*, including a setting forth of the many royal *cédulas* which have been despatched for the latter." Solórzano y Pereyra contributed largely to the codification of the laws of the Indies.

been permitted many privileges and powers denied to the audiencias of Spain. The most important of these powers were as follows: jurisdiction over *residencias* of *corregidores;* the right to send out special investigators (*pesquisidores*); supervision over inferior judges—seeing that they properly tried cases under their authority, care for the education and good treatment of the Indians in spiritual and temporal matters, and the punishment of officials who were remiss in that particular; the collection of tithes; the assumption of the rights and obligations of the royal patronage, as well as jurisdiction over cases affecting the same, the building of churches, the installment of curates and holders of benefices, and the inspection and possible retention of bulls and briefs.

The colonial audiencias were instructed to guard the royal prerogative, and were authorized to try all persons accused of usurping the royal jurisdiction. They were to see that officials, lay and ecclesiastical, did not charge excessive fees for their services, limiting especially those exorbitant charges which priests were apt to demand at burials, funerals, marriages and baptisms. The colonial audiencias were given supervision over *espolios*,[34] collecting, administering and disposing of the properties left by deceased prelates, and paying claims of heirs and creditors. Another duty was the restraining of ecclesiastical judges and dignitaries through the *recurso de fuerza*.[35] This authority had been permitted to the chanceries of Valladolid and Granada, only.

Although viceroys and governors were granted special jurisdiction over administrative matters, they were authorized to call upon the *acuerdos*[36] of the audiencias for counsel and advice whenever an exceptionally arduous case presented itself. The

---

[34] See Chapter X of this book.

[35] *Recurso de fuerza*, see footnote 3, Chapter XI of this work.

[36] The origin and nature of the *acuerdo* is explained in Chapter VI, note 78, of this book; see also Chapter III, note 37.

audiencias were permitted to entertain appeals against the rulings of viceroys and presidents, but these appeals could be carried again to the Council of the Indies. In the same manner that affairs of government belonged to the private jurisdiction of the executive, so did financial matters, according to Solórzano y Pereyra. In these, however, the viceroy or governor was assisted in the solution of perplexing problems by the *acuerdo general de hacienda,* a body composed of *oidores, oficiales reales*[37] and *contadores.* On the death, disability, or absence of the viceroy or governor and captain-general it was ordered that the government should pass under the charge of the entire audiencia. Lastly, Solórzano y Pereyra pointed out that while the sole duty of the Spanish *oidores* was to try cases, the magistrates of the colonial audiencias were called upon for a number of miscellaneous functions, such as those of *visitador,* or inspector of the provinces, or of other departments of the government, as *asesor* of the Santa Cruzada,[38] as inspector of ships, as *auditor de guerra,* as *asesor* of the governor, and as *juez de las executorías,* under commission of the Council of the Indies to collect and remit to the government receiver all money

[37] The *oficiales reales* consisted of the *tesorero* (treasurer), *contador* (accountant) and *factor* (disbursing officer and supply agent). See *Recopilación,* 8-4-34, 35; 8-2-5, 6.

The laws of March 2, 1618, and of November 17, 1626, ordered that in colonies having audiencias the *acuerdos de real hacienda* should be attended by the president (governor or viceroy), *fiscal,* senior *oidor,* and *oficial real,* respectively. In case there were no audiencia, the session should then consist of all the *oficiales reales* and the governor, and then the votes of the treasury officials should be final *(Recopilación,* 8-3-8, 11, 12). Under certain circumstances the *factor* was assisted by a *veedor* and a *proveedor.* The duties of the latter officials were largely administrative *(ibid.,* 8-4-38 to 39).

Bancroft *(History of Mexico,* III, 520) states that "the provinces of royal officials [*oficiales reales*] were merely revenue districts whose heads received their appointment from the king, and administered their office under a certain supervision from the viceroy and governors attending their councils; yet they were responsible only to the tribunal of finance in the viceregal capital, and this again reported direct to Spain." See also Priestley, *José de Gálvez,* 76-82.

[38] Bull of the Santa Cruzada, the apostolic bull by which the popes conceded certain indulgences to those who went to the conquest of

derived from fines and penalties imposed by official visitors (*visitadores*), judges of *residencia, etcetera.*[39]

With the exception of the entertainment of the *recurso de fuerza,* none of the above-mentioned functions could be exercised by the audiencias of Spain. Although the colonial audiencias were to a large extent patterned after those of Spain, they had greater power and exercised more extensive functions almost from the beginning. This was chiefly owing to the added responsibilities of government resulting from the isolation of the colonies and their distance from the home government. The audiencias in Spain remained almost purely judicial. There was no need or opportunity for them to encroach upon the executive, or to usurp its functions, because of the control exercised by its immediate representatives. In the colonies the audiencias were themselves established as the agents of the royal authority, with the special duty of limiting the abuses of the officials of the crown. In this capacity, aside from their customary duties, the tribunals exercised far-reaching authority of a non-judicial character.

It is desirable to point out in this connection that all the colonial audiencias utilized the same law in common. *Cédulas,* edicts, and decrees were issued to them from a common source, to be executed under similar circumstances, or on particular occasions when local conditions demanded such action. The great code of 1680, the *Recopilación de leyes de los Reinos de las Indias,* has already been described as containing laws, both general and particular, for the regulation of the colonial audiencias.[40]

Jerusalem, and later to the Spaniards who contributed alms to aid in the war against the Africans. It was called *cruzada* because the soldiers wore crosses as emblems (Escriche, *Diccionario,* I, 462). Funds for this purpose were raised in the Philippines, paid into the insular treasury and deducted from the subsidy at Acapulco *(Recopilación,* 1–20–24). As noted above, an *oidor* acted as *asesor* of these funds (*ibid.,* 2–16–23).

[39] Solórzano y Pereyra, *Política Indiana,* II, 271–279.

[40] The first attempt at the codification of the laws for the governing of the colonies was made in New Spain in 1545, when the ordinances for the government of that viceroyalty and audiencia were printed. This

In the foregoing paragraphs attention has been directed
briefly to the relations of the audiencias and executives with
each other, and with the central government. Some notice at
least should be given to the means by which the will of the
executive and judiciary was enforced and executed upon and in
the local units, the provinces and towns. We have already seen
that the offices of the *corregidores, alcaldes mayores* and the
alcaldes ordinarios developed in Spain, the first with jurisdiction
over the larger districts, the *alcaldes mayores* over the smaller
areas and large towns, and the *alcaldes ordinarios* in the munici-
palities. In a general sense, this system was carried into the colonies; the *corregidores* and *alcaldes mayores* were in charge of the

---

collection was given the royal approval in 1548. A similar compilation
was made in Perú in 1552 by Viceroy Mendoza. The first intimation of
a universal code is to be found in the recommendations of the *fiscal* of
the Council of the Indies, Francisco Hernández de Liebana, in 1552.
On September 4, 1560, Luís Velasco, viceroy of New Spain, was ordered
to print a compilation of laws for the Audiencia of Mexico. This commission was given to Oidor Puga of that tribunal and executed in 1563.
In 1569 Viceroy Francisco Toledo was ordered to make a similar compilation for Perú, but the work was not completed at that time. The
first volume actually printed by authority of the Council was accomplished in 1593. This was the beginning of the code of the Indies, but
the volume which was published pertained only to the regimen of the
Council of the Indies itself, and made no regulations for the colonies.
A more extensive collection of provisions, letters, orders and *cédulas*
was published on the authority of the Council by Diego de Encinas, a
clerk of that tribunal, in 1596. In 1603, the *Ordenanzas reales para la
Casa de Contratación de Sevilla y para otras cosas de las Indias* were
printed in the same city. Another ordinance was published for the
regulation of the *contaduría mayor*.

Various compilations were made by the *oidores* from time to time,
either for their own use, or in compliance with the royal commands.
Among the latter, perhaps the most famous and certainly the most
useful was that of Juan de Solórzano y Pereyra, *oidor* of the Audiencia
of Perú and later a member of the Council of the Indies. This collection
was made at Lima in compliance with the commission of Philip IV,
issued in 1610. The work, consisting of six volumes, received the
stamp of royal approval on July 3, 1627. In 1623 León Pinelo published
a *Discurso sobre la importancia, forma, y disposición de la recopilación
de leyes de Indias.* On April 19 of that year Pinelo was ordered to
make an examination of all the existing laws and *cédulas* relative to the
government of the colonies, printed or in manuscript, with a view to
codification. A magistrate named Aguilar y Acuña was ordered to
collaborate with him. The result of these proceedings was a *Sumario
de la Recopilación General,* which continued under process of compila-

large provinces and districts, the *alcaldes ordinarios* were the judges of the Spanish towns.

Much the same intercourse and relations existed between these officials in the colonies as had been characteristic of the similar ones of Spain. But there were some differences: while in Spain the *alcaldes* were in most cases city judges, subject to the *corregidores*,[41] in the colonies there was little or no difference between *alcaldes mayores* and *corregidores*. They were most frequently appointed by the executive, sometimes independently, sometimes by the assistance and advice of the audiencia, as judges and governors of the provinces, although the laws of the Indies provided for their appointment by the king. The practice developed of designating them locally, and of sending their names to Spain for confirmation. Each *alcalde mayor* or *corregidor* resided at the chief town of his province and combined in himself the functions of judge, inspector of *encomiendas*, administrator of *hacienda* and police, collector of tribute, vicepatron and cap-

---

tion for a half century. It was finally perfected and published in 1677. In 1668 Pinelo's work was issued as the *Autos acordados y decretos de gobierno del Real y Supremo Consejo de las Indias*.

Although the collection was practically ready by 1677, it was not officially accepted until May 18, 1680. On that day it was promulgated by Charles II, king of Spain. On November 1, 1681, the work was ordered published by the India House, and the *Recopilación de los Reynos de Indias* was issued at Madrid in four volumes. Subsequent editions were printed in 1754, 1774, 1791 and 1841. The last-mentioned contains in its index reforms down to 1820. A *Recopilación Sumaria* was published in Mexico in two volumes in 1787. The compilations of Zamora y Coronado, Rodríguez San Pedro and Pérez y López, cited repeatedly in this work, contain later laws, and serve in the place of the *Recopilación* for the more recent periods.

Authorities: Solórzano y Pereyra, *Política Indiana*, I, Introduction; G. B. Griffin, "A brief bibliographical sketch of the Recopilación de Indias" in Historical Society of Southern California, *Publications, 1887;* Fabié, *Ensayo histórico de la legislación española;* Puga, *Provisiones, cédulas*, (1563); Garcia Icazbalceta, *Bibliografía Mexicana del siglo XVI*, (1886), 25–26; Bancroft, *History of Mexico*, III, 550–5511; *History of Central America*, I, 225–288; Antequera, *Historia de la legislación española*, 480–483.

41 Altamira, *Historia*, IV, 165–166.

tain-general.[42] He was assisted by officials of a minor category, frequently natives, who exercised jurisdiction over their fellows. The law also provided for a *teniente letrado* to assist the *alcalde* or *corregidor*,[43] but in the Philippines there was no such official, except at irregular intervals in the Visayas.

These chiefs of provinces were responsible to the audiencias in matters of justice and to the viceroys or captains-general in administrative affairs. In Indian relations and in questions involving *encomiendas* they were subject to the executive, who had jurisdiction in first instance, with appeal to the audiencia. The tribunal could grant *encomiendas* in default of the regularly appointed executive. In financial matters the *corregidores* and *alcaldes mayores* were responsible to the executive, but they acted as the agents of the treasury officials (*oficiales reales*) in the collection of the revenue. In their provinces they supervised the building of ships, the construction of roads and bridges, the *repartimientos* or *polos*[44] of Indians, and the planting of tobacco when the tobacco monopoly existed in the Philippines. In these matters they were responsible to the governor, viceroy, or superintendent, and to the várious *juntas reales* and committees, of which at least one *oidor* was always a member.

Tributes from the Indians, tithes from the *encomenderos* and other kinds of local taxes were collected by the *alcaldes mayores* and *corregidores*. Acting for the vicepatron, these officials represented the subdelegated authority of the king over the monasteries and churches of their provinces. They officiated at the formal bestowal of benefices, they were expected to main-

---

[42] *Recopilación*, 5–2–2, 3, 7, 15, 19, 28. In this case a local military functionary.

[43] *Ibid.*, 37, 39, 41; Moses, *Establishment of Spanish Rule in America*, 83–84; Vander Linden, *L'expansion coloniale de l'Espagne*, 345–361.

[44] *Repartimientos* or *polos;* referring to the forced labor of natives on public works, such as ship and road-building. The provincial officials exercised supervision over this obligatory service, and were held responsible for the proper execution of the laws appertaining thereto (Blair and Robertson, *The Philippine Islands* [hereinafter cited as Blair and Robertson], XIX, 71–76).

tain harmonious relations with the priests and friars in their provinces, and to check, by their personal presence and intervention, if necessary, any tendency on the part of the churchmen to abuse the Indians or to impose upon them.

In like manner they were supposed to prevent the ecclesiastical judges from exceeding their power, and particularly from transgressing the royal jurisdiction, which frequently occurred in the earlier years when that authority had not become clearly defined or firmly established. As the churchmen with whom these officials had to deal derived their authority from the higher prelates and the provincials of the orders and often acted by their direction, their opposition to the local officials of the civil government was frequently so effective that the latter were obliged to appeal to the audiencia. The latter tribunal had the power necessary to deal with these cases, and to restrain the offending churchmen, by bringing pressure to bear upon their prelates and superiors.

The provincial governors also had certain military duties. In the northern provinces of New Spain they had charge of defense, with responsibility to the viceroy.[45] In the Philippines, however, and in certain parts of New Spain, where the captain-general took the place of the viceroy, *alcaldes mayores* and *corregidores* acted as lieutenants of the captains-general, exercising authority of a military character.[46] They were required to defend their provinces and districts against invasions, insurrections, Indian outbreaks, and disturbances. They were

---

[45] *Cartas y expedientes de gobernadores de Durango.* (1591–1700), *Archivo de Indias, Sevilla,* [hereinafter cited as A. I.,] 66–6–17, 18 (these numbers refer to archive place); *Cartas y Expedientes del Virrey de Mégico que tratan de asuntos de Guadalajara* (1698–1760), A. I., 67–2–10 to 13. These two series contain hundreds of letters on this subject, as do other series, relating to Nuevo León, Nueva Galicia, Nueva Vizcaya, and New Mexico.

[46] This was true of San Luís Potosí and Guadalajara in New Spain. See Bancroft, *History of Mexico,* III, 520; *History of Central America,* I, 297; Moses, *Establishment of Spanish rule in America,* 83.

authorized to impress men for military service. Local conditions
in Mexico, Perú, Central America, and the Philippines caused
some differentiation in these matters. This description will serve
to convey an impression of the nature of the duties of these
officials and the way in which they acted as the agents of the
captain-general, viceroy, and audiencia.[47]

It has been already pointed out that the *alcaldes mayores* and
corregidores had extensive judicial duties; a mere restatement of
that important fact will suffice at this time. In subsequent
chapters we shall study in detail numerous illustrations and
instances of the judicial functions of the provincial judges. It
has been noted also that the *alcaldes ordinarios* were the judges
of the Spanish towns. So they were in the Philippines, but, as
there were only four or five Spanish towns in the archipelago,
the *alcaldes ordinarios* do not assume great prominence in this
study. These *alcaldes* were usually chosen by the *ayuntamientos*
(municipal councils), though they were appointed on some
occasions by the governors. As the Spanish towns enjoyed
special privileges conferred by the king, their judges were not a
part of the regular judicial hierarchy, but were dependent on
their *ayuntamientos* or the governor. However, an *oidor* was
usually delegated to inspect the work of the *alcalde ordinario.*

---

[47] Bancroft (*History of Central America*, I, 297) defines the *corregidor* as a magistrate with civil and criminal jurisdiction in the first
instance, and gubernatorial inspection in the political and economic
government of all the towns of the district assigned to him. There were
corregidores letrados (learned in the law), *corregidores políticos* (political and administrative), *de capa y espada* (military) and *políticos y
militares* (administrative and military). When the *corregidor* was not
a lawyer by profession, unless he had an *asesor* of his own, the *alcalde
mayor*, if possessed of legal knowledge, became his advisor, which
greatly increased the importance of the last-mentioned official. The
alcalde mayor was appointed by the king. It was required that he
should be a lawyer by profession, twenty-six years of age, and of good
character. Practically, in cases of this kind, when the governor was
not a *letrado*, civil, criminal, and some phases of military authority devolved on the *alcalde mayor*; the first two ex-officio, and the latter as
the legal advisor of the military chief. In new colonies this officer was
invested with powers almost equal to those of the governor.—See *Recopilación*, 5–2.

With this introductory view of the general field of Spanish colonial administration, and this presentation of the characters and elements which are to assume important roles in this discussion because of their frequent relations with the audiencia, we may enter upon a more detailed study of a single institution. It has been emphasized especially that the audiencia in the Philippines was only an integral part of the governmental machinery used in the colonial empire of Spain. It is clear, therefore, that we are not studying an isolated tribunal, for every royal *cédula* promulgated to the Philippine audiencia was in some way related to those issued to ten or eleven other audiencias of equal status or similar character. Although the Philippines were apart physically, this institution, with its relation to the provincial and colonial governments on one hand, and the home government on the other, brought the colony as close as possible to Spain, and to the other colonies.

It is certain that the growth of audiencias was a part, not only of colonial, but of Spanish historical and institutional development. These institutions served the same purpose in the colonies that they accomplished in Spain; they were utilized for the administration of justice, and to check the excesses and abuses of officials. They were important because they facilitated a greater degree of centralization. They converged the provincial, colonial, intercolonial and home governments in the same manner as the audiencias in Spain brought about unity in provincial and national judicial administration.

CHAPTER II

THE ESTABLISHMENT OF THE AUDIENCIA OF MANILA (1583–1598).

The conditions which determined the establishment of an audiencia in the Philippines differed little, if at all, from those in Spain's other colonies. All of Spain's dependencies were situated at great distances from the mother country; the Philippines were farther away than any. Furthermore, the Philippines were isolated and could not be successfully maintained, if dependent on, or identified with any other colony; distance and other factors which we shall note made undesirable and impracticable a continuance of established relations with New Spain. If, however, the governor of the Philippines came to be almost absolute in his authority, his absolutism differed in degree rather than in kind from that of the governors and viceroys of other colonies. The contiguity of China and Japan, the constant danger of military invasion and naval attack by outside enemies and the dependence of the colony on the commerce of China also made the case of the Philippines somewhat different from that of the colonies in America. In general, the situation in the Philippines called for a distinct audiencia with the same powers and functions as were exercised by the audiencias of the other colonies.

A system for the administration of justice in the Philippines had been definitely established and organized before the audiencia was inaugurated in 1584. Many prominent features of the judicial and administrative systems of Spain and America had been already introduced into the Islands. At the head of both judicial and administrative affairs was the governor and captain-general, who was practically absolute, and whose authority was final except in certain matters of litigation which could be appealed to the Audiencia of Mexico. Subordinate to him were the *alcaldes mayores* and *corregidores*, whose functions have been already noted. In the Philippines, as elsewhere, the latter officials acted as magistrates and governors of provinces, combining judicial and administrative attributes. Directly subordinate to them were the *encomenderos*, whose holdings, including lands and Indians, may be said to have constituted the unit of the Spanish colonial land system until the close of the eighteenth century.[1] As in Spain, so in the Spanish towns of the Philippines, there were *alcaldes ordinarios*, or municipal

---

[1] The first *encomiendas* in the Philippines were granted by Legaspi in 1572 (Montero y Vidal, *Historia general*, I, 42–43). The *encomenderos* ruled the Indians in their care with little interference from *alcaldes mayores*, *corregidores*, or governors. Vander Linden especially emphasizes the fact that the *encomenderos* were not supposed to act as the private masters of the Indians on their holdings, but were to act as the representatives of the king (Vander Linden, *L'expansion coloniale de l'Espagne*, 345–346). The laws of the Indies specified that the *encomenderos* were to protect, aid and educate them, seeing particularly that they were taught the Catholic Faith *(Recopilación*, 6–8, 9, 10, 11; esp. tit. 9, laws 1–4).

The *encomenderos*, in the guise of benefactors, guardians and protectors of the Indians, supervised the labor of the latter on the *encomiendas*, drawing remuneration therefrom, collecting tribute from them, and retaining a share of that. Aside from the very intimate relationship of the *encomenderos* as the guardians of the Indians in spiritual and temporal things, they were not considered as officials in the same sense as were the *alcaldes mayores* and *corregidores*.

Dr. Pardo de Tavera characterizes the duties and relations of the *encomenderos* to the Indians as follows: "The encomenderos were the first Spaniards after the conquest and pacification of the colony who represented the civil authority of Spain in the Islands: they were obliged to maintain order and secure the well-being of the Indian residents of their encomiendas or holdings, and to defend their tenants against any encroachments on their rights by the Spaniards, soldiers, alcaldes, and judges; and to endeavor to bring their tenants together in towns and furnish them with opportunities to be converted to the Christian religion, and to help them build churches and convents . . . encomenderos were charged with the succor and support of the people on their holdings in case of any calamity, famine or public disaster, and they were prohibited from charging tribute in bulk against the various barangayes, that is to say, they should not make the chiefs of a family or tribe responsible for the payment of tribute by the various members, nor were the encomenderos allowed to use force to secure the payment of a tribute. When an encomendero received a tribute from

judges, elected by the citizens in some cases, or appointed by the governor in others.[2]

But the system as established was defective in many respects. The governor and captain-general was chief judge, executive, and commander of the military forces. In him were centralized all the functions of justice and government, exercised in the provinces through the *alcaldes mayores* and *corregidores.* The latter officials he appointed *ad interim,* supervised their administrative duties, and heard judicial cases appealed from them. He likewise exercised supervision over the *oficiales reales,* who were entrusted with the collection, care and expenditure of the funds of the colony.[3] During the period before the establishment of the audiencia, the governor exercised complete control over all branches and departments of the government,—provincial, municipal, and insular—in matters of justice, administration, and finance. The centralization of all this authority in the person of one official made his position responsible and powerful, but capable of much abuse. And it was the abuses incidental to the exercise of absolute power by the governor that led to the establishment of the Audiencia of Manila.

Probably the most important indirect reason for the establishment of an audiencia in the Philippines may be noted in the abuses connected with the administration of the *encomiendas.* These may be attributed both to the powerlessness and in-

---

his people, he thereupon was considered to have assumed the duty of acting as their protector" (Pardo de Tavera, *Philippines census* [1905], I, 330). Suffice it to say that, theoretically, the *encomenderos* were the fatherly protectors and benefactors of the helpless, childlike natives, and their every act was to be for the good of their wards.

[2] Antequera, *Historia de la legislación española,* 486–487; Bourne, "Historical introduction," in Blair and Robertson, I, 56.

[3] *Recopilación,* 6–8–38 to 39; 8–9–20 to 24. It seems that the *oficiales reales* merely supervised the collection of tribute, which was really accomplished in the provinces by the *alcaldes mayores* and *corregidores,* who acted as their agents. Martínez de Zúñiga, *An historical view of the Philippine Islands,* I, 2; Ordinances of Good Government, Blair and Robertson, L, 191–264; *Recopilación,* 6–5–64; Montero y Vidal, *Historia general,* I, 380–385.

efficiency of the governors, and to their cupidity and deliberate favoritism to the *encomenderos*. As a result of the rapid spread of these *encomiendas*,[4] settlements, or agricultural estates, for such they were, and their location in distant and widely separated parts of the Archipelago, the *encomenderos* came to have increased responsibilities and powers. They were far removed from the central authority at Manila. They were infrequently inspected by the *alcaldes mayores* and *corregidores* in whose districts they were situated. Indeed, the *encomiendas* had spread so rapidly in the Philippines that the governmental machinery provided by Spain was unable to provide for them. In 1591, for example, there were 267 *encomiendas* containing 667,612 souls. These were supervised by twelve *alcaldes mayores*.[5] One hundred and forty priests were provided to minister to this large congregation of natives. The Philippine government, with an autocratic military governor at its head, had been originally designed for one settlement or province, and not for an extensive

---

[4] The *Relación* of Miguél de Loarca, *alcalde mayor* of Arévalo, Panay, gives us a good idea of the rapidity with which this institution spread within ten years in the Philippines. It indicates the extent to which the *encomienda* was utilized as a means of opening up and settling the country. This report is dated June 12, 1582. At that time there were three principal centers of administration in the Islands: Manila, Cebú and Arévalo. About thirty *encomiendas* were located close to Manila, ten were near to Cebú, and fifteen near to Arévalo under the jurisdiction of Loarca. The latter group consisted of about 20,000 Indians. *Encomiendas* varied in size from 250 to 1500 natives, but the ideal *encomienda* was supposed to contain 500 souls. By *cédula* of August 9, 1589, royal authority was extended for the increase of the size of *encomiendas* in the Philippines to 800 or 1000 persons, if necessary, in order to bear the greater expenses of instruction and defense. This was bitterly opposed by the churchmen on account of the additional missionary labors incumbent on the priests assigned to these larger *encomiendas* (*Cédula* of August 9, 1589, A. I., 105–2–11). Philip II, on November 30, 1568, had ordered that no *encomienda* should yield more than 2000 pesos (*Recopilación*, 6–8–30).

Loarca states that there were also *encomiendas* in the Camarines provinces in southeast Luzón and in Ilocos, in the north of the same island. These *encomiendas* were under the jurisdiction of the *alcaldes mayores* and *corregidores* governing those provinces. (Relation by Loarca, Blair and Robertson, V, 35–187.)

[5] Report of Governor Dasmariñas on the *encomiendas* of the Philippines, May 31, 1591, in Blair and Robertson, VIII, 96–141.

military possession, distributed over a widely separated area, with insufficient means of communication and transportation.

Under the conditions outlined above, the *encomenderos* were permitted to forget the benign purposes for which they had been originally entrusted with the care and protection of the natives. The Indians on the *encomiendas* were reduced to the condition of slaves. They were mistreated, overtaxed, overworked, cheated, neglected, flogged, and abused.[6] Their protectors had become their exploiters. The churchmen who were supposed to act as their guardians and spiritual aids were insufficient in number to render effective service. Many of the latter served the interests of the *encomenderos,* and the latter were decidedly unfavorable to the introduction of more priests. The local officials of government and justice were in most cases too far away to care for and protect the natives, or even to visit the more remote *encomiendas* in their districts. Moreover, many of them were themselves *encomenderos,* perpetrating abuses on their own tenants, and accordingly little inclined to sacrifice their own interests for the protection of the natives on other *encomiendas.* Finally, the governor, located at the distant capital, was possibly ignorant of the real state of affairs; at any rate, he failed to enforce the laws which commanded humane treatment of the natives, leaving to the *encomenderos,* the *alcaldes mayores,* and *corregidores* the administration of the provinces and the supervision of the *encomiendas.*[7]

---

6 Blair and Robertson, VII, 269–294, Salazar to the Governor, January 25, 1591; Reply of the Governor [no date], *ibid.,* 294–300; *Carta del Obispo de Manila sobre la muerte de Ronquillo y los excesos que este cometió . . . ,* A. I., 68–1–32; *Memorial de las cosas . . . dignas de remediar en la Isla,* Zulueta Papers. Place numbers not given. These are examples of the hundreds of complaints, mostly by churchmen, against the abuses of the *encomenderos.* It would be impossible to cite them all.

The Zulueta Papers are transcripts from the Archive of the Indies of Seville, the National Library of Madrid, and the British Museum. They were copied under the direction of a Filipino scholar, Señor Zulueta. These Papers are now in the Philippines Library at Manila.

7 On June 4, 1620, the governor of the Philippines was authorized to

Efforts had been made for the correction of these abuses and to bring about a more effective control of the *encomiendas* by the governor. Early in the history of the Islands the king had empowered governors and viceroys to grant *encomiendas* for life, with thirty years' remission of tribute, to those who had participated in the conquest. Legaspi and Lavezares, the first two governors of the Philippines, had given *encomiendas* without limit to favorites, relatives, and friends; consequently, when Sande became governor, he was obliged to direct much of his attention to the eradication of the resultant evils, and he attempted to establish the *encomiendas* on a profitable and honest basis. He dispossessed many of the holders of these large tracts, and reserved them for the crown, as royal *encomiendas,* thus creating a revenue for the newly established and financially embarrassed government.[8] Sande made royal many of the hitherto unprofitable *encomiendas* which had been in private hands.[9] On account of these acts Sande became very unpopular

---

bestow *encomiendas,* with the provision that if he neglected to do so for a period of sixty days the vacant holdings should be bestowed by the audiencia. On October 24, 1655, Philip IV ordered that acting viceroys and acting governors should be limited to the faculty of providing *encomiendas ad interim,* subject to the subsequent ratification of the Council of the Indies (*Recopilación,* 6–8–8, 1–4, 5, 8, 11, 22).

[8] Blair and Robertson, III, 304–306.

[9] In this connection may be noted the distinction between the two classes of *encomiendas* which was made for purposes of administration. Private *encomiendas* were those which had been granted to private persons, conquerors, discoverers, soldiers, or persons who paid a regular rent, usually a third of the gross tribute collected. These were originally granted for life, and might be held for two subsequent generations. Later (after 1655), the usual period of confirmation was ten years, for persons who rented *encomiendas* as a business proposition. The royal *encomiendas* were situated near cities or ports and the income from them was reserved for the expenses and necessities of the royal estate, the payment of salaries, and other governmental expenses. Private *encomiendas* became royal on the death of an incumbent if he had no heirs, or on the expiration of the contract. The tribute from royal *encomiendas* was collected by the royal treasury. Morga's Sucesos, Blair and Robertson, XVI, 157; also *ibid.,* VIII, 27; see Bourne, "Historical introduction," *ibid.,* I, 39–40.

On June 7, 1597, the king, as a suggestion for the increase of funds for the maintenance of the government, wrote to the audiencia that a

in Manila, and so unpleasant were his relations with the residents that, having no protection or recourse, he was obliged to give up his command, practically driven from the Islands by his enemies.

The only person in the Philippines who exercised any sort of check on the governor was the bishop, with whom he was ordered to consult frequently. These consultations were often productive of bitter quarrels. The first prelate of the Philippines, Bishop Salazar, arrived in 1581, and throughout his ecclesiastical administration exercised influence of a far-reaching character. It was he who first showed the need of a royal audiencia to check the encroachments of the governor on the prerogatives of the church, for the protection of the natives, and for the safeguarding of the royal interests. Bishop Salazar was a determined opponent of Governor Sande, whom he accused of excessive indulgence in trade and the extortion of large sums from the *encomenderos.* On June 20, 1582, he wrote to the Council: "if I were as rich as Governor Sande, I would engage to pay any sum of money." He also testified that "the government here is a place for the . enrichment of governors; they

---

greater number of royal *encomiendas* should be established, and that the governor should not be permitted to assign so many to private persons (King to the Audiencia, June 7, 1597, A. I., 105–2–1). On February 16, 1602, the king again addressed the audiencia on the subject of the royal *encomiendas,* desiring to know why the tribute from them had so materially decreased, it having reached the low mark of 2500 pesos. In answer, the same reason for this falling off was suggested as in the letter above quoted, namely, that the governor had assigned many *encomiendas* to his friends (King to the Audiencia, February 16, 1602, A. I., 105–2–1). Francisco de la Misa, *factor* of the royal treasury of Manila, in a letter to the king, dated May 31, 1595, stated that the royal *encomiendas,* which had been established to provide revenue for the payment of the salaries of *alcaldes mayores, tenientes, oficiales reales,* and even that of the governor, had diminished greatly in number, so that not enough revenue was derived from them to meet the expenses for which they had been created. Misa concluded with a recommendation that eight royal *encomiendas* of the value of 8000 pesos a year should be established out of the first private *encomiendas* that were vacated (Misa to the King, May 31, 1595, A. I. 67–6–29).

carry away as much as 400,000 ducats, knowing that they will have to pay a share of it at the *residencia,* but they steal enough to do that also.''[10]

The government of the Philippines, prior to the establishment of the Audiencia of Manila, during the period 1565-1584, was subordinate to the viceroy and to the audiencia in Mexico. The time required for the transmission of documents and correspondence, the fewness of ships available for the voyage between the Philippines and New Spain, and the unsatisfactory means of communication resulting therefrom, seriously inconvenienced the residents of the colony. In matters of government and justice appeals had to be taken to Mexico. This proceeding involved great loss of time and expense, and was especially inimical to the administration of justice. The assignment and regulation of *encomiendas,* the supervision of financial affairs, the control of the Chinese trade, the dispatch of the galleons to New Spain, and the assignment of cargo-space on these ships, were all matters which, at that great distance, and at that time, called for divided control. The execution of all these duties was too great a charge for the human frailties of one man; the governor could do it neither honestly nor well. The necessity was apparent of having a central government in Manila which would be self-sufficient in itself; that is, independent of New Spain, and at the same time capable of repairing its own defects.

The relations which existed between the Manila government and the authorities of New Spain are illustrated by a letter which Governor Gonzalo Ronquillo de Peñalosa wrote a month later than the correspondence above alluded to. In this letter he announced the arrival of a ship from Mexico, which, he said, bore nothing but charges against him. These complaints, he alleged, had been formulated by agents of Dr. Francisco de Sande, his predecessor, whose *residencia* he had conducted and

---

[10] Salazar to the Council of the Indies, June 20, 1582, A. I., 68-1-32.

whom he had deprived of his office as governor. Ronquillo wrote that

nevertheless, Sande has been received in that royal audiencia of Mexico as *oidor*, as a result of which all those who love justice may well despair. They meddle with my government from Mexico, giving orders to my *corregidores* without consulting me, and addressing private individuals in regard to the supplies, directing them to keep watch over this or that matter; they impose grave penalties upon me, and no matter how small the affair may be, they refuse to listen to me or to hear my side of the question.[11]

He concluded by pointing out the inconsistency of his position, subject as he was to Sande, the man whom he had displaced because of the former's unfitness to occupy the post of governor. Although Governor Ronquillo de Peñalosa did not ask for an audiencia on this occasion, he did petition for an educated assistant to aid him in the administration of justice. "The trouble here," he wrote to the king, in the letter above quoted, "is that the people are of such a nature that, at the same time wheri justice is done to one, an enemy is made of another person." The rule of Ronquillo de Peñalosa as governor was distinctly typical of the possibilities of an absolute executive, far removed from the restraining influence of the courts, with scarcely any limitation upon his operations. Appointed as he had been for life, with proprietary attributes, and with the power of naming his successor, Ronquillo de Peñalosa was the first governor sent out from Spain in pursuance of the policy of entrusting frontier commands to military men who were fitted by profession and experience to deal with situations which demanded the qualities of the soldier, rather than those of the administrator and politcian. An attempt thus seems to have been made to remedy the ills which had been characteristic of the administration of Lavezares and Sande by entrusting the governor with more centralized power—an attempt to correct

---

[11] Ronquillo de Peñalosa to the King, July 15, 1582, A. I., 67–6–6.

the evils of absolutism with the mailed fist and more absolutism, backed by military power.

The bishop, who at this time kept the court well informed of the weaknesses of the government, as they appeared to him, sent many complaints against Ronquillo de Peñalosa, as other churchmen had done against former governors. Not only did the bishop himself write repeatedly, but he influenced the municipal and ecclesiastical chapters of Manila to send protests against the governor's misrule. It was largely owing to Salazar's influence that Captain Gabriel de Rivera (or Ribera) was sent to Spain with a petition signed by most of the influential men of the colony, asking for various reforms. Among these the establishment of a royal audiencia was especially requested.[12]

On the occasion of Ronquillo's death in 1583, the bishop called attention to the straits into which the colony had fallen as a result of the tyrannical methods of the deceased governor.[13] He described Ronquillo's efforts to prevent residents from appealing to the audiencia and viceroy of New Spain. He stated that the Indians had been unjustly treated by the *encomenderos* and *alcaldes mayores*, for when appeals had been made to the governor, the latter, on a plea of being too busy to occupy himself with such minute details, had ordered the *alcaldes mayores* to settle the questions at issue without disturbing him. Ronquillo was said to have engaged extensively in commerce, monopolizing the ships to the exclusion of the merchants, and forcing large loans from the officials and residents, who did not dare to refuse him, lest all their privileges be taken from them. He had established private *encomiendas* in nearly every town in Luzón, appropriating the income therefrom, instead of turning the proceeds into the royal treasury.[14]

---

[12] Morga's Sucesos, Blair and Robertson, XV, 59–60; *Carta del Obispo de Manila sobre la muerte de Ronquillo, y de los excesos que este cometio,* . . . A. I., 68–1–32.

[13] *Ibid.*

[14] The *cédula* of March 1, 1551, had forbidden the bestowal of *en-*

This the prelate conceded to be in accordance with the conditions of the governor's appointment, but it was nevertheless unjust, as the privilege of holding *encomiendas* was denied to other officials, and the treasury of the colony was in need of the revenue which had been daily enriching the governor. The bishop accused the governor of seizing Indians, placing them *en encomienda* wherever and whenever he found them, irrespective of whether they were already free, or whether they belonged on other *encomiendas*. These acts, he said, had caused the Indians to be dissatisfied and rebellious, and he evidently was of the opinion that a revolt was impending when he penned this memorial. "Many times I have prayed," he wrote, "that God should close the natives' eyes in order that they may not see the weakness and the little power with which we might resist them in case they should arise to put down these evils."

The bishop closed this memorial with a vigorous protest against the continuance of the hereditary principle in the succession of governors in the Philippines. He made the general recommendation that in the future governors should be appointed by the king, with a view to securing men of administrative and executive ability. He brought forth strenuous objections to the accession of the ex-governor's nephew, Diego Ronquillo de Peñalosa, who was not fitted to occupy the post of governor. If the latter assumed the government, the bishop could see nothing in store for the colony but a continuation of the evil days which had been extant throughout the administration of the elder Ronquillo, "who had spent all his time in gathering wealth for himself by means of trade, shutting his eyes and ears to those who asked justice of him." Salazar expressed the opinion that "had Gonzalo Ronquillo de Peñalosa

---

comiendas on ministers of justice, treasury officials, viceroys, ecclesiastics, and governors. According to the terms of the appointment of Gonzalo Ronquillo de Peñalosa as proprietary governor, he had been allowed an *encomienda* in each principal town. See *Recopilación*, 6–8–12.

spent as much of his time in making conquests and discoveries as he had in making packages [of merchandise], the prosperity of the Islands and the general welfare would have been his chief aim."[15]

Although the decree establishing an audiencia in the Philippines was promulgated before the above memorial reached court, there is no question but that the influence of Bishop Salazar did much towards bringing about the creation of a tribunal in the Islands. Indeed, Salazar has been given all the credit for this by more than one authority.[16] While the bishop did exert an important influence in bringing about this change, the support which he received from residents of the colony was also of immense advantage. Many individuals, aggrieved by the abuses of the executive, wrote vigorous complaints against "the tyranny of an absolute governor, who alone and unchecked, reserves to himself excessive power." Their letters emphasize the injustice of having appeals carried to Mexico, "where the people of Manila never get their deserts, and where they suffer on account of the distance." Various *encomenderos* had been wronged by the acts of the governor in dividing their *encomiendas,* and reducing the number of Indians thereon; they had appealed to Mexico, and after waiting over two years, had despaired of ever getting any return for the money and the time which they had spent in litigation at the distant capital. As a possible means of relief they requested the establishment of a royal audiencia at Manila.[17]

Another person who exerted considerable influence toward the establishment of an audiencia in the Philippines was Captain Gabriel de Rivera, who went to Madrid for that purpose.

---

[15] *Op. cit.*

[16] Including the two principal Spanish historians of the Philippines, Martínez de Zúñiga (*Estadismo,* I, 243) and Montero y Vidal (*Historia general,* I, 88).

[17] These letters, dated June 18, 1583, are among the Zulueta Papers at Manila.

He was the first *procurador general de las islas del poniente,* and it was his duty to represent at court the needs of the colony, and of its inhabitants.[18]   Rivera acted as the personal agent of Salazar in his advocacy of the establishment of an audiencia, and it was largely due to his efforts that the institution was established when it was.   In his memorial of February 16, 1582, Rivera criticized the existing administration in the Philippines, the proprietary governorship, and the control over commerce which the governor had exercised. The latter had levied the *almojarifazgo* and other customs duties in defiance of the royal *cédulas* forbidding them, and without consulting the wishes of the merchants or officials. Rivera alleged that the *almojarifazgo* and the *alcabala* were ruining the commerce of the Islands.[19]   His memorial treated

---

[18] A *procurador,* according to Escriche (*Diccionario,* II, 759), "is one who, by virtue of power or faculty conceded by another, acts in his name."   There were in later times several procurators representing different interests of the Philippines at the Court of Madrid.   The associated merchants had one or more, the *consulado,* each religious order, etc.   These *procuradores* were usually lawyers, not infrequently men who had been in the islands.   An interesting parallel might be noted between the *procuradores* and the American colonial agents of prerevolutionary days.   Zúñiga here gives Rivera entire credit for the bringing of the audiencia to Manila—*op. cit.,* I, 175.   See note 16, *supra.*

[19] The *alcabala (al que vale,* "according to value") was a percentage tax levied on goods (movable and immovable) sold or exchanged. Merchants were held accountable for the payment of this tax, and for this purpose their accounts were examined by royal officials at regular intervals (Escriche, *Diccionario,* I, 143).   It was first introduced into the Indies by Philip II in 1574, having been levied in Spain as early as 1079, though not in its perfected form.   In accordance with the tariff of November 1, 1591, it was exacted from merchants, apothecaries, *encomenderos* (having farms and cattle-ranches), ragpickers, clothmakers, silversmiths, goldsmiths, blacksmiths, and shoemakers.   An *alcabala* was paid on wine.   By the *cédula* of June 7, 1576, the rate of *alcabala* was fixed at two per cent.   In Perú it was raised to four per cent during the administration of the Conde de Chinchón as viceroy and was collected at that rate there until the *cédula* of July 26, 1776, raised it to six per cent.   This rate was paid thereafter in the Spanish colonies (*Recopilación,* 8–13–1 to 14, notes, 2 and 4), except for an increase in the rate to 8 per cent in 1782, to meet the added expenses of war.   The old rate of 6 per cent was restored in 1791 (transcripts of these *cédulas* exist in A. I., 87–1–20).

Exemptions from this tax were made in favor of churches,

extensively of the abuses which had occurred in the administration of the *encomiendas*, and he pointed out numerous defects in the judicial system of the colonies.

He suggested the establishment of a royal audiencia to consist of three judges, having criminal and civil jurisdiction, without appeal to any other tribunal than the Council of the Indies. The audiencia as outlined by him was to have administrative powers as well as judicial; it was to govern as a commission, with a governor at its head, chosen for a term of six years.[20] This scheme, he said, if put into operation, would re-

---

monasteries, and prelates when they bought or sold goods not for profit. When they engaged in commerce for its own sake they were obliged to pay the *alcabala* in the same way as laymen (*Recopilación*, 8–13–17). Goods belonging to the Santa Cruzada, provisions bought, sold or stored which were destined for the poor, and munitions of war paid no *alcabala* (*ibid.*, 18–23). Indians were also exempted under certain circumstances (*ibid.*, 24; see entire Title 13 of Book 8, *Recopilación*, for further specifications regarding the payment of this tax). In 1568 Philip II exempted the Philippines for thirty years. As noted above, the *alcabala* was not introduced regularly into the Indies until 1574, though it was levied in individual cases as early as 1558. Even earlier than this Pizarro had obtained the right to levy it in Perú for a period of a hundred years (*ibid.*, 8–13–1; note 1), but Philip II ordered it paid in the Philippines on August 9, 1589 (*ibid.*, 9–45–66).

The *almojarifazgo*, like the *alcabala*, had been utilized early in the history of the Peninsula and because a productive source of revenue, it was introduced into the Indies. The earliest law dealing with this tax in New Spain was promulgated by Charles V on October 18, 1553, exempting cargoes which had already paid the tax in Spain. On June 24, 1566, and on December 28, 1568, Philip II ordered a five per cent export tax on all goods leaving Seville for the Indies (the ordinance of December 28, 1562, having fixed it at two and a half per cent) and an import tax in the Indies on these same goods of ten per cent, making in all a tax of fifteen per cent. Wine was to pay a ten per cent import and export tax respectively, making a total of twenty per cent paid on that commodity (*ibid.*, 8–15–1, 2, 8). The law of April 21, 1574, ordered a two and a half export and a five per cent import tax on goods shipped between colonies (*ibid.*, 10). On August 9, 1589, a three per cent *almojarifazgo* was authorized in the Philippines, with exemptions on provisions, munitions, and other specified articles brought to the Islands by the Chinese, Japanese, Siamese, and Borneans (*ibid.*, 22, 24). The tax on Chinese merchandise was raised from three to six per cent on November 20, 1606 (*ibid.*, 23). Chinese goods from the Philippines paid a ten per cent *almojarifazgo* at Acapulco. This tax was also paid on leaving the Philippines or other New Spain ports and on entrance at Acapulco (*ibid.*, 21). For exemptions see *Recopilación*, 8–15–26 to 30.

[20] Rivera to the King, February 16, 1582, A. I., 1–1–2/24.

sult in no increased expense to the crown or colony. He proposed the abolition of the three *oficiales reales,* suggesting the substitution of three *oidores* in their places, thus extending the jurisdiction of the audiencia to matters of finance. The new tribunal should likewise take cognizance of the assignment of *encomiendas,* and see that in all cases the royal will was obeyed. The audiencia should exercise supervision over the *alcaldes mayores* in their relation to the *encomiendas,* with a view to remedying the existing abuses and seeing that justice was done to the Indians. The audiencia should hear cases appealed from the *alcaldes mayores* and *corregidores* instead of allowing these suits to be heard by the governor or sent to Mexico. Rivera also urged that there should be a special *defender of the Indians* as a part of the audiencia.[21]

Enough has been noted of the evils of the government as it existed before the establishment of the audiencia to under-

---

21 A legal defender of the Indians was wanted in this case to serve them in the courts. The bishop, at this time, was protector of the Indians and in that capacity had protested against the abuses of the *encomenderos.* The bishop, of course, could not enter the courts and defend the Indians in litigation.

The law of March 17, 1593, which ultimately established a defender of the Indians in Manila, filled the need voiced by Rivera. The law referred to read as follows: "The protection and defense of the Indians in the Philippines was entrusted by us to the bishops there, but having recognized that the latter cannot conform to the demands, *autos* and judicial summons which require their personal presence, we order that our president-governor shall name a protector and defender of the Indians, assigning to him a sufficient salary from the taxes levied pro rata upon the Indians who are under the royal jurisdiction and on private *encomiendas,* without touching the revenues of our royal *hacienda* which are for other purposes. And we declare that this does not signify that it is our intention to deprive the bishops of the superintendence and protection of the Indians in general" *(Recopilación,* 6–6–8).

Philip II, on January 10, 1589, restored the office of protector or defender of the Indians in the Indies generally. It was stated in this law that as a result of the earlier abolition of the office many inconveniences and injustices had arisen. The law authorized the appointment of a person of good character and morals to the office *(ibid.,* 1). The reform of April 9, 1591, required that the appointee should be a lawyer, and that there should be a defender of the Indians attached to each audiencia *(ibid.,* 3). The reform of March 11, 1784, provided that the *fiscales* should name these protectors in the future. *(Ibid.,* note 1.)

stand the reasons for the creation of the tribunal. The whole
matter summarizes itself in the excesses of the governor, and
the necessity of protecting all classes of society from his absolutism. These abuses called for the establishment of a tribunal
nearer than New Spain, which would, in a safe and expeditious
manner, impose the necessary limitations upon the governor,
insure an equitable collection and an economical expenditure
of the public revenue, and bring about particularly the elimination of official corruption. It was desirable to protect the
merchant in his legitimate business, to insure stability in the
relations of church and state, and to obviate the existing evils
in the administration of the provincial governments. The
latter meant the assignment of *encomiendas* in accordance with
the law to deserving individuals instead of to friends and relatives of the governors, or to other prominent officials of the
colony. It also meant that the natives on these *encomiendas*
should be protected from the rapacity of the *encomenderos*.
It was realized that an effort should be made to insure the imparting of religious instruction to the natives in partial return
for tribute paid by them. Finally, it meant the establishment
of a tribunal which would have power to enforce the law prescribing that the *alcaldes mayores* and *corregidores* should
exercise faithful supervision over these matters which were
within their jurisdiction. A tribunal was needed, not merely
to hear such appeals as might come to it by process of law,
but with authority to intervene actively in affairs of government, checking the abuses of the governor and protecting the
community from his absolutism.

The proposition to establish an independent audiencia in
Manila was opposed by the viceroy and audiencia of New Spain.
The latter tribunal wrote a letter of protest to the Council of
the Indies, demanding that in matters of government and justice the colony of the Philippines should continue to bear the
same relations to the viceroyalty of New Spain as did Guada-

lajara.[22] Rivera answered these objections in a special memorial, stating that the isolation of the Philippines alone justified the establishment of an audiencia and an independent government. He also pointed out that the nearness of Japan and China and the necessity of dealing with them required the presence of a sovereign tribunal in Manila. He asserted that the colony could deal directly with the Council of the Indies more profitably than through the Audiencia of Mexico. The latter mode of procedure was indirect and cumbersome and it exposed litigants to the meddling of the *oidores* of Mexico in matters which they did not understand.[23]

Finally, the Audiencia of Manila was established by decree of Philip II on May 5, 1583, in the following terms:

Whereas in the interests of good government and the administration of our justice, we have accorded the establishment in the city of Manila in the Island of Luzón of one of our royal audiencias and chanceries, in which there shall be a president, three *oidores*, a *fiscal*, and the necessary officials; and whereas we have granted that this audiencia should have the same authority and preëminence as each one of our royal audiencias which sit in the town of Valladolid and the city of Granada of these our realms, and the other audiencias of our Indies: now therefore we order to be made and sent to the said Island our royal seal, with which are to be stamped our decisions which are made and issued by the said president and *oidores* in the said audiencia.[24]

The jurisdiction of the tribunal, it is to be noted, extended throughout the Island of Luzón and the rest of the islands of the Archipelago, as well as over "the mainland of China, whether discovered or yet to be discovered."

The decree which provided for the foundation of the Audiencia of Manila consisted of three hundred and thirteen sec-

---

[22] The Audiencia of Guadalajara was at that time subordinate to the Viceroy of New Spain in matters of war, government, and finance (*hacienda*). *Ibid.*, 2–15–47, 49 to 54.

[23] Rivera to the King, June 26, 1583, A. I., 1–1–2/24.

[24] Foundation of the Audiencia, Blair and Robertson, V, 274–318; VI, 35–43; also in A. I., 1–1–3/25, the latter being the original *cédula*, signed by the king and ministers.

tions. Although the audiencia was subsequently abolished for
a few years, it was re-established in 1598 and these articles were
again utilized. It is therefore worth while to notice the most
important provisions of the law of establishment, which was
to serve as a foundation for the audiencia during a period of
approximately three hundred years. The first thirty-eight sections were devoted to the creation of the tribunal, to a definition of its jurisdiction over civil and criminal cases, and to a
determination of the proper method of procedure in them. The
audiencia was to have authority to try cases of appeal from
gobernadores, alcaldes mayores, and other magistrates of the
provinces; it also had jurisdiction over civil cases appealed
from the *alcaldes ordinarios* of the city and original jurisdiction over all criminal cases arising within five leagues of the
city of Manila. Appeals were to be tried by *revista* (review)
before the tribunal. Cases of first instance (*vista*) were not to
be tried in the tribunal, excepting those to which the government was a party, or the above-mentioned criminal cases. The
judgment of the audiencia was usually to be final in ordinary
suits, and always in criminal cases. Those involving the government, and civil suits exceeding a certain value were appealable to the Council of the Indies. Notice of appeal to the latter
tribunal had to be served within one year after the objection-
able decision was rendered, and the party appealing the case
was obliged to post financial bonds covering the expenses of
suit in case the final judgment were not favorable to him. The
decision of the audiencia was to be executed in all cases, even
though an appeal to the Council of the Indies had been made.
The procedure followed in the chanceries of Valladolid and Granada was to be enforced in the Audiencia of Manila except when
the contrary was especially ordered. Investigations might be
made by one judge, but the concurrence of two was necessary
for all decisions involving the reversal of a former judgment,
or in cases wherein a certain amount was at stake. In the latter

case, an assistant judge might be chosen from outside the audiencia to assist the regular magistrate.

The audiencia was forbidden to act alone in the selection of judges of *residencias* or *pesquisidores;* it was commanded not to interfere with governors of provinces, but it had the right, when charges had been made by private individuals, to conduct investigations of governors' official conduct. The audiencia was empowered to investigate the judges of provinces. Magistrates were forbidden to hear cases affecting themselves or their relatives, and when a case involving more than one thousand pesos was before the tribunal, and no *oidor* was eligible to try it, an *alcalde ordinario* might serve in the place of a regular magistrate, with appeal to the Council of the Indies. Criminal charges against the *oidores* were to be tried by the president, with the assistance, if need be, of such *alcaldes ordinarios* as the latter might select. No relative of the president or of an *oidor* could be appointed legally to a corregidorship or to an *encomienda.* *Oidores* were eligible for appointment by the president from time to time to inspect the administration of justice and government in the provinces.

Oidores were forbidden to receive fees from or to act as advocates for any private person, and they could not hold income-yielding estates in arable land or cattle. *Oidores* were forbidden to engage in business, either singly or in partnership, nor could they avail themselves of the compulsory services of Indians under pain of deprivation of office. Any person could bring suit against an *oidor.* As noted above, such cases would either be tried by the president or by an *alcalde ordinario* on the president's designation. Such cases might be appealed to the Council of the Indies.

The audiencia, according to the terms of its establishment, had extensive authority over matters of government. In case of the death or incapacity of the president, the audiencia was to assume control of affairs, the senior *oidor* filling the post of president and captain-general, with special charge over military matters. Under such circumstances the administrative and executive functions were to be administered by the audiencia as a body. The governor, who was also president of the audiencia, was ordered to make a complete report annually to the Council of the Indies on the state of the government and the finances of the colony, including an account of the gross income and expenditures, a survey of conditions of the *encomiendas* and *corregimientos,* as well as a report on the conduct of officials, including *oidores.* In fact, all matters that came regularly under the care of the executive were to be covered in the annual report of the governor and captain-general of the Islands.

The president was empowered to delegate the *oidores,* in turn, to make tours of inspection in the provinces. The magistrates, as visitors, were to inquire into the character of service rendered by the *alcaldes mayores* in the administration of government and justice. They were to note the state of the towns and their needs, the means taken for the construction and preservation of public buildings, and the condition of the Indians on the *encomiendas.* They were to see whether they were faithfully and efficiently instructed in religion, or whether they were permitted to live in ignorance and idolatry. Reports were to be made by the visitors on the state of the soil, the condition of the crops and harvests, extent of mineral wealth and timber in the provinces under investigation, weights and measures, and in fact, everything that had to do with the general welfare. On these trips the *oidores* were authorized to take such action as they felt to be necessary. Two *oidores* were also required to make weekly inspections of the prisons of the colony.

The decree of establishment also directed that certain phases of ecclesiastical affairs should claim the attention of the audiencia. The chief duty of the tribunal in that regard was to keep the ecclesiastical judges from exceeding their authority, and the practices of the audiencias of Spain were especially prescribed as a precedent for the local tribunal. The audiencia was charged with supervision over the assignment of benefices, and especially with the settlement of the property and estates of bishops and archbishops who died in the Islands. The audiencia was ordered to permit nothing to be done which would be in prejudice of the rights and prerogatives of the church. The tribunal was instructed to assist the prelates on all occasions when they petitioned for royal aid. It was also to see that properly accredited bulls were read and applied in the Spanish towns, but not in the native villages.

As noted above, suits involving the royal treasury and the collection of money for the government were to be reviewed and decided before any other that might come up in the royal audiencia. It was the duty of the *fiscal* to prosecute these cases in the interest of the government. At the beginning of each year the president and two magistrates were to audit the reports of the *oficiales reales,* and if these reports were not duly and properly rendered, the salaries of these officials were to be withheld. After auditing the accounts the committee was to count the money in the royal treasury. The *oidores* who did this extra work were to receive an allowance of twenty-five thousand *maravedís* (about 56 pesos) in addition to their regular salaries. The authorization of the audiencia was necessary for the payment of extraordinary expenses not appearing in the regular budget and these disbursements were made subject to the later approval of the Council of the Indies. The audiencia was held responsible in these matters by the Council. Full reports of expenditures made on the responsibility of the audiencia were to be made to the Council, and the *oidores* were held accountable in their *residencias* for their votes cast in the *junta* or *acuerdo de hacienda,* as the committee was called.

The audiencia was given supervision over the administration of the estates of deceased persons; it was to examine the accounts of executors and see that the wills of the deceased

were faithfully executed and that all was done in accordance
with the law. For this purpose an *oidor* was delegated each
year with authority to dispose of these cases in the name of the
audiencia. In a subsequent chapter the duties and activities
of this *administrador* or *juez de bienes de difuntos* will be enlarged upon.

Considerable space in this decree was devoted to prescribing the rules for the trial of cases involving Indians, with a
view to securing justice both in their administration by the *encomenderos* and in the supervision which the *alcaldes mayores*
exercised over the *encomenderos*. The provision was made that
"our said president and *oidores* shall always take great care to
be informed of the crimes and abuses which are committed
against the Indians under our royal crown, or against those
granted in *encomiendas* to other persons by the governors." The
audiencia was directed to exercise care that "the said Indians
shall be better treated and instructed in our Holy Catholic Faith,
as our free vassals."

The audiencia was required to exercise care that suits involving Indians were neither lengthy nor involved, that decisions were reached promptly and without unnecessary litigation,
and that the rites, customs, and practices to which the Indians
had always been accustomed should be continued in so far as was
practicable. The audiencia and the bishop were to see that there
was a person appointed in each village to give instruction in religion. *Alcaldes mayores* were ordered not to dispossess native
chiefs of their rule or authority; they were, on the contrary, to
appeal cases involving them without delay to the audiencia, or
to the visiting *oidor*. The audiencia was to devote two days a
week to hearing suits to which Indians were parties. *Encomenderos* were to be protected by the audiencia in the possession
of their *encomiendas*.

A proportionate amount of attention in this *cédula* is devoted
to outlining the duties of the *fiscal*, who, from many points of

view, was the most important official directly connected with
the tribunal. It was his function to appear as prosecutor for
the government in all cases tried before the audiencia, and he
was forbidden to serve as the advocate of any private person during his term of office. He should devote his attention
especially to matters involving the exchequer. He was to prosecute all cases of appeal from the *alcaldes mayores* and *corregidores* on behalf of the government, and "he was to take care to
assist and favor poor Indians in the suits that they have, and
to see that they are not oppressed, maltreated, or wronged."
The *fiscal*, ordinarily, was not to prosecute unless it were on the
complaint of some person, but in cases of notorious injustice,
or when judicial inquiry was being made, he could take the initiative on his own account. It was his duty to perform any
and all legal acts which were consistent with his position, and
which were designed to bring about justice or to secure the royal
interests.

The remaining sections of this decree, and, in fact, the greater
part of it, are devoted to establishing the duties of the *fiscal*
and the minor officials of the audiencia, to fixing a tariff of fees
to be charged for notarial and other legal work and to the determination of other matters which are of no great consequence
to the purposes of this chapter.

Among the minor officials attached to the audiencia were
the *alguacil mayor* and his two deputies. These were to act as
the executive officers of the court and were empowered to make
arrests, serve papers and execute similar functions. Their duties, as a whole, were much like those of the English or American constable or sheriff. They might arrest, on their own initiative, persons whom they caught in crime, as, for example, those
playing forbidden games of chance, or indulging in immoral
practices, typical particularly of the Chinese. The *alguacil* was
responsible for the maintenance of the prison of the audiencia;

for this purpose he could appoint a certain number of jail-wardens.

There were also clerks of court and notaries, chosen by royal appointment. Their duties were those customarily required of such officials, not differing from those of today. The audiencia likewise had official reporters, similar to the court reporters of the present day. Advocates and attorneys practicing before the audiencia had to fulfill certain prescribed requirements in regard to learning, training, and general ability. Receivers, bailiffs, jail-wardens and interpreters each received their due amount of space and attention in this *cédula*. The interpreters were to assist the Indians who were defending themselves in a Spanish-speaking court. Among their duties was the translation of the testimony of witnesses, of the questions of attorneys and the rulings of the courts into the native dialects, or into the Spanish language, as the circumstances might require. These interpreters were also required to assist the natives in the formulation of legal documents. All these minor officials were to be regulated in the collection of fees by a legal tariff. Finally, the audiencia was provided with an archive within which were to be deposited and kept the great seal of the government, and all official papers, including records of cases and official acts.

The new audiencia having been provided for, Santiago de Vera, the recently appointed governor and captain-general of the Islands and president of the new tribunal, arrived at Manila on May 28, 1584. In accordance with the new law, it was his duty to govern the Philippines in the capacity of executive and military commander, and at the same time preside over the audiencia in its respective judicial, advisory, and administrative capacities. The first session of the audiencia was held on June 15, 1584.[25] The new tribunal was officially brought into

25 *Ibid.*

being with much pomp and ceremony, including a procession of the president and magistrates in their robes of office, and the celebration of divine service in the cathedral by the bishop. The president and each of the *oidores* subsequently made lengthy reports to the Council of the Indies on the inauguration of the tribunal.

The most direct and striking consequence of the establishment of the audiencia in Manila was the discord which it engendered between the various officials and functionaries of the government. Whereas, before the inauguration of the tribunal, the chief ill of the colony had been the unrivaled absolutism and the high-handed proceedings of the governor, now, with the division of power newly effected, the creation of new departments, and the checking of one official against another, strife and contention took the place of despotism.

There were but few misunderstandings between the *oidores* over their judicial duties. The functions of the audiencia, as a court, were clearly defined and distinctly understood. Although appeals were made from the audiencia to the Council of the Indies, as appeals are always made from a minor court to a superior tribunal, there was little dissatisfaction with the body in the exercise of its purely legal functions. Its value in protecting the natives on the *encomiendas* from the tyranny of their masters, the facility rendered to the administration of justice by making appeal to New Spain unnecessary, and the advantage of having immediately at hand a tribunal with plenary powers were readily recognized.

The chief objection to the tribunal developed as a result of the audiencia's interference in matters of government and administration. Disputes arose between the governor and the *oidores*, and among the *oidores* themselves. The lack of experience in the local field of the president and magistrates may have been one of the causes of the unsatisfactory conditions immediately following the establishment of the audiencia. Another and possibly a more important reason lay in the nature and wording of the articles of establishment. A certain amount of confusion existed in the minds of all as to the extent of power which the audiencia should have in governmental and ecclesiastical affairs. No definite distinction had been drawn between the powers of the president and those of the *oidores* in matters of government, and the former at once accused the latter of infringing upon the jurisdiction of the executive. The *oidores,* on the other hand, claimed that their advice should be taken in all matters of appointment, defense, patronage—both ecclesiastical and secular—finance, commerce and interior administration. They began to intervene actively in those matters, to the displeasure of the governor and treasury officials. All the *oidores* as well as the *fiscal,* wrote lengthy memorials and reports to the king, offering advice on this affair or that, and criticising the governor, the bishop, and the *oficiales reales* for acts done within their own spheres of authority. In sending these reports and in making these suggestions, the magistrates did not question their own authority and they resented exceedingly the objections and charges of interference by those concerned.

An illustration may be noted in the letter written on July 3, 1584, by Oidor Melchoir Dávalos to the king. After several clear intimations that he would like to be governor in case a vacancy should arise and after modestly setting forth his own qualifications and virtues, Dávalos wrote a faithful and vivid account of the expeditions which had been made recently against the Mohammedan Sulus. He petitioned for a suspension of the law forbidding slavery in order that Spaniards might avail themselves of captive Moros as slaves.[26] He made several recom-

---

[26] Permission had been granted by Philip II on July 4, 1570, to enslave Mindanaos. A second *cédula* permitting the Spaniards in the Philippines to do this was promulgated by Philip III on May 29, 1620. This act was rendered justifiable in the eyes of the Spaniards by the fact that they were dealing with semi-savages who were of the Mohammedan faith, and accordingly the ceaseless enemies of the Spaniards. *Recopilación,* 6–2–12.

mendations in regard to the Chinese, stating particularly that he was devoting himself to a study of the kind of government best fitted for the Chinese in Manila. He complained that the Chinese merchants were draining the Islands of silver, bringing as many as thirty-four shiploads of Chinese cargo a year. Since nothing of commercial value was produced in the Philippines, they could take away nothing else than silver. This incessant drain on the coin imported from Acapulco was resulting in the impoverishment of the colony and constituted a source of danger to New Spain as well. The exportation of money was contrary to royal orders and distinctly prejudicial to the economic interests of the realm. Dávalos recommended immediate action in the matter. He then discussed military affairs, alleging that the pay of the soldiers was insufficient, and their condition miserable. The first and third of the matters touched upon by the *oidor* in his memorial, namely, the war in Mindanao and the condition of the soldiers, belonged to the private jurisdiction of the governor and captain-general,[27] the control of the Chinese coming later under the jurisdiction of the governor as captain-general, with special inhibition of the interference of the audiencia.[28]

This letter furnishes a good illustration of the interference of an *oidor* in matters of government. The desire to interfere does not seem to have been confined to one individual, but was apparently characteristic of all the magistrates of the audiencia.[29]

The extensive field over which the *oidores* claimed cognizance is shown by a series of memorials which were sent by the audiencia as a body to the court under the date of June 26, 1586.[30] They are noted here because they illustrate the diversity of the

---

27 *Recopilación*, 3–10–13, 14; see Chapter VIII of this book.

28 *Recopilación*, 2–15–55, promulgated November 4, 1606; see also 6–18–5 and 5–3–24.

29 Dávalos to the King, July 3, 1584, A. I., 67–6–18.

30 Audiencia to the Council of the Indies, June 26, 1586, A. I., 67–6–18.

interests of the *oidores*, and because their devotion to these various matters was characterized as unjustified meddling by the governor and the other opponents of the audiencia. The concern which the *oidores* manifested in the miscellaneous affairs of government constituted, no doubt, an indirect reason for the temporary removal of the tribunal in 1589.

These memorials suggested reform in many departments of government. The inadequate state of defense and the demoralized condition into which the garrison had fallen was the subject of one letter. Attention was called to the necessity of obtaining more funds for the fortifications of the Islands. Reference was made to the continual danger of Japanese invasion. Another letter dealt with financial affairs. The public exchequer was reported to be in bad condition, as there was not enough money in the treasury to pay the expenses of government. The *oidores* recommended that their own salaries should be paid out of the treasury of Mexico. They suggested an increase of tribute as a means of securing more money. This, they alleged, could be done in justice, since the amount of tribute paid by the natives of the Philippines did not equal that levied upon the Indians of New Spain.[31] The *oidores* reported an increase of 5000

---

[31] The *Recopilación* is singularly indefinite regarding the rate or amount of tribute to be assessed in New Spain. Beyond the stipulation that tribute levied under the supervision of viceroys, presidents, and audiencias should be moderate and just, practically nothing is said as to the amount that should be collected (See *cédulas* of June 19, 1536, and September 29, 1555, *Recopilación*, 6–5–21), excepting certain increases as stipulated in the law of November 1, 1591 (*ley 16*).

According to the laws just cited, the rate was to be fixed by the officials mentioned above. By *cédula* of December 19, 1534, the *oficiales reales* were empowered to fix the rate of tribute (*ibid.*, 28). Reductions in the rate of tribute were to be authorized by the *fiscal* and *oficiales reales* (*ibid.*, 29). Apparently the rate varied according to the locality (*ibid.*, 1 to 5, 16, 17), and in the *cédulas* of 1536 and 1555, cited above, consideration was given to the rate formerly paid by the Indians to their *caciques*. Fonseca y Urrutia (*Historia de la real hacienda*, I, 417 *et seq.*) tell us that the tribute paid in the province of Tlascala in 1572 was 13 *reales;* in 1564 the rate for New Spain was fixed at two pesos, and in 1600 it was reduced to one peso of eight *reales*. (Bancroft, *History of Mexico*, II, 586–9.)

pesos in the revenues of the colony as profits from the sale of certain offices which had formerly been bestowed gratis by the governor upon his friends, the righting of this wrong being effected through the influence of the *fiscal* and *oidores* who officiated as members of the *junta de hacienda.*

While ostensibly seeking means for the enlargement of the income of the Islands, as noted, the *oidores* protested against a recent royal order which had required that the proceeds returned from vacant *encomiendas* should be placed in the public treasury. They objected that this would take away all hope of reward from soldiers and subjects "who have served your Majesty, reducing them to poverty, with no means of support

---

Humboldt (Political Essay, II, 431–2) states that there had been a gradual diminution of tribute paid by the Indians during the hundred years preceding his visit. In 1601, he states, Indians paid 32 *reales* tribute and 4 *reales* additional, *de servicio*, in all, about 23 francs. It had been reduced, little by little, till the amount actually paid was from 5 to 15 francs, and, "in the greater part of Mexico," he states, "the head-tax amounts to 11 francs."

Archbishop Benavides, of Manila, writing in 1600 (Zulueta Papers, date and place number not given) pleaded for the abolition of the tribute in the Philippines, stating that while the collection of tribute in New Spain was justifiable because the natives had been accustomed to paying tribute before the Spaniards came, the custom was entirely new in the Philippines, since the native princes had never levied tribute. On the other hand, various persons writing from the Philippines at different times urged that the tribute there should be increased to the rate imposed in New Spain.

The money value of the tribute in the Philippines was fixed at eight *reales* by Legaspi. It could be paid either in gold or in kind. Morga tells us that the *encomenderos* made great profit by receiving the payment in rice, cotton, cloth, fowls, and other commodities, at a cheap rate, selling those same articles later to the improvident natives at greatly increased prices (Morga's Sucesos, Blair and Robertson, XVI, 159). When Dasmariñas arrived as governor in 1590, the tribute was raised from eight to ten *reales* (*cédula* of August 9, 1589, *Recopilación*, 6–5–65, also A. I., 105–2–11). While the eight *reales* were to be appropriated by the *encomenderos*, the additional two *reales* were to be distributed between the religious and military governments in proportions of one-half to one and a half (Blair and Robertson, XVI, 160).

In the instructions of May 23, 1593, to Governor Dasmarina, reference was made to a current rate of eight *reales* (*ibid.*, IX, 249), so it would seem that the local rate had been reduced from ten to eight *reales* at some date between 1589 and 1593. On February 16, 1602, the rate was restored at ten *reales* (*Recopilación*, 6–5–65), and was so con-

after a long career of service."[32] In other words, the audiencia
is here seen registering its objections to the conversion of private into royal *encomiendas,* notwithstanding the fact that this
would mean greater revenue for the government. The inconsistency of this attitude was pointed out by Magistrate Dávalos
in his letter of June 20, 1585.[33]

Another petition which may reflect some discredit upon the
audiencia was one which asked for the abolition of the one and
one-half per cent tax on imported money, and for the elimination of the three per cent *almojarifazgo.* Both of these taxes
bore heavily on the Chinese and on the Spanish merchants of
Manila. "These two taxes," wrote the *oidores,* "are drawing
the life-blood from the Chinese, who would otherwise bring
products of great value to our shores." The *oidores* had com-
menced this memorial by showing the financial needs of the
colony. They had requested assistance from the treasury of
Mexico, yet, in the same communication, they proposed to
abolish three of the most profitable sources of colonial revenue
that existed. These recommendations not only illustrate the
wide sphere of influence of the magistrates, but they also seem
to confirm the allegations which were often brought against
them, charges, indeed, which they proffered against one another—that each was more interested in trade than in the wel-

---

tinued until a subsequent regulation made optional on the part of the
natives the payment of the ten *reales* or four *reales* and a fowl. On
August 19, 1623, Fray Juan de Balmaseda complained that the *encomenderos* were making the natives pay ten *reales* in addition to the fowl
and that the above law was thus resulting in the payment of sixteen
reales tribute (A. I., 68–1–63). Accordingly, on November 21, 1625, a
cédula was issued which eliminated the substitution of the fowl, and the
rate was restored at ten *reales,* payable in gold or silver (A. I., 105–2–1).
The king, in response to complaints against the collection of tributes
in the provinces of Camarines and Albay, issued a *cédula* on September
25, 1697, ordering the observance in the Philippines of Book 6, Title 5,
of the *Recopilación de Indias,* which meant the correction of the abuse
above referred to (A. I., 68–4–12). It would seem that the rate of ten
reales was levied throughout the seventeenth century.

[32] Audiencia to the Council of the Indies, June 26, 1586, A. I., 67–6–18.

[33] Dávalos to the King, June 20, 1585, A. I., 67–6–18.

fare of the government. Notwithstanding the fact that the economic life of the colony depended on the Chinese trade, the evidence seems to indicate that, even this early in the history of the tribunal, its magistrates had personal interests to serve. In the letter referred to above, Dávalos, who seems to have been a dissenting party to all these proceedings, charged his contemporaries with being guilty of undue mercantile activity.

In this same memorial the *oidores* warned the Council against the Portuguese influence in China, deploring the existence of Macao as a rival to Manila as a trade emporium in the Orient. The audiencia warned the court against the influence and operations of Pedro Unamanú, the successor to Captain Gali, who had gone to China and Macao, supposedly to take on a cargo of Chinese silks. This was in defiance of the law which forbade Spaniards to trade in China, and it was also contrary to the instructions of the viceroy and audiencia of New Spain. In this connection the *oidores* stated that they had recommended to Governor Santiago de Vera that Unamanú should be arrested and punished for diverting his voyage in the interests of private trade. In accordance with the advice of the tribunal the governor had sent orders to Macao, summoning the leader of this expedition back to Manila; these instructions, however, the governor of Macao was unable to fulfill.[34]

This memorial shows that the *oidores* considered it to be their duty to inform the court fully as to the part which the audiencia played in this affair. The matter at hand constituted a question of disobedience of the law, and the Audiencia of Manila had done what it could to enforce it. The tribunal had assumed a role quite as important as that of the governor. The episode shows also that the audiencia was consulted by the governor in this matter, which was purely governmental. It would not be unfair to suggest that a potential factor in stimulating the

---

[34] Pereyra to Santiago de Vera, July 10, 1597, A. I., 68–1–33.

oidores and merchants of Manila to prevent the voyage of Pedro Unamanú or the Portuguese to China for trading purposes must have been the desire to safeguard the Spanish interests in the Chinese trade, and particularly those of Manila, which were the sole reliance of the colony. It was essential that this commerce should be prevented from falling into the hands of other individuals or nations.

This memorial also dealt with ecclesiastical affairs. In it was set forth the audiencia's arguments in certain contentions which the tribunal had had with the bishop, illustrating the fact that the audiencia was opposed not only by the governor but also by the ecclesiastical authorities. It appears that the king had formerly granted to the church courts a large share of temporal jurisdiction in the Islands. This former concession now stood in the way of the royal prerogative and caused endless conflicts between the civil and ecclesiastical judges. The audiencia took the ground that by virtue of its own establishment the authority of the church courts over civil matters was at an end. This the prelate declined to admit. Attention was also directed by the audiencia to the opposition which Bishop Salazar had manifested toward the claims advanced by the civil government for extending its jurisdiction over all the non-Christian tribes, the bishop alleging that Pope Alexander VI had ceded authority only over such Indians as had been christianized.[35]

In truth, the bishop had found after two years of conflict that the presence of the audiencia had not entirely solved the problems of administration, but, on the contrary, had increased the complexity of many of them. He had differed seriously with the *oidores* on several occasions. The ministers had opposed him not only in the larger questions of government and ecclesiastical administration, but in matters of ceremony as well. This

---

[35] This involves the *real patronato*, which will be dealt with in Chapter X of this book.

was more than the prelate could endure. He appealed some of these disputes to the governor and that official, after having neglected these matters for a long period, finally referred them to the audiencia, which promptly made the settlements in its own favor.[36]

Salazar's influence went far toward bringing about the removal of the tribunal, as it had helped in causing its establishment in 1584. The complaints of the bishop against the audiencia brought forth a royal reprimand for carrying on continual disputes with the audiencia. The prelate defended himself against these charges in a memorial dated June 24, 1590.[37] He stated that these petty matters of form and ceremony were of no great consequence. He accused the governor of seeking to stir up discord between him and the audiencia. As a matter of fact, he said, the relations between him and the audiencia were far more harmonious than they had been between the tribunal and the governor, and on many occasions he had been called in to settle disputes between the functionaries of the civil government. "It is well known," he wrote, "within the city and outside of it, that had I not entered as mediator between the president and *oidores* there would have been no peace. It would not have been possible for me to mediate if there had not been friendly relations between them and me."[38]

The unpopularity of the audiencia from 1584 to 1586 is proved by the fact that practically all the authorities in Manila— mercantile, ecclesiastical, political, and even the magistrates themselves—united in recommending its recall. On June 26, 1586, a series of petitions was directed to the Council from various personages and organizations of the city asking that the audiencia be removed. These included the municipal *cabildo*, the bishop, the governor, certain military officials, and,

---

36 Dávalos to the King, June 20, 1585, A. I., 67–6–18.
37 Memorial of Salazar, June 24, 1590, A. I., 67–6–67.
38 *Ibid.*

lastly, several *oidores* (all, in fact, excepting Dávalos). These greatly regretted the mistake which had been made in the establishment of the audiencia, conceded that it had been a failure, and represented that the financial burden which its presence had imposed had been too great for the colony to bear.[39] It is certain that the continual conflicts which had resulted from the presence of the audiencia had not produced a salutary effect on the government.

The audiencia itself wrote to the Council at the same time: "There has been in this tribunal, between the *oidores* and the president, continual misunderstandings as to jurisdiction, which we have decided to submit to your Majesty to ascertain whether precedence in these matters belongs to the president or to the *oidores*." The Manila *cabildo* recommended the re-establishment of the governorship with centralized authority: the power to grant titles, offices and *encomiendas*, with exclusive authority over the latter. This would include the power of appointing *encomenderos* in the name of the king. The recommendation was made by the *cabildo* that consultative authority in matters of government should be conferred on the ecclesiastical and military officials. It was also suggested that a defender of the Indians should be appointed other than the *fiscal*, for the latter, by nature of his office, was their prosecutor rather than their defender. It was the current opinion, this memorial went on to state, that the local prelate should be restored to his former place as defender of the Indians, and that he should have authority to dispossess *encomenderos*, if necessity for such action arose.

It has already been stated that Oidor Dávalos was the only official of importance who would not join in these representations. He believed that the audiencia was necessary to the prosperity of the colony, and that, if properly controlled, it

---

[39] Memorials of the organization and officials of Manila for the removal of the royal audiencia, June 26, 1586, A. I., 68–1–33.

would prove beneficial. He believed, moreover, that the governor was the chief element of discord in the colony, and that his influence had rendered inefficacious the efforts of the audiencia to keep peace and to enforce the laws. In a letter to the king,[40] just a year before the memorial described above, Dávalos had represented Governor Santiago de Vera as a schemer, aiming to get absolute control of the government. De Vera, he said, had gone so far as to influence the bishop and clergy to recommend, against their better judgment, the abolition of the audiencia. The governor realized that the tribunal was the one obstacle in the way of the fulfillment of his designs and had used every possible means to discredit and humiliate the audiencia and its magistrates. Dávalos asserted that the appeal of cases to Mexico would inflict great inconvenience on the people of Manila. He renewed the argument that Spain should have some sovereign body at that great distance from the mother country. He enlarged on the future possibilities of the conquest and rule of the entire Orient by Spain, pointing out the value of the Philippines as a base of operations. It was, therefore, of the greatest importance that the Islands should be provided with the proper sort of government.

Dávalos was especially bitter in his denunciation of Governor De Vera, who, he said, had even resorted to force in order to intimidate the magistrates and had called a council of military officials on one occasion for consultation in matters of justice and government. The governor was accused of violating the laws which had forbidden officials to hold *encomiendas;* he had given the best posts in the government to relatives, and had completely set aside the judgments which Dávalos had rendered in his capacity as *juez y administrador de bienes de difuntos.* The audiencia had been powerless to oppose De Vera, largely, Dávalos inferred, because a majority of the magistrates were under his influence.

---

40 Dávalos to the King, June 20, 1585, A. I., 67–6–18.

However unfavorable were the above comments on the governor, the picture which De Vera drew of himself in a letter to Archbishop Contreras,[41] at that time viceroy of New Spain, is exceedingly interesting by way of contrast. In his own words, the governor had grown "old and worn" in his Majesty's service. According to him, the audiencia was of no service to the government, and only a drawback, making his own duties as governor doubly heavy, especially "since the Council [of the Indias] so poorly seconds my efforts . . . everything concerning the government and war in these islands depends on the president. He must attend to everything punctually; and, in order to comply with his Majesty's commands, he must pay over and spend from the royal treasury what is necessary for the affairs of government and of war."

He complained that the audiencia had interfered with his administration of the finances and had suspended the payment of the drafts which he had drawn on the treasury. He had no recourse on account of the delay necessary before an appeal to the Council of the Indies could be answered. He complained that the audiencia had meddled with affairs of government on trivial pretexts, rendering him practically powerless.

During this period the internal troubles of the colony were supplemented by the interference of the viceroy and audiencia in Mexico. The latter had been reluctant to surrender their former authority over the Philippines. There were conflicts of jurisdiction between the viceroy and the governor and between the two audiencias over a number of matters, among which affairs of a commercial nature were preëminent. Both the authorities at Manila and those of Mexico claimed jurisdiction over the galleons which plied between Manila and Acapulco.[42]

---

[41] Santiago de Vera to Contreras, June 20, 1585, Blair and Robertson VI, 67–68.

[42] See *Recopilación*, 9–45, for regulations of the galleon trade between Acapulco and Manila. By these laws, promulgated from 1583 to 1636, the governor of the Philippines was given authority in Manila over

Numerous protests were made during this early period against what was considered the unauthorized interference of the Mexican authorities. Those in Manila felt that inasmuch as they had an audiencia which was co-equal in power with that of New Spain, they should be independent of the viceroyalty in all the affairs of justice, government, and commerce.

The combined memorials of the residents and officials of Manila, which we have already noted, were presented at court by a new procurator, Fray Alonso Sánchez. The latter, a Jesuit, was a churchman of high standing, and his abilities were recognized both at Madrid and in Rome. Besides carrying commissions from the secular officials, he represented the bishop, but the latter, distrustful of the influence at court of a Jesuit commissioned by the secular government, with which the prelate was constantly at war, determined to send one of his own supporters to Spain to represent his interests. The emissary of Salazar was Fray Francisco Ortega, of the Augustinian order. Ortega followed Sánchez to Spain and rendered valuable service as procurator of his order at Madrid.[43]

In written memorials and in personal interviews with the king and with members of the Council of the Indies, Sánchez summarized all the arguments heretofore given, asking for the abolition of the audiencia. The newness of the country, the sparseness of the population and the poverty of the inhabitants, according to his argument, made such an institution a financial burden. If it were continued, the salaries of the magistrates would have to be paid from Mexico. An audiencia in Manila was not necessary, he urged, since the chief element of the

---

the dispatching, manning, lading, and control of the galleon (see *Recopilación*, 9–45–3, 4, 20, 24, 29, 40, 41, 42, 44, 45, 59). He retained these powers until the latter part of the eighteenth century, when the abuses resulting from his control were eliminated (Martínez de Zúñiga, *Estadismo*, I, 268).

43 Montero y Vidal, *Historia general*, I, 94–95; Martínez de Zúñiga, *An historical view*, I, 183–186; see Ortega's Memorials to the King, Blair and Robertson, IX, 95–119.

population was military, and hence under martial law and jurisdiction. Even before the establishment of the audiencia it had been necessary to send but few cases to Mexico; indeed, alleged Sánchez, lawsuits seldom arose in the colony, and the presence of the audiencia encouraged rather than prevented litigation among the few merchants who lived in Manila. The discord caused by the presence of the tribunal and the continual lawsuits which it encouraged among the Spaniards had a disquieting effect on the natives, who had no need of such an institution, and who did not even understand its purposes. The audiencia, instead of serving as a protection to the natives, was an instrument of tyranny. The Spaniards, understanding the use of a court which would enforce the contracts made between them and the ignorant Indians, were often supported in the seizure of the latter's property, which act, in reality, amounted to deprivation and legalized robbery. Sánchez stated that the natives had been terrorized by the audiencia. The magistrates, versed in the legal customs and practices of Spain rather than of the Indians, were unfit to administer justice in the Philippines.

Sánchez also emphasized the international phases of the audiencia's existence in the Philippines, though with conclusions slightly different from those ' which we have already noted. He stated that the presence of the audiencia had caused the Portuguese, in China, formerly friendly, to be distrustful of the Spaniards, and this had resulted in a considerable diminution of trade. This change of attitude he attributed to the wording of the *cédula* by which the tribunal had been created, extending its jurisdiction throughout the "entire archipelago of China." Sánchez concluded his appeal with the statement that some act was necessary to restore the confidence of the Portuguese, whose influence, exerted upon the Chinese, could spell ruin for Spain's Far Eastern colony. The cancellation of that claim to China would remove all evidence of

Spanish bad faith; it would show to the Portuguese that the Spaniards had no desire to encroach on their rights, and through the restoration of commerce and prosperity the future of the colony would be assured.[44]

Sufficient has been presented to show that the audiencia, as established in 1584, was not a success. The chief objection to the tribunal was not its influence as a court; the real fault seems to have lain in the indefiniteness of the articles of establishment which gave it administrative powers, co-ordinate with the governor and captain-general. Almost every difficulty occurred in the administrative field. The audiencia also failed to preserve harmony between church and state and added to these complexities by itself having dissensions with the bishop. The petty character of the men who constituted this particular government, their personal selfishness, and their eagerness to take advantage, in dishonest ways, of the time and the distance which separated the colony from the royal control, contributed to the failure of the institution at that time. The audiencia was scarcely established, and it certainly did not have time to adjust itself to the new conditions with which it found itself surrounded, before it was removed. It would seem that the authorities in Madrid were somewhat hasty in withdrawing the audiencia, for it had proved its efficacy throughout the entire Spanish empire. The ill success of the Audiencia of Manila at this time does not prove that the institution was a failure, or that its establishment was a mistake, for seven years later it was returned and continued

---

[44] *Memoria y consultas de Fr. Alonso Sánchez* (no date given), A. I., 67–6–27; see also Juan de la Concepción, *Historia general de Filipinas* [cited hereinafter as Concepción, *Historia general*], II, 103–184. These agreements are interesting because they show how intensely nationalistic were the respective sentiments of the Spaniards and Portuguese with regard to their Asiatic colonies, notwithstanding the fact that since 1580 the home governments of the two nations had been united. This correspondence illustrates the fact that the Portuguese regarded their former colonies as still distinctively their own.

without interruption until 1898, and continues still as then reorganized. The statement of Philip II on November 25, 1595, "that experience had proved it to be unnecessary in a land so new and unsettled"[45] can hardly be justified in view of subsequent events.

The causes of the breakdown of the first audiencia may be found in the circumstances of the time, the personnel of the tribunal, the indefiniteness of the laws which created it, the novelty of the situation to magistrates and officials and their failure to adapt themselves to their duties and to one another. As an institution of reform the audiencia did not have time to adjust itself to a permanent status.

The king, in compliance with the demands of the various organizations and individuals of Manila as communicated by their respective envoys, abolished the Audiencia of Manila by royal *cédula* on August 9, 1589, ordering the Viceroy of New Spain to take the *residencias* of all officials who had been identified with the Manila government. To carry out these orders Licentiate Herver del Coral was sent from Mexico to Manila, where he arrived in May, 1590, in company with the new governor, Gómez Pérez Dasmariñas.[46] Santiago de Vera, the ex-governor, was promoted to a magistracy in the Audiencia of Mexico; the *oidor*, Pedro de Rojas, was made *teniente* and *asesor* to the governor, while the former *oidor*, Rivera, and Fiscal Ayala, were left without office.[47]

The regular organization for the administration of justice in the provinces was left precisely as it had been when the tribunal was in existence. The *alcaldes mayores* and the *corregidores* still functioned as judges of first instance and as governors of the provinces. The *alcaldes ordinarios* remained the

---

[45] Royal *cédula* for the restoration of the Audiencia of Manila, November 25, 1595, A. I., 106–4–19.

[46] Morga's Sucesos, Blair and Robertson, XV, 65–66.

[47] Suppressed Audiencia to the King, June 20, 1590, Blair and Robertson, VII, 208–211; also *Recopilación*, 2–15–181.

judges of first instance in the city of Manila. These judges tried cases with appeal to the governor, and the judgment of the latter was final in cases involving a value of a thousand ducats or less. Cases of a higher category might be appealed from the decision of the governor to the Audiencia of Mexico, and thence, if again appealed, to the Council of the Indies.

The audiencia of three magistrates and a *fiscal* was replaced by a governor, who was both captain-general and sole judge. He was assisted in the latter capacity, as above noted, by a *teniente* and *asesor*, a lawyer, who advised him in legal affairs and prepared his judicial decisions for him. This reform was made on the representation of Fray Sánchez, that Manila had no need of a judicial system more pretentious than that of any Spanish provincial town. That city was accordingly reduced to the rank of a city or district, with dependence in judicial and administrative matters on New Spain, in whose audiencia appeals from the governor of the Philippines were heard.

With these new reforms the leading authorities in Manila professed to be greatly pleased. Bishop Salazar, who was the most influential person in Manila at this time, expressed his satisfaction to the king in a letter dated June 24, 1590.[48] He suggested, however, that the continuance of the audiencia might have been satisfactory could its members have been paid from the treasury of New Spain. He reported the arrival of the new governor, and stated that the latter had already given evidence of a desire to govern wisely and justly.

Salazar's optimism in regard to the good intentions of the governor could not have been long continued, for Morga tells us that in the first year of the government of Gómez Pérez Dasmariñas the need of an audiencia was felt by many.[49] At that time, all the powers of government were centralized in the gov-

---

[48] Salazar to Felipe II, June 24, 1590, Blair and Robertson, VII, 252.

[49] Morga's Sucesos, Blair and Robertson, XV, 75.

ernor, and there was no immediate authority to which the people could apply for relief. Salazar had many disputes with the governor over questions relating to the respective spheres of the church and state, and from the decisions of the executive the prelate had no recourse. Dasmariñas, on reporting these matters to the king, stated that the bishop had interfered in the matter of the collection of the tribute, the government of the *encomiendas*, the Chinese trade (in which, the governor alleged that the prelate had an unpriestly interest), and in the administration of justice.[50] The prelate had interpreted the removal of the audiencia as constituting a re-establishment of the concession formerly made to the church of extensive control in the administration of government and justice. He claimed that ecclesiastical judges should have the same civil jurisdiction as they had exercised before the audiencia was first founded. This, of course, the governor would not tolerate.

Bishop Salazar was so displeased with the turn which affairs had taken in Manila that he determined to leave the Islands, and passage being placed at his disposal by the willing governor, the bishop set out in July, 1592.[51] On his arrival in Spain, Salazar concerned himself principally with religious matters, securing some valuable reforms. Among the latter was the erection of the Philippines into an archbishopric and the creation of three subordinate bishoprics. Salazar showed the desirability of the restoration of the audiencia as a preventive check on the excesses of the governor, but this change was not made as an immediate consequence of his recommendations.

A *cédula* was issued on January 17, 1593, which outlined with more definiteness a judicial system for the Islands. This

---

[50] Dasmariñas to Felipe II, June 20, 1591, Blair and Robertson, VIII, 142–168, *passim.*

[51] Salazar, on reaching the Spanish court, was made first archbishop of the Philippines. He died on December 4, 1594, before he could assume his new post.

reform confirmed the position of the governor as nominal head of the judiciary, with jurisdiction over appeals from the lower courts, but it decreed that these cases should be tried by a *letrado.* The governor's final and conclusive jurisdiction was extended to all cases not exceeding a thousand ducats in value. Cases of a greater value might be appealed to the Audiencia of Mexico.[52] The governor was given authority to name a protector of the Indians.[53]

The above changes were followed shortly by the *cédula* of August 18, 1593, by which the title of *teniente de capitán-general y asesor de gobernador y capitán-general de las Islas Filipinas* was bestowed on Don Antonio de Morga, who was probably the most efficient jurist and one of the most versatile officials that Spain ever sent to her Asiatic dependency.[54] Morga was at this time not only successor to the audiencia in judicial matters, but also attorney-general and sole legal adviser to the governor. His predecessor, Pedro de Rojas, was transferred to Mexico, in pursuance of the idea, as alleged in the order of transfer, of removing from the Philippines all the members of the old audiencia, so that the new scheme, as revised at that time, might be allowed to work itself out without prejudice. Before his departure, the *residencia* of Rojas was conducted by Morga.

Even the reforms of 1593 did not suffice to make the administration of justice satisfactory to all parties. From the

[52] *Cédula* of January 17, 1593, Blair and Robertson, VIII, 315.

[53] *Ibid.;* see also *cédula* of same date in *Recopilación*, 6–6–8.

[54] Morga remained in the Philippines throughout a period of eight years and during this time distinguished himself as a lawyer and judge, administrator, soldier, and later as a historian. It was due to his energies as senior magistrate that Van Noordt, the Dutch freebooter, was defeated at the entrance of Manila Bay. Morga, in his *Sucesos*, already quoted several times, has left us a scholarly view of conditions as they existed at the time of his residence in the Islands. Morga left the Philippines on July 10, 1603, with a promotion to the Audiencia of Mexico; he served in New Spain for several years and in 1616 he was again promoted to the post of president of the Audiencia of Quito.

large amount of correspondence which exists, embodying complaints against the harsh methods of Dasmariñas and his successor, Tello, three letters may be cited which show the attitude of the various officials of the colony towards the re-establishment of the audiencia. The first of these was written by Governor Dasmariñas himself, and it may be in some ways surprising to note that he asked for the restoration of the audiencia. His reasons, in part, however, were different from those advanced by his contemporaries. Dasmariñas was of the opinion that an audiencia would be effective in the nullification of the interdicts and excommunications imposed by the archbishop and the local prelates, which he claimed were working havoc with the civil government.[55]

The treasury officials complained that the absolute government of the executive was contrary to the interests of *real hacienda*. Their objections to the prevailing system were voiced in the second of the memorials alluded to above, that of Francisco de la Misa, *factor* of the royal treasury of Manila.[56] Misa said that under the former arrangement the audiencia had audited the accounts of the royal treasury and of the city of Manila each year. In this way the accounts had been well kept and the funds properly accounted for. The removal of the audiencia had left the governor with authority over the nomination of the officials of *real hacienda*, as well as the supervision of the accounts. Since Dasmariñas had been governor, no accounts had been rendered by the minor officials of the treasury, and, as a consequence, their superiors had been unable to make up their reports for the Contaduría of Mexico. The governor's attention had been called to this deficiency repeatedly, but the latter had displayed no interest in the state of the colony's finances, which, said Misa, exceeded all other matters in importance. "This comes," the *factor* observed,

---

55 Dasmariñas to the King, December 6, 1595, A. I., 67–6–18.
56 Misa to the King, May 31, 1595, A. I., 67–6–29.

"from placing in charge of Your Majesty's finances a soldier, unfitted to do else than command troops, and then unchecked by an audiencia, so far distant from your royal person." The laxity of the governor and of his subordinates seems to have resulted in the loss of much revenue.

Misa also showed that there had been many irregularities in the sale of offices, deficiencies which the presence of an audiencia would have checked. Instead of selling the minor clerkships of the exchequer, the governor had given them to his friends. Two offices, which were by no means insignificant, those of the chief clerkships of government and of justice, respectively, had been sold formerly for four thousand pesos each. The governor, however, had preferred to have them on his civil patronage list; this would not have been permitted had an audiencia been present to enforce the law.

The governor was charged by Misa with extravagance in the expenditure of the revenue of the colony. The payment of the salaries of new appointees to offices, friends of the governor, had made heavy drains on the treasury. The king, by repeated *cédulas,* had forbidden the designation of an excessive number of *alcaldes* and *corregidores* because of the desirability of economizing the resources of the colony. While the audiencia was in existence its consent had been necessary for the creation of new judicial districts, but since the recall of the tribunal, the governor had trebled the number of provincial officials, and, in addition, had permitted each to have a salaried assistant.

According to Misa, various other evils had resulted from the absolutism of the governor, among which were numerous abuses which he had tolerated in the galleon trade. It was alleged that Spanish merchants in Mexico had sent money to agents in Manila, and in that way had caused the legal amount brought from Acapulco for investment on the annual galleon to be exceeded.[57]

---

[57] The amount legally permitted to be taken to the Philippines at this time was 500,000 pesos (subsequently 1,000,000 pesos). The gal-

This, the *factor* stated, was due partially to the laxity and corruption of the Acapulco officials, who had permitted the galleon
to leave that port with more than the authorized amount of
money. The governor of the Philippines, however, could have
prevented this abuse had he been so inclined, as the ships'
manifests were always subject to his inspection on arrival
at Manila. The money sent by the merchants of Mexico was
invested in merchandise in the Islands and these goods were
shipped back to Acapulco on the galleon, thus excluding the
commerce of the local merchants. The latter were growing
poorer daily while the governor and his friends were waxing
richer. The governor had also exercised favoritism in the distribution of cargo space, thus rewarding his friends and punishing his enemies.[58] Since the suppression of the audiencia these
abuses had increased, as there had been no authority in Manila
to hold the governor in check.

This memorial, from Misa, which was carefully considered
at court, went far toward demonstrating that the restoration
of the audiencia would have beneficial results, so far as the
administration of *real hacienda* was concerned.

The third of the letters referred to as reflecting the attitude
of the Manila officials toward the re-establishment of the
audiencia and ultimately contributing to its restoration, was
directed to the court by Antonio de Morga, the efficient
lieutenant-governor. Morga, as did Misa, placed great emphasis on the need in Manila of a more efficient system for the
administration of the exchequer. Morga was moderate in his

---

leon, on the voyage from Manila to Acapulco, could carry merchandise
to the registered value of 250,000 pesos (later 500,000 pesos). This
regulation was first enacted January 11, 1593 (*Recopilación* 9–45–6, 9).
On the same date residents of New Spain were forbidden to trade in
the Philippines and the entire Philippine and Chinese trade was expressly reserved to subjects in the Philippines. The latter were given
the exclusive privilege of sending goods to New Spain (*ibid.*, 1). They
were permitted to buy only from the Chinese merchants who came to
Manila (*ibid.*, 34).—See Martínez de Zúñiga, *Estadismo*, I, 266–270.

[58] *Cédula* of January 11, 1593, *Recopilación*, 9–45–44.

characterization of the governor, alleging that Dasmariñas had been brought completely under the influence of the ecclesiastics. He expressed the belief that an audiencia would aid in combatting what he termed the retrogression of the colony under the influence of the priests. "There should be someone," he wrote, "to oppose the ecclesiastics in a land so far away from the Audiencia of Mexico; for, no matter what question is sent there for decision, at least two years must elapse before despatches can be returned."[59] No official was better qualified to explain the needs of the colony in matters of justice than Morga, for he was at that time, in reality, the supreme court of the Islands.

The audiencia, after an interregnum of seven years, was restored by a *cédula* promulgated by Philip II, November 26, 1595.[60] The tribunal was to consist of a president, who should also be governor and captain-general, four *oidores*, a *fiscal*, and various subordinates. The history of the former audiencia and the reasons for its suppression and re-establishment are summarized in the *cédula* as follows:

I established an audiencia in that city and province in order that everything might be governed by means of it, and that justice might be administered with the same universal equality, mildness, and satisfaction desirable; after its establishment I ordered it suppressed as experience proved it unnecessary in a land so new and unsettled; in its place I sent a governor, and though his administration was excellent, yet, inasmuch as that community had grown, and I hope that it will continue to grow, I have thought it advisable to found and establish the said audiencia again.

In this *cédula*, which was addressed to Governor Tello, the king pointed to the increased importance of the Philippines, and to the many expeditions by which the Island of Luzón and other islands of the Archipelago had become pacified and

---

[59] Morga to Philip II, July 6, 1596, Blair and Robertson, IX, 271.

[60] Ordinance for the re-establishment of the Audiencia of Manila, November 26, 1595, A. I., 106-4-19; also in Blair and Robertson, IX, 189-191.

more densely settled. The increase of commerce with the Chinese was also cited as a reason for providing the Islands with a more stable government. It was stated that in the administration of justice there should be as much efficiency as possible without the loss and inconvenience involved in appealing cases to Mexico. The governor would have more time for his increasing administrative and military duties if disengaged from his former judicial functions. The *cédula* continued:

> You [the governor] may find it advisable to have by you persons with whom to take counsel, in order that matters may be considered with the requisite conformity and by a sufficiently large body of advisers; for these reasons I have decided to form an audiencia; . . . you shall be its president, holding that office with those of my governor and captain-general.[61]

Together with this decree of re-establishment the king issued special instructions to Tello, prescribing in detail the relations which the governor was to observe with the audiencia. These instructions, in general, sought to prevent the recurrence of the misunderstandings which had been so fatal to the earlier tribunal. The governor and *oidores* were ordered to co-operate in the formulation of commercial regulations, with a view, particularly, to securing the Chinese trade, in the en-

---

[61] The Archbishop of Manila, in a letter to the king, on August 15, 1624, stated that the principal motive which influenced Philip II to re-establish the audiencia at the time of Governor Tello, was that in a district so remote and distant from his royal presence the governors might not be so absolute, but that there might be a superior arm to check them, and to prevent their extortions from innocent people (Blair and Robertson, XXI, 95). It is certain, too, that the audiencia was also destined to champion the royal prerogative in the face of the encroachments of the higher officials of the church. This need was especially urged by Morga.

Grao y Monfalcón, the procurator of the merchants of Manila at the court in 1636, wrote on June 13 of that year: "In the year 590 the royal Audiencia of Manila was suppressed . . . and its suppression must also be reckoned among the hardships of that city . . . because of those which it suffered until the year 597, when the Audiencia was reëstablished (*sic*)." (Blair and Robertson, XXVII, 189).

forcement of the *pancada*,[62] the consideration of ways and
means to prevent money from passing to China, in matters of
taxation and finance, *encomiendas,* and the pacification and
government of the wild tribes. By these instructions, it is important to note, the function of advising the governor in administrative matters was definitely bestowed upon the *oidores.*
"Matters of importance," the *cédula* prescribed, "the said president-governor shall discuss with the *oidores* of the said audiencia,
so that the latter, after consultation, may give him their
opinion."[63]

The governor and the magistrates were jointly charged to
do all possible to discourage Indians and Spaniards from
wasting their means in fruitless and petty lawsuits. The natives, according to this new *reglamento,* should always be protected against the designs of those who would take undue
advantage of them. The governor was moreover instructed to
confer with the archbishop and audiencia in ecclesiastical
affairs, and the prelates were especially forbidden to excommunicate and issue declamations from the pulpit against the
officials of the civil government, such as were constantly proclaimed when Salazar was bishop. Priests were not to meddle
with the civil government, or with the *pancada,* or with any
form of trade.

The audiencia as reformed, with the powers and duties
noted, began its life in Manila on May 8, 1598. The inaugura-

---

[62] *Pancada*, the wholesale purchase of the goods brought to Manila
by the Chinese. These goods were bought by a committee of two or
three persons, acting for the governor and *ayuntamiento,* then sold or
apportioned among the merchants of the city in proportion to the
amount of money which they were able to invest. This arrangement
was designed to give all the merchants a chance to buy and at the
same time to prevent the Chinese from selling at exorbitant prices
(*Cédula* of January 11, 1593, *Recopilación,* 9–45–34.)

[63] *Cédulas* of May 5, 1583, and May 25, 1596, *Recopilación,* 2–15–11.
It will be noted that this authority was granted to the first audiencia
established in Manila. This same faculty was conferred by the *Ordenanzas nuevamente formadas para el régimen y govierno de la audiencia nacional de Manila,* Art. I, Chap. 1, Sec. 1 (A. I., 106–4–19).

tion of the tribunal was attended with general rejoicing, and a celebration characterized by great formality and pomp. The royal seal was conducted through the city in a procession which was composed of all the royal and clerical dignitaries. Church, state, and citizenry united in expressing satisfaction at the restoration of the tribunal, with its consequent prospect of an efficient government and administration of justice.

Reforms were made in the scope and composition of the audiencia at various times during its existence. It developed from a commission of three magistrates, with a president at its head, with definite and ill-expressed powers over a vast archipelago, whose population was sparse and scattered, to a double-chambered tribunal of appeal in second and third instance, with definite jurisdiction over a well-organized commonwealth. It would be highly desirable, did space allow, to review chronologically the important reforms which were made in the organization, scope and jurisdiction of the Audiencia of Manila throughout its history. The most important of these, however, will be noted incidentally in the following pages.

The audiencia, from the time of its renewal onward, typified and represented the royal authority, and its tenure was more continuous than the governorship. Eight times subsequently did the audiencia assume the reins of government in lieu of the governor. It became the most reliable channel through which the royal authority made itself felt in the Islands, and it was especially utilized by the court as a check on the governor.[64] Whenever occasion arose, the audiencia interposed as the intermediary and arbiter between dissenting

---

[64] Martínez de Zúñiga has this to say concerning the work and purpose of the tribunal: "The royal audiencia was established to check the despotism of the governor, whom it has never impeded, because its learned members were always the weaker, and the governor may send them as prisoners to Spain, exile them to the provinces to take census, or imprison them in Fort Santiago, as has been done" (Martínez de Zúñiga, *Estadismo*, I, 244).

parties in the name of the sovereign, and its decrees were listened to with respect. It was no longer a temporary organization, and so firmly established was it henceforth that no person seriously considered its recall a possibility. Through a period of three hundred years the audiencia exercised its functions. It was first and always a judicial body. It shared executive and administrative duties with the governor. It frequently exercised attributes of an advanced legislative character. It participated in the government of the provinces. It shared the authority of the royal patronage in the control of ecclesiastical affairs. These various activities will be studied in subsequent chapters.

CHAPTER III

THE JUDICIAL FUNCTIONS OF THE AUDIENCIA

The audiencia was first and always a tribunal of justice. It was established for the purpose of trying cases and settling disputes. Had it no other functions than the purely judicial, however, it would not have played the important part which it did in colonial administration during two hundred years of its existence. Its chief interest to the student of history and government will not be so much its activity as a judicial institution as the relations it bore to other departments of the government. Its extraordinary powers and functions developed incidentally at first through the establishment of the institution in colonies where no other agency existed to deal with the unforeseen problems and necessities which arose from time to time. The gradual assumption and exercise of non-judicial functions are therefore the chief characteristics to be noted in the history of the Audiencia of Manila.

The aim of this chapter, however, will be to study the audiencia in its capacity as a civil judiciary and to clear the way for the discussion in subsequent chapters of the wider, and from the present viewpoint, more notable fields of its activity. An effort will be made to describe its judicial procedure, the kinds of cases which it tried, the limitations on its jurisdiction—what courts were inferior to it, and what authority was superior. This investigation will be made from the viewpoint of the historian, rather than from that of the student of jurisprudence, subject to such limitations as a lack of knowledge of the law may impose. We shall first consider the procedure of the audiencia as authorized by the laws of the Indies, illustrating this procedure by the citation of actual cases in practice.

The powers and duties of the Audiencia of Manila as defined in the special decree of establishment of May 5, 1583, have been set forth in the preceding chapter. By this decree the audiencia was granted civil and criminal jurisdiction in cases of appeal from the lower courts and original jurisdiction in those affecting the government and the conduct of its officials. The authority of the audiencia in the latter cases was exercised through the appeals which came to it from the special investigators and visitors who tried these officials in first instance.

The laws of the Indies, after prescribing the time of meeting and the hours of the daily sessions of the audiencia, made their first important judicial regulation by forbidding viceroys and presidents to assist in the determination of suits. Cases must be tried by the properly qualified *oidores,* yet the president (viceroy or governor) was to sign the decisions with the magistrates.[1] Unless the president were a lawyer, he was even denied cognizance of military cases. The audiencia had jurisdiction over appeals from the viceroy or governor in all government matters to which any official or private citizen might take exception.[2] In case of disagreement between the audiencia and the president, it was prescribed that the question at issue should be carried to the Council of the Indies. In case the majority of the audiencia agreed to follow a certain course of action, the viceroy or president was forbidden to contravene or oppose that action. Instead, he was ordered to abide by it, appealing to the Council of the Indies for final settlement of the contention.[3]

There were many laws regulating the relations between the audiencia and the governor, most of which will be noted in greater detail in a subsequent chapter. The most important were

---

[1] *Recopilación,* 2–15–32.
[2] *Ibid.,* 34–36, 44.
[3] *Ibid.,* 41.

the laws which ordered that the viceroys of New Spain and Perú
should leave to the audiencias entire jurisdiction over *residencias,*
questions involving the marriage relation[4] and the administration of property of deceased persons.[5] A law especially referring to the Philippines ordered the Audiencia of Manila to abstain from interfering with the government of the Chinese in
the Parián.[6] This did not forbid the trial on appeal of cases
relating to the Chinese, since in practice the audiencia had
authority to take cognizance of such cases. Certain extra
duties were required of the oldest *oidor* of the audiencia, who
was known as the *decano.* He was given complete authority
over the tribunal in the absence of the president. He might
assign cases to the magistrates, designate judges for special
duties and determine all matters relating to the interior
organization and government of the tribunal. These functions
were assumed, after 1776, by the regent, and the prerogatives
of the office of *decano* became merely nominal, except when
the regent was absent. In audiencias whose size permitted it,
the oldest *oidor,* or the regent, after that office was created,
could determine whether sessions should consist of one or two
salas.[7] An audiencia was legally constituted, however, if only
one magistrate were present.[8] The audiencia was commanded
to guard its proceedings with great secrecy, and such rules were
formulated for its magistrates as would enable the tribunal to
uphold its dignity, and command the respect of the commonwealth.

---

[4] Certain phases of these questions remained within the jurisdiction of the church courts.

[5] *Recopilación,* 2–15–53.

[6] Parián, a market-place; the name given to the quarter set aside by
the government wherein the Chinese were confined. This restriction
was imposed in 1603, to give added security to the city of Manila, en-
dangered by a Chinese uprising at that time.—See Montero y Vidal,
Historia general, III, 146–148; *Recopilación,* 2–15–55; 5–3–24; 6–18–5.

[7] *Ibid.,* 2–15–64; 2–16–16 to 20.

[8] *Ibid.,* 2–15–180.

Cases of first instance were tried by inferior judges who were below the category of *oidores*.[9]   As noted in a former chapter, these judges were the *alcaldes ordinarios, alcaldes mayores,* and *corregidores.* The former tried civil and criminal cases in the towns and cities and the last two exercised extensive jurisdiction in the provinces.   Cases were appealed from them to the audiencia.[10]   The audiencia was forbidden to concern itself with cases of first instance, excepting certain criminal suits which originated within five leagues of Manila.[11]

A separate *sala* for the trial of criminal cases was created in the audiencias of Lima and Mexico.   The magistrates serving in these *salas* were designated as *alcaldes del crimen.* They had jurisdiction in first instance over the criminal cases arising within five leagues of the capital, as referred to above, and in second instance over those appealed from the provincial judges.[12]   The *oidores* in these audiencias confined themselves to civil suits, but in audiencias where there were no *alcaldes del crimen,* the *oidores* were authorized to try both civil and criminal cases.[13]   The magistrates of the Audiencia of Manila had both criminal and civil jurisdiction, as that tribunal belonged to the latter class.   ˙When the number of *oidores* present was insufficient to do the work of the audiencia, *alcaldes ordinarios* or *alcaldes mayores* who had the necessary qualifications might be transferred temporarily to the tribunal. When acting as *oidores* they could not try cases over which they had formerly exercised original jurisdiction.[14]

A system of procedure was prescribed for the trial of cases before the audiencia and the order fixed in which these should come up for consideration.   It was ordered that two slates

---

9 *Ibid.,* 70.   See Chapter I of this book.
10 *Ibid.,* 71.
11 *Ibid.,* 3, 5, 67.   See Chapter I, note 20, for distinction between *oidores* and *alcaldes del crimen.*
12 *Ibid.,* 68; 2–19–2.
13 *Ibid.,* 1, 3.
14 *Ibid.,* 2–15–63, 71.

should be kept, one for cases classified according to their importance and another for those to be tried by rotation. Cases of the first category and those which were especially urgent might supersede the latter, but when there were none of the former the second slate was to be adhered to.

Cases relating to *real hacienda* took precedence over all others. The president was instructed to see personally that these cases should not be subjected to delay and that at least one day a week should be set aside for their adjudication. Next in importance were cases involving infractions of royal ordinances and laws. Probate cases were given one day a week. Two days weekly were set aside for the consideration of suits which arose between Indians and between Indians and Spaniards. Cases involving the poor, however, were to take precedence over these. The audiencia was made responsible for the good treatment of the Indians and it was charged with the obligation of seeing that all suits to which Indians were parties should be tried without loss of time. Delays resulting from the carelessness of lawyers and from their eagerness to profit at the expense of the natives were discouraged. Matters of slight importance which pertained to the Indians were to be dispatched by decrees of the audiencias and viceroys; this provision was designed to avoid contentious litigation, to which the natives were characteristically inclined. It also sought thereby to protect them from dishonest judges and lawyers. Any and all of the cases mentioned in this paragraph were considered to be of such importance that they were classified among the first to be tried and determined prior to those involving property, commercial affairs, and ordinary transactions. Of the latter cases those already decided were to be reopened before the hearing of new cases of the same class. Cases involving the poor were to be given speedy consideration.[15] Length of

---

15 *Ibid.*, 2–15–74 to 85.

waiting should be the criterion for the consideration of the remaining cases.

The audiencia was empowered to compel testimony from all persons and authorities.[16]   As already noted, the *oidores* of audiencias which did not contain *alcaldes del crimen* were authorized to entertain appeals from persons who had been condemned to death.[17]   The same was true of all other criminal cases that were admitted to appeal.   Members of religious and military orders were not exempted from the jurisdiction of the audiencia.[18]

The laws regulating the audiencia's jurisdiction in civil cases seem to have varied according to the time and the policy of the government.   The audiencia exercised both original and appellate jurisdiction, as we have already noted.   Most of the civil suits tried by the tribunal were appealed to it from inferior judges.   A law was made in 1563 ordering that cases involving less than twenty pesos might be tried by verbal process.[19]   This law would seem to have excluded cases of less than that value from appeal to the audiencia, as the processes had to be committed to writing in order to be appealed.   The *cédulas* of November 26, 1573, and August 10, 1574, fixed the minimum amount that might be appealed at six pesos of eight *reales,* or 3000 *maravedís.*[20]   Charles V in 1542 promulgated an important law for the regulation of appeals to the audiencia.   It provided that the smallest amount that might be appealed should be 300,000 *maravedís* (667 pesos).[21]   This law

---

16 *Ibid.,* 90–91.

17 *Ibid.,* 93.

18 Exemption from the jurisdiction of the civil authority having been claimed by the military and religious orders of Santiago, Calatrava, and Alcántara, Philip IV, on April 1, 1635, gave jurisdiction over these orders to the audiencias.—*Ibid.,* 96.

19 *Ibid.,* 5–10–1.

20 *Ibid.,* 2.

21 According to the *Recopilación,* 5–13–1 (laws of October 20, 1545, February 13, 1620, and the Ordinance of Audiencias [1563]), the value of the peso was fixed at 450 *maravedís.*

was re-promulgated on September 24, 1568, and on September 22, 1626.[22] The provisions of these laws, however, probably applied only to such cases as might come from provincial justices, since appeals from city judges and *ayuntamientos* could be taken over by the audiencia with less trouble and expense, because of the proximity of the tribunal. As a matter of fact, this opinion is seemingly substantiated by a new law, dated June 13, 1634, which ordered that an appeal from an *ayuntamiento* should not be received in an audiencia unless the suit involved a sum greater than 60,000 *maravedís,* or 133 pesos.[23] This was considerably less, it will be seen, than the amount fixed as the limit by the law immediately preceding it, which was promulgated in 1626.

The laws establishing the finality of the jurisdiction of the audiencia were also altered from time to time. The earliest law on the subject, dated April 24, 1545, ordered that no appeal should be made from the tribunal in cases involving less than 6000 *maravedís* (13.3 pesos).[24] This limit was raised to 200 pesos by *cédulas* of April 4, 1558, and March 4, 1559, and by the ordinance of 1563.[25]

In 1542, the jurisdiction of the audiencia was made final in all cases appealed from the ordinary courts.[26] The execution of all decisions which were not appealable was rigidly required.[27] By the ordinance of 1563 it was stipulated that sentences of review which had been confirmed by the audiencia could not be appealed again, no matter how large a sum was involved.[28] This was partially abrogated by the law of February 13, 1620, which ordered that cases involving 6000 pesos of 450 *maravedís*

---

[22] *Recopilación,* 2–15–88.
[23] *Ibid.,* 5–12–20.
[24] *Ibid.,* 5–12–29.
[25] *Ibid.,* 5–10–3.
[26] *Ibid.,* 5–13–8.
[27] *Ibid.,* 4, 7.
[28] *Ibid.,* 5–10–4.

each, already terminated on review by an audiencia, might be further appealed to the king.[29]

Decisions were reached by the concurrence of a majority of the magistrates trying the case. When there were only two *oidores* present a decision had to be unanimous. In case the full quota of magistrates were present and the votes were equally divided, the *fiscal* might be called in to decide the case, but if the latter were prosecuting the case, or were otherwise incapacitated, a duly qualified lawyer might be chosen to serve as a special magistrate.[30] This rule did not apply to the revision of sentences in civil cases wherein the value exceeded 300,000 *maravedís;* in these the concurrence of three magistrates was necessary.[31] A record of the judicial decisions of the magistrates was kept in the official journal of the audiencia. Decisions and legal papers had to be signed by the magistrates involved. *Oidores* who registered dissenting opinions were obliged to affix their signatures to the *autos* with those who had voted in the affirmative, but the negative votes were also recorded.[32]

While the audiencia might repeal the written opinion of an inferior judge in review of sentence, the revision of verbal decisions of *alcaldes ordinarios* could be accomplished only when the *alcalde* in question had been summoned before the tribunal and the reasons for his decision had been investigated in his presence.[33] The audiencia, therefore, exercised appellate jurisdiction over civil and criminal cases tried in first instance by the judges of the provinces.

If an *alcalde mayor* or other inferior judge failed to comply with the instructions laid down for his guidance, or if he were

---

29 *Ibid.*, 5–13–1.

30 *Ibid.*, 2–15–97.

31 *Ibid.*, 88.

32 *Ibid.*, 103, 107, 108.   Magistrates were forbidden to sign decisions during office hours—valuable time which should be devoted to hearing cases (*ibid.*, 109).

33 *Ibid.*, 105.

guilty of an abuse in the administration of justice, he was held to account by the visiting *oidor* who was dispatched at regular intervals for the inspection of the provinces—and for the judicial scrutiny of the provincial courts. In cases of notorious injustice special *pesquisidores,* usually *oidores,* were sent at once for the correction of the abuse in question, at the expense of the offending officials.[34] These, if found guilty of wilful disobedience, were punished in accordance with the gravity of their offenses. The audiencia had appellate jurisdiction in these cases.[35] The visiting *oidores* imposed fines in accordance with a tariff which had been formulated by the audiencia and approved by the Council of the Indies.[36] All fines levied by the audiencia, either upon officials or individuals could be remitted by the president with the consent of the *acuerdo.*[37]

It was the policy of the government to give the audiencia final jurisdiction in as many cases as possible. It was desirable to endow the colonial tribunals and authorities with sufficient power to make them worthy of respect. At the same time it was necessary to relieve the Council of the Indies of the duty of hearing the vast number of individual suits which would inevitably come to it if that tribunal were made too accessible. The Council was occupied with appeals in government and justice from all of Spain's colonies. It has been noted that the limit of value of cases which could be appealed from the audiencia to the Council of the Indies was raised in 1620 from 200 to 6000 pesos. This

---

[34] *Ibid.,* 117. *Pesquisidores* were special investigators with extraordinary executive and judicial powers who were sent out by the home or central government when need arose to correct abuses in colonial or provincial administration. *Visitadores* (visitors) were sent regularly to inspect the government of a province or colony. The governor was supposed to dispatch visitors to examine the work of *alcaldes mayores* and *corregidores* every three years.

[35] *Ibid.,* 118.

[36] *Ibid.,* 178.

[37] *Recopilación,* 5–15–21. *Acuerdo,* the joint consultative action of the governor and audiencia. See Chapter VI of this book and note 78 of the same chapter.

would seem to indicate a growing tendency to confine suits involving individuals to the colonial tribunals, thus increasing the importance of the audiencias, and at the same time making the Council of the Indies more exclusively a tribunal of administration.   This change, however, was never completely effected, despite the various expedients adopted to discourage the appeal of individual cases.   Persons appealing were obliged to guarantee the expenses of suit.   The great cost, the delays, and the distance altogether made appeal difficult.   Appeals of longer standing than two years were not received from the Philippines in the Council of the Indies.[38]   An investigation of the records shows that most of the cases appealed to the Council of the Indies involved administrative law in some form, having to do either with the prosecution of officials, their removal from office, the prosecution of bondsmen, *residencias*, conflicts of jurisdiction, or with appeals from the decision of the audiencia in commercial and ecclesiastical matters.

The gradual extension of the jurisdiction of the audiencia over *encomiendas* may be cited as an example of the changes in the authority of the tribunal and in its relation to the Council of the Indies.   The first important legislation in regulation of the *encomienda* was the celebrated law of Malines, promulgated in that city by Charles V, on October 20, 1545, and enunciated at successive dates until 1610.   The law prescribed the course which was to be pursued by the audiencia in suits between individuals relative to *encomiendas* or the Indians thereon.   In these contentions the Council of the Indies and not the audiencia was the final arbiter.   The duty of the latter tribunal was to collect evidence in these cases, taking the testimony of witnesses

---

[38] *Ibid.*, 5–13–3.   The periods of validity of cases appealed from the audiencias of Ultramar varied with the distance and the time necessary for the transmission of *autos* to the Council.   The time assigned by the laws of the Indies was as follows: Chile, one and a half years, Tierra Firme, New Granada, Santo Domingo, New Spain, one year, and the Philippines, two years.   This law was promulgated first on September 24, 1621, and again on March 30, 1629.

for both sides and remitting all papers, sealed, to the Council of the Indies. The council, on consideration of the evidence, rendered the final decision. The audiencia had to conclude its part of the investigation and file its report within a period of three months. This time limit was extended to six months in 1554. The purpose of this law was to guarantee justice in the assignment and retention of *encomiendas* by removing them from the control of the audiencias, whose magistrates, as experience had proved, often allowed themselves to be influenced by local prejudices. *Encomiendas* were to be assigned by the king, in theory at least, and no other authority save the monarch and his council could exercise jurisdiction over them.[39]

The audiencia was, however, authorized to act as the protector of persons holding Indians on *encomiendas,* to see that they were not unjustly deprived of or wrongfully disturbed in their holdings. In case a person were thus deprived of his Indians, the audiencia was empowered to restore conditions to their former state. If the aggressor persisted, or cared to contest the right of his opponent to the Indians in question, the audiencia was ordered to observe the law of Malines, collecting all the evidence in the case, and forwarding it to the Council of the Indies for final decision. The frequency of litigation, however, and the vast number of unimportant cases which arose under the provisions of the law of Malines came to demand too much of the time and attention of the Council of the Indies, thereby causing many delays in suits involving *encomiendas.* In order to remedy this defect, Philip III, on April 17, 1609, conferred on the audiencia jurisdiction over all cases involving *encomiendas, repartimientos,*[40] tributes, and despoliations of Indians up to the value

---

[39] *Recopilación*, 2–15–123 to 133.

[40] *Ibid.*, 133 (1563). Helps (*Spanish conquest*, I, 102, 103–104) states that the *repartimiento* system was originated in 1496, from the requirement of Columbus that the natives of Hispaniola should pay him a certain quantity of gold as tribute. In view of the inability of the natives to meet the demands of the Spaniards in regard to the

of a thousand ducats.[41]   Cases involving a greater value were
still to be settled in conformity with the law of Malines. Finally,
in 1624 it was ordered that in suits which did not involve more
than three Indians and in cases wherein the costs of litigation
exceeded the amount in dispute, the decree of the governor
should prevail. For obvious reasons, the audiencia could not
concern itself with such cases, but when the value of the Indians
justified the attention of the tribunal, its decisions were final,
taking precedence over those of the governor.[42]   This, then,
was the final status of the jurisdiction of the audiencia over
encomiendas as set forth in the laws of the Indies. In the

---

precious metal, "the villagers were ordered to make (and work) the
farms in the Spanish settlements.   This may be considered as the
beginning of the system of *repartimientos*, or *encomiendas*, as they
were afterwards called."

In a subsequent chapter the same author tells of the difficulty which
Ovando had in compelling the Indians to live among the Spaniards,
to pay tribute and accept religious teaching.   Ferdinand and Isabella,
in a letter dated December 20, 1503, directed Ovando to compel the
Indians to deal with the Spaniards, to work for wages, to go to mass,
to be instructed in the faith, and further, that they should do all these
things "as free persons, for so they are."   . . .   "Ovando adopted the
following system," says Helps; "he distributed Indians amongst the
Castillians, giving to one man fifty, to another a hundred; with a deed
that ran thus: 'to you, such a one, is given an *encomienda* of so many
Indians, with such a Cacique, and you are to teach them the things
of our Holy Catholic Faith'.   The word *encomienda* . . . was a
term belonging to the military orders, corresponding to our command-
ery or preceptory; and this term naturally enough came into use
with the appointment, as governors in the Indies, of men, who held
authority in those orders, such as Bobadilla and Ovando."   (See also
Bancroft, *History of Central America*. I, 262.)   "With respect to the
implied condition of teaching the Indians 'the Holy Catholic Faith' it
was no more attended to from the first than any formal clause in a
deed, which is supposed by the parties concerned to be a mere
formality."

"We have now arrived," continues Helps, "at the climax of the
repartimiento system.   That which Bobadilla did illegally, was now
done with proper formalities on parchment: . . .   We may notice
again that the first *repartimientos* made by Columbus . . . apportioned to any Spaniard, whom he thought fit, such and such lands, to
be worked by such a Cacique and his people—a very different procedure to giving *men*—a feudal system, not a system of slavery."—Helps
Spanish conquest, I, 138–139.

[41] *Recopilación*, 2–15–129.

[42] *Ibid.*, 127.

Philippines the authority of the tribunal in regard to them was neither executive nor legislative, except in such cases and on such occasions as we shall refer to later. The judicial authority of the Audiencia of Manila over *encomiendas* was indisputable.

Having indicated the general basis upon which the authority of the audiencia rested, we may more precisely define its jurisdiction by reviewing a few of the most characteristic cases which were tried in the tribunal in accordance with the laws already discussed. The statement has been made that at the time of its establishment the audiencia was needed as a court of justice and that it was removed in 1589 for political reasons rather than because of the inadequacy or failure of the institution as a tribunal of justice. In the preceding chapter we saw that the audiencia was designed to relieve the executive of judicial duties, such as the trial of cases appealed from the *alcaldes mayores* of the provinces and the *alcaldes ordinarios* of the city. These functions, up to the time of the establishment of the audiencia, had been exercised by the governor. This had resulted in favoritism and in a perversion of justice to the private ends of the governor and of his friends. Perhaps the chief evil under the system had proceeded from the governor's double jurisdiction, as both executive and judge, over cases involving *encomiendas* and *encomenderos*. The governor assigned *encomiendas* in the name of the king, and he was also judge with final jurisdiction over all suits involving them, the law of Malines being impossible of execution in the Philippines before the establishment of the audiencia, and after its withdrawal in 1589.[43]

The same was true in regard to commercial cases, and complaints were ever arising against the governor's high-handed proceedings in the allotment of cargo space on the galleons to his friends, and his monopolization of the best Chinese goods that

43 *Ibid.*, 5–15–181.

came to Manila. The governor, as in the assignment of *encomiendas,* enjoyed an undue advantage in these matters, for at the same time that he was the executive with the power of bestowing these favors, he was the sole judge in all contentions which arose regarding commerce. It was therefore distinctly in the interests of justice that a supreme court should be established, and it is easy to understand why those who had profited by the absence of the audiencia should oppose its restoration, and why others should take the opposite view.

Soon after the audiencia was abolished in 1589, arguments were presented at court for its restoration. From the large number of petitions that were presented, two, aside from those discussed in the preceding chapter, may be cited here because they illustrate the disadvantages from a judicial point of view of having the administration of justice in the hands of the governor, with appeal to Mexico. Francisco de la Misa, *factor* of the treasury of Manila, wrote a memorial to the king on May 31, 1595,[44] referring to the delay which had arisen in the trial of suits involving *encomiendas:* the jurisdiction of the governor was not final; appeals had to be carried to the Audiencia of Mexico and cases involving a thousand ducats or more had to be taken from that tribunal to the Council of the Indies;[45] this meant two appeals and much delay. He mentioned certain cases which had been pending two years, and showed that, because of the delay to which they had been subjected in Mexico, it would be at least two years more before the decisions could be returned. Misa said that conditions had reverted to the state which had existed before the audiencia was established; a much larger number of cases was awaiting trial than the governor and his

---

[44] Francisco de la Misa to the King, May 31, 1595, A. I. 67–1–29.

[45] In this and in other letters of officials in the Philippines we find the amount frequently referred to as 1000 pesos, although in the *Recopilación* (2–15–129 [1609]) the jurisdiction is fixed at 1000 ducats. According to law 181 (1589), the authority of the governor (the audiencia had been suppressed) was extended to cases of the same value.

lieutenant could attempt to try. These difficulties were multiplied by the fact that there was no *fiscal,* an officer whose services as legal adviser to the government and as prosecuting attorney were indispensable.[46]

Misa petitioned for a reform of the law which had established the governor as judge of ultimate recourse in cases involving one thousand pesos (ducats) or less. He believed it advisable to reduce the limit of the value of cases settled in the colony from one thousand to four hundred pesos and appeal all those exceeding the latter sum to the Audiencia of Mexico. It would result in a more equitable administration of justice, he stated, if the trial of important cases were conducted in second instance before that tribunal. This practice, though subject to great delay, would have the advantage of guaranteeing the review of these cases by a competent and properly qualified magistracy rather than by a biased and tyrannical executive. He alleged that four hundred pesos in the Philippines meant as much as a thousand elsewhere. Another suggestion advanced by Misa was that suits and investigations involving *real hacienda* should be tried by competent judges, rather than by the governor, whose own personal interest in the cases was often too great to ensure fair trial. Another evil pointed out by Misa, and a fairly typical one throughout the history of the colony, was the delay and uncertainty of the *residencia.* This defect was particularly apparent at this time because all cases of *residencia* had to be sent to Mexico, since there was no tribunal in Manila with jurisdiction on appeal over these official investigations. Misa described the plight of various *alcaldes mayores, corregidores,* and other officials who had been investigated and suspended from office, awaiting the outcome of the *residencia.*

---

[46] It is probable that Misa meant that there was not sufficient distinction between the governor's *asesor* and the *teniente de gobierno.* This combined post was filled by Pedro de Rojas until 1593 and then by Antonio de Morga. These officials were the private advisers of the governors in legal matters, and active magistrates at the same time.

There were no persons to take their places; as a result, the suspended officials were without gainful employment, while their districts and offices reverted to a state of lawlessness, barbarism and disorder, without governor, judges, or incumbents. The governor had attempted to remedy the trouble by making temporary appointments from among the removed officials, but this he had no authority to do; moreover, the reinstatement of officials whose conduct was under investigation was subversive of the best interests of government and justice. The governor's action in these cases had raised a storm of protest in the colony, yet he was forced to take these steps in preference to leaving the natives without government and protection. Misa presented this picture of the state of affairs in the colony to show the evil results of the absence from the Philippines of a tribunal with authority to conduct *residencias* and to provide offices.

While this series of complaints was not followed by an open advocacy of the establishment of a royal audiencia in Manila, the defects which were pointed out showed the desirability of putting an end to the governor's intervention in judicial matters. There can be no question but that the arrival at court of such letters showed clearly the need of a tribunal at Manila for the administration of justice.

Complaints were also directed against this state of affairs by Antonio de Morga, lieutenant-governor of the Islands. This official argued that the commonwealth required an audiencia in order to secure a more equitable administration of justice.[47] He called attention to the overcrowded docket of the court over which he presided and emphasized the impossibility of the satisfactory termination of the cases waiting to be tried. That the defects referred to in these communications were appreciated at court is evidenced by the *cédula* of May 26, 1595, which emphasized

---

[47] Memorial of Antonio de Morga, July 6, 1596, Blair and Robertson, IX, 271 *et seq.*

the necessity of administering justice in the Philippines with "universal equality, mildness and satisfaction."[48]

Nevertheless the presence of a tribunal had the effect of encouraging the inhabitants of the Islands to litigation. It has been said that there have been more lawsuits in the Philippines than in any other country of the same size and population, which remark probably would apply to any country where the Spanish judicial system had lately obtained. This condition was no doubt due to the fact that adequate facilities existed whereby the natives could go to law. Lawyers and judges were ever unduly ready to encourage and hear any suits which might arise if there were any way in which profit might be derived therefrom. Pardo de Tavera, in discussing these phases of the legal history of the Islands, states that the laws protected the native, but at the same time they kept him in a state of perpetual tutelage. Judgments were passed by native magistrates in suits between natives in the later days of Spanish rule, but in general throughout the period of Spain's domination suits were prosecuted under the direction of a *protector of the Indians* in case one party to a suit was a Spaniard, or when the rights of the natives were in any way jeopardized or injured by a Spaniard. "In this manner Spanish prestige was preserved, inasmuch as it was no longer an Indian who asked for the punishment of one belonging to a superior race, but a Spaniard who took up the Indian's cause and conducted the suit against another Spaniard."[49] Thus it may be seen that in Spain's judicial system the means were provided, in theory at least, whereby the meanest native could obtain justice, not only among his fellows, but in cases to which members of the superior Spanish race were parties.

The declared purpose of the whole system of legislation for the Indies was the material and spiritual well-being of the

---

[48] *Cédula* of May 26, 1596, A. I., 106–4–19.
[49] Pardo de Tavera, in *Census of the Philippine Islands*, I, 335.

Indians.[50] The officials of the government, the churchmen, and the *encomenderos* were especially charged in their commissions and in official correspondence to make the protection and welfare of the Indians their chief concern. Attention has just been directed to the office of protector of the Indians. The *fiscal*, or one of his assistants, attended to that duty in the Audiencia of Manila, while agents (*agentes fiscales*) were especially commissioned by the *fiscal* to act in that capacity in the provinces.[51] We have also noted that the *oidores* were charged with the duty of protecting the Indians when officiating as visitors in the provinces. Such cases, also those involving decisions of *corregidores* and *alcaldes mayores* by which the natives were dealt with unjustly, were appealable, under certain circumstances, to the audiencia. These cases commanded the immediate attention of the tribunal, to the exclusion of other business.[52] Among the vast number of cases at our disposal which illustrate the jurisdiction of the tribunal over such matters, the following may be selected as typical. On May 16, 1796, the *fiscal* brought a charge in the audiencia against the governor, exposing the sufferings inflicted upon the Indians of the *barrio* of Santa Ana by the *corregidor* of Tondo[53] in connection with the construction of a road. The audiencia refused to consider the case in first instance, as the matter was not contentious, but it recommended that the *fiscal* should make the charges before the governor and have him render a decision upon the matter; if exception were taken to his decision the case could be appealed to the audiencia. The *oidores* found that they were without

---

[50] *Recopilación*, 1–1, 2, 3; 5–1.

[51] King to the President and Oidores, February 16, 1602, A. I., 105–2–1; *Cédula* of October 25, 1870; *Colección legislativa de España*, CV, 449–463; *Cédula* of April 12, 1875, *ibid.*, CXIV, 516–524.

[52] *Recopilación*, 2–15–81, 83.

[53] Tondo is now a district or ward of the city of Manila. At the time referred to here, the *barrio* of Santa Ana (small district under a *teniente* of a *corregidor* or *alcalde mayor*) was within the jurisdiction of the *corregimiento* of Tondo.

jurisdiction over the case in first instance and they declared that their entertainment of the suit would be in violation of the laws of the Indies.[54] The *fiscal* appealed from the judgment of the audiencia. The Council of the Indies, in a return communication dated May 13, 1798,[55] approved the ruling of the audiencia, affirming that in cases of the nature referred to, the *fiscal*, as protector of the Indians, should submit testimony in behalf of the latter to the governor, who should consider whether the Indians had been wronged and render his decision accordingly. If exception were taken to the decision of the governor, the case could then be appealed to the audiencia. While these appeals and this litigation were in progress, the Indians were being subjected to repeated hardships.

This case is illustrative of the ineffectiveness of the system for the administration of justice in Spain's colonies. It had taken two years for this appeal to be carried to Spain and receive the attention of the Council of the Indies. The answer had yet to be returned, probably requiring at least a year more for the return of the Vera Cruz and Acapulco galleons and for the proper proceedings to be carried on in the Manila tribunal. It is questionable whether the Indians in whose interests this was ultimately done ever received any benefit from these legal proceedings.

The case which has just been described involved the trial and punishment of a *corregidor* in the defense and protection of the natives. It is important to note that this case was ordered to be tried in first instance by the governor and not by the audiencia. The jurisdiction of the latter tribunal in second instance was confirmed by the king on this occasion. By the law of October 9, 1812, and by others made pursuant to the Constitution of 1812, the audiencia was given jurisdiction in first

---

[54] *Recopilación*, 2–15–71, which forbade the trial of *alcaldes* and provincial officials before the audiencia.

[55] Council of the Indies to the *Fiscal*, A. I., 105–2–10.

instance over cases involving provincial officials, and particularly judges. In regard to the care and protection of the Indians, which was involved in this controversy, the law provided that such cases should be treated originally by the *corregidores* and *alcaldes mayores* with appeal to the audiencia.[56] But this case dealt primarily with the official conduct of a *corregidor*, over whom the governor had more direct jurisdiction. The *cédula* of May 13, 1798, which constituted the reply of the king to the appeal of the *fiscal* in the case described above, ordered that henceforth in cases affecting the relations of the *corregidores* and *alcaldes mayores* on the one part and the Indians on the other, the *fiscal*, audiencia, and governor should act in *acuerdo*, in that way avoiding friction and quarrels over jurisdiction.[57]

That the audiencia did not always try cases relating to the Indians with requisite promptness, is evidenced by the many and repeated letters of the king to the tribunal, to the *fiscal*, as protector of the Indians, and to the regent, chiding these officials for delay. On many occasions the royal zeal for justice in the treatment of the Indians, based on a lack of knowledge of the true nature of the Filipino, completely overruled all considerations of practicability and common sense. As an illustration of this, on June 20, 1686, certain natives of the province of Bulacán sent false evidence to the Council of the Indies; this testimony was taken in preference to that remitted by the audiencia, the decision of the latter body being reversed by the Council of the Indies. The audiencia refused to allow the execution of the new judgment; the *oidores* all offered to resign in protest, and the regent, at the risk of removal, reopened the case. It was proved by the testimony of a number of officials and by the confessions

---

[56] *Recopilación*, 5-2-3; 2-15-81, 83.

[57] This decision conforms with the *Recopilación*, 5-2-3, 4, and 2-15-68; 117. These laws give to the audiencia and the governor jurisdiction over excesses of the provincial judges and executives, and over cases appealed from them. *Ibid.*, 2-16-44 gave jurisdiction to the viceroy over criminal charges against *oidores* and *alcaldes*.

of the natives who had perjured themselves that the evidence upon which the Council had acted was false.[58] A record of these proceedings was remitted to the Council and that tribunal promptly reversed its former decision.

Further illustrations of the authority of the audiencia in cases involving natives may be seen in suits which arose from time to time over the illegal treatment of the latter by the friars and the unjust occupation of the natives' lands by the religious orders. These suits afford illustration, also, of the services of the audiencia as an agency to force persons to show their titles to lands which they held.[59] This jurisdiction will be given more detailed treatment in the proper place, but the brief citation of one or two cases among many seems advisable to illustrate the activity of the audiencia in protecting the Indians, both by trying suits involving them and by actually intervening in their behalf.

Various revolts broke out among the Indians near Manila from 1740 to 1750. These insurrections were said to have been provoked by the encroachments of the Augustinians and Dominicans on the lands of the natives. The matter was called to the attention of the home government, and Pedro Calderón Enríquez, an *oidor*, was ordered to investigate the charges made against these religious orders and to ascertain the validity of their claims to the lands in question. The friars, when ordered to submit titles to a secular judge, refused to comply, claiming ecclesiastical exemption. In the face of their opposition, Calderón dispossessed the friars of the lands which they were said

---

58 Council of the Indies to Audiencia, December 16, 1687, A. I., 105-2-1. The facility with which witnesses may be procured is from one point of view a great aid to the administration of justice in the Philippines today. See Elliott, *The Philippines to the end of the military règime*, 246-8.

59 Royal decree on Usurpation of Indian Lands, November 7, 1751, Blair and Robertson, LXVII, 27-34. See Cunningham, "Origin of the friar lands question in the Philippines" in *Political science review*, X, 465-480.

to have usurped and which they were continuing to hold without legitimate title, restoring the lands to the crown. The case was appealed to the audiencia and that tribunal upheld the visitor.

Calderón also found that the University of Santo Tomás and the Dominicans, in collusion with a clerk of the audiencia, had taken lands from the native town of Sílang in 1743. Calderón restored the lands to their rightful owners and his act was approved in judicial review by the audiencia. The friars took exception to this by appealing to the Council of the Indies. The Council notified the audiencia of its affirmation of the judgment of Calderón and further stated that the lands of Sílang, Imús, San Nicolás, and Cavite had been unjustly seized and should be restored. This was not only an affirmation but an extension of the sentence of the *oidor,* made by the Council after the royal *fiscal* (of the Council of the Indies) had reviewed all the evidence presented in the case. This suit shows the efforts made to carry out the royal intention that the natives of Spain's colonies should be justly treated. It also shows the respective jurisdictions of the audiencia and Council of the Indies as courts of review and appeal in adjusting disputes between the church and the Indians.

In addition to the above, the audiencia exercised jurisdiction over the religious themselves, both as individuals and as subjects of the king, punishing them for violation of the civil laws of the realm to which they were amenable as subjects. An illustration of this is furnished by the following case which occurred in 1617. Two Augustinian provincials were murdered, one, Fray Gerónimo de Salas, by poisoning, and his successor, Fray Vicente Sepúlveda, by strangulation. A tribunal of friars, composed of nine prominent members of the Augustinian order, was appointed by the bishop for the investigation of the crime. This body, after due consideration, caused six members of the order to be apprehended; four of them were believed to be guilty of the murder and two were suspected of connivance at the crime. On July 31, 1617, these six culprits were handed over to the civil government, and on September 2 of that year, the four guilty ecclesiastics were condemned to death by the audiencia, while the other two were sentenced to six years of service in the galleys. This case illustrates the extent of ecclesiastical jurisdiction exercised respectively by the church and government tribunals under the *fuero mixto*.[60] The former, on this occasion, made the preliminary investigations and handed the culprits over to the secular authority with recommendations; the latter conducted the trial, passed sentence and saw to its execution. The trial and conclusion of this case covered the remarkably short period of thirty-three days.[61]

Speaking generally, the authority of the audiencia over ecclesiastical affairs extended to disputes between orders, between the government and the church, or its representatives, to cases relating to land titles, to those alleging abuses of the Indians by the friars, to cases involving the royal patronage, and to cases of *fuerza*.[62] As the question of the ecclesiastical jurisdiction of the audiencia will be discussed more fully in subsequent chapters, no effort will be made at this time to particularize concerning its authority over church affairs, it being merely desirable to suggest the fact here that the audiencia had jurisdiction in suits involving the church and the civil government and in those which had to do with the protection of the natives from the abuses of the ecclesiastics.

Records of thousands of cases exist to show the different

---

60 *Fuero mixto*, in this case a *fuero* or concession to the ecclesiastical government of jurisdiction over secular matters. See note 53, Chapter XI, of this volume.

61 Audiencia to the King, September 27, 1617, A. I., 67–6–20. Three of these friars were hanged at once, and one, Juan Ocádiz, escaped to New Spain. He was said to be the illegitimate son of Doña Ana of Austria (see Blair and Robertson, XVIII, 82–88).

62 *Recopilación*, 2–15–134 to 153; 2–16–15; 2–18–29, 30; 1–4–3, 20; 1–6–26, 39, 57; 1–7–18, 29 to 31; 2–15–146, 147, 149. See note 3, Chapter XI, of this volume.

kinds of suits tried judicially in the audiencia. Civil and criminal matters came up in the tribunal as in all other courts of
law, and hence, as such, merit only passing attention. Among
civil cases possibly the most typical were those relating to
encomiendas. It must be borne in mind that the Spaniard,
however mistakenly from the theoretical point of view, regarded
the *encomiendas* as property in the same sense as a modern
farmer regards his farm as property. He paid a rental or tax
to the government, he engaged in agriculture for gain, and, as
we have seen, the moral duty of protecting, uplifting, or edu-
cating the Indians rested but lightly on his conscience. Therefore, as these cases are discussed in the following pages, the
value of the property and not the treatment of the Indians on
the *encomiendas* is the first consideration. As already stated,
the law of Malines reserved for the Council of the Indies final
action in all *encomienda* suits involving more than one thousand
ducats.[63]

Many suits involving *encomiendas* came up prior to the
establishment of the audiencia; the defects apparent in the trial
of these cases by the governor show clearly the need of an
audiencia at that time. The earliest case noted in this connection was prosecuted in 1580 by the *asesor* of the governor against
Doña Lucía de Loaxa, the widow of an *encomendero*, with the
object of dispossessing her of an *encomienda* held at Butuán,
Mindanao.[64] She was charged with having nullified her title by
marriage to another *encomendero*, since the law forbade married
women to hold *encomiendas*. In her defense she alleged that
the desire of the governor to enforce the law was only pretense,
since many married women in the Philippines held *encomiendas*.

---

[63] *Recopilación*, 2-15-129.

[64] This case and the others dealt with in this section involving
encomiendas are to be found in the *Inventario de los pleytos en la real
audiencia de Manila que se hallen en el rl. y supremo consejo de las
Indias y remiten al rl. archivo en Sevilla según rl. orden de Julio de
1787*. The key to the above exists in the *Inventario de autos de la
Essma. la Cámara de Indias*, IV, 453, A. I.

She stated that the governor desired to deprive her of her property in order that he might bestow it upon a friend. This case was carried to the Council of the Indies, and it illustrates the effectiveness of the law of Malines, which took from the governor authority over a case in which he was interested and gave final jurisdiction to the tribunal in Spain. The papers pertaining to this case were returned to the governor with orders to do as the law commanded. The defendant was accordingly removed from the *encomienda*.

Another case was disposed of in a slightly different manner. On January 22, 1581, Juan Gutiérrez de Figueroa, second husband of Magdalena Rodríguez, widow of an *encomendero* of Mindanao, filed suit before the governor praying to be continued as possessor of an *encomienda* which his wife had held prior to her marriage to him. He brought the suit on the grounds that he was a soldier and was accordingly deserving of reward. This case, in accordance with the provisions of Malines, came within the jurisdiction of the governor. He denied the petition, but the soldier appealed the case to the Council of the Indies and that tribunal again reversed the decision of the governor on May 23, 1584.

In January, 1582, Bishop Salazar, as protector of the Indians, brought suit before Governor Ronquillo de Peñalosa against Juan de Ayala, a Spaniard holding various *encomiendas* in different parts of the Island of Luzón, but resident in Manila. Two specific charges were brought against Ayala. He was said to have reduced the Indians on his *encomiendas* to the status of slaves, which was forbidden by the law of November 9, 1526.[65] He had also violated the law which prescribed that *encomenderos* should live on their *encomiendas*,[66] and give their personal

---

[65] *Recopilación*, 6–2–1. This prohibition was first imposed by Charles V on the above date and subsequently by Philip II and Philip III (see laws 1 to 14, same title).

[66] *Ibid.*, 6–9–11, 13.

attention to the Indians thereon. Ayala adduced testimony
to prove that this law was a dead-letter and that it was disregarded by most of the *encomenderos*. He even showed that
there were many of them residing in Spain who held *encomiendas* in Spain and Perú. Governor Ronquillo felt that the evidence at hand was insufficient to justify a decision in this case,
so he permitted it to be carried to the Council of the Indies.
The latter tribunal rendered its decision on June 24, 1584, communicating to the Audiencia of Manila its ruling that Ayala
should be allowed to retain the *encomiendas* in question, but
the president and *oidores* were especially charged to enforce the
law prohibiting slavery in the Indies.

The procedure in these cases confirms the laws already
alluded to, which were promulgated before the establishment of
the audiencia, that the governor should have jurisdiction in
suits involving less than a thousand ducats, with appeal to the
Council of the Indies. It would also appear, from the data at
our command, that the audiencia inherited the governor's former
authority in these matters.

During the period from 1583 to 1589, and after the re-
establishment of the audiencia in Manila, this tribunal exercised
authority over suits involving *encomiendas*. There is so much
sameness in the nature of these cases that little would be added
by describing them. There appears evidence of considerable
conflict of jurisdiction, however, between the governor and the
audiencia over the adjustment of the latter to the new situation
relative to the *encomiendas*. Governors Acuña, Tello and
Fajardo sought on various occasions to retain jurisdiction over
suits involving *encomiendas* on the basis of the law of Malines,
notwithstanding the fact that the audiencia had been given the
duty of trying such cases. When appeals were made to the
Council of the Indies, that tribunal made clear its determination that the audiencia should try suits involving *encomiendas*,
but that in administrative matters relating thereto the will of

the governor should prevail, unless his decision were contested through legal channels. An illustration of such difference of opinion may be noted in the letter written by Governor Juan Niño de Tavora on August 4, 1628, to the Council of the Indies. Tavora complained of the action of the audiencia in regard to the disposal of a case involving an *encomendero* who had married the widow of another *encomendero,* and who had tried to unite and hold both their *encomiendas* after marriage. The governor contended that two persons holding *encomiendas* by previous right should choose the more desirable one and relinquish the other, in accordance with the practice in other places. Especially should this be done in the Philippines, he held, because there were so few *encomiendas* in the Islands. The *fiscal* approved of this suggestion and made a motion before the *acuerdo* of the audiencia that this course should be pursued, but, as no laws had been promulgated on the subject, there was no precedent to follow. The audiencia accordingly declared that such a course as the governor had suggested would not be legal. Tavora petitioned the Council of the Indies for a ruling on the subject. The Council sustained the governor in its *consulta* of January 15, 1630.

There was apparently no limit to the value of suits involving *encomiendas* which might be tried in the audiencia, and appealed to the Council of the Indies. There exists the record of one case in which the *encomienda* was valued at 223,000 pesos. In this suit the *fiscal* proceeded against Doña Juana Leal and Francisco de Rebolledo, residents of Mexico, for possession of an *encomienda* held in the Philippines. This case affords an illustration of the delays to which the course of justice was subject, it being appealed to the Council of the Indies in 1612, and not finally settled till 1620. A suit involving an *encomienda* valued at 430,102 pesos came before the audiencia in 1703, when two residents of Manila, named Delgado and Abaurrea, were dispossessed of an *encomienda* by the governor.

The *encomienda* was awarded immediately to Juan de Echevarría and Antonio de Endaya. The latter were prosecuted in the audiencia by the dispossessed *encomenderos*, and the tribunal, in compliance with the law of Malines, made the prescribed investigation, recommending that the governor's action should be disapproved, since the evidence showed that the persons installed on the *encomienda* were distant relatives of the governor. The Council adopted the recommendations of the audiencia in this case, ordering that the original *encomenderos* should be restored to their estate, and that this breach of royal commands should be registered against the governor to be answered in his *residencia*.

Another suit, of a similar nature to that described above, was brought in the audiencia in 1713 against Juan de Rivas, who had been assigned two *encomiendas* in Leyte and Cebú, respectively, by the governor, thus depriving one Saramiento who had held them formerly. The plaintiff claimed that he had made great improvements on these estates, spending all his income thereon, and as yet had received no profits from the lands. He petitioned, therefore, that these *encomiendas* should be bestowed upon him for another term.[67] The audiencia withheld its judgment on this case, referring it to the Council. That body, after seeking the advice of the royal *fiscal* and

---

[67] The laws of the Indies *(Recopilación,* 6–19–6) authorized the governor of the Philippines to assign *encomiendas ad interim* for the period of six years (promulgated August 25, 1646). By the laws of May 1, 1774, and June 8, 1792, the period was made five years in all the colonies except Perú; in the latter it was six years (note to *Recopilación,* 8–22–1). We have record of the extension of an *encomienda* in the Philippines to the Hospital of San Juan de Diós for four years by Governor Marquina on July 10, 1789. The *cofradía* had held this *encomienda* for ten years, and on its petition the governor made this additional concession, subject to royal confirmation (A. I., 107–5–18). The above episode is at variance with the statement of Bancroft *(History of Central America,* I, 264) that the *encomienda* system came to an end in 1721. Helps states that the *encomienda* system "remained in full force until the reign of Charles The Third of Spain, at which period, it appears, it was annulled."—See Helps *Spanish conquest,* IV, 240.

contador, recommended to the king that Saramiento should be allowed to retain the *encomiendas* for another term, and it was accordingly done, a royal order to that effect being expedited on May 29, 1715.

It is notable how frequently the action of the audiencia or that of the governor was confirmed by the Council of the Indies. In most of the cases which have been described, the original papers, including letters, *autos* and *testimonios,* each *expediente*[68] containing from one hundred to two thousand pages, are marked "seen by the Council", "action of the governor confirmed", or "no action to be taken"; the original decisions being thus confirmed. It may be concluded, therefore, from this brief study that the audiencia had appellate jurisdiction as a court of law over suits involving *encomiendas,* and, furthermore, that the tribunal acting in that capacity placed a very effective and definite check on the governor in his executive control over *encomiendas.*

Property suits, aside from those involving *encomiendas,* were numerous. One noted case may be cited in which the heirs of Governor Fausto Cruzat y Góngora in 1703 brought suit to recover money owed by Gaspar Sánchez and Bernardo de Guirós to the ex-governor. The audiencia failed to award the sum, which approximated 8000 pesos. The case was appealed to the Council of the Indies and the decision was reversed, the plaintiffs being awarded the money originally sued for, with costs

---

68 *Expedientes* are defined in Blair and Robertson, LII, 72, note 28, as "all the papers belonging to any matter, judicial, legislative, or executive, consisting of orders, opinions, reports, and all other measures." A *testimonio* is a duly attested and certified statement or number of statements submitted as proof or evidence concerning a given matter. *Testimonios* include transcripts of letters, *cédulas, autos,* and *expedientes* on a particular subject, usually bound together. They may extend over a period of a hundred years or more, showing step by step the factors leading up to the formulation of any *auto,* or *cédula,* or given as reasons for a particular action taken by an official or tribunal. *Testimonios* form a large part of the material in the Archive of the Indies. They are of the same value as originals, and they are certainly more available and legible because frequently more recently written.

of suit. A similar case was brought by the children and heirs of Governor Bustamante against Juan de Nebra, *general* of the galleon. The case was tried in the audiencia and the tribunal decided in favor of the defendant. The case was appealed to the Council of the Indies and the decision was reversed.[69] In 1736 Gaspar Thomé, a Frenchman, sued the estate of a deceased debtor, Juan de Olerte, for 2000 pesos.[70] The case was appealed to the Council of the Indies, and fully two hundred pages of documentary material exist, carefully annotated and digested, to show how thoroughly and with what formality a suit of even that small import was tried. We have already noted the tendency of the government to discourage the appeal of property suits to the Council of the Indies. The jurisdiction of the audiencia was final, for the most part, in suits involving sums from 200 to 6000 pesos.

As matters of trade were always important in the life and politics of the Islands, commercial suits commanded a large share of the attention of the audiencia. Up to 1769 the jurisdiction of the audiencia was supreme in matters relating thereto,[71] but on December 13 of that year a *consulado* was established at Manila, thereby relieving the audiencia of much of its former control over commercial affairs.[72] The *consulado*, from the time of its establishment, was an ever-present thorn in the side of the audiencia and conflicts over the respective jurisdictions of the tribunals[73] were continually arising. We may

---

[69] *Inventario, op. cit.*

[70] Note the appeal of a case involving less than 6000 pesos, which was contrary to the laws of the Indies. (*Recopilación*, 5–13–1).

[71] Martínez de Zúñiga, *Estadismo*, I, 245.

[72] Decree for establishment of the *Consulado*, in Manila, December 13, 1769, A. I., 108–3–17.

[73] The *consulado* was an organization of the merchants of certain authorized cities of the Spanish empire. A *consulado* had to be established by royal authorization. The tribunal of the *consulado* was composed of two consuls and a *prior*, who were chosen for terms of two years and one year respectively. They were chosen by twelve electors who in turn were designated by the members of the *consulado*. The

briefly cite one or two cases to illustrate the respective jurisdictions of the audiencia and the tribunal of the *consulado*. On December 26, 1806, action was brought by two Spaniards against the British firm of Jacob Smith and Company on account of the inferior quality of goods sold to the plaintiff by that firm.[74] Suit was brought originally in the audiencia, but the *consulado* applied to the governor for jurisdiction in the case on the ground that, as a commercial suit, it should be tried in the *consulado*.[75] The governor awarded jurisdiction to the audiencia. The *consulado* re-appealed the case, but the Council sustained the governor's decision on the ground that this was a suit between a private individual and a merchant which should be tried in the audiencia, the tribunal which usually tried cases between individuals. The function of the *consulado*, the royal decree stated, was to try suits of a commercial character which arose between merchants.[76]

An occasion on which the jurisdiction of the audiencia was unquestioned may be noted in the suit which was appealed to the Council of the Indies from the audiencia in 1698, over the wrecking of the galleon "San Francisco Xavier". The admiral, Don Esteban Ramos, was held accountable for the silver carried on the ship and the merchants of Manila sued him for what they had lost in the wreck.[77] It was charged that Ramos had landed the silver, but was seeking to conceal that fact, claiming instead that it was lost. The case was appealed to the Council by the defendant.[78] The Council referred the case to the *Junta*

---

tribunal de alzadas was composed of an *oidor* and two merchants. The latter constituted the final court of appeal in the colony in commercial cases and exception to their decisions could be taken only in the Council of the Indies.—Martínez de Zúñiga, *Estadismo*, 245–246.

[74] Council of the Indies to the Audiencia, January 21, 1808, A. I., 105–2–18.

[75] *Recopilación*, 9–46–40.

[76] *Ibid.*, 9–46. This section of the laws of the Indies establishes the *consulados* of Lima and Mexico, and lays down regulations for them.

[77] This was before the time of the Consulado of Manila.

[78] *Inventario, op. cit.*

de Guerra,[79] and that tribunal reversed the decision of the
audiencia, declaring that Ramos was a faithful servant of His
Majesty, and still a poor man. There was no possibility of his
having the silver. Ramos was transferred to the Atlantic
flota.[80] The royal *fiscal,* in the opinion rendered for the guidance of the *junta,* made the comment that frequently the *oidores*
of colonial audiencias were influenced, against their own ideas
of justice, by the opinions and wishes of the most powerful
residents. Such was possibly the case in Manila on this occasion. This statement at least shows that those in control at
Madrid were aware of some of the fundamental weaknesses of
the colonial audiencias.

Another typical case, indirectly connected with commerce,
occurred in 1713, when the *fiscal* of the audiencia prosecuted
three captains, Enrique Boynont, Fernando Gall and Diego
Brunet, who had arrived at Cavite in command of French
merchant and exploring ships, without the royal permission to
trade in the Islands. These captains, who were foreigners, of
course, were charged with smuggling, and were brought before
the royal audiencia. The charges against them were not proved,
and in due time the cases were dismissed.[81] The laws of the
Indies authorized the governor and the *alcaldes del crimen* to
try cases of strangers,[82] but in Manila, where there were no
magistrates of this category, such cases were tried by the
audiencia.

Perhaps the most important commercial suit that was ever

---

[79] The *Junta de Guerra* was the committee of the Council of the
Indies with jurisdiction over military and naval affairs. When ques-
tions of this nature came to the Council they were referred to the
Junta, where decision was made and referred back to the Council.
See notes 17 and 36, Chapter VII of this book.

[80] *Inventario, op. cit.*

[81] *Ibid.*

[82] *Recopilación,* 2–1–14; see also 9–27–35, 37, 2–2–39, also 9–27–3, 5,
13, 28, 29, 40, 47. These laws forbid the entrance of foreign ships and
individuals to the ports of the Indies.

tried in the Audiencia of Manila, came before that tribunal in 1656, when several residents of Mexico were excluded from the use of the galleon and their goods confiscated. This action was in accordance with repeated *cédulas* and regulations which reserved the space in the galleon for the exclusive use of the Manila merchants and authorities. Mexican traders, who had from time to time shipped goods on the galleons, were forbidden to crowd out the Manila merchants, who depended on that trade exclusively. The fine levied on this occasion amounted to 273,133 pesos. The case was appealed to the Council of the Indies, the aforesaid decision was upheld, and the sum was finally ordered paid in Mexico.[83]

During the greater part of the audiencia's existence there was no *consulado* in Manila and the jurisdiction of the audiencia in commercial cases extended to suits between merchants for space on the galleon. The tribunal had jurisdiction over the trial of officials for dishonesty in the assignment of galleon space: investigations of officials charged with reserving more than their due share of space, and such other cases as are mentioned in the laws of the Indies as being the concern of the *consulados* of Lima and Mexico.[84] Officers of the galleons were tried for mistreating seamen, for smuggling, for exceeding the limit of merchandise allowed, for giving passage to lewd women and to persons travelling on the galleons without permission. They were tried for carrying more slaves than they were allowed by law to carry, for charging exorbitant prices of passage, and for failing to turn in accounts of money collected. Commanders were often held criminally responsible for carelessness in navigation and for shipwrecks. These cases were tried in the tribunal of the *consulado* after 1769.

---

[83] *Real Acuerdo de 17 de Julio, 1656,* A. I., 67-6-22. (The final action of the Council is indicated without date on the margin of the *auto* of the Audiencia.)

[84] *Recopilación,* 9-46-28; 9-45-13.

The audiencia had appellate jurisdiction over all residents of the colony, both natives and Spaniards. All crimes committed within five leagues of the city of Manila were ordered to be tried by the *oidores* in first instance,[85] but unless they were of extraordinary importance, special investigators, usually *alcaldes mayores* or *alcaldes ordinarios,* were delegated to try them in the name of the audiencia.[86] As already stated, most of the criminal cases arising in the colony were tried in first instance in the provinces by the *alcaldes mayores.* Cases appealed to the audiencia were reviewed in that tribunal. The trial consisted of an examination of the summary or abstract of the case as it was originally tried by the lower judge and, if errors were found to exist, the decision was either reversed or the case was remanded to the judge who first had tried the case, for second trial.[87] The audiencia did not try the case with the defendant present. It merely reviewed the proceedings of the lower judge. Criminal cases were not ordinarily appealable to the Council of the Indies.

The procedure in criminal cases was generally so similar to that already described that it is unnecessary to give any illustration of the audiencia's criminal jurisdiction. Most of the cases that eventually reached the audiencia involved Spaniards, native *caciques,* and half-castes. Natives who were charged with robbery, murder, and crimes of a depraved nature were usually of a class unable to finance appeals to the audiencia. This fact probably accounts for the scarcity of criminal cases appealed during the first two centuries of the audiencia's existence.[88] However,

---

85 *Ibid.,* 2–15–111.

86 *Ibid.,* 71.

87 Foreman, *Philippine Islands,* 241. The laws regulating the trial of cases on appeal may be noted in *Recopilación,* 5–9, 10, 11, 12, 13.

88 The following figures have been taken from various reports of the audiencia to the Council of the Indies, and they show the number of criminal cases tried in the tribunal in the years designated:
1710— 51 cases......report dated December 11, 1711; A. I., 105–2–9.
1774— 34 "   "   "   "   25, 1776; *ibid.*

the reforms of the nineteenth century brought an increased number of cases into the audiencia by systematizing the administration of justice, differentiating the judgeships from administrative offices, and providing for greater facility of appeal.[89]

It is probable that in criminal as well as in civil cases, Spaniards derived considerable benefit from the fact that the audiencia was composed of magistrates of their own nationality. High officials, no doubt, escaped the consequences of their misdeeds more easily than did men of more modest social and political attainments. This is shown by the well-known case of the murder by Governor Fajardo of his wife on July 21, 1621; this came up before an audiencia which was com-

---

1776—	48 cases	. . . . . . report	dated	March,	1778;	*ibid.*
1779—	53 "	"	"	July	30, 1780;	"
1786—	99 "	"	"	May	1, 1778;	A. I., 105–2–10.
1789—	51 "	"	"	June	4, 1790;	"
1795—	38 "	"	"	April	4, 1798;	"
1822—	641 "	"	"	July	3, 1823;	A. I., 106–4–21.

According to Desdevises du Dezert ("Vice-rois et capitaines gènèraux des Indes espagnoles," in *Revue historique CXXVI*, 59, 60) the Audiencia of Lima decided 89 civil cases on appeal from February 11, 1788, to January 5, 1789. At the end of this period there were 122 cases waiting on the docket. In the chamber of first instance of the same audiencia 72 cases were tried and 124 remained to be tried at the end of approximately the same period. In the criminal *sala* during the year 1788, there were 7 death sentences rendered, 16 sentences for robbery, 14 cases tried involving personal injury, 15 for carrying arms in face of the prohibition of the law, and 6 cases of adultery. The magistrates excused themselves for this rather contemptible showing by alleging that the membership of the tribunal had not been complete, to which the king made answer that there would have been sufficient judges had not the latter continually absented themselves on the smallest pretexts. The charge of indolence was also frequently brought against the magistrates of the Audiencia of Manila.

[89] See *colección legislativa de España*, LXIV, 105–147 (Royal Decree of January 30, 1855). *Cédula* of December 6, 1858, in Rodríguez San Pedro, *Diccionario de legislación ultramarina*, VII, 69. *Cédula* of March 10, 1857, *ibid.*, VIII, 39. Royal Decree of July 4, 1861, *Colección legislativa de España*, LXXXVI, 1–45. The basic principle of these reforms are to be found in the Constitution of 1812, Martínez Alcubilla, *Diccionario*, III, 408–458, and in *Las Ordenanzas Nuevamente Formadas para el Régimen y Govierno interior de la Audiencia Nacional de Manila en cumplimiento de la Ley de 9 de Octre de 1812, sobre arreglo de tribunales.* A. I., 106–4–19.

posed of judges who were largely under the governor's domination. The tribunal gave the matter a cursory investigation,
after which the governor was allowed to go unpunished.[90] We
shall see that proceedings were different, however, when officials under investigation were charged with offenses against the
government. The *residencia,* which dealt with such charges,
was a pitiless form of inquisition in which the officiating
magistrate was in duty bound to find his victim guilty, if
possible.

Criminal cases of a character slightly different from those
described above were prosecuted by the government for the
infraction of any governmental regulation, or for the evasion
of the payment of taxes or duties. The collection of revenues
devolved upon the *oficiales reales* and they were ordered to
accomplish their duties in this particular, if possible, without
the assistance of the courts.[91] Numerous cases did come up
in the audiencia, however, involving the prosecution of individuals for violations of the *alcabala, quinto,* and the tax on
the export of silver *(comisos).* Persons assisting in the apprehension of violators of these laws were rewarded with a
part of the proceeds of the fine, the remainder becoming the
property of *real hacienda.* On October 6, 1783, the final
jurisdiction in cases of smuggling and non-payment of the
king's fifth was taken from the audiencia, appeals being authorized to the Council of the Indies.[92]

Reference has already been made to the services of an *oidor*
as special *auditor de guerra.* This, as well as other matters
relating to the jurisdiction of the governor and captain-general over military matters, wherein the audiencia had no
authority, will be noted when an examination is made of the

---

90 Blair and Robertson, XX, 35–43, 147, 168, 196–198.

91 *Recopilación,* 8–10–16.

92 *Cédulas* of October 6, 1783, and of November 19, 1805, A. I., 105–
2–18.

relations of the governor and audiencia in a subsequent chapter. Suffice it to say here that the audiencia did not have jurisdiction as a court over soldiers or military affairs.

Closely related to the subject of the defense of the Islands, and the exercise of judicial authority over soldiers was the special jurisdiction which the governor had over matters relating to the Chinese. This subject will be treated in greater detail when we discuss the relations of the audiencia and the governor.

During the first two centuries of its existence the audiencia had jurisdiction as a judicial tribunal in the cases and instances which have been noted. It had civil and criminal authority, original and appellate. Its decisions were final in civil suits on claims for six thousand pesos or less. Criminal cases were settled in the audiencia.

The judicial authority of the audiencia was impeded during the greater part of its history by the failure of the government to entrust it with complete jurisdiction in all civil and criminal matters, and by the tendency of the latter to interfere in matters of minute and insignificant detail, which should have been left to the magistrates of the tribunal. The Constitution of 1812 and the reforms made in pursuance thereof really effected the changes which had long been needed. The audiencia's jurisdiction was made final in all civil suits and increased in administrative cases; thereafter no appeals were made to the Council of the Indies unless they involved administrative law. Cases involving official dishonesty, incapacity, *residencia, pesquisas,* treason, disputes between audiencias and other tribunals over conflicts of jurisdiction, and questions of the interpretation of the law were still carried to Spain. These were important steps for the improvement of colonial judicial procedure; they served to simplify it, preventing a multiplicity of cases from being carried to Spain which should have been settled within the colony. These tardy reforms left to the home government more time in which to occupy itself with questions of governmental policy, leaving to the audiencias more authority and responsibility in purely judicial matters, thus giving to them a greater prestige in the commonwealths wherein they were situated.

The qualifications for the magistracy were also raised at this time, although it cannot be said that the magistrates of the audiencias were at any time incompetent or lacking in ability. The audiencias of the colonies were given equal status with those of the Peninsula, and were thus elevated in dignity and standing to the rank of tribunals of the first order. The chief defects of the colonial judicial system of the seventeenth century were thus corrected, though somewhat tardily. It is unfortunate indeed that these changes applied only to a mere skeleton of Spain's former colonial empire.

In this chapter we have discussed the audiencia as a formal court of justice, with methods, practices, and traditions little different from those of any tribunal of justice. However, it had judicial authority more extensive and far-reaching than has yet been indicated. Among the different kinds of cases over which the audiencia had jurisdiction, perhaps none was more important, and certainly none was more exclusively peculiar to the Spanish judicial system than suits of *residencia*. So distinct and extraordinary was that phase of judicial activity that it merits consideration apart from a discussion of the audiencia's functions as an ordinary court of law. In the following section we shall note its jurisdiction as an administrative court over suits wherein the government was a party and wherein the object was not only to punish offenders, but to act as a preventive of official misconduct.

CHAPTER IV

JUDICIAL FUNCTIONS OF THE AUDIENCIA; THE RESIDENCIA[1]

The purpose of the *residencia* was to uphold the morale of colonial service by making officials answer for all their acts in a judicial examination held at the close of their terms. It may be said that the fear of the *residencia* was almost the sole incentive to righteous official conduct or efficient public service, and it will be seen that the audiencia exercised very pronounced authority in this. Indeed, the audiencia had general supervision in a semi-judicial capacity over the services of officials and public servants in the colonies. It was the function of the audiencia to send reports to the court relative to the conduct, work, or attitude of any employee or official of the government, or of any resident of the colony. These reports were known as *informaciones (pareceres) de servicio.*[2] The tribunal itself was ready at all times to hear complaints against provincial governors and judges, treasury officials, magistrates, governors, or, in fact, any and all officials holding their positions by virtue of the king's commission.[3] Charges might be made by a wronged party or by anyone whose knowledge of an abuse was sufficient to justify charges. Heavy penalties were imposed upon persons making false or unsubstantiated charges.[4] Complaints against *alcaldes mayores* and *corregidores* were most likely to be made during the regular investigation of the visiting *oidor*, which, as we have noted, occurred every three

---

[1] See Cunningham, "Residencia in the Spanish colonies," in the *Southwestern historical quarterly*, XXI, 253–278.

[2] *Ibid.*, 2–33, 1, 6; literally, a report on character of services.

[3] *Ibid.*, 5–11.

[4] *Ibid.*, notes 1 to 4.

years, but sufficient complaint might be made to justify the dispatch of a special investigator at any time.[5]

The findings of the above inspections might be reviewed by the audiencia and lead to the suspension and dismissal of the official under investigation.[6] The final action had to be confirmed by the Council of the Indies in case the person concerned were a royal appointee, but in these matters the action of the local officials was usually approved. For the removal of *oidores* and *oficiales reales* a slightly different method was pursued. A magistrate of the audiencia was designated to investigate the case, the evidence was submitted to the Council of the Indies and final action was taken by it and not by the audiencia.[7] Any and all charges brought against an official in these investigations, even though he were cleared at the time, might be revived in the *residencia*.

Suspensions from office were made by the governor with the advice and consent of the audiencia. The governor had the legal right to make temporary removals, but on account of the seriousness of such an act, and the considerations depending upon it, he usually preferred to have the support of the magistrates in the matter. The governor, as vicepatron,. could suspend prelates and other church officials, but he seldom, if ever, exercised his powers to the full extent. The audiencia at Manila, on the other hand, actually drove the archbishop from the city on various occasions. The suspension and the removal of members of the ordinary clergy from their districts was a frequent occurrence, but churchmen were not subject to *residencia*. The audiencia had no authority to suspend or remove the governor, though the magistrates could and frequently did bring charges against the governor which led to his dismissal. Governors actually suspended and removed *oidores* at

---

5 *Ibid.*, 2–31–1.

6 *Ibid.*, 5–12–9.

7 *Ibid.*. 5–11–6; see also, 5–12–14.

times, though such acts were protested as violations of the law which authorized only the Council of the Indies to remove these officials.

Briefly, the procedure in making these removals was as follows: the governor and audiencia investigated the conduct of an official whenever circumstances demanded it; the latter was either suspended and recommended for removal, such recommendations being made by the audiencia to the governor or to the Council of the Indies, according to the rank of the official, or the tribunal could make the removal itself.[8] If exception to the action of the audiencia were taken, all the papers relative to the case were forwarded to the Council of the Indies, and if good reasons were found to exist for the action of the lower court the Council approved its action.[9] This, was not the *residencia* as usually considered.

Of the various authorities at our disposal, Bancroft gives the most acceptable characterization of the *residencia*. He defines it as an examination held, or an account taken, of the official acts of an executive or judicial official within the province of his jurisdiction during the term of his incumbency. This, Bancroft says, was done at the expiration of the term of office or at stated periods, or, in case of malfeasance, at any time.[10] The principle underlying the institution of the *residen-*

---

[8] *Ibid.*, 5–15–36 to 39; 7–1–10 to 13.

[9] *Ibid.*, 5–12–7 to 9.

[10] Bancroft, *History of Central America*, I, 250–1. Special emphasis should be placed upon the last clause of the above definition. The periodical *residencia* was not the sole means for the removal of officials in the Spanish colonies. The conclusion seems to have been reached by many historians that officials were permitted to conduct themselves carelessly, running their offices to suit their own personal convenience from the date of their appointment, in the assurance that their tenure was sure until the termination of a specified term, and that the periodical *residencia* was the only occasion on which they might be held to answer for their sins. Only the most scant attention has been given by modern writers to the *residencia*. See Bourne, "Historical introduction," in Blair and Robertson, I, 50–52; Moses, *Establishment of Spanish rule in America*, 172; Vander Linden, *L'expansion coloniale de l'Espagne*, 349.

cia was bequeathed to the Spaniards by the Romans, being similar to and probably derived from their law which gave the right of accusation to any Roman citizen against an office-holder. The *residencia* was conducted by a judicial official, and it combined the features of a general survey of the career of the official under investigation, an auditing of his accounts and a formal trial. Its purpose was to ascertain whether or not the official had faithfully executed his duties and it served to clear him if he were proved honest, giving him a clean certificate of recommendation. If he were found guilty of official misconduct or dishonesty he was apprehended, degraded, and punished, according to his deserts.

Professor Bourne has written in regard to the *residencia:*

The *residencia* . . . was an institution peculiar in modern times of the Spanish colonial system. It was designed to provide a method by which officials could be held to strict accountability for all acts during their term of office. . . . To allow a contest in the courts involving the governor's powers during his term of office would be subversive of his authority. He was then to be kept in bounds by realizing that a day of judgment was impending, when everyone, even the poorest Indian, might in perfect security bring forward his accusation. In the Philippines the *residencia* for a governor lasted six months and was conducted by his successor and all the charges made were forwarded to Spain. . . . The Italian traveller Gemelli Careri who visited Manila in 1696 characterizes the governor's *residencia* as a "dreadful Trial", the strain of which would sometimes "break their hearts."

Professor Bourne stated that it was the opinion of De Pons that "the severities of the *residencia* could be mitigated, and no doubt such was the case in the Philippines. By the end of the eighteenth century the *residencia* seems to have lost its efficacy."[11]

It is important to note at the outset that the *residencia* was not conducted periodically alone, but that it might be held at

---

[11] Bourne, "Historical introduction," Blair and Robertson, I, 51–52; see De Pons, *Voyage*, II, 25; Churchill, *Voyages*, IV, 427–428; see also Barrows, "The governor general of the Philippines, under Spain and the United States," in *The Pacific Ocean in history*, 246.

any time in the career of an official. The term *pesquisa* was applied to the form of *residencia* which was carried out by a special investigator (*pesquisidor*), sent when serious charges were made against the conduct of an official.[12] In the investigation which took place the official might be fined, or if grave offenses were proved, he might be removed from office. Appeals might be made from the *pesquisidor* to the audiencia and to the Council of the Indies. In fact, the judgments of the *pesquisidor* were always reviewed in the local tribunal unless the investigating judge had been commissioned by the Council of the Indies.

The distinction which has been made here between the formal *residencia* which occurred at the close of the term of office and the *pesquisa* which might take place whenever serious charges were made, was first emphasized in laws promulgated by Charles V in 1538, and by Philip II in 1591; these aimed to put a stop to the excesses of certain governors, *corregidores,* and ministers of justice, who, relying on the practice then prevailing of taking *residencias* only at the close of the official term, had committed unlimited excesses. The new laws, above referred to, stated that although it had never been the royal wish that *residencias* of royal appointees should be taken without notice having been sent first to the monarch, the above circumstances had made it necessary for them to be taken when charges were made. This *cédula,* therefore, authorized the taking of *residencias* whenever the best interests of the service required it.[13]

This *cédula* was followed by another which forbade the sending of special investigators or judges of *residencia* against governors of provinces, unless persons of responsible character presented charges against them, giving bonds to cover the costs. An investigator was thereupon sent to conduct the trial of the

---

[12] *Recopilación*, 7–1; 2–15–117.
[13] *Ibid.*, 5–15–19.

official under examination.[14] This matter is covered in slightly
different terms in the law of June 19, 1620. According to that
enactment, a *receptor*[15] might be sent to conduct the preliminary investigations of *corregidores* and ordinary justices when
these demanded instant attention and could not await the
formal *residencia*. If, as a result of this inquiry, the guilt of
the official seemed apparent, a more complete investigation was
made by a judge appointed by the president and audiencia in
acuerdo.[16]

The authority to determine whether cases merited investigation or not and whether an inquiry should be made, belonged
to the *acuerdo,* while the designation of the judge rested
with the governor.[17] The judges sent on these missions
were not at first authorized to pass final sentence, their decisions being subject to review in the audiencia before execution.
However, by the law of May 5, 1576, this added authority was
bestowed upon the *oidores* who conducted special investigations,
or *residencias*.[18] Appeals might be made to the audiencia and,
if the sentence imposed the death penalty or permanent removal from office, the appeal might be carried to the Council of
the Indies.[19] The final approval of the Council was required
before action could be taken with regard to any royal appointee,
except in those cases wherein the fine did not exceed one
thousand pesos.[20]

The *oidores,* it seems, did not always act as impartial
judges when entrusted with these investigations; they were

---

[14] *Ibid.,* 20.

[15] A *receptor* was a clerk of court, who on special authorization or
commission of a tribunal was dispatched to institute judicial proceedings on behalf of the court.—Escriche, *Diccionario,* II, 794.

[16] *Recopilación,* 7–1–16.

[17] *Ibid.,* 5–15–21.

[18] *Ibid.,* 7–1–14.

[19] *Ibid.,* 5–12–31.

[20] *Ibid.,* 5–15–38.

often influenced by the extra reward obtained for these services, and frequently by prejudice against the officials under
investigation. Such were the charges implied by Governor
Fajardo in 1619 when he wrote:

> It is always to be believed that the auditors (*oidores*) to whom the
> inquiries are entrusted, ought to make them, not only as judges, but as
> interested parties, so that sinister inquiries should not be sent to your
> Majesty's royal Council to defraud your royal treasury and the merits
> of those who have served well, I assure your Majesty that I have
> heard that many inquiries have been made with less justification than
> might be advisable.[21]

A typical illustration of the jurisdiction of the audiencia
in an investigation of this sort, and of the delay to which the
minor officials were subjected, is shown in the case of Antonio
Pimentel, governor of the Marianas,[22] whose *residencia* was taken
in the decade following 1711. In this case may be seen the
distinction between the formal *residencia,* conducted at the
close of the regular term of office, and an investigation of
charges brought during the incumbency of the official. This
case illustrates both forms of investigation, for it originated in
a charge of treason brought against Pimentel, who, it was said,
had furnished food and water to the crews of two English
vessels, enemies of Spain, and subsequently these same ships
had captured the galleon, "Nuestra Señora de la Encarnación".
The conduct of the case was given to magistrate Torralba, who,
on his arrival at Guam, sent Pimentel in chains to Manila.
Notwithstanding his defense of ignorance of a state of war
existing between Spain and England, he was sentenced to the
forfeiture of the bonds which he had posted on assuming office,
and in addition was deprived of his position as governor at
Guam. This sentence was rendered January 23, 1712, and was

---

21 Fajardo to Felipe III, August 10, 1619; Blair and Robertson, XVIII, 276.

22 The Marianas were the islands of the Ladrone Group situated 1200 miles east of the Philippines.

approved by the audiencia in review on July 24, 1714.[23] The tribunal sentenced Pimentel to prison and ordered that his *residencia* should be taken; accordingly, an examination was made of all his official acts as governor. Pimentel, therefore, had not only to stand investigation for the particular act which had brought about his removal, but he was also subjected to a *residencia* covering his entire career as governor. It may be noted that the two forms of investigation were separate and distinct on this occasion.

Owing to the death of Governor Lizárraga, to the imprisonment of Oidor Villa, and to the state of anarchy surrounding the administration of Torralba as governor, Pimentel was forced to languish in prison several years while he waited *residencia*. The appointment of Luís de Tagle as his successor and judge of *residencia* was dated June 25, 1717. This occasion was one on which the successor of a governor took his predecessor's *residencia,* owing, the commission said, to the distance and the irregularity of communication between Manila and Guam. A letter of the audiencia, dated August 9, 1718, advised the governor that there were 427 unfinished cases on the docket of the tribunal, and chief among those that ought to be decided without delay was the review of the *residencia* of Pimentel; it was added that there seemed to be no prospect that a boat could get to Guam before 1719. The record of the termination of this case probably reposes somewhere in the archives, tied in an aged, yellow packet, bound by Spanish red tape.

In summary, it may be said that there were two kinds of investigations of official conduct, one taken at the completion of the regular term of office and the other at any time when the needs of the service required it. They both had the same ultimate purpose of holding officials responsible for misconduct

---

23 *Expedientes relativos á la residencia de Don Antonio Pimentel, Governador de las Marianas*, A. I., 68–4–17 and 18.

in office, of giving to all persons an opportunity of having justice done to them and of deterring office-holders from future misdeeds.

Practically all of the colonial officials were subject to *residencia*. The most sensational and widely known *residencias* were, of course, those of viceroys and captains-general, but *oidores*, treasury officials, *encomenderos, alcaldes mayores, corregidores*, admirals, generals, captains, and constructors of galleons were likewise examined in this way.[24] The visitors and special investigators who were sent to examine the government of the provinces and the state of the Indians on the *encomiendas* were also subject to *residencia*. *Residencias* were exacted of all minor officials at the same time that their superiors were examined.[25] Clerks, notaries, secretaries, *alcaldes ordinarios, regidores*, and other officials of a minor category were investigated at the same time that the governor was examined, an *alcalde* or an *oidor* being delegated by the new president to review their official conduct. The examination of these minor officials seems to have become more and more perfunctory and there was a tendency during the latter part of the nineteenth century to continue them in office, even without investigation. When, for instance, Governors Basco y Vargas and Marquina gave up their offices this formality was omitted.[26] The practice of taking the *residencias* of minor officials was definitely abandoned on August 24, 1799, and a rigid inspection by the audiencia of their official acts was authorized.[27]

Much contradictory legislation appears in the laws of the Indies relative to the method of taking *residencias;* this due to

---

[24] *Recopilación*, 5–15–3, 4, 8, 10–18.

[25] *Ibid.*, 5–15–11, 24.

[26] Having been excused by the *cédulas* of July 7, 1789, and January 15, 1795, A. I., 105–2–5.

[27] *Recopilación*, 5–15, notes 4, 11. When the *residencia* of a viceroy or president was taken, the *oidores* were also held responsible for all opinions given conjointly with him in the *acuerdo*.

the reforms made from time to time. These laws were formulated for a growing empire. A chronological review of them
will show that the *residencia* was at first more or less of an
experiment. Indeed, all the colonial institutions were in the
early periods passing through an experimental stage and these
seemingly contradictory laws were promulgated or repealed,
according to their success or failure when put into effect.
Whenever, therefore, two laws appear to be in conflict, the one
of later date will be found to supersede and repeal the
earlier one.[28] In illustration of this characteristic of the laws of
the Indies we may note the following example: The *cédula* .of

---

[28] Sinibaldo de Mas, the able Philippine critic of the nineteenth century, says in regard to the above characteristic of the *Recopilación*
and its laws: "Since the *Leyes de Indias* are not a constitutional
code, but a compilation made in the year 1754 [a footnote amends this
statement with the information that the *Recopilación* was first made in
1681] of royal orders despatched at various epochs and by distinct
monarchs, . . . there results . . . a confusion of jurisdictions."
—Mas, Internal political condition of the Philippines, Blair and Robertson, LII, 70.

Dr. James Alexander Robertson, in his article on "Legaspi and
Philippine colonization" (see American Historical Association, *Annual
report, 1907*, I, 150 and note), characterizes the laws of the Indies as
"that mass of contradictory legislation," largely "ecclesiastical in tone,"
ill-digested, and "utterly at variance with one another." Dr. Robertson
also states that "it is from a too close following of these laws and a
too great neglect of actual conditions that writers on the colonial
policy of Spain have at times fallen into error." On the other hand, it
may be said, that not enough use has been made by modern writers of
the laws of the Indies, and there is need of such investigation as will
test that oft-repeated statement that the laws of the Indies were not
enforced. Up to the present, Latin American scholarship has been
content with a rehasing of Helps and Prescott, for the early periods,
omitting the seventeenth century and the greater part of the eighteenth
altogether, and fixing on Juan y Ulloa, Robertson, and Humboldt as the
great all-determining authorities for the latter periods of Spanish
colonization. These, indeed, have been supplemented by a few ecclesiastical histories, each of which has been written to prove a particular
thesis. The present writer dares to believe, after some attempt to
harmonize the laws of the Indies with actual practice, that these
laws were actually used as a basis of colonial government, and that,
while not always effectively enforced, they were by no means a dead-
letter until Spain actually lost her colonies and are not today, for it is
easy to see in the laws of the Indies the fundamentals of the institutions of present-day Spanish America.

December 4, 1630, ordered that the *residencia* of the governor
should be taken by his successor. This law was seldom, if ever,
observed. Owing to the distance from Spain and New Spain,
and the consequent length of time consumed in voyages, to the
unhealthful climate, and to the dangerous military campaigns in
which the governors were compelled to engage, death frequently
intervened before the successor of a governor arrived. These
conditions (which were characteristic of all of Spain's colonies)
did not prevent the *residencia* from being taken, but caused the
law to be modified by the *cédula* of December 28, 1667, according
to which judges for the *residencias* of viceroys and presidents-
governor and captains-general were to be designated by the
court. The period of four months, which had been authorized
for the taking of *residencias* by the *cédula* of August 30, 1582,
was extended to six months.[29] A change was necessary, the
new law declared, in order to put a stop to the incessant
strife, and the malice which had been shown by viceroys, governors, and ministers in the taking of *residencias*. The king determined that henceforth the judge of *residencias* should be designated by the court. The magistrate usually named was the
decano. After 1776 the regent almost invariably conducted
these investigations. The important reform of August 24,
1799, ordered that judges of *residencia* for governors, viceroys, presidents, governors-intendant, corregidor-intendants, and
presidents of the Council of the Indies should be appointed by
the king.[30]

The first *residencia* to be conducted in the Philippines in
accordance with the new law of November 28, 1667, was that of
Governor Salcedo, in 1670. This governor had been removed
by the commissary of the Inquisition on October 10, 1668, and
Francisco Coloma, the *decano*, was ordered to take his *resi-*

---

[29] *Recopilación*, 5–15–1.
[30] *Cédula* of August 24, 1799, in Rodríguez San Pedro, *Legislación
ultramarina*, III, 280–281.

dencia.[31]   Coloma's intervention in the matter was protested
by the audiencia in a letter to the Council of the Indies, dated
April 7, 1670, on the grounds that the senior *oidor* was also
the *asesor* and possible successor of the governor, and for that
reason he was disqualified from taking the latter's *residencia.*[32]

The audiencia suspended the proposed action of Coloma,
pending the reply of the Council of the Indies.   In addition to
the protest of the audiencia, the *fiscal,* on May 20, 1670, sent
a report of the case to the court, which act was in fulfillment
of his regular duties as *fiscal,* as prescribed by the laws of the
Indies.[33]   The notes from Manila were effective in bringing
about the desired results.   Upon receipt of the communications,
the Council of the Indies, on June 17, 1671, ordered the nullification of all former *cédulas,* cancelled Coloma's appointment
to take the *residencia* in question, on the grounds that he had
been the governor's *asesor,* and appointed Fernando de Montemayor, the *oidor* next in rank, to conduct the *residencia* of the
governor.[34]   Salcedo had already been dead three years, and
two more transpired before his *residencia* was completed and
the *autos* thereof reviewed by the Council.

The laws provided ample opportunity for appeal in cases of
residencia.   The *cédula* of November 17, 1526, ordered that
appeals might be made to the Council of the Indies from
judges of *residencia* in cases involving liabilities in excess of 600
pesos.[35]   Many appeals were made to the Council in accord with
this law, and the time of the tribunal was consumed in the

---

31 *Papeles relativos á la residencia del gobernador Salcedo, Inventario, op. cit.;* also A. I., 67–6–10, 67–6–11, 67–3–4.

32 Since all legal advice was furnished the governor by his *asesor,*
Coloma would be examining his own acts.

33 *Recopilación,* 2–18–27.

34 *Cédula* of June 17, 1671, A. I., 82–6–10. In view of these proceedings, Salcedo's letter of June 25, 1665, in praise of the services of
Coloma and Montemayor is interesting (A. I., 67–6–9).

35 *Recopilación,* 5–12–8; 2–16–46, provided for appeal of cases carrying death penalty.

consideration of matters comparatively of small importance. To obviate this defect the law was changed on August 7, 1568, to provide that no case could be appealed to the Council of the Indies unless the sentence imposed capital punishment or deprivation of office.[26] The *cédula* of June 23, 1608, ordered that if the fine imposed upon the governor and ministers of the Philippines did not exceed one thousand pesos the case should be finished in the audiencia.[37] Cases involving a greater amount were to be appealed to the Council. Sentence of judges of *residencia* were not to be executed pending the trial of appeals to the audiencia and the Council of the Indies.[38]

Philip IV initiated further reforms in regard to appeal in 1636. *Ordenanza LVI*, promulgated at that time, provided that "the said Council [of the Indies] may only have jurisdiction over the visits and *residencias* of the viceroys, presidents, *oidores,* and officials of our audiencias and accountants and officials of the tribunals of accounts, officials of the treasury and those of the governors provided by the Council with our titles."[39] *Ordenanza LXII*, issued at the same time, ordered that "in the visits and *residencias* which are seen and determined in our Council of the Indies," cases did not have to be referred to the king for consultation, excepting when, in "the *residencias* of viceroys, presidents, and *oidores, alcaldes del crimen,* and *fiscales* of our royal audiencias of the Indies and governors of the principal provinces there, condemnations of corporal punishment, privation or suspension from office result against them."[40] In these cases the Council was ordered to submit its decisions and all papers bearing thereon to the king before passing judgment, so that the final judgment might be rendered by the sovereign in person. The

---

36 *Ibid.*, 5–12–31.
37 *Ibid.*, 5–15–38.
38 *Ibid.*, 39.
39 *Ibid.*, 2–2–58.
40 *Ibid.*, 64.

Council could take final action in the *residencias* of military and naval officials without consulting the king. It was, of course, impossible for the sovereign to give his personal attention to any of these matters, but the last word was pronounced in these suits by responsible ministers of the court who stood high in the royal estimation.

Officials were usually obliged to submit to *residencia* before leaving the colony, also before their promotion to higher posts.[41] Owing, however, to the paucity of ships plying to New Spain and to the length of time elapsing between sailing dates, officials could give bonds and leave before the *residencia* was completed.[42] This was permitted only to men of good character, whose services had been uniformly satisfactory, and who were destined to some other post wherein their services were indispensable. The investigation was then conducted in the absence of the official concerned.[43] It was decreed by the *cédula* of December 30, 1776, that an annual deduction of one-fifth of the total salary of the governors and viceroys respectively should be made, until sufficient money had been taken out to cover the probable costs and liabilities of their *residencias*.[44] This was a special assessment, distinct from the *media anata*,[45] and the money deducted thereby was to be re-

---

[41] *Ibid.*, 5–15–3.

[42] There were two kinds of bonds, those posted at the beginning of a term of office, and special bonds of *residencia*, given at the time of that investigation. The last-mentioned were not required if the office were not a responsible one or if the charges were not sufficiently serious.

[43] *Recopilación*, 5–15–3; this *cédula* was annulled by that of May 21, 1787; see note to law 3 of the same title.

[44] King to Basco y Vargas, December 30, 1776 (A. I., 107–5–20). These annual deductions of one-fifth were first authorized on August 26, 1757, on the recommendation of the Council of the Indies. They were discontinued by the *consulta* of March 2, 1773, it being ordered that governors should only post the customary bonds with the president of the Council of the Indies. We see here that the practice was restored on December 30, 1776. This requirement seems to have been confined to governors of the Philippines (A. I., 105–2–21).

[45] *Recopilación*, 8–19; see notes 11 and 13, Chapter V of this book.

turned if nothing detrimental were proved in the *residencia*. The last year's salaries of *alcaldes mayores* and *corregidores* were withheld, pending investigations of their official conduct and a rendering of accounts of collections made by them.[46] If an official were cleared of all guilt, the money which had been withheld was returned and the costs of *residencia* were defrayed by the royal treasury.[47] In case the official were found guilty of misconduct, he had to forfeit his deposits, back-salary, bonds, and frequently to pay a large fine in addition. The amount of the penalty, of course, depended on the extent of the guilt. It may be said that in the Philippines the royal treasury suffered no serious embarrassment through having to bear costs of *residencia*.

The judges of *residencia* who served as such in addition to their regular duties, received an additional compensation which varied according to the place where the *residencia* was held, its distance from the capital, and other circumstances.[48] This was modified by a reform of the nineteenth century which awarded extra pay only in the case the official were fined. This, of course, was intended to afford the examining judge a stimulating interest in the case. Still later the system of giving extra pay for *residencias* was abolished.[49]

A detailed survey of the governor's *residencia* in the Philippines would illustrate the influence of the audiencia in such investigations. Unfortunately the story would be long and little space remains for such a purpose. During the first two centuries of Spanish rule in the Islands the *residencias* of the governors were especially stringent, many of these officials suffering deprivation of office, imprisonment, and exile. The

---

[46] *Recopilación*, 8–26–17.

[47] *Ibid.*, 5–15–42.

[48] *Ibid.*, note 12.

[49] Royal decree of November 20, 1841, in Rodríguez San Pedro, *Legislación ultramarina*, I, 282; see also royal order of December 3, 1844 (for Cuba), *ibid.*, 287.

families and dependents of some were reduced to the last extreme of poverty, while the victims themselves spent years in
some distant province, unable to defend themselves from their
enemies. Many victims of the *residencia* were purposely put
aside in order that no appeal could be heard from them. One
would occasionally find relief at last in a tardy pardon or in
a modification of sentence, obtained through friends at home,
when these could be reached, but more often death would intervene before the exercise of executive clemency or revision
of sentence could be obtained.

The factors of petty spite, malice, and personal ambition
entered to an extensive degree in the rendering of testimony
at a *residencia*. A governor, recently arrived in the colony,
would be full of zeal and ardor to inaugurate a successful
administration, and make a good record for himself. The first
duty that presented itself on his arrival was that of taking or
supervising his predecessor's *residencia*. Frequently, before
arriving at Manila, the new governor would be in full possession of a complete record of the misdeeds of his predecessor,
and the *residencia* of the latter was as good as taken.[50]
Oidores, merchants, *alcaldes,* treasury officials, and churchmen,
compelled to stand aside and see a governor take his choice
out of the best things, leaving for them only the husks, were
not slow in bringing charges at the official *residencia*.[51]   A

---

[50] Officials, desirous of ingratiating themselves into the favor of the
new executive, frequently journeyed by land and sea from Manila as
far as the Straits of San Bernardino. The privilege thus gained of
returning to Manila in company with the new governor, gave then
the unrestricted or unqualified opportunity to poison his mind with
tales of the misdeeds of the incumbent, and insinuations as to the
wealth which the latter had heaped up for himself through the exercise of dishonest methods.

[51] The *residencia* of a governor presented a splendid opportunity
to his enemies for revenge. A governor was always in a fair way to
make enemies; consequently any such awaited the *residencia* of their
former oppressor with great eagerness. In case a governor did make
fair profit out of his office, and there were many opportunities for

new governor, desirous of demonstrating his intention of start-
ing an 'honest and vigorous administration, hearing nothing
but evil of his predecessor, would naturally lend himself as an
instrument to the malcontents. A *fiscal*, after spending six
years in conflict with a governor, could be depended on to
bring strenuous prosecution against him. A magistrate with
enmity in his heart for the governor whose *residencia* he was
to take, was no fit person to conduct an impartial investigation.

While as a rule the *residencias* of governors were severe,
due largely to the presence of the audiencia, that of Dr. Sande,
the first governor to submit to this investigation, illustrates the
evils of the *residencia* as conducted before the establishment
of the audiencia. His successor, Governor Ronquillo de
Peñalosa, conducted Sande's *residencia* and sentenced him to
pay a heavy fine, but he appealed the case to the Audiencia
of Mexico, by which tribunal, in the meantime, he had been
commissioned *oidor*. We have noted in an earlier chapter
Ronquillo's comments on the abject state into which the administration of justice had fallen when a man could be promoted to a magistracy in a tribunal which had jurisdiction
over his own case on appeal.[52] However, after the establishment of the audiencia, and until the close of the nineteenth

---

profit, commercial and otherwise, legitimate and illegitimate, his
enemies gave him no rest at the time of his *residencia*. (According
to Martínez de Zúñiga [*Estadismo*, I, 242] the emoluments of the governor, aside from his salary, aggregated 20,000 pesos a year.) It is probable that most of the governors were dishonest, as the opportunities for
corruption were numerous, and the temptations offered by the position
were too powerful to be resisted by any human being. Thousands of
miles from Spain, in an age of slow communication, entrusted with
the assignment of all sorts of lucrative offices, *encomiendas*, and commercial privileges, and having friends, relatives, and special interests
to serve, a governor was surrounded by countless officials who were
eagerly awaiting their share of booty, and who were ready at a
moment's notice to turn traitor if they could gain by such an act. It
may be said of the Spanish colonial governor as was said of Verres of
old, that in stealing, one must steal threefold, once for himself, once
for his judges, and once to pay the penalty.

52 Chapter II of this book.

century, the *residencia* went to the other extreme, and was, as a rule, exceedingly rigorous.

We may briefly note a few of the most severe *residencias* in which the influence of the audiencia told against the victim. In 1625, Gerónimo de Silva, temporary governor, was imprisoned by the audiencia because he failed to pursue the Dutch after their defeat in 1617. The real difficulty lay in the fact that Silva had incurred the enmity of the senior *oidor,* who ultimately conducted the *residencia,* because Silva's arrival in the Islands deprived that magistrate of the command of the military and naval forces of the Islands. Again, Governor Corcuera, after nine years of very successful rule, during which he distinguished himself in several campaigns of conquest and incidentally aroused the hostility and jealousy of the *oidores,* was arrested on charges made by the audiencia on the arrival of Governor Diego Fajardo in 1644. An *oidor,* who was the personal enemy of Corcuera, was designated to conduct the *residencia,* the ex-governor was fined 25,000 pesos and was imprisoned five years while the magistrates of the audiencia delayed the transmission of the papers which permitted a rehearing of the case. At last his defense was sent to the Council, the fine was remitted, he was given salary for the period of his exile, and the post of governor of the Canaries was conferred upon him. Although the audiencia was responsible for the injustice in this case, Fajardo, as president and governor, was held answerable in his own *residencia* for his conduct toward his predecessor.

Governor Simón de Anda y Salazar, one of the most successful governors the Islands had ever known, was made to suffer from the personal malice of the *oidores* when he gave his last *residencia* in 1776.[53] Among the offenses which were

---

[53] Montero y Vidal, *Historia general,* II, 253–258. Anda, as it will be noted later, spent an earlier term of service in the Philippines. He

proved against him was that of exercising prejudice in conducting the *residencia* of Oidor Villacorta, conducted under his
supervision. The *residencia* had been rigorous, due no doubt to
personal enmity between the *oidor* and the governor, extending
over a period of many years. He was also fined 4000 pesos as a
price for his excessive zeal in the prosecution of the *residencia*
of his predecessor, Governor Raón, who had friends in the audiencia to defend his memory and champion his cause.[54] Anda
was also shown to have absolved certain officials of *real hacienda* of financial responsibility, permitting them to leave the
Islands without the consent of the audiencia. These and other
charges proved against him were said to have caused his pre-
mature death in 1776.

Governor José Basco y Vargas, another very efficient gov-

first came to the Philippines during the administration of Governor
Arandía, as *oidor* of the audiencia. He had therefore been obliged to
submit to *residencia* on a previous occasion; in 1764 a review was made
of his official conduct as *oidor*, and especially of his acts in defiance of
Archbishop Rojo, in setting up claims to the governorship of the Islands
and resisting the British. His conduct was approved, and he received
high honor and promotion at the court, being advanced to membership in the Council of Castile. On November 19, 1769, he was granted
an annual pension of 3000 pesos for life. On September 8, 1777, this
pension was continued in favor of his eldest son (A. I., 106–4–4).

[54] Anda had more than the usual number of *residencias* to supervise at the beginning of his term. Owing to some misapprehension on
the part of his predecessor, Governor Raón, no *residencia* was required of La Torre, the *teniente del rey* who took over the government in 1764. Owing to the anarchical condition in Manila consequent
upon the invasion of the British, and the ecclesiastical rule preceding
that event, neither Arandía, Espeleta, nor Rojo had given *residencia*.
The audiencia and Raón in *acuerdo* on October 26, 1768, voted that
governors' *residencias* should be dispensed with, and apparently believed that this action settled the matter. On November 9, 1770, the
Council of the Indies disapproved of this stand, fined Raón (who had
died the preceding July), and ordered Anda to take the *residencias* of
Arandía (governor, 1754–1759), Espeleta (archbishop-governor, 1759–
1761), Rojo (archbishop-governor, 1761–1764), Oidor Villacorta, and
Governor Raón. These orders he complied with, conducting the investigations with his characteristic thoroughness, though Rojo and
Raón were dead. Villacorta was imprisoned and heavily fined. The
sentences against Arandía, Raón and Villacorta were moderated
by the Council of the Indies on September 9, 1772.—A. I., 105–2–31.

ernor,[55] but one who had been opposed throughout his term of office by the audiencia, was heavily fined in 1787 by the *oidor* designated to conduct the investigation. The decision of the judge of *residencia* was reversed by the Council of the Indies, however, and Vargas' exceptional merits were recognized to the extent of his being appointed to the governorship of Cartagena, with the rank of rear admiral. In taking the *residencia* of Vargas, the audiencia had disagreed so completely that the tribunal was obliged to resort to the extreme measure of appointing a churchman as arbiter. Fray Gerónimo Caraballo, the curate of Quiapo, was designated for that duty.

Aside from the above brief references to notable cases in which the audiencia exercised jurisdiction over the *residencias* of governors, allowing itself to be influenced by considerations other than those of justice, it seems desirable to review in detail at least one case of the *residencia* of a governor, to show more particularly just what authority was exercised by the tribunal, and just how that authority was exercised.

We may select for this purpose the *residencia* of Governor Felix Beringuer de Marquina, which was the last to be conducted under the old laws, and the last, accordingly, of the severe *residencias*.[56] As governor and superintendent of *real hacienda* Marquina assumed such power as no other governor had ever exercised. He was opposed at every turn by the

---

[55] As we shall note in another chapter, José Basco y Vargas inaugurated the reforms of the intendancy in the Philippines, retaining the post of governor, while Ciriaco Gonzales Carvajal was first *intendente de guerra y real hacienda.*—A. I., 105–3–5 and 107–5–19; see Chapter V, note 20, of this work.

[56] This *residencia* was held under the same laws that had prevailed throughout the seventeenth and eighteenth centuries. A feature common to them all, particularly, was the fact that the regent, or some other colonial magistrate conducted the investigation and gave sentence, which might be appealed to the Council of the Indies. This gave an opportunity for great injustice to be done to the governor by his enemies, and it did not give him an impartial hearing. The laws of 1799 still permitted a local magistrate to collect the evidence, but the decision was rendered by the Council of the Indies.

audiencia and probably no other governor ever had so many
of his measures vetoed or opposed by the home government as
he. The *fiscal* and *oidores* brought many charges against him;
these finally culminated, before the expiration of his term, in
the royal order of February 19, 1792, for the taking of his
residencia. The regent, Agustín de Amparán, was put in pos
session of the special charges which had been made against
Marquina. According to these the governor had been careless
in defending the Islands against the Moros, who had insulted
and robbed with impunity the various settlements, with no
effort having been made to check their advance. The governor
had transgressed in numerous instances the sphere of the
audiencia and had substituted his own authority. He was said
to have been guilty of immoral relations with certain Spanish
women of the colony, having deliberately and maliciously separated an intendant from his wife on one occasion by ordering
the former to a post of duty where no woman could go; he
had amassed a great fortune through trade and by diverting
the proceeds of the royal revenue to his own private advantage;
he had permitted merchants to conduct business without proper
licenses; he had allowed foreign merchants to remain in
Manila under conditions forbidden by law.[57] These and many
others were the charges brought against Governor Marquina.
They may be considered as typical of the accusations which
were usually brought against governors in their *residencias*.

Amparán was commanded by the royal order above-mentioned to remove Marquina to some spot outside Manila where
he could not interfere with the *residencia*, but whence he could
be summoned at any time, to give testimony in his own behalf.[58] The regent was instructed to ascertain from the treasury officials whether Marquina should not be required to post
more than the usual amount of bonds in view of the grave

---

[57] Audiencia to the King, June 28, 1791, A. I., 108-4-18.
[58] Instructions to Amparán, February 19, 1792, A. I., 105-2-10.

charges against him. It seems that the law already cited requiring an annual deduction of one-fifth of the governor's salary to cover *residencia* had been abrogated by a royal order dated February 13, 1782; hence there was some apprehension lest Marquina had not deposited sufficient money.[59]

In compliance with these orders Marquina was relieved of his office in September, 1792, and was sent to Laguna de Bay, about thirty miles from Manila. After five months' delay, the investigation was inaugurated and it was concluded by July 22, 1793, but Aguilar, the new governor, intervened and suspended the sentence on the ground that Marquina had not been given sufficient opportunity to defend himself. Up to this time Marquina had not testified directly. Aguilar ordered that the ex-governor should be brought to Manila and that a lawyer should be appointed for his defense. This was done and the charges which had been made against him were duly answered. This evidence could not be incorporated in the official papers of *residencia*, for they had been finished and closed by the regent, but it was forwarded to Spain under separate cover.[60]

The official papers of Marquina's *residencia*, as formulated by the regent of the audiencia, arrived before the Council of the Indies in due time, together with Marquina's defense which

---

[59] Instructions were also given at the same time for investigations of the official conduct of numerous persons who had been identified with the government of Marquina. Among these were Helarión Pastor, *fiscal de la real hacienda*, Manuel de Sota, *contador de cuentas*, Francisco Múñoz, *teniente del rey*, Rufino Suárez Rivera, *asesor*, and Miguel Formento, clerk of the treasury. A separate commission was made for the *residencia* of each of these.

[60] The just and honorable conduct of Marquina's successor on this occasion may be contrasted with that of his various predecessors, whose unfairness, bigotry, and stupidity had caused governors Corcuera, Silva, and Torralba, victims of· *residencia*, to be seized, imprisoned, and exiled without opportunities for defense, while their investigations were being conducted. This case serves well to illustrate the fact that by the close of the eighteenth century the *residencia* had grown more humane.

had been sent separately. The glaring injustice of the investigation as conducted by Amparán and of the official evidence transmitted, was patent to the *fiscal* of the Council. He refused to receive any testimony not incorporated in the official papers of the case. Marquina was allowed a retrial by the Council. This resulted in a further delay of three years; during this period Marquina remained in the provinces with the exception of the time spent in Manila giving testimony in his second *residencia,* which was taken under the direct supervision of Governor Aguilar. Immediately after his second trial Marquina was transferred to Mexico, but he was obliged to deposit an additional 50,000 pesos before his departure from Manila.

In the ultimate judgment Marquina was pronounced guilty of many offenses in addition to those mentioned in the charges previously outlined. He had shown favoritism in the dispensation of official favors; he had authorized the expenditure of public money for private ends; he had neglected defense and agriculture; he had been negligent in the supervision of the various departments of *real hacienda* and particularly of tobacco; he had infringed on the jurisdiction of the royal audiencia. He had indulged in private trade and had granted special favors to foreign merchants.[61]

The regent fined him 40,000 pesos outright and, moreover, he was condemned to pay into the royal treasury an additional fine of 16,000 pesos to cover certain illegitimate profits made through granting unlawful trading concessions to an Armenian merchant. This sentence was not executed immediately, as it

---

[61] He was charged with having entered into a conspiracy with an Armenian merchant to secure trade which should have gone to Spanish merchants. In this particular venture he had made a profit of 16,000 pesos and in so doing he had not only violated the laws of the Indies which forbade officials to trade (*Recopilación*, 2-16-54, 62), but he had connived at the infraction of another law which forbade trade to foreigners (*ibid.*, 9-27-1, 5, 7 and note 2).

had to be confirmed by the Council of the Indies. On review of the findings and recommendations of the regent, the Council declared that since the proceedings at the trial of Marquina had been irregular and the governor had already suffered the consequences of his own misdeeds, the fine imposed by the judge of the *residencia* in Manila might be reduced to 2000 pesos with costs of trial. Marquina on October 12, 1797, asked to be excused from the payment of the 2000 pesos, but the Council denied his petition, declaring that he had been treated with great consideration and mercy and that nothing more could be done in his behalf, especially since he had not been adjudged innocent of the charges which had been made against him.[62]

Marquina's trial illustrates all the characteristics, the delays, terrors, and ramifications of a typical *residencia* of the seventeenth and eighteenth centuries. Continued complaints against him caused Marquina's *residencia* to be taken before the expiration of his official term. The regent of the audiencia was commissioned by the court to conduct the investigation because Marquina's successor had not arrived. That magistrate was prejudiced against Marquina on account of having witnessed the governor's continual malfeasance in office. He was unable to conduct an impartial investigation, and the audiencia, likewise prejudiced, would not intervene in behalf of the ex-governor. The wrongs done to Marquina in his trial

---

[62] It is an interesting commentary on Spanish methods that, notwithstanding Marquina's misgovernment in the Philippines, he was promoted to the post of viceroy of New Spain, which position he held from 1800 to 1803.

Desdevises du Dezert, in his article on "Vice-rois et capitaines gènèraux des Indes espagnoles" (*Revue historique*, CXXV, 241), shows that Marquina continued his peculations while viceroy of New Spain, engaging in the smuggling trade with Jamaica, and enriching himself to the extent that in thirty-two months he was able to send twelve million pesos on his own account to Spain. Desdevises du Dezert inadvertently refers to Marquina as having come from the Marianas to Mexico. He came from the Philippines and not from the Marianas.

were so patent that the Council of the Indies ordered a new hearing. A severe sentence was finally passed by the judge in Manila, but it was modified by the Council of the Indies through considerations of justice. The *residencia* occupied ten years, and during the greater part of that time the ex-governor remained in exile—a victim of his own misdeeds, the faulty *residencia* system, and the hostility of the audiencia. The customary severity of the *residencia* was only mitigated in this case by the presence of an impartial governor, who, unlike most governors whose desire was to harass their victims, sought to secure a fair trial for his predecessor. To accomplish this he was obliged to work against, rather than in cooperation with the audiencia.

The above method of conducting *residencias* of governors, presidents, viceroys, and superintendents was modified, as already mentioned, by the reform of August 24, 1799. The new law provided that the court, instead of the new governor, should appoint the examining judge. The latter was no longer empowered to pronounce sentence of any sort. He was only to conduct the investigation in the future, remitting the *autos* of the case to the Council of the Indies for final determination and sentence.[63] Again, on March 16, 1797, the royal order of December 30, 1777, was re-enacted and the practice was revived of deducting annually one-fifth of the salaries of officials whose incomes were 8000 pesos a year or more.[64] This law was again promulgated on January 18, 1848. Its purpose was to secure the retention of a sufficient sum of money to guarantee all losses incident to the *residencia*. It apparently continued in force until July 7, 1860, when governors and captains-general were declared exempt from these discounts.[65]

---

[63] *Recopilación*, 5–15, notes 4 and 5.

[64] *Reales resoluciones del Consejo, 4 de Marzo*, 1794, A. I., 106–4–18; Royal Order of January 18, 1848, Rodríguez San Pedro, *Legislación ultramarina*, I, 290.

[65] These discounts were "considered subversive of their authority

We shall now examine more particularly the jurisdiction of the audiencia over the *residencias* of minor officials of the colony. It has already been pointed out that the *residencias* of provincial judges and governors, *alcaldes ordinarios* and *reales oficiales* were taken by judges appointed by the president of the audiencia, with appeal to the tribunal. These cases, under certain circumstances, might be taken on second appeal to the Council of the Indies. The practice in these investigations may be best understood by noting the development of the law regarding them, for, as we have already noted, the *residencia* was the product of years of administrative experience, during which various methods were tried, and rejected or adopted as they were found respectively inadvisable or efficacious.

The earliest *cédula* on the subject, that of November 17, 1526, ordered that the audiencia should try all appeals from judges of *residencia*, wherein the amount involved did not exceed 600 pesos. A law of Philip II, dated 1563, forbade viceroys, presidents, and audiencias from sending judges of *residencia* or other investigators against judges of provinces, unless complaint had been lodged against those officials by a person willing to post bonds and pay the costs in case the charges proved to be false.[66]

The *cédula* of September 3, 1565, laid down the principle that the *residencias* of officers appointed by viceroys and presi-

---

[that of the governors]; . . . the best guarantee of their acts is not a discount of some thousands of pesos, which is always penurious when compared with the honor and dignity of the persons called, on account of their elevated character and distinguished services, to hold these posts, and if, in former times, this practice had some foundation in the tardiness of communication between the Peninsula and these provinces, it does not exist today in view of the frequency of communication which enables said authorities to consult with the government of Her Majesty in all the steps which are considered necessary in the territory of their command."—Royal order of July 7, 1860, in Rodríguez San Pedro, *Legislación ultramarina*, I, 287.

[66] *Recopilación*, 5–15–20.

dents should be taken by commission of those who appointed them.[67] As regularly appointed *corregidores* and *alcaldes mayores* held royal commissions,[68] they did not, according to this law, give *residencia* to judges appointed by the governor. The Council of the Indies, therefore, should name judges to investigate the official conduct of its own appointees. As a matter of fact, however, the Council delegated this authority to the governor and audiencia. This latter practice was authorized by a clause in the *cédula* of September 3, 1565, which provided that *residencias* of the officials referred to should be taken under supervision of the audiencias in the districts wherein the officials resided. This meant that while the audiencia was not to interfere in the taking of the *residencia* itself, the tribunal was to see that the laws regarding *residencias* were faithfully executed. The law of March 11, 1591, ordered that if the conduct of *corregidores, alcaldes mayores,* and other magistrates demanded that their *residencias* should be taken before the completion of their term of office, the viceroys, presidents, or governors should appoint judges for the purpose.[69] Nothing was said in this *cédula* relative to the authority of the audiencia in this matter, but the law of January 19, 1608, gave to the audiencia the right to try *residencia* cases on appeal from the sentences of these special judges.

The laws of June 3 and June 19, 1620, provided that the governor and audiencia should decide in *acuerdo* whether the *residencia* of a *gobernador, corregidor,* or an *alcalde mayor* should be taken. Neither the governor nor the audiencia was to have complete authority in the matter, but each should participate, the audiencia assisting in the decision as to whether the case merited investigation and the governor making out the commission and appointing the judge if an investigation were

---

67 *Ibid.*, 4.
68 *Ibid.*, 5–2–1, 2, 7.
69 *Ibid.*, 5–15–19.

necessary. The audiencia, alone, was authorized to appoint judges of *residencia* for judicial officers only.[70] The interference of the audiencia in the *residencias* of governors, *corregidores, alcaldes mayores,* and other justices and ministers provided by royal appointment was definitely forbidden by the *cédula* of April 20, 1639, as this jurisdiction was declared to belong to the Council of the Indies.[71] Although we have evidence that the Council did exercise such jurisdiction, it was always on review of cases appealed from the audiencias. While the above prohibition forbade the audiencia from taking the *residencias* of these officials it did not restrain the tribunal from participating in the decision as to whether a *residencia* should be taken, or in the review of the *autos* of *residencia*.

An illustration of the intervention of the Council of the Indies in *residencias* of *alcaldes mayores* is shown in the case of Josef Tormento, *alcalde* of Caragara. On June 6, 1786, he was sentenced in *residencia* to a pecuniary penalty, perpetual deprivation of office, and two years' exile from Manila. This sentence was confirmed in review by the audiencia on October 8 of the same year. The Council modified this sentence, however, approving the fine, but cancelling the other provisions.[72] In 1803 the incumbent of the same post, Antonio Mateo, was incarcerated by order of the audiencia, pending investigation of the charge made against him that he had used the funds of his office for private trade. It was shown, however, that this official knew the location of a quicksilver deposit of great value, whereupon the governor had him removed from prison, ordering the suspension of the charges against him, notwithstanding the protests of the *oidores*. The *fiscal* concurred in the action of the governor. The audiencia appealed the case to the Council of the Indies, alleging con-

---

[70] *Ibid.*, 7–1–16; 5–15–21.

[71] *Ibid.*, 2–15–69; see 2–2–58, 64.

[72] King to the Fiscal, September 29, 1788, A. I., 105–2–10.

spiracy between the governor and the *fiscal*. The Council, however, on examination of the case, approved their action, ordered the charges to be dismissed, and gave directions that the *alcalde mayor* should be restored to his former position or given another of equal category as soon as possible.[73]

Although the *cédula* of August 24, 1799, gave the audiencia the right to conduct the *residencias* of *corregidores* and *alcaldes mayores*, this case involved certain interesting features which should be pointed out in this connection. In the first place, it shows the manner in which the Council of the Indies exercised ultimate authority in matters of *residencia*. Again, it reveals the influence which the *fiscal* and even the governor might have in determining whether suit should be brought,[74] and finally it indicates that expediency might constitute an important factor in the ultimate results of a case of this kind.

The practice of granting jurisdiction over the *residencia* of an official to the authority that appointed him seems to have been followed repeatedly. This principle was enunciated in the *cédula* of August 20, 1758, but on August 8, 1764, a royal decree authorized viceroys and presidents to name judges of *residencia* for all officials holding royal appointments, with the condition that the *autos* should be forwarded to the Council of the Indies. This law was repealed on April 23, 1769.[75]

The *cédula* of August 24, 1799, which has been mentioned several times in this chapter, was a reform of the greatest importance in the history of the *residencia*. Prior to its promulgation, all officials had to give *residencia*, but this law abolished that universal requirement. It provided that *residencias* of *corregidores*, *alcaldes mayores*, and subdelegate-intendants should be taken only when charges had been made against them. This might occur at any time during their term

---

[73] King to the Audiencia, October 6, 1806, A. I., 105–2–18.

[74] *Recopilación*, 2–18–27.

[75] *Ibid.*, 5–15, note 4.

of office, or at the close of their service. These investigations had to be concluded within four months, but if charges were not made against an official his past record was not investigated.

The length of time consumed in all *residencias* except those of viceroys was limited to four months. The period allotted for these investigations was divided into two parts.[76] During the first half, edicts or notices of *residencia* were posted throughout the district of the official concerned. These were printed in Spanish and in the common dialect, so that natives and others concerned might read and know that the official was giving up his post and that charges might be brought against him, setting forth any misconduct, undue harshness, tyranny or dishonesty of which he had been guilty during his term of office. These notices invited them to register any complaints which they might wish to make and gave them sixty days in which to do it. At the close of this period the judge of *residencia* opened an investigation in the town wherein the official under examination had resided, usually the capital of the province. The actual trial of *residencia* might consume sixty days, or it might be perfunctory in its character and occupy a much shorter period, the entire question of time depending on the amount of evidence presented against the retiring official. On the other hand, as we have seen, the *residencia* of a governor might occupy ten years.

If the judge were taking a *residencia* in the provinces he was frequently delayed in arriving at his post of duty, owing to the pressure of other business, or to the uncertainty of transportation facilities. In that event, he could not open the judicial investigation until the allotted period had almost transpired.

In the trial, two distinct lines of investigation were usually

---

[76] *Ibid.*, 5–15–27 to 49.

pursued: charges which had been made against the official were investigated and the records of his office were examined. The discovery was frequently made through this procedure that the official had embezzled money belonging to the government, usually investing it in private ventures. The inquiry might show that he had been careless in the execution of the duties of his office, remiss in his attention to *encomiendas,* particularly neglecting the Indians thereon, or too ignorant and incompetent to try properly, record, and transmit the *autos* of the cases which had come to him in first instance. These defects might not become apparent until they were revealed in this examination.

The judge of *residencia* would seem to have been well occupied during the time that he was conducting the investigation. He received and reviewed all charges made. In addition to auditing the records of the office, he had to pursue inquiries as to the truth of these charges. He examined witnesses both for and against the defendant, and was supposed to give the official under investigation every opportunity to defend himself. He was relieved, however, of the trouble and responsibility of checking up the financial accounts of the official under *residencia.* This important matter was turned over to the treasury officials, who ascertained shortages, and held the bondsmen of the official under investigation responsible.[77] The judges of *residencia,* and the *oidores* making investigations and reviewing cases of *residencia* were ordered to confine their examinations to "criminal and legal matters and charges which result against those under *residencia.*"[78]

After all the evidence had been taken and the case had been duly tried, the judge of *residencia* was authorized to render sentence. Sentences were executed by the examining judge if

---

[77] *Ibid.,* 8–1–28; 5–15–35. Heavy penalties were prescribed for those who offered insecure financial guarantees (*ibid.,* 5–15–33 to 36).

[78] *Ibid.,* 34.

the penalty did not exceed twenty-five thousand *maravedís*. The latter cases were not appealable. If the fine were less than two hundred ducats and the defendant desired to appeal, he was obliged to pay the fine or deposit the amount thereof. His case would then be reviewed by the audiencia and in order to effect this, notice of appeal had to be submitted in sufficient time to permit the record of the entire case to be reduced to writing. If, on review, the audiencia found that the defendant was not guilty of the charges which had been brought against him, the money taken as a fine or deposit was restored. If the amount of the fine exceeded two hundred ducats, or if the defendant had been convicted of serious crimes, the judge was authorized to take the proper and necessary steps for the detention of the prisoner and the seizure of his property pending a new trial in the higher tribunal.[79] Cases involving more than one thousand pesos could be carried to the Council of the Indies.

A thoroughly typical case, illustrating all of the ramifications of a provincial official's *residencia,* was that of Francisco Fernández Zéndera, *alcalde mayor* and military captain of the province of Ilocos.[80] It was investigated first by a judge appointed by the *acuerdo,* it was reviewed by the audiencia and it was finally carried to the Council of the Indies. It was characteristic in another sense, namely, in that twelve years passed before the matter was settled.

After Zéndera had occupied his post three years, complaints against him were brought to the attention of the *fiscal.* In his capacity as prosecuting official and as protector of the Indians, he made a motion before the audiencia in *acuerdo,* that a judge of *residencia* should be sent to conduct an investiga-

---

79 *Ibid.,* 39, 40.

80 *Expediente de Don Frco. Fernández Zéndera, alcalde mayor y capitán de guerra de la provincia de Ilocos. . . . su residencia pendiente de informe de la audiencia, 1794,* A. I., 106–5–4 and 5. The papers relating to this trial easily aggregate 4000 pages.

tion of Zéndera's official conduct. The following charges against Zéndera had been sent to the governor, and on the basis of these, the *fiscal*, governor, and audiencia decided to conduct the investigation: First, Zéndera had compelled natives to work for him on his own estates, building houses, granaries, fences, tilling the soil and planting crops, from two hundred to three hundred men having worked for him continually, without pay or food; second, the arbitrary methods of this *alcalde mayor* left the natives without money with which to buy their food or to pay their tribute; third, not only were the men forced to labor, but the women were obliged to sew, spin and embroider without pay, and the product of their labor was confiscated by the *alcalde mayor*.

The audiencia and the governor, in *acuerdo*, having taken note of these charges, commissioned Angel Moguel, chief secretary of the government, to conduct the *residencia* of the *alcalde*. Moguel was put in possession of the necessary documents and departed at once for Vigán, the head city of the province. On November 7, 1782, he posted notices to the effect that Zéndera's *residencia* was to be taken, calling on the residents to make formal charges against him. Moguel suspended Zéndera from office and accepted 20,000 pesos from two of his friends as bonds to cover the *residencia*, this sum offsetting the valuation of the properties for which Zéndera was responsible. These were additional to other bonds which Zéndera had posted on his accession to office.

For some unassigned reason, only twenty-five days were allowed for the filing of complaints, but during this time eighty-eight charges were made, most of which were variations of those mentioned above. Zéndera was said to have been uncompromising in his administration of justice; he had imposed excessive fines; he had imprisoned the natives without giving them opportunities for defense; he had refused to allow them to appeal their cases.[81] Not being a lawyer, he lacked sufficient qualifications for the proper conduct of trials; moreover he had refused to employ a *teniente* or *asesor*. He had failed to supervise and enforce the instruction of Spanish, and he had done nothing to assist in the education of the natives. Zéndera was charged with having suppressed all commerce except his own, going so far as to arrest merchants of other provinces who came to Ilocos to trade. This he had done to secure his own monopoly in commercial matters. He had, moreover, suppressed the trade of the Ilocanos with the Igorrotes. He had failed to segregate the men from the women in the provincial prison. It was said that he had neglected to publish the governor's edicts (*bandos*) from Manila. He had shown partiality to Spanish priests in preference to the native clergy. He was charged with having taken rice as tribute at a low price, turning it over to the treasury officials at a higher rate, thereby making great profits for himself.

Zéndera was found guilty of almost every charge made against him. The sentence of *residencia* was pronounced by the judge commissioned for the purpose on August 13, 1782. The defendant was fined 8000 pesos and sentenced to depriva-

---

[81] It was said that he had shown favoritism in his dealings with some of the *barangay* (district) chiefs, allowing them unbridled license in the collection of tribute and in the enforcement of compulsory labor, most of which they utilized for their own, or for his, benefit. One chief was said to have gone so far as to forcibly take carabaos from the natives when the latter were working them in the fields. Zéndera had, of course, extended favors to these *barangay* chiefs in exchange for reciprocal advantages. (The *alcaldes mayores* ruled the native population through these chiefs at this time. Later they utilized the *gobernadorcillos*, who were native or *mestizo* governors of the small towns.—See Malcolm, *The government of the Philippine Islands*, 64–72.)

It was also charged that he had allowed cock-fights whenever requested, instead of restricting these to holidays and Sundays as the law prescribed. On these occasions he collected two *reales* from each entrant, and in addition he took the slain birds, alleging that they were for the consumption of the inmates of the provincial prison. Testimony was produced to show that the prisoners had never eaten fowl.

tion of office for a period of eight years.[82] The audiencia, in turn, reviewed the case, and that tribunal, on May 20, 1783, finding the *autos* of the case incomplete, ordered Moguel back to Vigán for a second time to complete the investigation. The judgment of *residencia* after this second investigation was made was the same as before, and the case was carried to the Council of the Indies on November 7, 1785. It seems that in this case the audiencia was somewhat slow in granting the appeal, for on February 19, 1788, a *cédula* was expedited which ordered the audiencia to forward all the *autos* in its possession bearing on the case. The final judgment of the Council of the Indies was rendered March 23, 1794. The fine of 8000 pesos was reduced to 3000 pesos, and the portion of the sentence which had ordered a deprivation of office was remitted altogether.[83]

The *cédula* of August 24, 1799, already referred to, greatly altered the applicability of the *residencias* to provincial as well as insular officials. Its greatest importance was due to the fact that it authorized investigations of *corregidores, alcaldes mayores,* and sub-delegate intendants only when charges were made against them; otherwise it was assumed that their official conduct had been satisfactory, and accordingly no *residencias* were held. Before the officials could be transferred to

---

[82] In taking the *residencias* of *corregidores* and *alcaldes mayores* the audiencia frequently took great responsibility upon itself. On July 10, 1800, on taking the *residencia* of Luís Rodríguez Varela, *alcalde mayor* of Pangasinán, the audiencia suspended the decoration of the *pequeña cruz,* which had been conferred upon this official by the royal authority. The deprivation, in this case, was tentative, pending the investigation of the charges which had been made of shortages in the finances of his province.—Audiencia to the King, July 10, 1800, A. I., 106–4–18.

[83] The original sentence probably denied to Zéndera the privilege of holding the office of *alcalde mayor* only, since he occupied the post of *regidor* of the city of Manila, pending the appeal of his case to the Council of the Indies. It is evident, therefore, that the sentence which was pronounced upon Zéndera did not apply to all positions of honor and trust.

other posts they were obliged to show certificates of clearance from former positions. The audiencia was given final jurisdiction over the *residencias* of these officials, with inhibition of appeal. At the same time the tribunal was denied jurisdiction in any instance over the *residencias* of viceroys, captains-general, presidents, governors, treasury officials, *oidores*, and intendants.[84] After the suppression of the Council of the Indies on March 24, 1834, the latter cases were finished in the Supreme Tribunal of Justice, and that tribunal continued to exercise this jurisdiction till the close of the nineteenth century.[85]

The *cédula* above referred to abolished the *residencias* of *tenientes letrados, alcaldes ordinarios, regidores,* clerks, procurators, syndics, *alguaciles,* and other minor officials. In place of the formal investigation and judgment after the term of office was completed, the audiencia was given more complete control over their official acts, with the duty of seeing that justice was administered, jails inspected and kept clean, prisoners

---

[84] *Cédula* of August 24, 1799, *Recopilación,* 5–15, notes 4 and 5; see also Rodríguez San Pedro, *Legislación ultramarina,* I, 282.

[85] Escriche, *Diccionario,* I, 578; see also royal order of November 20, 1841, and of January 18, 1848, in Rodríguez San Pedro, *Legislación ultramarina,* I, 282; 290. When the Intendancy was established in 1784–7, an effort was made by the newly created officials to escape the *residencia.* The entire term of the first intendant, Carvajal (or Carbajal), had been devoted to an assertion of his independence of the governor and audiencia. Carvajal interpreted the law requiring all officials of the government to give *residencia* every five years to the Department of Justice as not applying to him or his subordinates. He pointed to the stipulation in the ordinance which created his department, and established its independence of the executive and judiciary. The king disapproved of his attitude and ordered that henceforth the officials of *real hacienda* should give *residencia* in the same manner as other officials, in accordance with the laws of the Indies. (King to Carvajal, July 29, 1788, A. I., 107–5–19, citing *Recopilación,* 2–15–69; 5–15–15 and *Ordenanza de Intendentes de Buenos Ayres,* Art. 305.) This decree ordered that the *residencias* of the intendants and their assistants should be submitted to the audiencia. The *cédula* of August 24, 1799, so frequently cited in this chapter, gave final jurisdiction to the audiencia over the *residencias* of *intendentes-corregidores,* but it decreed that superintendents should give *residencia* directly to the Council of the Indies.

given a speedy trial and not molested with undue exactions, and the police supervised. The tribunal was also empowered to see that the *ayuntamientos* conducted their elections impartially and that the municipal officials executed their duties faithfully. In this way the formal investigation at the close of the term of these minor officials was replaced by a more efficient supervision of their acts by the audiencia. The constitutional reforms of the early nineteenth century gave to the audiencia original jurisdiction over the trial of judges of first instance, with appeal to the Supreme Tribunal of Justice. This authority was suppressed in 1815, and continued so until 1835, when it was restored to the audiencias of the colonies.

Although the reform of August 24, 1799, recognized the *residencias* of *alcaldes mayores, tenientes,* and *corregidores,* merely transferring jurisdiction over these to the audiencias, it would seem that this investigation retained less of its former severity from this time onwards. In fact, some authorities infer that the *residencia* was abolished after 1799.[86] This was not the case, however, as the *residencia* was recognized by laws promulgated as lately as 1870.[87]

---

[86] Martínez Alcubilla (*Diccionario,* XI, 477) and Escriche (*Diccionario,* II, 819) state that the *cédula* of August 24, 1799, abolished the *residencia.* The latter states that the *residencia* was eliminated because of the corruption of judges, and as the judges of *residencia* had proved to be a grave infliction on the towns, mistreating witnesses and defendants on many occasions, it was thought advisable to discontinue the practice of holding these investigations. Escriche also quotes extracts from the laws of August 24, 1799, September 26, 1835, and November 20, 1841, wherein were provided regulations for the future continuance of the *residencia.* Cases involving viceroys, captains-general, and presidents of audiencias were to be tried in the Supreme Tribunal of Justice in first instance. *Alcaldes mayores, corregidores,* military and political governors who were not presidents were to be tried in the audiencias which exercised jurisdiction over their districts.

[87] See *Cédula* of July 7, 1860, in Rodríguez San Pedro, *Legislación ultramarina,* III, 287; royal order of July 25, 1865, *ibid.,* X, 99; royal order of October 25, 1870, *Colección legislativa,* CV, 442–465.

The eminent authority, Manuel Bernáldez Pizarro, writing from Manila on April 26, 1827, deplored the laxity which was characteristic of the method of conducting trials of *residencia,* and recommended

The audiencia also had jurisdiction over the *residencias* of galleon officials. These had to submit to *residencia* at the termination of each voyage. An *oidor* was designated by the governor for the inspection of the ship, for the examination of its papers, for the consideration of complaints against the officers of ill-treatment of passengers and crews during the voyage.[88] An investigation was conducted on the occasion of the loss of a ship. Then a thorough inquiry was made in an endeavor to discover negligence on the part of the admiral, general, or other officials. The exercise of a similar authority over cases involving the loss of galleons has been discussed in the preceding chapter.

In pursuance of this authority, Magistrate Torralba was commissioned in 1710 to take the *residencia*s of the officers of the galleon ''Nuestra Señora del Rosario y San Vicente Ferrer'', which was wrecked in the Straits of San Bernardino on the voyage from Acapulco in 1709.[89] As great diligence had been shown by them in landing the treasure and sending it overland, the matter was dropped. A similar investigation was conducted in 1743 in the case of the galleon ''Cobadonga'', which was captured by the British. The charge was made that neither the ''Cobadonga'' nor her convoy, ''El Pilar'', had offered any resistance, and that the latter had deserted the

---

that they be made more effective and just. He criticized especially the prevailing system of holding the *alcaldes mayores* to a strict accountability; who, he wrote, "as they have permission to trade, are more tempted to evade or infringe the laws; and many persons are appointed to that office 'who lack all the qualifications necessary for any public office whatever.' . . . not only have they used their authority to possess themselves of the property of the Indians . . . and defrauded the Indians with unjust exactions; but they have humiliated the religious, stolen moneys from the king . . . [and] have thrown the provinces into a condition of effervescence and of conspiracy against the government." (Blair and Robertson, LI, 212, 212–213.) Pizarro recommended a more stringent *residencia* as a means of remedying these defects.

88 *Recopilación*, 5–15–17 and 18; 9–45–42.

89 Governor to Council of the Indies, January 4, 1710, A. I., 68–4–15.

galleon and had taken refuge in flight.[90] The officers were arrested and thrown into prison on charges brought by the *fiscal,* but they were cleared in the investigation which proved that the ships were not in a condition to fight.

The various laws and cases which have been cited in this chapter show that the trial of *residencia* of captains-general, treasury officials, *oidores,* intendants, *alcaldes mayores,* and *alcaldes ordinarios* was a judicial function over which the audiencia had a large share of authority. It is safe to say that no *residencia* was ever taken in the Philippines, after the audiencia had been established there, in which that tribunal did not exercise some degree of authority. As the laws and regulations of the *residencia* varied at different times, the extent of the jurisdiction of the audiencia in this matter was not always the same. The audiencia either assisted in the examination of the charges or in the designation of the judge. The magistrate selected was usually an *oidor.* *Oidores* were liable to designation to conduct inquiries, and the audiencia, as a tribunal, tried these cases in review. The tribunal exercised supervision over the work of the investigating judge. The case was either finished in the audiencia, or reviewed there and appealed to the Council of the Indies through the action of the audiencia. The Council of the Indies was the supreme arbiter in all cases, prior to 1799. Subsequently the Council, or the Supreme Tribunal of Justice after 1834, retained final jurisdiction over the *residencias* of the higher officials only. In the *residencias* of provincial or local officials the jurisdiction of the audiencia was final.

---

[90] Concepción, XI, 132–234 (Anson's depredations).

CHAPTER V

THE SEMI-JUDICIAL AND ADMINISTRATIVE FUNCTIONS OF THE AUDIENCIA.

Aside from the activities which have been described, the magistrates of the audiencia rendered important services in various administrative capacities. From the beginning until the end of the eighteenth century the *oidores* were assigned to special commissions or judgeships with jurisdiction over such miscellaneous secular and ecclesiastical matters as did not come readily under any other department or authority. In practically all cases these functions involved the *oidores* in their individual capacities rather than as magistrates of a tribunal of justice. Though their work was independent of the audiencia, their decisions were reviewed in the audiencia in many cases. In short, it may be said that when any unforeseen or unclassified matter came up for solution, it was usually assigned to a magistrate of the audiencia.

The exercise of these extra functions was especially characteristic of the history of the audiencia down to 1785, when the reforms of the intendancy were introduced throughout the Spanish colonial empire. These important reforms grouped these administrative functions about a central head, the superintendent, and lessened the duties of the *oidores* in these matters, confining the magistrates more particularly to judicial duties. It may be said, however, that the *oidores* exercised these extra functions practically till the end of the eighteenth century, which period comprised the greater part of the existence of the colonial audiencia.

The laws of the Indies empowered the president of the audiencia to designate *oidores* to serve on these commissions.

Additional compensation and travelling expenses were given for these extra services.[1] The president was forbidden to send magistrates on commissions to places outside the district of the audiencia, which, of course, would have been impossible in the Philippines. Appointment to some of these commissions was considered by the magistrates as highly desirable. Frequent disagreements arose over these appointments, and the king was obliged to issue pacificatory *cédulas*, from time to time, to allay the discord and strife which arose over the appointments to the more lucrative of these places. The principle was laid down repeatedly that special commissions should be assigned fairly among the ministers, and that in their distribution only the aptitude of the magistrates for the particular tasks should be considered.[2] The term of service for these special posts was a year. No change was allowed in the incumbency of a particular commission unless on account of death, sickness, or removal for incompetency. Appointments to these extra duties were made in the royal name, and appointees were obliged to make reports to the court on the termination of the commission held. Magistrates were held responsible for their service in this capacity in their *residencias*. In large audiencias such as Mexico, Lima, and Buenos Ayres in the eighteenth century, many commissions of this character were served by regular commissioners who held no other posts, but in the smaller colonies such as the Philippines, Puerto Rico, and Cuba, they were held by *oidores* when the duties connected with the commissions did not entail sufficient work to occupy all the time of the appointee.

The most important and profitable commissions were awarded to the senior magistrate of the audiencia. He was charged

---

[1] *Recopilación*, 2–16–40; see also 7–1–15.
[2] Law of November 10, 1818, A. I., 106–4–19; see *Real instrucción dada á los regentes de las audiencias, 20 de Junio de 1776*, in Rodríguez San Pedro, *Legislación ultramarina*, VII, 22–28; Zamora y Coronado, *Apéndice*. 19–33.

permanently with the duty of seeing that all the decrees, fines, and decisions of the Council of the Indies were executed, collections being made in accordance with the instructions of that body. These included fines imposed in *residencia* and other penalties exacted on different occasions by the audiencia, or by the Council of the Indies. Among the latter were confiscations of property and fines for smuggling, for the illegal exportation of silver, and for the evasion of the king's fifth,[3] the *alcabala* and the *almojarifazgo*. The senior magistrate was authorized to retain as compensation three per cent of the amount collected, and he was ordered to give account to the audiencia of collections made by him in accordance with the law.[4] Another magistrate was *asesor* of the Santa Cruzada, and it was his duty to give legal advice and to act as special attorney for that department of ecclesiastical activity.[5] The president, *fiscal*, and the senior *oidor* concurred in the *acuerdos* which treated of matters pertaining to *real hacienda*.[6] This was known as the *junta ordinaria*. A tribunal of appeals above the *junta ordinaria* was created later, and in its activities, also, the magistrates of the audiencia participated.[7] The audiencia also

---

[3] A tax on silver, gold and other metals (as well as on pearls) mined in the Indies. This tax was first authorized on February 5, 1504 (*Recopilación*, 8-10-1). Philip II conceded a commutation of this tax to ten per cent in favor of *adelantados*, their successors and other early settlers (*ibid.*, 4-3-19). A draft of a letter exists in A. I., 106-6-6, written about 1585 by Governor Sande of the Philippines, asking for an extension of this dispensation.—See Blair and Robertson, IV, 87, par. 114 and note. On August 8, 1609, the king inquired of the Manila audiencia whether the tax was a fifth or a tenth.—A. I., 102-2-1.

[4] *Ibid.*, 2-16-19 to 22.

[5] *Ibid.*, 23.

[6] *Ibid.*, 24. This *junta* is to be distinguished from the *real contaduría*, which was composed of the *oficiales reales*. See Martínez de Zúñiga, *Estadismo*, 246.

[7] This was the *junta superior de la real hacienda*, created for Manila by the law of July 24, 1784. It was one of the reforms of the intendancy. It cannot be said, however, that these reforms became effective until 1787, though the *cédulas* of July 17 and 24, 1784, which ordered them, were received in Manila on December 5, 1785. These

heard judicially certain cases of appeal involving the royal treasury, but magistrates who had participated in the *junta* mentioned above were not allowed to hear again the cases in which their previous vote had been given. Each *oidor* served in turn for the period of six months on the board of auctions.[8] Magistrates were appointed by the governor, yearly, in turn, to serve as inspectors of the government. In this capacity they were expected to examine and report on the administration of justice and on the work of the audiencia, the royal treasury and the officials connected therewith, visitors, provincial officials and those of the city of Manila. The inspecting magistrate was authorized to examine the records of these officials and to use any other legitimate means in performance of his special duties.[9]

An *oidor* was designated by the president to make periodical inspections in the provinces. This official had to attend to a variety of matters while on visits of inspection. He was required to make a census of the towns, and inquire into the prosperity of the inhabitants; to audit the accounts of the town officials, and to see whether the provincial governor or

---

cédulas ordered the formation of a government locally, which would conform to the general principles of the intendancy and which were laid down in the *cédulas* referred to. These plans had to be referred to Spain on appeal. Subsequently the Ordinance of Intendants of Buenos Ayres was applied to the Philippines.—A. I., 107–5–14. Until January 11, 1791, all appeals from the *junta superior* were heard in the Audiencia of Manila. The *cédula* of that date, received in Manila on June 30, 1793, ordered that such appeals should be carried to the Council of the Indies.—A. I., 107–5–22. The *junta superior de real hacienda* did much toward relieving the audiencia of its advisory functions as in matters of finance and commerce. Many evidences of this may be noted in the reports and correspondence of the *superintendente de real hacienda de Manila.*—A. I., 107–5–14; 107–5–15 to 31; 107–6–1 to 31; 107–7–1 to 21. Priestley (*José de Gálvez*, 338–9) shows that even after the establishment of the intendancy in New Spain, the audiencia retained the administration of crown lands, notwithstanding the provisions of the new laws which ordered that they should be controlled by the *junta superior*. See also *ibid.*, 302–3.

8 *Recopilación*, 2–16–34.

9 *Ibid.*, 2–15–169.

magistrate had been faithful in the execution of his duties. He was supposed to visit the *encomiendas* and note the treatment of the Indians thereon, to find out whether the natives were properly and sufficiently instructed, or whether they were permitted to remain in idolatry and idleness. He inspected the churches and monasteries, seeing that they contained the requisite number of religious and no more, and noting whether the natives under the charge of the ecclesiastics were well treated. In the same way he inspected the curacies of the towns. The visiting *oidor* was especially required to give careful attention to the *corregidores* and *alcaldes mayores,* inspecting their judicial and administrative activities and holding them responsible for any irregularities, especially with regard to the treatment of the Indians. The visitor was required to inspect inns and taverns, to ascertain whether they observed the regular tariffs, and whether the drugs sold in the provinces were of good quality. He also inspected highways and bridges. If the visitor found anything wrong he was authorized to take immediate steps, on his own responsibility, to remedy the defects, reporting any action taken to the audiencia without delay. As seen in the last chapter, the immediate consequence of the visit was frequently the *residencia* of the official inspected. The visitor was provided with sufficient funds to defray his expenses, so that he would not be a burden on the *encomenderos* or Indians. The president of the audiencia was forbidden to order visits to the same province more frequently than once every three years, unless, after an investigation, such action was declared necessary by vote of the *acuerdo.*[10]

The audiencia exercised supervision over certain matters of church finance. These included tithes, the funds of temporalities, and of certain charitable societies, and jurisdiction over the adjustment of estates and properties left by deceased pre-

---

10 *Ibid.,* 2–31–1 to 3.

lates. In connection with the latter was the duty of auditing the accounts of benefices which were subject to the royal patronage whenever a transfer of occupants was made. These matters, though miscellaneous in their character, and accordingly pertinent here, may be reserved for a subsequent chapter which will be dedicated to a discussion of the relations of the audiencia and the Church.

An *oidor* in the Philippines served as judge of *medias anatas*.[11] These taxes were levied upon the salaries of all officials of royal appointment, except ecclesiastics, these exactions varying in amount from one-half the first year's income to one-tenth of the gross salary of each official. The *cédula* of June 2, 1632,[12] ordered the judge-commissioner of *medias anatas* to surrender the money which he had collected to the treasury officials who in turn were to transmit it to Spain.[13] More definite information as to the nature of the duties of the judge-commissioner of these funds may be gathered from the *cédula* of December 14, 1776, by which Oidor Félix Díaz Quejada y Obrero was appointed as commissioner of *medias anatas* in the Philippines. This magistrate was authorized to retain four per cent of all that he collected. This percentage, the *cédula* stated, was the same as was paid to the commissioner of *medias anatas* of New Spain. The *cédula* ordered Quejada to collect this tax from

---

11 *Ibid.*, 8–19 (general subject of *medias anatas*). Holders of ecclesiastical benefices were subsequently obliged to pay the *media anata*, although they were especially exempted by the *cédula* of June 2, 1632. The *media anata* (civil and ecclesiastical) was paid until December 28, 1846, when this tax, together with the *lanza* (a tax formerly paid by the nobility, but subsequently required of all classes in lieu of military service) was abolished (Martínez Alcubilla, *Diccionario*, I, 407).

12 *Ibid.*, 8–19–1 and 2.

13 The *cédula* of July 3, 1664, reorganized the system of *medias anatas*, authorizing their division into two separate allotments, one payable at the court on the appointment of the official concerned, and the second within or at the end of eighteen months after his appointment, at the capital of the district wherein he served. Guarantees had to be given that the second payment would be made when due, and interest was charged at the rate of eight per cent a year on the amount remaining to be paid (*ibid.*, 4).

all royal appointees, but not from governors of towns or Indian *caciques* who were elected yearly, and who, of course, were not royal appointees. Appeals from judgments of the commissioner of *medias anatas* were to be entertained in the Council of the Indies only, and not in the audiencia.[14]

It has been pointed out already in this chapter that the effect of the reforms of the intendancy was to limit the jurisdiction of the *oidores* over special commissions. This is especially true of those relating to finance. An illustration of this is shown in the disputes which occurred between the *oidores* and the governor, over the conservatorships of betel,[15] wine, tobacco, playing-cards, and cockpits. When these sources of income developed in the latter part of the seventeenth century, their supervision, as usual, had been conferred on *oidores* with title of *asesores* or *jueces-conservadores* (judge conservators).[16] This was done in disregard of the laws of the Indies, wherein was expressed the desirability of conferring these assessorships, if possible, on properly qualified officials, other than *oidores*. The magistrate holding a commission was to attend to the legal duties and adjudicate all suits in connection therewith. The latter regulation was made in order that when the cases were brought to trial the magistrate might not be incapacitated by having rendered decisions in them ahead. The law continued in the following strain:

---

[14] *Cédula* of December 14, 1776, A. I., 105–2–16.

[15] The extensive use of the betel-nut by the natives of the Philippines encouraged the Spanish government to monopolize its production and sale, and a considerable revenue was derived from it. In 1786 the profit from the sale of betel was 16,770 pesos (Report of Intendant, January 8, 1788, A. I. 107– 5–15), and the next year the sum collected was 15,207 pesos (Report of Intendant, June 21, 1789, 107–5–18). Other monopolies during the same period yielded as follows: Tobacco, 258,743 pesos; wine, 73,636 pesos; cockpits, 8,375 pesos; tributes, 174,494 pesos (Report of Intendant, June 21, 1789).

[16] *Juez conservador* (civil), a judge named *por privilegio del rey*, with private jurisdiction over the civil affairs of some community or guild, for the protection of its interests and estates or the collection of its rents (Escriche, *Diccionario*, II, 260).

when a case so urgent and extraordinary offers itself that an *oidor* must be appointed, warning is hereby given that . . . the same magistrate who tried the case originally may not be judge.[17]

This law conceded that *oidores* might serve when other magistrates were not available.

Governor Marquina, *superintendente subdelegado de real hacienda* from 1789 to 1793, refused to permit *oidores* to serve as *asesores* of the monopolies of betel, wine, and tobacco. These magistrates claimed, however, that they were entitled to the appointments, since they had occupied these positions before July 26, 1784, the date of the creation of the intendancy in the Philippines. They conceded that they had been relieved of jurisdiction over these rents on that date, and that the authority formerly exercised by them had been assumed by the intendant.[18] By the *cédula* of November 23, 1787, however, the intendancy had been abolished and the government restored to "the state and condition which had previously existed."[19] This would mean that the *oidores* should again hold these *asesorías,* and on the basis of this reasoning they demanded that the governor should return them.

The *oidores* did not tamely submit to a deprivation of their posts as *asesores* on the occasion of the establishment of the intendancy. They complained to the king, alleging that these appointments belonged to them by their own right. The king inquired of Governor Basco y Vargas why the *oidores* had not been designated for these duties. The governor replied that the supervision of the rents had been assumed by the intendant, but that their direction belonged at that time to the governor and superintendent, by virtue of the *cédula* of November 23,

---

[17] *Recopilación,* 3–3–35.

[18] Report on the establishment of the Intendancy in Manila, December 5, 1785, A. I., 107–5–19.

[19] *Testimonio* and transcript of the royal *cédula* of November 23, 1787; King to Marquina, June 15, 1791, A. I., 105–2–10.

1787.[20]   He stated that the *oidores* had no right of their own to these *asesorías*, since the faculty of appointing *asesores* had been conferred on the governor (or viceroy) by the laws of the Indies,[21] and in times past governors had appointed lawyers who were not *oidores*. There was therefore no obligation on the part of the governor to give these places to *oidores;* indeed, the laws of the Indies had emphasized the undesirability of doing so.[22]

Basco y Vargas, in pursuance of this conception of his rights and duties, combined all of these *asesorías* under the direction of one office, placing them under the orders of his own *asesor,* leaving *oidores* in charge of each minor *asesoría,* except that of tobacco, which was placed under the immediate direction of the governor's *asesor*. The king approved this action, giving the new official a new title, that of *asesor de todo lo directivo y lo económico de la superintendencia subdelegada de la real hacienda de Filipinas.*[23] The local authority appointed Magistrate Castillo y Negrete to this new position at once, but the king, on the ground that the law[24] forbade an *oidor* to hold such an office, disapproved of the appointment and gave the place to Rufino de Rivera, who had formerly been *auditor de guerra* and *asesor de gobierno*.

As soon as Governor Marquina assumed office, he relieved the magistrates of the audiencia of all share in the administration of these monopolies, combining all these branches of *real hacienda* under the *asesor* above mentioned. On August 3, 1791,

---

[20] The first intendant, Ciriaco Gonzales Carvajal, was given the title of *intendente de guerra y real hacienda,* by virtue of the *cédulas* of July 17 and 24, 1784. By the reform of November 23, 1787, the duties of his office were united to those of the governor, whose title, under the new arrangement, was *gobernador y capitán general y superintendente de la real hacienda* (A. I., 105-3-5 and 107-5-19; see Chapter IV, note 55, of this work.

[21] *Recopilación,* 3-3-35.

[22] Basco y Vargas to the King, May 9, 1786, A. I., 107-5-19.

[23] *Cédula* of March 20, 1790, A. I., 107-5-19.

[24] *Recopilación,* 3-3-35.

the audiencia protested against the acts of the governor, basing its claims to a continuance of authority on the *cédula* of March 20, 1790, by which the king had authorized the *oidores* to administer all the monopolies except tobacco.

On August 16, 1791, Governor Marquina answered the complaint of the audiencia in a memorial of his own, in which he set forth his position in summarized form, giving a history of the entire contention, and defining his position with precision and clarity.[25] He claimed that the *cédulas* which had been issued up to that time had recognized the right of the governor to dispose of these *asesorías*, which did not and never had belonged to the *oidores* by their own right. As superintendent of *real hacienda*, he (the governor) was judge-conservator of all the *asesorías*, and by *cédula* of March 20, 1790, he had been authorized to control them through his *asesor*. The latter official had also been ordered to administer the rent of tobacco directly as the agent of the governor and to supervise the others in the governor's name. The *oidores* had been forbidden to hold these positions, except under exceptional circumstances, which, in Marquina's judgment, did not exist at this time,[26] since there was present in the colony a special *asesor* whose duty it was to supervise these monopolies. The audiencia would have to try certain cases on appeal as a judicial body, and *oidores* who had already rendered decisions as judge-conservators could not justly render decisions when the same cases were appealed. He declared that he had the approval of the king in his contention, and was therefore confident of his position.

The governor's will prevailed, and the magistrates were deprived of the commissions which they had formerly held; these were given over to regular officials of *real hacienda*. Contentious cases, however, that did not pertain exclusively to

---

25 Marquina to the Audiencia, August 16, 1791, A. I., 107–5–19.
26 *Recopilación*, 3–3–35, cited in notes 21 and 24 of this chapter.

finance were tried on appeal in the audiencia and that body exercised regular, but not special, jurisdiction in them thereafter.

One of the most important offices which the *oidores* were called on to perform was that of *juez de difuntos*. The duties of this office consisted largely in the administration of the funds and property of persons who died intestate, or without heirs in the colony. This work was entrusted to the colonial audiencia as a body in 1526, and any judge therein might be delegated from the tribunal for the adjustment of an estate.

The first law providing for a special administrator was proclaimed at Valladolid on April 16, 1550. It stated that many of the heirs of persons who died in the colonies had been defrauded of their rightful dues by the carelessness, omission, illegal procedure, and usurpation of the ministers who had diverted the property to their own uses; this condition of affairs made reform imperative. Viceroys and presidents of royal audiencias, while retaining power of removal for cause, were commanded henceforth to name, at the beginning of each year, an *oidor* from the local audiencia to act as *juez de difuntos*.[27] This judge was authorized to collect, administer, rent, sell, and have general supervision over the property of deceased persons to the same extent that the audiencia previously had. The acts of the judge were appealable to the audiencia of the district wherein he officiated. On December 15, 1609, a law was proclaimed by Philip III which extended the term of this judge from one to two years. The early laws provided no extra salary for the *juez de difuntos*. It was prescribed that his decisions should be respected by the audiencia and by the other officials of the government, the viceroys and presidents being especially instructed not to allow any other official to usurp his functions.

---

27 *Ibid.*, 2–32–1.

In case the *juez de difuntos* should fail to execute his duties, or should exceed his powers, it was the duty of the *fiscal* to bring the abuse to the attention of the audiencia, and that tribunal was supposed to see that the proper methods were enforced. The jurisdiction of this special magistrate was to extend to the settling of the estates of intestates, and of testates leaving property to persons in Spain. His authority was valid over the property of deceased officials, merchants, and *encomenderos,* and it might be extended to the cases of foreigners. He also assisted in the disposal of property left by clerics. When the latter died intestate, the proceeds of their estates were added to the fund known as the *bienes de difuntos.* No distinction was made between property left by them and that left by civil employees of the government or private citizens. If these priests had made testaments, it was the duty of the *juez de difuntos* to see that the property reached the donees without the interference of the prelates.[28]

As in other cases noted in this and in former chapters, so in the administration of the estates left by intestate decedents the laws seem to have undergone considerable change. In 1526, Charles V ordered that such estates were to be administered under the supervision of the audiencia. In 1550, the place of special *juez de difuntos* was created in each audiencia, the post to be filled by a magistrate designated by the president. In 1653, Philip IV added to the importance of the office by decreeing that all intestate cases should be administered by a special *juez de difuntos,* irrespective as to whether the heirs were in Spain, or at the place where the death took place.[29] This law provided that if children or descendants were left whose legitimacy was unquestioned, the heirs being in the colony, or if a will legally attested and witnessed were left, the case was to be settled in the ordinary courts. If there

---

[28] *Ibid.,* 7 and note; 8.
[29] *Ibid.,* 43.

were doubt, however, as to the validity of the claims of persons representing themselves as descendants, or if there were no heirs, the case would then be administered by the *juez de difuntos*. Settlements made by the ordinary justices were not reviewed in the royal audiencia. The authority accorded them frequently afforded pretexts for their intervention in cases which should have been settled by the *juez de difuntos,* particularly when heirs were left in Spain and in other colonies. A number of disagreements arose over this point, but all doubt was conclusively settled by the *cédula* of January 31, 1772, which awarded such jurisdiction to the *juez de difuntos.*[30] This was confirmed by the law of September 28, 1797. Foreigners residing outside the dominions were not allowed to inherit property left to them in the colonies, even though they were lineal descendants.[31] Heirs or others claiming property left by deceased persons must appear in person, or have others appear for them, properly authorized, and must prove conclusively their rights as heirs or creditors.

The *cédula* of September 28, 1797, was a codification and a reclassification of all previous laws on the subject of this jurisdiction. The provisions of this law, briefly stated, were as follows: (1) These judges should not under any circumstances have jurisdiction over property left by will, or without will, when the heirs were present and when there was no question of their right to the property. (2) In order that these judges

---

[30] *Ibid.,* 42, note 4; 47, note 7. These cases may be noted in A. I., 68–4–12.

[31] *Ibid.,* 44. The *cédula* of July 16, 1776, ordered the confiscation of property left by foreigners, forbidding that it should be sent outside of the realm either by the *juez de difuntos* or by the testamentary executor. In accordance with this regulation the superintendent, in 1800, seized the property of a Spaniard who had married a lady of Madras. The Spaniard had left a will providing for the transfer of his property to his wife, naming an executor to administer the will. This was opposed by the *juez de difuntos,* but when the case was appealed the action of the superintendent was approved (Aguilar to Soler, July 8, 1800, A. I., 107–5–24).

have power of intervention, it must be well known or appear by judicial process that either all the heirs or the greater number of them were absent. (3) They were not to have jurisdiction over property left by Indians or *caciques*. (4) They should not usually have authority to settle up the estates or property of native clerics, because their heirs would presumably be present. These cases were therefore subject to the jurisdiction of the ordinary courts, unless it were shown that there were heirs in Spain. Under no circumstances should the ecclesiastical authorities have intervention in these cases. (5) When the heirs were present, the audiencia was ordered to enforce the law which forbade the intervention of both the *juez de difuntos* and the ordinary judge.[32] In these cases the heirs were allowed to assume their property intact, without its being sold and thereby costs incurred. (6) The practice which had hitherto been followed by the *juez de difuntos* of diverting a fifth of the property of those who died intestate for the repose of the souls of the dead should cease from that time onward, and the proceeds of said property should be handed over without deduction to the heirs and relatives of the deceased, in accordance with the *cédula* of June 20, 1766.[33] (7) The *juez de difuntos* was forbidden to intervene in the settlement of estates or property left to heirs by will.[34]

It would appear, then, that the *oidor* detailed as *juez de difuntos* had jurisdiction over cases of intestacy, over the settlement of property when no heirs were apparent, or when there was doubt as to the existence of heirs, and in cases where

---

[32] See *Recopilación*, 2–32–42.

[33] A case appealed to the Council of the Indies on June 4, 1806, involved the property of Antonio Rodríguez de la Peña, deceased. Rodríguez had bequeathed 35,875 reales to his father; the Augustinians claimed 11,875 reales, or one-third of the entire estate, for prayers said in behalf of the soul of the departed one. The *contaduría general* in Madrid refused to allow payment (Aparici to the Council of the Indies, June 4, 1806, A. I., 107–3–8).

[34] *Recopilación*, 2–32, note 7.

the designated testamentary donees were outside the colony. The ordinary justices administered estates in two capacities, namely, when testaments were to be executed, the heirs being present, or when they acted as agents for the *juez de difuntos*. The latter was privileged to call upon the *corregidores, alcaldes mayores,* and other ordinary justices to execute provisions in the provinces, and these officials were obliged, when so designated, to settle estates subject to the supervision of the *juez*.[35]

When the heirs were resident in Spain, or in some colony other than the Philippines, the estates of deceased persons were sold and the money was set aside to be remitted to Spain. The collective sum of these properties, sold and unsold, was designated as the *bienes de difuntos*.[36] At stated periods the *juez de difuntos* was required to turn over the funds that he had collected, or received in the execution of his duties, to the *oficiales reales*, first deducting three per cent of their gross amount for his services.[37] His accounts, which were sent to the Council of the Indies, were also audited by these officials, and the audiencia likewise held him accountable for any abuses or errors other thân financial. He was also held responsible in his *residencia*. The *fiscal* was his prosecutor in case of suit. The *juez de difuntos*, on his part, was authorized to require reports from the agents and administrators who served him in the provinces, and all necessary safeguards were taken for his protection.[38]

Theoretically, the *juez de difuntos*, acting through the *oficiales reales*, sent such money as he had collected to the *Casa de Contratación* of Seville, or, after June 18, 1790, the date of the extinction of that body, to the *juez de arribadas* in Cádiz.[39] Thence it was distributed among the heirs in various

---

[35] *Ibid.*, 10.
[36] *Ibid.*, 32–33, 40, 60.
[37] *Ibid.*, 16, 32, 33.
[38] *Ibid.*, 16–18, 27–29, 31.
[39] *Ibid.*, 46, and note.

parts of Spain, or, in case no heirs were found, it was to remain in a fund by itself, until otherwise appropriated or disposed of by the crown. The money was sent at the risk of the heirs, eighteen per cent of the gross amount being deducted to pay the costs of transfer.[40] In actual practice, however, the

---

[40] *Ibid*, 48–56, 59.

The report to the Council of the Indies of Pedro Aparici, general superintendent of *real hacienda*, on July 8, 1805, shows in detail the method of settlement in Spain. This report was submitted to cover the administration of the property of Alberto Reyes, who died in Manila in 1803. The statement was as follows:

Total property left	123,700 r.
Executor's commission	741 r. 16 m.
Administration	1,237 r.
Expenses	123 r. 18 m.
Total deductions	2,102 r.
Balance to be distributed among heirs	121,598 r.
Two–thirds left to brother as per will	81,066 r.
One–third left to parents as per will	40,532 r.

Another illustration of the disposal of money left under slightly different circumstances may be noted in the Royal Order of February 14, 1800, to the *juez de arribadas* at Cádiz. The king ordered the transmission of 8024 pesos to the royal treasury because of the impossibility of finding the heirs of Antonio Manuel Pereda, who died at Manila in 1767. By the terms of his will, 2000 pesos had been left to the Third Order of St. Francis, 200 pesos to poor widows and orphans, and the balance was left to his mother. The lady had died, however, and as there were no heirs apparent, the money was ordered transferred to the royal treasury (A. I., 107–3–9).

These large sums, constantly on hand, intact and available, were always a source of grave temptation to governors and treasury officials. Loans were frequently taken from this fund for ordinary or unusual expenses of the government. At first the *juez de difuntos* objected forcibly to the governor's seeming disregard of the royal instructions regarding these funds. The laws of the Indies had commanded that they should be held inviolable (*Recopilación*, 57, 70). As noted above, the practice had arisen of making deductions from the subsidy equivalent to the amount of *bienes de difuntos* produced in the Philippines, and of retaining the money in Acapulco. This practice worked havoc with the fulfillment of the law which had ordered that these funds be preserved intact. The governor and the treasury officials had fallen into the practice of appropriating such available funds as existed in the *caja de difuntos* for purposes of local administration, with the assurance that the money would be properly accounted for in Mexico. Governor Anda seems to have been a leading offender in this matter. In 1767 he borrowed 19,729 pesos from the *juez de difuntos* and in 1768 another sum of 30,000 pesos was taken (Landazurri to the Council

funds derived from the Philippines were retained at Manila, itemized accounts of them being forwarded to Acapulco, the proper amount being deducted there from the annual subsidy.[41] This rendered unnecessary the actual transfer of money. The *juez de difuntos* in Mexico received the funds from the Philippines, together with reports and accounts relating thereto, and remitted them to Spain. There occurred many instances in which this magistrate in Mexico found mistakes in the reports rendered by his subordinate in Manila. A great deal of criticism was made from time to time, of alleged irregularities in

---

of the Indies, May 22, 1770, A. I., 107–3–9). By the *cédula* of October 9, 1777, the king approved the action of Governor Anda in borrowing from these funds on three other occasions to the extent of 25,000, 14,206, and 24,477 pesos, respectively, for the fortification of the city. It was ordered that this should not be done again, however, except under extraordinary circumstances (A. I., 107–3–9).

After being permitted for a long period of time, the practice which the Manila authorities had followed of making these deductions was finally disapproved by the home government. In 1806, because of the non-arrival of the galleon with the subsidy, the governor (and superintendent) authorized an advance of 54,049 pesos from the *bienes de difuntos*, which sum constituted the entire amount on hand. On April 25, 1815, the *fiscal* of the *contaduria general de las Indias* handed down an adverse opinion on this action (A. I., 107–3–9). Although the practice of allowing small loans from the funds of deceased persons had been practiced in the Philippines in case of exceptional circumstances, it was his opinion that the whole proceeding had been contrary to the laws of the Indies (*Recopilación*, 2–32–57). He advised that in the future there should be no interference with this money until the deduction had been authorized by the *juez de difuntos* in Mexico, and the judge should act only after he had received the report of the corresponding official in the Philippines.

If the above advice were followed, at least a year would pass before the report of the Manila judge could reach Mexico, and be returned. It was not to be supposed that the officials in the Philippines would wait for any such formality when in need of money for the current expenses of government. This is another example of the cumbrousness and lack of expedition of Spanish colonial administration, as affected by time and distance. It will be noted, also, that this practice had been going on since the time of Anda (1768), and the Council of the Indies did not pronounce against it decisively until 1815. The particular litigation which brought about its condemnation arose in 1806 and continued throughout a period of nine years.

[41] *Ibid.*, 60. See the articles on the Philippine *situado* by E. G. Bourne and James A. Leroy in the *American historical review*, X, 459–461, 929–932; XI. 722–723.

the administration of these funds in the Philippines; in fact, successive royal *cédulas* repeatedly charged the Philippine officials with maladministration.[42] The general superintendent of finance, Aparici, in a report to the Council, stated on July 19, 1797, that these funds had never been properly accounted for, and that glaring defects—even dishonesty, had always existed.[43] These faults, he alleged, were owing to the fact that the funds were not directly administered, but were paid into the treasury of Mexico, and that because of this roundabout method direct control could not be exercised. Although this high official pointed out these defects and made recommendations for the betterment of the service, no change was made, and the funds continued to be remitted to Mexico until 1815, when the suspension of the regular galleon eliminated the possibility of this practice.[44]

The *juez de difuntos* was frequently opposed in the exercise of his special jurisdiction by other officials of the colony. Many cases involving these conflicts of jurisdiction were appealed to the Council of the Indies. Among the most frequent were the quarrels which took place between the captain-general

---

[42] *Cédulas* of November 26, 1776, September 9, 1778, October 13, 1780, June 12, 1783, February 17, 1786, A. I., 107-3-9.

[43] Aparici to the Council of the Indies, July 19, 1797, A. I., 107-3-9.

An examination of a few typical accounts of this department will show that the sums involved were always considerable. On June 6, 1767, the *juez de difuntos* in Manila had 45,563 pesos on hand; on June 17, 1781, 31,009 pesos; on June 29, 1783, 27,636 pesos; on July 28, 1801, 40,827 pesos (see reports of various *jueces de difuntos*. A. I. 107-3-9). The total receipts of the office of *juez de difuntos* in Manila for the year terminating January 25, 1819, were 10,750 pesos. Payments against the fund that year were 27,747 pesos, which were made possible by a balance on hand at the beginning of the year of 52,900 pesos (Report of Vicente de Posadas, *Juez de Difuntos de Manila*, January 25, 1819, A. I., 107-3-9). On March 31, 1828, the funds of this department amounted to 32,657 pesos (A. I., 107-3-9).

[44] The last state galleon left Manila for Mexico in 1811, and the last ship sailed from Acapulco to Manila in 1815 (Foreman, *Philippine Islands*, 243; and Montero y Vidal, *Historia general*, II, 413, note. The galleon service was suppressed by decree of the Cortes, September 14, 1813.—*Ibid*, 412.

and the *juez de difuntos* over the question of the special military jurisdiction of the latter, and the claim of the *juez de difuntos* to administer the property of military and galleon officials. For example, on July 6, 1757, the *juez* appealed to the Council for jurisdiction over the property of a deceased galleon official on the basis of the rights conceded to him by the laws of the Indies;[45] the governor claimed the right to administer this property on the ground that the galleon officials were appointed by him, and that they were held by the laws of the Indies to be under the military jurisdiction. This case was decided in favor of the *juez de difuntos,* and may be considered as having established a precedent for his subsequent jurisdiction over such cases.[46]

Probably the most notable case of conflict between the civil and military jurisdictions and one which involved the *juez de difuntos* occurred at the time of the death of the lieutenant-governor and king's lieutenant, Pedro Sarrio. The latter had left his property by will to his brother, the Marqués de Algorja, a resident of Alicante. He had appointed a resident of Manila as executor. The governor claimed that the right to administer the property belonged to the executor. The *juez de difuntos,* on the ground that Sarrio had left heirs in Spain, contended that the funds should be administered by him, as the executor did not have authority to transmit the property to Spain. This case was carried to the Council of the Indies; no record appears of its ultimate solution, but it is illustrative of the commonly accepted principle that the *juez de difuntos* should have authority over the administration of all property which had to be transmitted to Spain for distribution

---

45 *Recopilación,* 2–32–7.

46 Villacorta to the Council of the Indies, July 6, 1757, A. I., 106–4–15. The evidence of this case also exists in A. I., 107–3–9, and is cited in connection with a later dispute of the same character.

among heirs.[47]   The governor's contention against it was based
on the fact that Sarrio was a military official.   As we have already seen, the law of August 29, 1798, authorized the settlement of the property of soldiers by special military courts.[48]

Other sources of frequent dispute were the respective
claims of the *juez de difuntos* and the *oficiales reales* for jurisdiction over property left by persons who were indebted to
the royal treasury at the time of their death.   On the occasion
of the death of the *corregidores* of Tondo and Ilocos, in 1776 and
1778, respectively, without having made wills, the *oficiales reales*
took steps to make an immediate seizure of the property of the
deceased officials.   They demanded that all documents and papers
pertaining to the cases should be surrendered at once into their
hands in order that the amount owing to the government might
be collected.   Governor Basco y Vargas interposed on the ground
that since these officials had died intestate, the settlement of
their property should be effected by the *juez de difuntos;* it
being incumbent upon the *oficiales reales* to present the claims
to the judge.[49]

Shortly after this decision had been rendered, the *alcalde
mayor* of Tayabas died, leaving a deficit of 7000 pesos, and the
officials of the royal treasury immediately brought suit in the
audiencia on the basis of the laws of the Indies for jurisdiction in the case prior to that of the *juez de difuntos*.   They
alleged that the law provided that the treasury officials should
have precedence in collections, and that debts due to the *real
hacienda* should be settled prior to all others.   Moreover, they
claimed that all officials should assist them in making these
collections and that no restrictions should be placed upon their
activities.   Further evidence in support of the contentions of

---

[47] Marquina to the Council of the Indies, June 18, 1790, A. I.,
107–5–18.
[48] *Recopilación*, 2–32, note 2.
[49] *Ibid.*, 5–12–14.   Basco y Vargas to the King, June 6, 1778, A. I.,
105–2–9.

the treasury officials was submitted in the substance of the royal *cédula* of April 23, 1770, which declared that these judges should be entrusted exclusively with the collection of royal funds. "Furthermore," the *cédula* stated, "if any case shall arise which pertains to finance and at the same time to the *juez de difuntos,* the latter may not make the advocation, because, however favorable may be his jurisdiction, that of the royal treasury is more favorable."[50] The *oficiales reales* insisted that they should not be required to go before the *juez de difuntos* for any purpose, since the laws of the Indies[51] gave them the power of inspecting the accounts of the *juez de difuntos* and of keeping and administering these funds.[52] The more recent *cédula* of October 13, 1780, had decreed that the accounts of the *juez de difuntos* should be approved by the treasury officials, and on this basis they were able to advance claims to seniority.

This dispute, though brought for adjudication before the audiencia, was not settled by the tribunal. The evidence pertaining to the case was collected and referred to the Council on December 22, 1786. The *cédula* which finally disposed of the matter was issued May 4, 1794, in the following terms:

It is indisputable that the ministers of our *real hacienda* are authorized to have jurisdiction over all debtors of my royal treasury . . . with preference to the ordinary jurisdiction of the *juez de difuntos,* or to the judge commissioned to settle property of intestates or to pay creditors; . . . the accounts of my *real hacienda* shall be settled by my royal judges before the *juez de difuntos* may have cognizance.[53]

By this decree it was definitely established that the treasury officials should have precedence over the regular judges in the settlements of estates of officials and individuals against whom

---

[50] *Cédulas* of April 23, 1770, October 13, 1780, and May 4, 1794, A. I., 105–2–10.
[51] *Recopilación,* 2–32–28.
[52] *Ibid.,* law 25.
[53] *Cédula* of May 4, 1794, A. I., 105–2–10.

the royal treasury had claims. After the demands of the government were paid, those of private individuals might be settled, and it was ordered that the *juez de difuntos,* as the champion·of individual claims, should always give precedence to the *oficiales reales* who represented the interests of the government.

The organization for the administration of these funds presented a complete hierarchy. The actions of the *juez de difuntos* were subject to review by the Audiencia of Manila. The funds from the Philippines were deducted from the subsidy at Acapulco, and forwarded to the *Casa de Contratación* of Seville (or the *juez de arribadas* at Cádiz, after 1790) by the *juez de difuntos* of Mexico. The heirs in Spain were then found, and the money transferred to them, less discounts covering costs of transmission to Spain. In case appeals were made from the decision or settlement of the *juez de difuntos,* the records of his proceedings in the case under consideration were reviewed by the Council of the Indies. The method of procedure there was to refer these documents and accounts to the *Contaduría General,* where all accounts for the Council were audited and settled, and the recommendations of that tribunal were accepted. The constitutional reforms of the nineteenth century gave the audiencia increased authority in the final settlement of these matters, and its decision was made final in practically all contentious cases, though, of course, final judgments involving heirs who were resident in Spain might still be appealed by them to the Council of the Indies or the Supreme Tribunal of Justice.

Aside from the activities of the magistrates as members of the *juntas de hacienda,* described earlier in this chapter, it would perhaps be safe to assert that the tribunal exercised general supervision over financial affairs in the colony until the time of the establishment of the intendancy (1785-87). Correspondence between the Council of the Indies and the

Audiencia of Manila would seem to indicate that the magistrates were expected to transmit, and did send, in fact, reports on colonial finances to the Council of the Indies. Among the reports of the *oidores* about twenty of these periodical statements have been found, covering irregularly the period from 1609 to 1780. No doubt a complete set exists. These generally embody a detailed audit of the accounts of the *oficiales reales*. Numerous commissions were also sent to the audiencia from time to time, ordering the magistrates to give special attention to financial affairs, such as the collection of licenses from Chinese; to see that tithes were efficiently collected and reported, to see that the tax on metals (mined) was paid, and offering special rewards in case of apprehension. It has already been shown that the king on August 8, 1609, asked the audiencia whether the king's fifth had been commuted to a tenth in the Philippines. On July 21, 1756, the audiencia reported on the number of ships that had entered the harbor of Manila during the year before. On May 4, 1760, Francisco Leandro de Viana, the *fiscal*, charged the merchants of Manila with wholesale fraud in the payment of the *almojarifazgo*, paying only 3% when the law of 1714, then in force, had ordered the payment of 8%. Viana's report charged the *oidores* with responsibility for this deliberate violation of the law, alleging that the *oidores* had been profiting thereby. It was on this occasion that the *fiscal* recommended the establishment of a *consulado* at Manila, which would remove from the magistrates of the audiencia all temptation to use their positions for private profit in violation of the commercial laws of the realm.[54] The part played by the magistrates in the administration of the trade with Acapulco may also be mentioned here. This will be discussed in a subsequent chapter.[55]

---

[54] A. I., 106–4–17; 108–3–17; 105–2–10 to 32. See Bibliography under "Manuscripts used."

[55] The author has at his disposal abundant data for each subject

Apart from the extra duties and commissions already noted, the audiencia was utilized for a variety of purposes which are too miscellaneous to be classified, but too important to be omitted from this discussion. Duplicates of executive orders relating to subjects far removed from the jurisdiction of the audiencia as a court, were sent to it, with instructions that the tribunal take note of numerous matters, such as seeing that the laws were properly executed, observing the effect of reforms, and reporting on their availability and adaptability at various times and places. Copies of new laws relating to civil and ecclesiastical affairs were sent to the audiencia for its information.

The above practices were never more prominently evident than during the constitutional reforms from 1810 to 1823.[56] That period, of course, was a time of change and stress, and the audiencia seems to have been regarded as the one stable authority in the Philippines. *Cédulas* and executive orders were issued to the audiencia without regard to the department of government to which they applied. By the *cédula* of June 14, 1811, the audiencia was made responsible for the execution of all the orders of the superior government. On March 18, 1812, oaths of all civil and judicial officials were ordered to be administered by the audiencia. A royal order was received by the Audiencia of Manila on January 19, 1813, which forbade the existence of free-masonry in the Islands. The audiencia was made responsible for the execution of all these *cédulas* and decrees. On August 6, 1813, the tribunal acknowledged

---

covering each decade and century, showing that the powers mentioned were characteristic throughout. It is to be hoped that the reader will appreciate the impossibility of giving more than a few citations for each case, not because they are not available, but because there is not room for them. It was the writer's original plan to write two additional chapters, one on the commercial duties of the audiencia, and another on the financial powers. Because of a lack of space these chapters have been omitted.

[56] A. I., 106–4–18.

receipt of the law of April 25, 1810, which forbade foreigners to land in the Islands without passports. The audiencia was again made responsible for the execution of the reforms of 1812, 1815, 1823, 1834, and 1835, by which the entire administrative and judicial systems of the colony were reorganized.

The conduct of officials was continually under the observation of the *oidores,* and special reports were frequently sent to the Council from the audiencia in review of the progress of the government in general, or in elucidation of some special phase of it.[55] A few more examples of these investigations which were charged upon the *oidores* may be reviewed here, together with the reports made by the magistrates in compliance with royal instructions.

The king, on August 9, 1609, wrote to the audiencia, asking for information concerning the truth of a certain report which had come to him regarding a custom practiced among the natives before the arrival of the Spaniards, and which was said still to be in operation. It had been asserted that the children of a free man and a slave woman would be half-slave and half-free, and the progeny of these children by subsequent marriage would be classed as a fourth, an eighth, or a sixteenth slave or free. It was said that the natives recognized varying degrees of freedom and slavery. The king, in the letter above referred to, expressed a desire to know the truth of these reports, and he ordered the audiencia to instruct him fully concerning these alleged practices and customs. He called attention to the existing law which forbade Spaniards to hold slaves, and he requested information as to how great a hold this barbarous custom had upon the natives, and how it might be eradicated with the least possible inconvenience and loss.[56]

---

55 As noted in the preceding chapter.

56 King to the Audiencia, August 8, 1609, A. I., 105–2–1.

The audiencia was required to submit data regularly concerning the religious orders, showing the number of friars belonging to each order and designating the provinces that were held by each. The tribunal was often asked to make recommendations for the regulation of the religious. As we shall note in a subsequent chapter, one of the regular duties of the audiencia was to send in a yearly report on the number of religious arriving in or departing from the Islands. The tribunal had jurisdiction over the royal colleges and universities; it exercised supervision over courses of study and instruction given in them, and the *oidores* reported concerning these matters from time to time.

The audiencia kept the court informed as to the number of Spaniards in the Islands, the occupation of each, and his attitude toward the government. It reported on the number of Chinese and other foreigners in the Islands, the amount of tribute paid by the Chinese, and the extent of the Chinese trade. From time to time the magistrates were asked by the court to make special reports on these or other subjects. They were required to report from time to time on the number and services of the officials of the government, major and subordinate, whether they were all needed, the quality of their services, and what reforms could be made to effect greater economy and efficiency. The audiencia was especially charged with the duty of seeing that the provincial officials were not so numerous as to be a burden on the natives. The government realized that oppression of the Indians would result from the presence of too many Spaniards among them, and the effort was continually made to limit the number of these undesirables. The audiencia, in short, was the representative of the king in all these matters.

On several occasions the audiencia assumed the initiative, or assisted materially, in the accomplishment of various functions of an extraordinary character. It played an important

role in checking the epidemic of smallpox which ravaged the
Islands from 1790 to 1794. On January 18, 1790, Governor
Marquina reported that this disease had been playing havoc
with the Indians in various parts of the Islands.[57] He had
raised 2385 pesos by voluntary contributions from different
officials and corporations, and had appointed a committee to
administer the funds. This committee consisted of representatives of the different religious communities and the *consulado,*
the archbishop, the chief of the *contaduría,* the *fiscal,* the
regent and the magistrates of the audiencia. Soon after this
letter was written Marquina's *residencia* was taken, and the
king, on January 24, 1794, wrote to the regent, asking him to
act as executive of the general committee already appointed to
conduct the campaign against this epidemic, and to report
what progress had been made in combatting it, suggesting
that a general committee of sanitation should be constituted to
handle such cases in the future.[58]

In the *cédula* of November 26, 1765, we find another illustration of the extraordinary functions of the magistrates of the
audiencia. The governor was ordered on this occasion to appoint a committee to consider ways and means of remedying
the damage done to agriculture and commerce in the Islands
as a result of the depredations of the English upon their
occupation of various parts of the Islands. This committee
was to consist of the *fiscal* as president, the *oidores,* the chief
of the *contaduría,* the *alcaldes ordinarios* of the city, and the.
alcaldes mayores of the districts immediately outside the city.
It was ordered to meet at stated periods to discuss and recommend ways and means of improvement, proper taxation,
and other measures calculated to bring about a revival of agriculture. This committee was the forerunner of the *Sociedad*

---

[57] Marquina to the King, January 18, 1790, A. I., 105–2–10.
[58] King to the Regent of Manila, January 24, 1794, *ibid.*

de Amigos del País, which was established during the administration of Governor José Basco y Vargas.[59]

The variety of the functions of the audiencia is well illustrated by a report made on July 20, 1757, in compliance with
a royal order of inquiry as to how much money should be
expended by the Philippine government on the inauguration
ceremonies of the governor.[60] Besides noting an added duty
of the tribunal, this is illustrative of the pomp and ceremony
utilized to impress the inhabitants of the colonies with the
grandeur of Spain and her government. After a lengthy investigation, the audiencia stated. in reply that the government
of Perú had been authorized to spend 12,000 pesos in the
reception of a viceroy, while New Spain could spend 8000
pesos. As much as 4000 pesos had been spent in Manila in
times past. Since the Philippines was a colony of less importance than these, and the governor there was of inferior
rank to the viceroy, and as even these sums were extravagant,
it was the opinion of the tribunal that the government at
Manila should limit itself to an expenditure of 2000 pesos.
This may be considered as an example of the work accomplished by the *oidores* in checking the excesses of the other
officials and departments of the government.[61]

The audiencia had general authority over the inspection and
censorship of books which were printed in the colony or imported. This power was conceded by a series of laws promulgated at different times from 1556 to 1668.[62] At the earlier

---

59 See, *Plan económico del gobernador de Filipinas José Basco y
Vargas, 1 de Septre, 1779, y carta que lo acompaña, No. 157, de 11 de
Dicre de 1779* (printed); A. I., 106–1–14; see Barrows, *History of the
Philippines,* 242.

60 Memorial of July 20, 1757, A. I., 106–4–15.

61 See Moses, *South America on the eve of emancipation,* 27–31,.
for an account of the festivities and formalities at the installation
of the viceroy at Lima. It will be noted that the audiencia played
an important part in the ceremonies. Professor Moses here utilizes.
a description contained in Juan y Ulloa, *Voyage,* II, 46–50.

62 *Recopilación,* 1–24–1 to 15.

date it was ordered that no book treating of the Indies should be printed without first having been inspected, approved, and licensed by the Council of the Indies, and none could be introduced into the Indies without the express permission of that body.[63] Books of fables and other profane publications were not allowed in the colonies under any circumstances. The Council of the Indies, by enactment of May 8, 1584, authorized the audiencia to publish books and dictionaries in the native dialects, and a later law stipulated that twenty copies of each book should be sent to the Council of the Indies to be placed on file there.[64] The *oidores* and the *oficiales reales* whose duty it was to inspect the ships which arrived from New Spain were ordered to search for forbidden and heretical books, but in doing this they must act in conformity with the expurgatories of the Inquisition.[65] By *cédula* of October 10, 1575, and of December 2, 1580, the right to print books of prayer and of divine service for Spain and the Indies was conceded to the monastery of San Lorenzo. This same *cédula* ordered that viceroys, presidents, and *oidores* should see that no other service-books were used in the churches and monasteries, and that books printed by any other agency should not be permitted to enter the Islands.[66]

In conformity with the above regulations, the Audiencia of Manila, on July 21, 1787, suppressed a book which had been written by the commissary of the Inquisition, on the ground that this functionary had published it on the authority of the archbishop alone, and without authorization of the Council of the

---

[63] *Ibid.*, 1 and 2.

[64] *Ibid.*, 3; 15. The *cédula* of October 10, 1752, gave to the audiencia the right to authorize the publication of legal treatises, ordinances and enactments. The regent was given control over this matter by the *Instrucción* of June 20, 1776 (A. I., 106–212). See Montero y Vidal, *Historia general*, III, 304 and 485, with reference to the publication of the *autos acordados* of 1866.

[65] *Ibid.*, 7 and 12.

[66] *Ibid.*, 8.

Indies, as was required by law. The case was appealed by the commissary to the Council, and the latter body, while approving the action of the audiencia in suppressing the book, and reprimanding the archbishop, after an examination of the volume, allowed its publication in conformity with the laws of the Indies.[67] Taken together, the relations of the audiencia and the commissary of the Inquisition in most matters, and particularly in the publication of books, were harmonious, and the same strife and trouble did not occur in the Philippines that developed in Mexico, Naples, and Perú over the question.[68]

On January 26, 1816, the audiencia forbade the publication of any book without its express permission.[69] As a result, considerable trouble arose with the governor and the *fiscal,* neither of whom had been consulted when the *auto* was passed. The *fiscal* contended that the audiencia was violating the law which had reserved to the Council the power to give licenses for the publication of books; moreover, it was asserted, the law required the governor and audiencia to act in *acuerdo* in matters pertaining to the suppression and licensing of books, the tribunal not being authorized to proceed alone. The audiencia contended in reply that these laws could no longer be interpreted to mean that the governor should have authority over matters of a purely judicial nature, such as these were, because he was no longer president of the audiencia, and hence not a judicial official.[70] The tribunal furthermore based its

---

[67] *Ibid.,* 1 and 2.

[68] See Lea, *The Inquisition in the Spanish dependencies,* 70, 204, 265; 444–446.

[69] *Acuerdo* of January 26, 1816, A. I., 106–4–19.

[70] The constitutional reforms of 1812 included the separation of the governorship from the presidency of the audiencia. In 1814 the governor was again made president, and the offices were not entirely separated until 1861. The governor's intervention in matters of justice was merely nominal, however, after the creation of the office of regent, in 1776.—*Cédula* of March 11, 1776, A. I., 106–2–12; Royal Instruction to Regents, June 20, 1776, in Rodríguez San Pedro, VII, 22–23; *Ordenanzas para el gobierno de la Audiencia de Manila. 9 de Octubre, 1812;* A. I., 106–4–19; *Acuerdo de 15 de Enero, 1814, ibid.*

contention on two enactments—one, a royal order dated October 1, 1770, which directed certain prelates to apply to the audiencia for permission to have a religious work published, and the other, dated July 21, 1787, already cited, by which the king confirmed the refusal of the audiencia to allow the publication of a work prepared by the commissary of the Inquisition, when he had failed to seek the authority of the audiencia. It is clear, however, that on this occasion the audiencia was guilty of deliberate misinterpretation of the law in its own favor. The Council of the Indies had the final right to decide as to the contents of the book, and the audiencia merely suspended publication, pending the action of the Council. The audiencia was never given the power to pass finally on the contents of books, except those dealing with languages and dialects. The ultimate right of passing on all religious publications was retained by the Council of the Indies, while the audiencia was authorized merely to suspend the publication and circulation of books which had not complied with the above royal ordinances. After the suppression of the Council of the Indies and the establishment of the Supreme Tribunal of Justice, there was a tendency toward giving the colonial governments a wider degree of latitude in such matters.

It has been noted already, in the *cédula* of October 9, 1812, and in subsequent reforms, that all matters of a contentious nature should be settled in the audiencias and not carried to the tribunal in Spain. A further reform in the censorship of books was made on October 4, 1839, when the control of these matters was placed in the hands of two censors, appointed by the *acuérdo* and the archbishop, respectively. In case a decision were made to suppress a certain book, a legal proceeding had to be instituted before the *fiscal*, who became the arbiter if a disagreement arose between the censors. Seizure was justified on the grounds that the publication contained something contrary to the legitimate interests of the throne or of the religion. Condemned books were not only seized, but sent from the colony.[71] The responsibilities of censorship were thus shared until October 7, 1856, when, on account of the many disagreements which had arisen as a result of this divided authority, the superior government decreed that a standing board of censors should be created, to consist of eight members, four to be appointed by the archbishop and four by the governor. This board was to be presided over by the *fiscal* of the audiencia.[72]

Among other important functions of a non-judicial character was the audiencia's duty of keeping the archives of the government. The tribunal had a number of records in which entries were made concerning its work.[73] A registry was kept of the votes of the *oidores* in suits involving a hundred thousand *maravedís* or more. Further, separate records were kept of all resolutions of the *acuerdo* relative to government and finance, respectively, Thursday afternoon of each week being devoted to the latter. Likewise, a book of *cédulas* and royal provisions was kept by the audiencia, and on the basis of these the tribunal formed all judgments and gave advice when requested. Separate files were kept for copies of all royal orders, *cédulas* and letters, one for secret, and the other for open correspondence. In another volume an account was kept of the amounts received from fines and from funds liquidated for the expenses of justice. As already stated, lists were also maintained of all persons residing in the colony, with an account of their quality and work, their attitude toward the government, their occupation, and, if they were officials, the nature and character of their services.[74] The audiencia kept a

---

[71] Montero y Vidal, III, 30.

[72] *Ibid.*, 251.

[73] *Recopilación*, 2-15-156 to 166.

[74] On the basis of this the governor compiled and sent to Spain a yearly report on the work of the magistrates, prosecutors, and subalterns of the audiencia, setting forth the salaries paid and character of services rendered, making recommendations for promotion or complaints against these officials. Vacancies in the tribunal were reported at the same time and in the same manner.

book of *residencias,* which has been described in a former chapter. Also records of persons coming to and leaving the Islands, with appropriate entries concerning them, were preserved in this archive.

Besides the special duties of the *oidores* indicated in this chapter, there were others which will be described later in more detail. The *residencia* has been already treated. Other duties will be noted in connection with the relation of the audiencia and the governor. Some are more closely related to the religious and the ecclesiastical institutions of the colony, and merit special treatment in that connection. The audiencia, moreover, had extensive functions in relation to the commercial and economic life of the colony. A fuller comprehension of these numerous activities may be gained in the following chapters where they are discussed in connection with two of the most powerful factors in the colony's life—the governor and the church.

CHAPTER VI

THE AUDIENCIA AND THE GOVERNOR: GENERAL RELATIONS

The audiencia was brought into closer and more frequent relationship with the governor than with any other authority in the colony. The governor was president of the royal audiencia and hence was nominally its chief magistrate. This brought him into touch with its functions as a court. The governor was chief executive of the colony, and in that capacity was responsible for administrative, financial, and military affairs. It will be noted that the audiencia, in various ways, exercised powers of intervention in all of these matters.

The official title of the governor of the Philippines up to 1861 was governor, captain-general, and president of the royal audiencia,[1] a combination of three important functions. In his capacity as governor, he was chief executive of the civil government, with authority over all administrative departments, including finance, and over ecclesiastical affairs. As

---

[1] *Recopilación*, 2–15–11. Note the brief discussion of this relationship in Smith, *The viceroy of New Spain*, 152–156. Dr. Smith shows that the chief purpose of the Spanish government in establishing the viceroy and audiencia together was to guarantee a check and balance of one upon the other. Quoting Revilla Gigedo (*Instruction*, Article 20), he says: "The presidency of the *audiencia* places the viceroy at the head of that body but not to give orders to it, as even his acts in matters of justice are subject to it; and although he is present at its sessions, which is very difficult, considering the grave and continuous occupations which so vast a command imposes upon him, he does not have a vote in matters which are regularly dealt with there—that is, matters of justice." Dr. Smith shows (162) that the effect of the later laws of the eighteenth century was to deprive "the viceroys absolutely of any part in the procedure of the administration of justice, either alone or in company with the other judges, voting with them in the audiencia" (from Revilla Gigedo, *Instruction*, Article 64). The limitation of the governor of the Philippines in legal matters is discussed further on in this chapter.

captain-general, the governor was commander-in-chief of the military forces, with the special duty of providing for the defense of the Islands. As president of the audiencia, the governor retained his authority as executive while entering the field of the judiciary. Though he could not act as judge, himself, nevertheless we have seen in former chapters that he exercised extensive authority over the tribunal, its procedure, and its magistrates.

It will accordingly be our aim in this chapter to discuss the general relations of the audiencia and the governor. These include administrative, financial, and ecclesiastical functions, and those involving the government of the provinces. To these will be added such further observations as remain to be made concerning the judicial relations of the governor and audiencia, leaving apart for discussion in another chapter as an integral subject, the military jurisdiction and the respective participation of the audiencia and the governor in the matter of defense.

Generally speaking, the governor of the Philippines occupied the same relative position, within and without the colony, as did the viceroy in New Spain, and during the greater part of the history of the Islands he was independent of the government of New Spain and was responsible to the Spanish court directly, in the same manner as the viceroy.[2] The independence of the Philippine government may be said to have been practically complete, with such exceptions as will be men-

---

[2] See Moses, *Establishment of Spanish rule in America*, 70–71.

Philip III ordered the viceroy of New Spain to "give aid to the governor and captain-general of the Philippines in whatever may occur, and above all . . . to send him on demand whatever may seem necessary of arms, men, munitions, and money for the conservation of those Islands, salaries, and *presidios*, and other matters under his care (*Recopilación*, 3–4–13)." The viceroys also exercised a certain degree of authority over the despatch of the galleons from Acapulco (*ibid.*, 9–45–25 to 31, 47, 74 to 76). Aside from the points indicated, the Philippines were normally as independent of New Spain as the latter was independent of the Philippines.

tioned in a subsequent chapter, treating of the *ad interim* rule, after the re-establishment of the audiencia in 1598. The governor was the chief administrative official of the colony, and the provincial governments derived their authority from him; he was the royal vice-patron, and in this capacity he bore the same relation to the church in the colony as the king did to the church in Spain. Likewise as the king was the theoretical head of the state, and was limited and assisted in the exercise of his authority over the empire by the Council of the Indies, so the governor and captain general of the Philippines (and the viceroy in New Spain and Perú) was the head of the colony, and was limited by the audiencia. The audiencias of all the colonies were equally dependent on the Council of the Indies.

Professor Bourne very aptly characterizes the office of governor of the Philippines and its relations to the audiencia. He writes:

The Philippine Islands were constituted a kingdom and placed under the charge of a governor and captain general, whose powers were truly royal and limited only by the check imposed by the Supreme Court (the *Audiencia*) and by the ordeal of the *residencia* at the expiration of his term of office. Among his extensive prerogatives was his appointing power which embraced all branches of the civil service in the islands. He also was *ex officio* the President of the *Audiencia*. His salary was $8000 a year, but his income might be largely augmented by gifts or bribes. The limitations upon the power of the Governor imposed by the *Audiencia*, in the opinion of the French astronomer Le Gentil, were the only safeguard against an arbitrary despotism, yet Zúñiga, a generation later pronounced its efforts in this direction generally ineffectual.[3]

Juan José Delgado, who gives us perhaps the most comprehensive and realistic survey of the Philippines of any of the ecclesiastical historians of those Islands, describes the nature of the office of governor as follows:

The governors of these Islands have absolute authority to provide and to attend to all that pertains to the royal estate, government,

---

[3] Bourne, "Historical introduction," Blair and Robertson, I, 49–50.

war; they have consultations in different matters with the *oidores* of the royal audiencia; they try in the first instance the criminal causes of the soldiers, and they appoint *alcaldes, corregidores*, deputy and chief justices of all the Islands for the exercise of government, justice, war, . . . and besides many other preëminences conceded by royal decrees to the presidency of the royal audiencia and chancery.[4]

The governors of these Islands [he wrote] are almost absolute, and are like private masters of them. They exercise supreme authority, by reason of their charge, for receiving and sending embassies to the neighboring kings and tyrants, . . . they can make peace, make and declare war, and take vengeance on those who insult us, without awaiting any resolution from the Court for it. Therefore many kings have rendered vassalage and paid tribute to the governors, have recognized them as their superiors, have respected and feared their arms, have solicited their friendship, and have tried to procure friendly relations and commerce with them; and those who have broken their word with them have been punished.[5]

The governor of the Philippines, like the viceroy of New Spain, was the administrative head of the colony, and as such exercised supervision over all the departments of the government, likewise over ecclesiastical affairs. He was directed to devote himself to the service of God, and to labor for the welfare of the souls of the natives and inhabitants of the provinces, governing them in peace and quietude, endeavoring to bring about their spiritual and moral uplift and their numerical increase. The governors (or viceroys) were instructed by the laws of the Indies

---

[4] Delgado, *Historia de Filipinas*, 212–215.

[5] Delgado illustrates this statement as follows: "The legitimate King of Borney, who had been dispossessed of his kingdom . . . begged for help from Don Francisco Sande, Governor of these Islands. Governor Sande went with his fleet, fought with and drove away the tyrant, and put the legitimate king in possession; the latter rendered obedience to the governor, appointed in the place of the King of España, and subjected himself to this crown as vassal and tributary." Further on he writes, "His Majesty also ordered Sande, by a decree of April 9, 1586, to sustain friendship with China, and forbade him to make war; for, as some authors say, Sande had the intention of conquering that Empire, . . . although it may be said that the idea was simply speculative; the Council forbade it, and ordered him thenceforth to observe what was prescribed" (*ibid.*, see Blair and Robertson, XVII, 317–320, whose translation differs slightly from the above).

to provide all things which are convenient for the administration
and execution of justice, . . . to maintain the government and defense
of their districts, exercising very special care for the good treatment,
conservation and augmentation of the Indians, and especially the collection, administration, account and care of the royal exchequer.

They were instructed, in short, to do all for the provinces
under their charge[6] that the king, himself, might do. The
laws of the Indies ordered the audiencia, the religious authorities and the civil officials to acknowledge the governor [or
viceroy] as their chief. The laws emphasized as the special
duties of the governor the supervision and augmentation of the
finances, the defense of the colony, and general supervision
over all officials, executive and judicial, central and provincial.

Foremost among the responsibilities of the executive was that
of supervising the administration of the colonial exchequer.
In this, however, he was assisted by the audiencia. The customary *oficiales reales* were among the first officials created for
the Philippine government, and they were responsible to the
governor. At the time of the creation of the audiencia, it was
ordered that the governor and two *oidores* should audit the
accounts of the *oficiales reales*, but this power was transferred to
Governor Dasmariñas when the audiencia was removed in 1589.
In 1602 the right of inspection of accounts was returned to the
oidores,[7] but the governor, it was stated, as executive head of
the government, was responsible, and he exercised direct intervention in these matters, limited only by the annual inspection of
the *oidores*. During the greater part of the history of the Islands
the governor exercised supervision over the collection and the
administration of the public revenue, in accordance with the
law,[8] and he was required to be present at the weekly
meetings of the *junta de hacienda*, of which two magistrates

---

[6] *Recopilación*, 3-3-2; 63, 64; 3-14-1, 33.

[7] Instructions to Acuña, February 16, 1602, Blair and Robertson,
XI, 273-4.

[8] *Recopilación*, 3-3-55; 3-2-33.

were members, there to pass on all financial measures and to
authorize expenditures.[9] The governor had control over the sale
of offices, jointly with the *oficiales reales,* but from the correspondence on these subjects it is clear that the audiencia was
designed to check the governor's authority in that particular.[10]
The governor was forbidden to authorize extraordinary expenditures from the treasury without express royal permission, except
in cases of riot, or invasion.[11] This regulation was almost impossible of faithful execution, and as his duties increased and
became more complicated, the governor was unable to give as
complete attention to these matters as the laws of the Indies
prescribed.   Although the governor had these financial powers,
he could not decide cases appealed from the *oficiales reales.*
These were regarded as contentious cases and as such were
resolved by the audiencia.[12]   In Mexico and Lima, wherein there
were higher tribunals of accounts than in Manila (*contaduría
mayor*), the audiencia did not have this jurisdiction.

From 1784 to 1787 the governor was temporarily deprived
of the leadership in financial matters by virtue of the Ordinance
of Intendants, but the *oidores* retained membership in the
colonial board of audits, together with the intendant, who had
taken the governor's former place as the responsible head of
the colony's finances.   In 1787 the governor was restored to his
former position with respect to the exchequer, with the official
title of *superintendente subdelegado de real hacienda.*   It is
sufficient to say that the governor's relation to this new department did not materially lessen the authority of the audiencia with regard to the finances of the colony.

Although the appointing power was claimed by many gov-

---

[9] *Ibid.,* 3-3-56; 2-15-159.
[10] King to the Audiencia, December 4, 1777, A. I., 105-2-9.   It was
seen in the preceding chapter, that the audiencia reported to the
Council of the Indies on the finances of the colony.
[11] *Recopilación,* 3-3-57.
[12] *Ibid.,* 2-15-76 and 77.

ernors as their sole prerogative, the audiencia imposed a very decided check on their exercise of this authority. The governor had the right to make appointments in all departments of the government, except in certain so-called offices of royal designation, to which the governor made tentative appointments, subject to subsequent royal confirmation.[13] Although the law of February 8, 1610, exempted appointments made by the governor of the Philippines from the necessity of royal confirmation,[14] in practice these nominations were sent to the court for approval in the same manner as were those from Spain's other colonies.

The audiencia intervened in the matter of appointments in two ways. In case it succeeded to the government on the death of the governor the tribunal exercised all the prerogatives of appointment.[15] When the governor was present he was obliged to refer the names of all candidates to the *acuerdo*.[16] This was made necessary because the governor, being new to the Islands and unfamiliar with local conditions, was not so well fitted to pass upon the merits of candidates for office as were the *oidores* who had become permanently identified with the interests of the colony and whose opinion was of weight in these matters. Thus it came about that the audiencia exercised joint authority with the governor in making appointments.[17] The question of the relative authority of the audiencia and governor in making appointments was a source of conflict throughout the history of the Islands.

When the governor submitted the name of a candidate to the *acuerdo* it was the duty of the magistrates to furnish all

---

13 *Ibid.*, 3–2–1 to 6; 2–15–172. Governors and viceroys were authorized by the *cédula* of April 20, 1776, to make permanent appointments to offices whose salaries did not exceed 400 pesos (*ibid.*, 3–2, note 2).

14 *Ibid.*, 3–2–67.

15 *Ibid.*, 3–2–1, 10 to 12, 47, 48; 8–4–24.

16 *Ibid.*, 3–2–8.

17 Villacorta to the King, July 6, 1767, A. I., 106–4–15.

the information possible regarding the character. fitness, and ability of the person under consideration for the position. If the audiencia and the governor should disagree and the latter still persisted in an appointment, it was the duty of the audiencia to submit, forwarding all evidence relative to the candidate to the Council of the Indies, the latter body ultimately taking such action as it deemed best. When the nominations of the governor reached the Council of the Indies for confirmation, that tribunal relied extensively upon information furnished by the audiencia concerning the candidates under consideration.

As already stated, the king retained the right to appoint certain so-called "officials of royal designation." These varied at different times, but, in general, included *corregidores, alcaldes mayores, oficiales reales, oidores,* regents, and, of course, viceroys, governors, and captains-general.[18] All these officials, except those last named, could be temporarily designated by the executive. Although the law placed *corregidores, alcaldes mayores,* and *oficiales reales* in this category, their designation by the court, like the confirmation of *encomiendas,* was usually nominal. Many of these offices were filled in Spain and Mexico, while some appointees were named from the Philippines, and probably in the majority of the latter cases the royal appointment merely amounted to a confirmation of a temporary appointment made by the governor. The post of governor of the Philippines was filled temporarily by the viceroy of New Spain until about 1720. In the same manner the governor of Ternate was named by the Philippine executive, with the advice and consent of the audiencia. These *ad interim* appointments were valid until the king made them regular by confirmation, or sent persons from Spain to hold them permanently.

When a vacancy occurred among the offices of royal desig-

---

18 *Recopilación*, 3–2–3, 4 and note, 21, 22, 47, 70; 5–2–5, 7, 8–4–1.

nation, it was the governor's duty to forward a list of candidates, or nominees, and from this list the king, or the Council of the Indies in his name, made a permanent appointment.[19] In the meantime a temporary appointment was often made by the governor, in *acuerdo* with the audiencia, and the name of the appointee was placed first on the list remitted to the court. This procedure was followed in the appointment of *encomenderos, corregidores, alcaldes mayores,* and treasury officials. It was seldom done in the cases of *oidores* and *fiscales,* who, because of their special or professional character, were usually sent directly from Spain or from New Spain. Unless there were special reasons to the contrary, for instance, the filing of an adverse report by the audiencia, or a protest on the part of residents, the governor's temporary appointments were usually confirmed and made permanent. Temporary appointees with salaries exceeding 1000 pesos a year only received half-salary until their appointments were confirmed.[20] At least two years and frequently four transpired before the regular appointment arrived, and as the terms were from three to five years for the majority of these offices, the governor's candidate was usually the incumbent a considerable portion of the time, whether his nomination were confirmed or not. Neither relatives nor dependents of governors or *oidores* could be legally appointed to any office.[21] This mandate was often violated, as we shall see. It was the duty of the regent and the *fiscal* to certify to the court that appointees were not relatives of the governor or *oidores.*[22]

In an instruction directed exclusively to the Philippine audiencia, the king ordered the tribunal to see that offices were

---

[19] *Ibid.,* 3–2–1, 2, 3, 8–4–1.

[20] *Ibid.,* 51. After February 20, 1785, this regulation applied only to offices yielding more than 2000 pesos a year.—*Ibid.,* note 17.

[21] *Ibid.,* 27.

[22] *Ibid.,* 33, 38.

bestowed only upon persons "who by fitness or qualifications
are best able to hold them."[23]   It appears that this law, or
another promulgated about the same time, gave to the *fiscal*
and the *oidores* the right to pass on the qualifications of
encomenderos, alcaldes mayores, corregidores, and other minor
officials, on condition that preference should be given to conquerors, settlers, and their descendants.   Governor Alonso Fajardo remonstrated that this new practice hampered the work of
the governor, and created difficulties between him and the
oidores.[24]   A yet later law, dated October 1, 1624, gave the
governor (and viceroy) the right to make temporary appointments of all judicial officials, without the interposition of the
audiencia.[25]   On February 22, 1680, the power of making permanent appointments of *alcaldes mayores* and *corregidores* was
vested in the governor and the audiencia.[26]   In view of this
law, the Audiencia of Manila claimed and actually exercised
authority in the appointment of provincial officials from that
time onward.

Vacancies in the audiencia itself were filled temporarily by
the governor.   In case the audiencia were governing *ad interim*
it could designate magistrates from the outside to try cases,
but the power of the audiencia, as provided by these laws,
was secondary to that of the governor if he were present.
Under no circumstances were permanent appointments to the
audiencia to be made by any authority other than the king and
Council.   In case there were a vacancy in the office of *fiscal*
the junior *oidor* was authorized to fill the place.[27]   Conversely,
it also occurred that when an extra *oidor* was needed, the

---

23 King to the Audiencia, August 9, 1609, A. I., 105–2–1.
24 Fajardo to the King, December 10, 1621, Blair and Robertson.
XX, 138–140.
25 *Recopilación*, 2–15–34; 5–12–24; 2–16–29.
26 *Ibid.*, 2–2–70.
27 *Ibid.*, 3–2–45; 2–16–29.

fiscal might be temporarily designated to fill the place.[28]   It was also ordered that if the *fiscal* could not be spared from his office on account of his numerous and important duties, a lawyer might be named to act as *fiscal ad interim.*[29]   In New Spain an *alcalde del crimen* took the place of the junior *oidor* when the latter occupied the *fiscalía.*   There were no *alcaldes del crimen* in the Philippines, but the *cédula* of February 8, 1610, above cited, was always quoted as furnishing justification for the appointment of *oidores ad interim* by the governor.[30]   In a subsequent chapter we shall refer to several occasions on which this was done; indeed, entire audiencias were re-constituted by certain governors.

The audiencia was required to see that the appointees designated by the governor duly complied with the requirements of *residencia;* likewise that they were properly installed in office, and that they did not serve in offices for which they had neither authority nor qualifications.[31]   Notwithstanding the variety and the conflicting character of the laws bearing on matters of appointment, a careful consideration of law and practice leads to the conclusion that the governor, as chief executive, had the power of making appointments, but in the execution of this duty he was ordered to consult the audiencia, although, strictly speaking, he was not obliged to follow its advice.   If there were good reasons for not appointing an official recommended by the governor, the *oidores* could send representations to the Council of the Indies, setting forth their

---

28 Although a sufficient number of *oidores* were usually present in Manila to suffice for the judicial needs of the audiencia, on many occasions there were only two or three available.   When but few cases were before the tribunal, the junior *oidor* could easily be spared to act as *fiscal.*   However, when a magistrate was needed, owing to the multiplicity of cases to be tried, or the absence of two or more magistrates on special commissions, the need was very urgent, and the *fiscal* was then liable to be called upon to serve.

29 *Recopilación*, 2–16–30.

30 *Ibid.*, 3–2–67.

31 *Ibid.*, 2–15–173 and 174.

objections, and the Council might confirm or nullify the appointment, as it chose. The audiencia could make appointments if it were in temporary charge of the government. The authority which the audiencia exercised in regard to appointments varied according to circumstances. If the governor were new at his post, weak or indulgent, the audiencia exercised more extensive authority than was conceded by the laws. If the governor were experienced, efficient, and a man of strong personality and dominating character, the tribunal exercised less power in regard to appointments, and, in fact, in all other matters pertaining to government.

Closely related to the appointing power was the duty which the governor had of submitting annually to the court a list of all the officials of the colony, with comments on the character of their services, and with recommendations for promotion or dismissal from office.[32] The *oidores* were included in these reports.[33] It was also the function of the governor to report on the administration of justice.[34] The governor was instructed to inform the court in case the *oidores* engaged in forbidden commercial ventures, either directly, through the agency of their wives, or through other intermediaries.[35] He was authorized, moreover, to investigate and report on the public and private conduct of the magistrates and of their wives as well[36] and to exert himself to see that their actions were at all times in consonance with the dignity of their rank and positions and of such a character as would reflect credit on the royal name

---

[32] *Ibid.*, 3–3–70.

[33] *Ibid.*, 3–14–6, 7; Felipe III to Fajardo, December 13, 1620, Blair and Robertson, XIX, 174–175.

[34] *Recopilación*, 3–14–5, 6, 8.

[35] *Ibid.*, 2–16–59, 62 to 64; 3–3–39. A confirmation of the latter was so often reported that it seems to have been expected, and nothing was done about it. It would seem that practically every official in the colony conducted a mercantile business as a side-issue.

[36] Felipe IV to Fajardo, October 9, 1623, Blair and Robertson, XX, 259; *Recopilación*, 2–16–66, 67.

and entitle them to the respect of the residents of the colony. The confidential reports of the governor to the king might include all of these matters, and many others too numerous to mention. On the other hand, the audiencia, as a body, was authorized to direct the attention of the Council to any irregularities of which the governor might be guilty, and thus a system of checks and balances was maintained.[37] However, the *oidores* were forbidden to make charges individually. This injunction was so frequently disregarded that it was practically a deadletter.

Typical of the governor's authority over all the officials of the colony, and incidentally over the *oidores*, was his power to grant or withhold permission to marry within the colony. The earlier laws on this subject absolutely forbade viceroys, presidents, *oidores*, *alcaldes*, or their children to marry within their districts.[38] Deprivation of office and forfeiture of salary were the penalties for infraction of these regulations. These laws were followed by others which required the president (viceroy or governor) to report immediately to the Council the case of any magistrate guilty of violating the law forbidding the marriage of officials.[39] It was not until 1754 that a law was promulgated providing for special marriage dispensations to be granted by the Council of the Indies upon the recommendation of the president of the audiencia.[40] In 1789 the president was authorized to concede permission to accountants and treasury officials, but not to *oidores*.[41] The prohibi-

---

[37] *Recopilación*, 2–15–36, 39, 40.

[38] *Ibid.*, 2–16–82 to 84.

[39] *Ibid.*, 87.

[40] *Ibid.*, 82, note 20 (*Cédula* of January 23, 1754).

[41] *Cédula* of July 13, 1789, A. I., 107–5–20. On June 21, 1784, the Council of the Indies recommended that permission to marry within his district be accorded to Oidor Ciriaco Gonzales Carvajal (A. I., 105–3–2); the same concession was recommended in the case of Oidor Felipe Cisneros, June 30, 1788 (A. I., 105–3–4), and again to Francisco Xavier de Mendieta, January 22, 1791 (A. I., 105–3–5).

tion was applied to magistrates until 1843, and the only condition under which they were permitted to marry within the colony was by virtue of the express permission of the supreme tribunal in Spain. In 1848, the president of the audiencia was authorized to grant marriage licenses to magistrates on condition that the contracting parties were "of equal quality, customs, and of corresponding circumstances," permission having first been obtained from Spain,[42] the president alone passing upon the requisite qualifications.

The chief reason for the restrictions and prohibitions placed on the marriage of magistrates seems to have been the conviction that officers of justice would compromise themselves by marriage, acquiring vast numbers of relatives and dependents, thereby making it impossible to render impartial decisions or administer justice as evenly and dispassionately as they would were they not so familiarly known in their districts. It was also necessary to prevent officials from lowering their dignity by union with natives and half-castes. The marriage of officials with natives of the Philippines was not regarded with favor at any time by the Spanish government.

It seems that the above prohibition did not apply with the same force to *fiscales* as to magistrates. This is illustrated by a case which arose in 1804 when Fiscal Miguel Díaz de Rivera was deprived of his office by royal decree for having married without the permission of the Council of the Indies.[43] The *fiscal* had married the daughter of the *corregidor* of Pangasinán, who was a colonel in the Spanish army. The mother of the girl was a Eurasian from Madras, and had been a subject of Great Britain. Under the date of May 27, 1805, Díaz sent a petition to the king, bearing the endorsement of Governor Aguilar, demanding his restoration to office. Among

---

[42] Royal order of April 3, 1848; Rodríguez San Pedro, *Legislación ultramarina*, VII, 79.

[43] Royal order of December 2, 1804, A. I., 106–4–18.

the reasons cited for the proposed reinstatement of the *fiscal*, it was said that Díaz, being a prosecutor and not a magistrate, was not subject to the same regulations and conditions as the *oidores*, whose judicial duties rendered impossible their marriage within the Islands. Aguilar stated that the purpose of the law had been to debar ministers from making such marriage connections as would diminish the respect which the community should have for them as *oidores* of a royal audiencia, thus undermining their standing as magistrates. In this instance there could have been no case of degradation because of the high standing of the mother and father. Moreover, a *fiscal* could not be regarded as a magistrate, and the same laws did not apply to both classes of officials. As an outcome of these representations Díaz was restored to office by the royal decree of October 13, 1806.[44]

A duty similar to that just noted, inasmuch as it was indicative of the authority of the governor over the *oidores*, was his power to examine and try criminal charges against the magistrates. A law which was in force from 1550 to 1620 ordered that the president should be assisted in the trial of criminal charges against *oidores* by *alcaldes ordinarios*. On September 5, 1620, this law was modified by the enactment of another, which ordered that in cases involving imprisonment, heavy fines, removal from office, or the death penalty, the governor should make the investigation and refer the *autos* to the Council of the Indies for final judgment.

This law still left the trial of *oidores* for misdemeanors in the governor's jurisdiction, but in cases of sedition or notorious offenses which required immediate action in order to furnish a public example for its effect on the natives, the president was required to confer with the audiencia, and to act in accordance with its judgment. By this law the president was forbidden

---

[44] Royal decree of October 13, 1806, A. I., 106–4–18.

to make more than temporary suspensions of *oidores* from their offices. In no case could they be permanent unless first approved by the Council of the Indies.[45] Notwithstanding this law, it may be noted that certain governors went so far on some occasions as to remove, imprison, and exile magistrates and to appoint a new audiencia.[46] The judicial power of the governor over such cases was further altered by the Royal Instruction of Regents of June 26, 1776, by which he was forbidden to impose any penalty on the *oidores* without the concurrence of the *acuerdo* and the regent.[47] The president and the *acuerdo* could rebuke and discipline *oidores*, privately, when their conduct demanded it. Even on such an occasion as this the magistrate was to be given full opportunity to defend himself. If a private investigation of the conduct of an *oidor* were necessary, the inquiry could be still conducted by the senior magistrate.[48] *Oidores*, on the other hand, had no jurisdiction over the trial of charges against the president, unless it were in his *residencia*. In this event the investigation might be conducted by a magistrate designated by the governor or by the Council of the Indies.[49]

Aside from his executive and military duties, the governor was president of the royal audiencia. This arrangement had the advantage of giving him an opportunity to know and appreciate the legal needs of the colony. It brought him in constant contact with judicial minds, and his position in this regard was no doubt calculated to keep him in the straight and

---

[45] Laws of May 3, 1605 and September 5, 1620, *Recopilación*, 2–16–43 and 44.

[46] This was done, for example, by governors Fajardo and Bustamante, while this law was still in force (1618–1624 and 1717–1719 respectively). The observation of this law in Chile was commanded in a royal order expedited to the president of the audiencia there on September 22, 1725; see *Recopilación*, 2–16, note 13.

[47] *Ibid.*, note 14.

[48] *Ibid.*, 2–16–51.

[49] Discussed in Chapter IV of this treatise.

narrow path of the law. Nevertheless, the governor, who was usually a soldier, but seldom a lawyer, did not participate as a magistrate in the trial of cases, and his activities in the tribunal were directive, rather than judicial. His opinions in all legal and administrative matters were prepared by his *asesor.*[50]

As president of the audiencia the governor exercised two important powers. One authorized him to divide the audiencia into *salas* and to designate *oidores* to try cases within the tribunal, to inspect the provinces, to take *residencias,* or to attend to semi-administrative matters, such as have been noted in the preceding chapter.[51] The other was the power to decide whether a contention was of judicial, governmental, military,

---

[50] Governors, captains-general, and viceroys were assisted by an *asesor,* or legal adviser, who gave his opinion in all matters of law that came up for solution. The necessity for this official developed through the fact that as most governors were soldiers, they were incapable of rendering judgment on legal and administrative questions. As counselor to the governor, this official bore the same relation to the executive as the *fiscal* did to the audiencia. The *asesor* was held responsible in the *residencia* for all decisions rendered by the governor in matters of justice, and in governmental affairs the governor and *asesor* were jointly responsible. Frequently the *asesor* was able to block completely the work of the audiencia and his opinion nullified the judgments of magistrates who were as learned in the law and as well qualified, if not better, than he. Martínez de Zúñiga (*Estadismo,* I, 224) discusses the influence of the *asesor* in the following terms: "*Expedientes* are sent to one of the two royal *fiscales* to ascertain their legality; afterwards they are sent to the *asesor* whom the governors must consult; the latter place (of *asesor*) is a very good one, . . . besides 2000 pesos as salary it has its private revenues in addition to 500 pesos yearly from each of the royal monopolies (discussed in Chapter V of this volume). There are many persons in Manila who are exempted from ordinary justice through their military connections or on account of being employed in the royal monopolies, and as they depend on him, he exercises great power; . . . there are few who desire him for an enemy, for when they least think of it they are in need of his favorable opinion in some *expediente* which they have brought before the government." The laws of the Indies forbade that an *oidor* should act as the governor's *asesor* if any other appointee with the requisite qualifications were available *(Recopilación,* 3–3–35, and note). See *cédula* (and accompanying *expedientes)* of September 26, 1756, A. I., 106–4–16.

[51] *Recopilación,* 2–15–61 to 63, 169; 2–16–12, 31, 32.

or ecclesiastical character, and to assign it to the proper department or tribunal.[52] This power was significant because it made the governor the supreme arbiter between all conflicting authorities in the colony. Frequently he decided disputes between the audiencia and the ecclesiastical courts, between the audiencia and the *consulado*, or between the *oidores* and the *oficiales reales* in matters relative to the jurisdiction of these tribunals over questions at issue.

While the magistrates were allowed to proceed practically without interference in affairs of justice, the governor was instructed to keep himself informed concerning the judicial work of the audiencia.[53] While forbidden to alter the judgments of the tribunal or to tamper with its sentences,[54] he could excuse or remit fines with the consent of the *oidores*. The governor could commute sentences in criminal cases. The final pardoning power rested with the king and it was exercised upon the recommendation of the governor or the prelates[55] and

---

[52] *Ibid.*, 2-15-38.

[53] *Ibid.*, 3-3-36, 38.

[54] *Ibid.*, 3-3-60. Relative to the relations of the viceroys and audiencias of the Spanish colonies, Robertson (*The History of America*, IV, 19-20) says: "The Spanish viceroys have often attempted to intrude themselves into the seat of justice, and with an ambition which their distance from the controul (*sic*) of a superior rendered bold, have aspired at a power which their master does not venture to assume . . . the viceroys have been prohibited, in the most explicit terms, by repeated laws, from interfering in the judicial proceedings of the courts of Audience, or from delivering an opinion, or giving a voice with respect to any point litigated before them. In some particular cases, in which any question of civil right is involved, even the political regulations of the viceroy may be brought under review of the court of Audience, which in those instances, may be deemed an intermediate power between him and the people, as a constitutional barrier to circumscribe his jurisdiction. But as legal restraints on a person who represents the sovereign, and is clothed with his authority, are little suited to the genius of Spanish policy; the hesitation and reserve with which it confers this power on the courts of Audience are remarkable. They may advise, they many remonstrate; but in the event of a direct collision between their opinion and the will of the viceroy, what he determines must be brought into execution, and nothing remains for them, but to lay the matter before the king and the Council of the Indies."

[55] *Recopilación*, 3-3-27, promulgated July 19, 1614, conferred general pardoning power on the viceroy.

the Council of the Indies. There were exceptional occasions, however, on which the governor assumed the responsibility of pardoning criminals.

After the creation of the office of regent in the audiencias of the colonies, in 1776, the governor's position as president of the audiencia became purely nominal, the regent actually officiating as chief justice, though the president was still legally required to affix his signature to all judicial decisions of the tribunal. The frequent and extended absences of the governor from the capital and the multiplicity of his administrative duties prevented him from attending to these matters with requisite promptness, and injustice consequently resulted from the requirement. Many complaints were made from 1776 onward against this condition of affairs, with the result that a modification in the existing law was made on October 24, 1803, making valid the signature of the regent to all decisions of the audiencia, when the governor was absent from the colony on expeditions of conquest or tours of inspection.[56] At all other times the governor, as president, affixed his signature to all legal acts and *autos*, although he did not participate in their decisions. The law remained thus until 1861, when the governorship was separated from the presidency, the *acuerdo* was abolished, and the regent was made president of the audiencia with authority to sign all judicial decisions.[57]

We have already noted that the governor exercised special judicial powers, independent of the audiencia. Among these the military jurisdiction stands pre-eminent, and it will be discussed separately in the following chapter. The governor was also empowered to try Indians in first instance, with appeal to the audiencia.[58] The actual trial of these cases,

---

[56] Regent to the King, July 9, 1793, A. I., 106–4–18; *Cédula* of October 24, 1803, A. I., 105–2–10.

[57] Royal decree of July 4, 1861, *Colección legislativa*, LXXXVI, 1–45.

[58] *Recopilación*, 3–3–65. It is to be noted that the New Laws of

however, was delegated to the *alcaldes mayores* and *corregidores* with appeal to the audiencia. It was impossible for the governor, occupied as he was with the multitudinous affairs of his office, to concern himself personally with the thousands of petty cases among the Indians, or between Indians and Spaniards. He had jurisdiction over suits involving the condemnation of property through which public roads were to pass.[59] The special jurisdiction of the governor, assisted by the audiencia, over cases affecting the royal ecclesiastical patronage will be discussed later.

The laws of the Indies would seem to indicate that both the governor and the audiencia exercised independently the power to exile undesirable residents from the colony. It was stipulated that if sentence of exile were passed by the governor and the offenders were sent to Spain, the necessary papers, issued by the governor, should accompany them.[60] If the decree of banishment were imposed by the audiencia in its judicial capacity, the governor was forbidden to commute the sentence or otherwise interfere in the matter.[61] The audiencia frequently sentenced criminals or other undesirables to spend terms of varying lengths in the provinces or in the Marianas.

1542 conferred on the audiencias the duty of protecting the Indians. Professor Moses, in his *Spanish dependencies in South America*, I, (212–3), says: "The audiencias were commanded to inquire into the treatment which the Indians had received at the hands of governors and private persons; and, in case of excesses and ill-treatment, the guilty parties should be punished. . . . While it was acknowledged that some persons had a sufficient title to hold Indians, it was ordered that when the number held was excessive, the audiencia should gather the necessary information and reduce the allotments made to the said persons in a fair and moderate quantity 'and place the rest under the Crown'."

[59] *Ibid.*, 53.

[60] *Ibid.*, 3–3–61; 3–4–7. We have a notable illustration of this in the banishment of Archbishop Poblete by Governor Salcedo (1663–1668) as a result of the resistance of the former to Salcedo's intervention in ecclesiastical matters on the basis of the royal patronage. Salcedo did not solicit the aid or intervention of the audiencia in this matter.

[61] *Ibid.*, 2–16–8.

This, as we have seen, was commonly one of the trials connected with the residencia. We have a noteworthy illustration of the action of the audiencia in *acuerdo* with the governor in the banishment of Archbishop Felipe Pardo, who was exiled by the *acuerdo* of the audiencia and Governor Juan de Vargas Hurtado, in 1684. Vargas was succeeded the same year by Governor Curuzaelegui, who recalled the prelate from exile and forced the audiencia to endorse the act of recall.

Closely related to the governor's jurisdiction over banishment was his jurisdiction over cases of persons entering the Islands or departing from them without royal permission.[62] He exercised final jurisdiction here over civil and ecclesiastical authorities, *encomenderos,* and private persons. The law forbade any person to enter or leave the Islands without the royal permission, and the governor was charged with the execution of this law. *Encomenderos* were not to leave the Islands on pain of confiscation of their *encomiendas.*[63] While the laws of May 25, 1596, and of June 4, 1620, gave authority to the governor over the religious, relative to their entrance into the Islands and departure therefrom,[64] the *cédula* of July 12, 1640, authorized the audiencia to enforce the law on this subject; especially was the tribunal to see that no ecclesiastics departed for Japan and China without the proper authority.[65] Although there can be no doubt of the finality of the governor's jurisdiction in this matter, yet the audiencia exercised an advisory power, and an authority to check irregularities, particularly with a view to seeing that the governor did his duty and fulfilled his obligations in the matter. Numerous instances exist to show that whenever this subject was treated in a royal order or decree, copies of the law were sent to the audiencia

---

[62] *Ibid.,* 3–3–58; King to Audiencia, March 6, 1781, A. I., 105–2–9.
[63] Instruction to Tello, May 25, 1596, Blair and Robertson, IX, 229, 232–233, 238–239.
[64] *Recopilación,* 1–14–29 to 31.
[65] *Ibid.,* 31.

for its information. On other occasions when there was reason to believe that there had been irregularities in the procedure of a governor, the audiencia complained to the Council of the Indies. This was done for example in 1779 when Governor Sarrio conceded permission for several priests to go to Mexico. This action the audiencia claimed to be irregular, since the Council of the Indies had not been notified or consulted. The king, on March 6, 1781, approved the action of the governor on the basis of the laws above referred to.[66]

Besides his judicial authority the governor shared legislative functions with the audiencia. We have noted in an earlier chapter that the *acuerdo* passed ordinances for the domestic welfare and local government of the colony. It prescribed rules and issued regulations for merchants, *encomenderos,* and religious, in accordance with the rulings for royal ecclesiastical patronage. The *acuerdo* developed from the advisory power of the audiencia. The king in his first decrees ordered the viceroys and presidents to consult with the *oidores* whenever the interests of the government demanded it,[67] and if necessary the opinions of the magistrates could be required in writing. When an agreement was reached upon a given subject, they voted in *acuerdo* and gradually that *acuerdo* came to have the force of law. On many occasions the *acuerdo* prevailed over the governor's will. There was no constitutional basis for this, and the *acuerdo,* when it became a legislative function in passing ordinances and overruling the governor himself, assumed prerogatives which were never exercised by the audiencias of Spain.[68]

The laws of the Indies established the governor as the sole executive, and forbade the audiencia to interfere with the gov-

---

[66] King to the Audiencia, March 6, 1781, A. I., 105-2-9.

[67] *Recopilación,* 3-3-45.

[68] This is treated in the first chapter of this book. See Solórzano, *Política Indiana,* II, 271-279.

ernment.[69] The governor, occupied by his extensive administrative and military duties, came to devote less attention to the judicial side of his office, which was left almost entirely to the audiencia. So it developed that the *acuerdos* in reference to judicial matters—the establishment of tariffs and rules for their observance and the dispatch of *pesquisidores* and visitors to the provinces, came in the latter eighteenth and early nineteenth centuries to be increasingly the concern of the audiencia. The authority of the tribunal in these matters was recognized by the Constitution of 1812 and the reforms made in pursuance thereof.[70]

In the same manner the *acuerdo* came to be recognized in governmental and administrative matters. The enactments of these legislative sessions of the audiencia were known as *autos acordados.* They ultimately came to embrace a wide field. The audiencia passed laws for the regulation of the provinces; it made rulings which the *alcaldes mayores* and *corregidores* were to follow in the collection of tribute; it prescribed their relations with the parish priests; it issued regulations for the conduct of the friars and the ordinary clergy relative to the royal patronage. Laws were passed for the encouragement of agriculture and industry and the regulation of commerce. Rice, tobacco and silk culture, the production of cinnamon and cocoanuts, the breeding of fowls, the regulation of cock-fighting, cloth-making and ship-building all came in for their share of attention in the *acuerdo.*[71]

---

69 *Recopilación,* 2-15-11.

70 Constitution of 1812, Martínez Alcubilla, III, 408 *et seq.; Acuerdo* for the promulgation of the Constitution of 1812, Montero y Vidai, III, 404; *Acuerdo* of January 15, 1814, *Ordenanzas.* etc., A. I., 106-4-19; *Cédula* of September 26, 1835, Zamora y Coronado, *Apéndice,* 41-138; Royal Decree of January 30, 1855, *Colección legislativa,* LX, 105-147; see also Royal Instruction to Regents, June 20, 1776, and *Cédula* of April 8, 1778, in Rodríguez San Pedro, *Legislación ultramarina,* VII, 22-28.

71 Ordinances enacted by the Audiencia of Manila, June 13 to December 19, 1598, Blair and Robertson, X, 293-316; Ordinances

The audiencia, in the exercise of the *acuerdo* power, passed ordinances for the enforcement of the laws forbidding the unauthorized departure of persons from the Islands; it helped to fix the rate of passage on the galleons and on the coast-wise ships. It made regulations for the Chinese in the Parián, it prescribed the conditions under which licenses might be issued to Chinese merchants and it passed ordinances for the better enforcement of the laws prohibiting the immigration of the Chinese. The *acuerdo* concerned itself with the maintenance of prisons and the care of prisoners, the *residencias* of provincial officials, the auditing of accounts, the collection of the revenue, and the supervision of the officials of the treasury. Ordinances were passed enforcing the general law which ordered that the natives should not live together in Christian communities without marriage, that they should attend religious ceremonies, that they should be instructed in religion, and that they should not be exploited, either by the civil or ecclesiastical authorities. It is, of course, understood that the audiencia in no way trespassed the authority of the church in issuing these regulations; indeed it was quite the contrary; these ordinances were passed on the basis of the authority of the royal patronage, with the design of assisting the vice-patron (the governor) in the execution of his duties, and the church was aided rather than impeded thereby. It must be remembered, of course, that the governor, as president of the audiencia, presided in these *acuerdos,* and that in most cases, actually, as well as in theory, these *autos acordados* were his will.

---

etc., January 7, to June 15, 1599, *ibid.,* XI, 1–81. Reference may also be made to the five volume *Colección de autos acordados de la real audiencia . . . de Manila,* 1861-1866; see also *Estadísticas de las causas y expedientes de gobierno despachadas por la audiencia de Filipinas durante el año de 1876.* For New Spain we have the *Recopilación sumaria de algunos autos acordados de la real audiencia de Nueva España,* Mexico, 1787. Of similar import and character was the well-known collection of Puga, cited in the bibliography of this volume. See also Solórzano, *Politica Indiana* (2 vols.).

There were many occasions in the history of the Islands when the *acuerdo* was influential in the formulation of far-reaching reforms. The well-known "Ordinances of Good Government," issued by Governor Corcuera in 1642 for the observance of the provincial officials, and repromulgated with modifications by Cruzat y Góngora in 1696 and by Raón in 1768 were formulated by the *acuerdo*.[72] Similarily were those formulated that were proposed by Marquina in 1790. The local regulations for the *consulado*, established in 1769, were formulated by the audiencia largely on the recommendations of the able *fiscal*, Francisco Leandro de Viana. In the same manner the new plan of constitutional government given to the Philippines in 1812 was drafted by the audiencia at the request of the Council of the Indies.[73] Likewise the plans for the government of the intendancy were submitted to the *acuerdo* by Governor Basco y Vargas in 1785. Indeed, these, as well as the scheme of 1787-8, were actually written by two magistrates of the audiencia, the former plan by Oidor Ciriaco Gonzales Carvajal, subsequently intendant, and the latter by Oidor Castillo y Negrete.[74]

There were occasions when the audiencia enacted administrative measures in which the governor failed to participate. These were especially noticeable during the administrations of Acuña, Fajardo, and Corcuera—governors who spent much of their time away from Manila. A more recent instance of this occurred in 1790 when the natives of the province of Ilocos revolted against a tyrannical and dissolute *alcalde mayor*. The

---

[72] Blair and Robertson, L, 191–264; see, also, Montero y Vidal, *Historia general*, I, 380–385, also correspondence relative to the modifications of these ordinances by Raón in A. I., 105–4–5. Marquina's efforts along this line may be noted in A. 1., 105–4–6.

[73] *Acuerdo* of January 15, 1814, A. I., 106–4–19; see also Montero y Vidal, *Historia general*, III, 404; 430.

[74] Carvajal to the King, December 5, 1785, A. I., 107–5–14; Carvajal to the Audiencia of Manila, December 29, 1787, A. I., 107–5–15; *Testimonio del expediente sobre poner la real jurisdicción y el gobierno y policía de estas islas en el ser y estado que tenían antes*, December 20, 1788, A. I., 107–5–18, 105–3–5.

acuerdo, notwithstanding the objection of Governor Marquina, removed the offending official and appointed another, and this action was subsequently approved by the king.[75] According to the laws of the Indies the authority of removal and appointment of such officials rested with the governor.[76] The tendency of the *acuerdo* to act in civil affairs without the advice or presence of the governor was checked by the royal order of November 12, 1840, wherein the audiencia was ordered not to attempt to carry its *acuerdos* into execution without the authority of the superior government.[77] The evil effects of the audiencia's intervention in provincial government were pointed out in 1842 by Sinibaldo de Mas, when he wrote: "the government of the provinces is in charge of an alcalde-mayor, who is at once judge of first instance, chief of political matters, subdelegate of the treasury, and war-captain or military commandant, for whose different attributes he is subject to authorities distinct from one another."[78]

---

[75] King to the Audiencia, August 13, 1793, A. I., 105–2–10.

[76] *Recopilación,* 3–2–70 (after 1680), 67.

[77] Rodríguez San Pedro, *Legislación ultramarina,* VII, 67.

[78] Mas, "Internal political condition of the Philippines," in Blair and Robertson, LII, 70–73. Mas was a Spanish diplomatic official stationed in China, who visited the Islands in 1842 on a semi-official mission. This writer was not favorably impressed with the effectiveness of the *acuerdo.* He wrote: "Whatever difficulty occurs in the fulfilment of an order, it must be solved by means of a conference and advice [*consulta*], from which a reply is not obtained until from twelve to fourteen months." Instead of governmental matters being referred to the *acuerdo,* Mas stated that they were referred to Spain, hence there was great delay. He stated that the governor scarcely decided any question by himself, and those which were solved in the colony were referred to the *asesor,* and "from this practice," he continued, "arises the system of expedientes, which reigns, and which is so fatal to the prosperity and good government of the country, since very often the arrangement that appears good to some, is contrary to the opinions or interests of others. . . . Thus much valuable time is lost and the expedientes result in only a waste of paper, besides great injury to the islands. The governor often has to conform to the opinions expressed in the expediente, although he knows they will be the cause of injustice. On the other hand, the governor is often directly at fault, because he enforces his own opinion on his assessor (sp.), who has often obtained his

The audiencia was deprived of its *acuerdo* power in in governmental matters by the Constitution of 1812, but it was still retained in judicial affairs. In 1815 and again in 1823 on the restoration of the monarchy, the full *acuerdo* power as practiced before 1812 was resumed by the audiencia. Official recognition of the *acuerdo* was made publicly by Governor Torres, who succeeded Enrile on March 18, 1834. In his inaugural address this governor avowed his purpose to be the extension and improvement of commerce, the army and agriculture, "but, in order to develop these to their highest extent, and to realize the utmost success in my administration," he said, "I count on the co-operation of all the authorities, and particularly of the *real acuerdo*, of which I have the honor to be president."[79] The audiencia was finally excluded from the *acuerdo* in administrative matters by the reform of July 4, 1861; since then the tribunal has been purely judicial, the legislative

---

position through favoritism and is not a lawyer, and decides questions according to the will of the governor. . . . The chiefs of the various departments carry on correspondence with the directors-general of their respective departments in Madrid, without the knowledge of the governor, a fact that increases the confusion and disorder." (See also Revilla Gigedo's description of the evils of the expediente in New Spain [1790]. Smith, *The viceroy of New Spain*, 190–191.)

This description of the Philippine government in 1842 would seem to indicate that aside from the limitations imposed upon his rule by the audiencia, the governor was obliged to contend with a number of other officials, departments, and regulations, which effectively prevented him from exercising absolute power, even at the sacrifice of efficiency. We note in this description, moreover, that tendency of Spanish colonial government which has been emphasized so often in this treatise— namely, the failure of the home government to leave to the colonial officials sufficient scope of action or authority to deal adequately with the ordinary problems of government. Up to the end of the eighteenth century the audiencia was the only civil authority or tribunal present to exercise any check on the executive in administrative affairs. However, in the last century the importance of the audiencia in this regard was diminished by the creation of other departments, ministries, and offices, by the elimination of time and space, due to the progress of invention, which brought the colonies nearer to Spain, and finally by the fact that the tribunal itself was more and more confined to judicial affairs.

[79] Governor Torres to the Queen, March 18, 1835, A. I., 106–4–21.

functions of government having been assumed by the Administrative Council (*Consejo de Administración*) of which the president and *fiscal*, and usually two *oidores* at least were members. Thus, even after the reform of 1861, the *oidores* continued to participate in legislative functions, though the audiencia as a body did not.[80]

Typical of the multitudinous duties of the governor, and illustrative at the same time of his relations with the audiencia, were the various subjects treated in the Instruction of the king to Governor Pedro de Acuña, dated February 16, 1602,[81] which is chosen for citation here because of its comprehensive character, and also because of its availability. Beginning with the reminder that the governor should confer with the Viceroy of New Spain whenever necessary, this comprehensive paper treated first of the defense of the Islands against the Japanese, and of the maintenance of a garrison in Mindanao. The matter of tribute was taken up, and the desirability was shown of having the natives pay tribute in kind rather than in money. It was said that the latter method encouraged the natives to indolence, for as soon as they had earned enough money to pay their tribute they ceased work altogether. The governor was advised to consult with the audiencia in regard to this matter. The king ordered the governor to cut down expenses and to economize by the elimination of as many offices as possible. He recommended, in particular, the abolition of the offices of *corregidor* and *alcalde mayor*.

---

[80] *Colección legislativa de España*, LXXXVI, 1–45. Elliott, in his *Philippines to the end of the military regime*, p. 242, states incorrectly that this reform took place in 1865. Mr. Elliott did not make use of the sources. It is to be noted, too, that Dr. Barrows in his article on "The governor general of the Philippines," in *The Pacific Ocean in history* makes contradictory statements relative to this matter. On page 242 he asserts that the governor was president of the audiencia till 1844, and on page 248 the statement occurs that "a further specialization of 1861 deprived the governor-general of his judicial powers."

[81] Instruction of the King to Governor Acuña, February 16, 1602, Blair and Robertson, XI, 263–88.

The king warned Acuña against a continuation of the dishonesty of past governors in the lading of ships for New Spain. He declared that thereafter the allotment of freight should not be left to the friends of the governor, but the matter should be personally supervised by the governor and an *oidor*. The frauds which had been common also in the assignment of *encomiendas* in the colony must cease; to effect this the governor was temporarily deprived of jurisdiction over this matter. Who was to assign the *encomiendas* in the future was not divulged.[82]

The governor was instructed to see that the salable offices were not conferred on the relatives of the *oidores,* nor given to his own relatives, but that they should be disposed of to persons offering the most money for them. It had been charged that governors and audiencias had connived together in the past to deprive persons of offices to which they were legitimately entitled. This had been done by allowing favorites to hold more than one office, and by favoritism in the sale of these positions. These abuses must be stopped, the king said; it was ordered that in the future no person should be allowed to hold more than one office, that as many of these as possible should be sold, with unrestricted competitive bidding.

The governor and the *fiscal* were ordered to exercise care and diligence in the inspection of the returning galleon, to see especially that it brought no unregistered money from persons

---

[82] Fray Sánchez, in his memorial of July 26, 1586, stated that the audiencia had stopped the practice of conceding *encomicndas* (A. I., 67–6–27), which the governors had followed prior to its establishment. Nevertheless the governor's authority to bestow *encomiendas* was recognized by the royal instructions to Governor Dasmariñas, issued May 25, 1593 (Blair and Robertson, IX, 232). The statement of Sánchez may be interpreted to mean that the audiencia had stopped the abuses which had been perpetrated by various governors in bestowing *encomiendas* on their friends. *Encomiendas* were conceded by different governors in the Philippines throughout the eighteenth century. This matter has been discussed in an earlier note.

in Mexico. Acuña's predecessor, Tello, had recommended that west-bound galleons should stop at the Ladrones to leave priests and soldiers, and to minister to the needs of Spaniards already there. This was authorized and the governor was instructed to see that it was done. The governor was also ordered on this occasion to make an investigation of the audiencia. Complaints had been coming to the court for a long time against the laxity of the tribunal in the administration of justice, and of the commercial activities of the *oidores*. The governor was to aid the *fiscal* in the prosecution of any *oidores* who were remiss, to the extent of sending them under arrest to New Spain if the charges against them justified such action.

This Instruction, it will be noted, required the governor to intervene actively in practically all the governmental affairs that came up in the colony. He was to exercise authority with regard to defense, finance, and revenue. He was to exercise supervision over provincial affairs so as to insure the good treatment of the natives and the beneficent administration of the *encomiendas*. He was to give his attention to the galleon trade and to the disposal of offices within the colony. If doubt or difficulty arose in any of these matters of administration, he was to demand from the audiencia, its assistance, counsel, and support. The governor was also authorized to see that justice was administered effectively, though he was not to intervene directly in that matter, except to see that abuses were erradicated. This Instruction shows that the governor was regarded as the chief executive of the government. He was the responsible head in the judicial, administrative, and military spheres. The audiencia, on the other hand, had consultative functions, aimed to assist the governor when he required it, but to restrict him when he sought to exceed his powers. Instructions similar to this were given to many succeeding governors. A citation of these would prove nothing new, however.

In the same manner that the Instruction to Acuña gives us

an idea of the relative functions of the audiencia and the governorship in 1602, so the criticisms of the able Spanish diplomat, Sinibaldo de Mas, written in 1842, aid us in estimating their respective spheres in the nineteenth century. This opinion is valuable because it summarizes the result of two hundred and fifty years of the interaction of these political institutions in the Islands. Mas showed the reason for the establishment of the intendancy, and the conferring of added powers upon the audiencia and criticized the relations existing between the governor and these institutions in the following terms:

> To set some balance to his power (that of the governor), because of the distance from the throne, certain privileges and preëminences have been granted to other persons, especially to the Audiencia, even to the point of making of the latter a court of appeal against the measures of the chief of the islands. Besides, the revenues have been removed from his jurisdiction, and the office of the intendant has been constituted, who obeys no others than the orders communicated to him by the ministry of the treasury from Madrid. It is very obvious that this single point is quite sufficient to paralyze completely the action of the governor-general. Besides, since there are many matters which require to be passed on by distinct ministries, it happens that two contrary orders touch the same matter, or that one order is lacking, which is enough to render its execution impossible . . . a chief may detain a communication, even after he has received it, if it does not suit him. This system of setting obstacles in the way of the governor of a distant colony is wise and absolutely necessary, . . . there results rather than a balance among the various departments of authority a confusion of jurisdictions, the fatal fount of eternal discord.[83]

---

[83] Mas, "Internal political conditions of the Philippines, 1842," Blair and Robertson, LII, 69–70 and note. The keen observations of this official on social and governmental conditions in the Philippines are peculiarly pertinent, and they are as true in many regards today as they were seventy-five years ago. He recommended a regency to govern the Philippines, consisting of the governor as president, a military commander and an intendant of finance. The audiencia, according to his plan of reform, was to be limited to judicial affairs, with appellate jurisdiction over civil, criminal, and commercial cases. Instead of the audiencia as a court of appeals against the governor, the regency was to entertain appeals from the audiencia. Many of his ideas were incorporated into the new laws of the last half of the nineteenth century (*ibid.*, 78–85).

Mas made extensive quotations which were calculated to show "the great confusion and contrariety of the orders to governor and audiencia." This characteristic of the laws of the Indies has repeatedly been referred to in this treatise, and we shall note its results in a subsequent chapter dealing with the conflicts of jurisdiction between the audiencia and the governor.

It is clear, therefore, that the decision of the governor was not final in administrative affairs. Persons dissatisfied with his executive actions or decisions in such matters were privileged to appeal to the audiencia. If the findings of the tribunal differed from those of the governor, and if the governor were still unyielding, his will was to be obeyed but the case was thereupon appealed to the Council of the Indies.[84] If the case were one of law and justice the governor, on the other hand, was instructed to abide by the decision of the audiencia, but he was privileged to carry the case to the Council of the Indies. Thus it was that each of these authorities had a sphere wherein its word was law, and its decisions final in the colony.

It was prescribed, however, that when there were differences of opinion between the governor and the audiencia an effort should be made both by the governor and the audiencia to avoid notorious disagreements which would furnish a bad example to the natives, or otherwise degrade the dignity of the royal tribunal or governor. Viceroys, presidents, and audiencias were forbidden to take action in cases wherein there was doubt as to their jurisdiction, or wherein there was a question as to the advisability of taking final action.[85]

It would appear, therefore, from this survey of the laws, that the audiencia was provided with ample means for restraining the action of the governor. This it could do either by admonition, by appealing from his decisions in administrative

---

[84] *Recopilación*, 5–12–22; 2–15–35; 36, 41.
[85] *Ibid.*, 3–3–51.

matters, or by blocking him in the *acuerdo*. It was evidently
the design of those who planned the legislation of the Indies
to guard at all times against the excesses of an all-powerful
executive. Such was certainly the purpose of the establishment
of the audiencia, both in the Americas and in the Philippines.
Taking into consideration the three hundred years of Philippine history, however, it cannot be said that in the actual
operation of the government these precautions were entirely
effective.

According to the laws of the Indies the governor, as executive, had his own sphere in which the *oidores* were forbidden
to interfere.[86] In the light of our investigation, however, it
would appear that this exclusive field was exceedingly limited,
and that even it was continually subject to the encroachments
of the audiencia. In the exercise of his military authority the
governor was independent of the tribunal, although we shall
see that on some occasions the audiencia exercised military
jurisdiction in an executive capacity, and that there were times
when the governor was glad to call upon the audiencia for
assistance in this matter. As president of the audiencia the
governor exercised considerable authority during the first half
of the history of the colony, but from 1776 to 1861 his position as president was merely nominal, and at the latter date
it was abolished. He was the chief administrative official of
the colony, and his authority in this particular was more far-
reaching than in any other. In this, however, he was limited
by the *acuerdo* of the audiencia, which developed, as we have
seen, from an advisory to a legislative function, and ultimately
had the effect of limiting the governor in his hitherto exclusive
field.

---

[86] *Ibid.*, 2–15–35, 36, 41; 3–3–2, 34, 42; 3–14–1; 5–12–22.

CHAPTER VII

THE AUDIENCIA AND THE GOVERNOR: THE MILITARY JURISDICTION

The isolation of the Philippines, their distance from the home country and New Spain, and their proximity to the colonies and trade routes of rival nations, made the problem of defense the foremost consideration. This was almost equally true of New Spain, Perú, and the West Indian colonies, all of which were exposed to the attack of outside enemies, though, of course, they were neither as isolated nor as far away as the Philippines.

The necessity of being ever on the alert, constantly prepared to resist invasion and to put down insurrection, gave a military character to the governments of these colonies. The viceroys and governors were in most cases trained soldiers. In addition to their other prerogatives, they exercised the office and title of captain-general and as such they commanded the military and naval forces of their colonies, inadequate as these forces sometimes were. During the first two hundred years governors and viceroys were largely selected on the basis of their past military exploits on the continent or in America. The administrations of the different Philippine governors of the sixteenth and seventeenth centuries were characterized rather by their devotion to military affairs than by economic improvements or administrative efficiency. The supervision of judicial and governmental affairs was thus left for long periods in the hands of other officials and authorities, to be reclaimed or fought over by the governors when their time was not taken up by military conquests.

It is practically agreed among all authorities who have written on the Philippines that the leading consideration and necessity of the government during two hundred years was military defense. These writers comprise officials who saw service there and commentators who visited the Islands and studied the government. In their recommendations and comments they unite in urging that the defense of the Islands should not be neglected; that the governor should be given adequate forces with sufficient jurisdiction over them and over the other elements of the colony to defend it successfully from invasion or insurrection.

It was the policy of the government throughout the history of the Islands to conserve and keep intact the governor's military jurisdiction. We have noted in an earlier chapter that one of the main reasons for the suppression of the audiencia in 1589 was that it interfered too extensively with the military jurisdiction of the governor. During the decade following the extinction of the tribunal, the military governors were given almost unlimited powers, until their abuses led to the re-establishment of the tribunal to guard against these excesses. We shall see in the following chapter that the limitations placed upon them by the audiencia were always a source of complaint by the various governors. Governor Acuña went so far as to recommend the suppression of the tribunal because the needs of the colony were military and had to be met by the firm action of a soldier, without the interference of a body of magistrates.[1] Similar recommendations were made by a majority of

---

[1] Acuña to Felipe III, July 15, 1604, Blair and Robertson, XIII, 235. Acuña stated that the soldiers and military officials were "discontented and grieved at the ill-treatment which the said auditors accord them; and at seeing that they are hindered by them, an auditor commanding at his will the arrest of a captain, official, or soldier, without cause or reason, and interfering in all the details of service—even going so far as to inspect their quarters, and send them to the public prison, for very trivial affairs, against all military precedents." The governor said that when affairs went on in a peaceful and orderly way, it was because the *oidores* were not interfering with them. He stated that it was the opinion of all right-

the succeeding governors, but more especially by Fajardo, Corcuera, Vargas, Arandía, and even by Anda who had risen from
the post of *oidor* to that of governor and military commander.[2]

The conviction that the government should be pre-eminently
military was not held by governors alone. Fernando de los
Rios Coronel, procurator of the Philippines at the Court of
Madrid in 1597, urged that the government should be of a
military character and that the practice of sending soldiers to
govern the Islands should be continued.[3] This opinion was also
advanced by Fray Alonso Sánchez, procurator of the Islands
at Madrid in 1589, and the emissary whose arguments were
chiefly instrumental in bringing about the suppression of the
audiencia.[4] Francisco Leandro de Viana, the most efficient *fiscal*
that the Islands ever had, and afterwards councillor of the
Indies, recognized the military attributes of the governor's
position. He urged a separation of the spheres of the governor and the audiencia, recommending that the former should
attend solely to war and government, while the latter should
confine itself to matters of justice.[5]

This opinion was shared by Juan José Delgado, the able
Jesuit historian, who expressed the conviction that the ''islands
need disinterested military governors, not merchants; and men
of resolution and character, not students, who are more fit to
govern monasteries than communities of heroes.''[6] Delgado recommended that governors of the Philippines should be picked

---

thinking men that soldiers were of more use in the colony than
judges (*ibid.*, 237).

[2] The terms of these governors were as follows: Fajardo, 1618–
1624; Corcuera, 1635–1644; Vargas, 1678–1684; Arandía, 1754–1759;
Anda, 1762–1764, 1770–1776.

[3] Rios Coronel to the King, June 27, 1597, A. I., 67–6–19; see
also Bourne, "Historical introduction," in Blair and Robertson, I,
53, note.

[4] These arguments are noted in detail in Chapter II of this
volume.

[5] Viana to Carlos III, May 1, 1767, Blair and Robertson, L, 126–135.

[6] Delgado, 212–215, reproduced in Blair and Robertson, XVII,
316.

men, selected for their military qualities. The distance and isolation of the colony and its proximity to the great empires of China and Japan made defense the first requisite. Delgado believed that a soldier would be less amenable to bribes and that commercial ventures would be less attractive to him.[7] He recommended that governors should be absolute in affairs of government and war and that all departments and officials of the government should be subject to him.

While most of the independent commentators writing on the subject seem to have conceived of the duties of the governor as savoring more of war than of peace, we may note that Manuel Bernáldez Pizarro, for many years a resident and official in the Philippines, writing in 1827, urged that the governors there should be efficient administrators rather than soldiers. It must be remembered, however, that the political conditions in the Philippines during his period were widely different from those of the seventeenth and eighteenth centuries when the Islands were constantly exposed to the attack of outside enemies and liable to insurrections within. The chief problems of the nineteenth century were administrative, rather than military. He pointed out that governors had already exhibited too much of the militant spirit in dealing with the problems of government, "not heeding the opinions and customs of the country, but depending on the force of arms," or their *asesores*.[8] This had the effect of causing dissensions between the governor and audiencia, and the resultant discord had furnished a very bad example for the natives and residents of the colony.

The characteristic tendency throughout the history of the

---

[7] "But," he continued, "if a man come to these islands with the intention of escaping his natural poverty by humoring the rich and powerful, and even obeying them, the wrongs accruing to the community are incredible" (*ibid.*, 317).

[8] Reforms in Filipinas, April 26, 1827, by Manuel Bernáldez Pizarro, Blair and Robertson, LI, 219; see 213–218.

Islands to lay stress on the military side of the governor's position was commented on by Montero y Vidal, the modern historian of the Philippines, in the following terms:

> The authority of the governor-general is complete, and so great a number of attributes conferred on one functionary, incompetent, as a general rule, for everything outside of military affairs, is certainly prejudicial to the right exercise of his duty; . . . since 1822 the government has always devolved upon an official; a general, and in the case of his death, a *segundo cabo*, and, in case of the death of the latter, a commandant of the naval station.[9]

The preservation of the peace and the maintenance of the defense of the Islands was the chief responsibility and the most important duty of the governor and captain-general. Although the audiencia was ordered to do all that it could to assist, nevertheless the tribunal was strictly forbidden to restrict or hinder the governor in the execution of his military duties.[10] The governor's position as commander-in-chief of the king's forces, and his pre-eminence in military affairs, were generally recognized.

Notwithstanding the fact that the early laws conferred exclusive military powers on the governor, a glance at three hundred years of Spanish colonial history will show that the audiencias participated in these matters in two different ways. In fact, an analysis of the military jurisdiction shows the presence and the exercise, in general, of two kinds of activity. These consisted, first, of a special judicial system for the trial of persons under military law and distinct from the civil jurisdiction, and second, of the control and disposition of the military forces of the Islands, and their utilization for defense. One,

---

[9] Montero y Vidal, *Archipiélago Filipino*, 162–168. "The Spanish régime in Filipinas lasted 333 years. . . . During that time there were 97 governors—not counting some twenty who served for less than one year each, mostly *ad interim*, and the average length of their terms of office was a little less than three and one-half years, a fact which is an important element in the administrative history of the islands" (Blair and Robertson, L, 74, note 46).

[10] *Recopilación*, 3–3–3.

therefore, was judicial, the other was administrative, but both of these forces of activity were within the military sphere. The problem of this chapter, therefore, consists in determining the conditions, circumstances, and extent of the audiencia's participation in military affairs, and of its relation to the authority and jurisdiction of the governor and captain-general.

As commander-in-chief, the governor was at the head of a special judicial system for the trial of soldiers under the military law. This judicial system was independent of the audiencia, and the latter body, during the greater part of the history of the Islands, was denied jurisdiction in these cases, even on appeal.[11] We have already noted, however, the tendency of the law to excuse these busy executives from direct participation in ordinary judicial activities. Notwithstanding the governor's status in the above-mentioned particular, he seldom intervened personally in the trial of such cases. His position with regard to the military jurisdiction was similar to his relation with the audiencia, of which he was president, but over which he seldom presided.

The actual trial of the criminal cases of soldiers was conducted in first instance by military tribunals and magistrates. Most prominent among the latter were the *castellán* and the *maestre de campo*. The captains, themselves, had certain judicial authority within their companies.[12] Appeals were made from these military judges of first instance to the captain-general. If there had been notorious injustice or a grave infraction of the law in the trial of a case of first instance, it was the governor's duty either to refer the case to some other magistrate than to the one who originally tried it, or to a special judicial tribunal. An *oidor* might be designated to serve in this tribunal. When the magistrates served in this

---

11 *Ibid.*, 3–11–1 to 3.
12 *Ibid.*, 3–11–1, 2, 3 to 10; 3–10–3, 11; 5–10–15.

capacity they were responsible entirely to the governor and were not identified with the audiencia. *Oidores* frequently objected to this service, but the governor was usually able to enforce these demands, which were in accordance with the laws and approved by the home government.

The captain-general exercised the pardoning power. Under some circumstances cases might be appealed to Spain, but in these suits, most of which involved personal crimes and misdemeanors, the decision of the captain-general or the local military tribunal was usually final, if for no other reason than the fact that the soldiers in Manila lacked the means to carry their cases further. Those cases which were appealed usually involved principles of law desirable to be tested by reference to a higher tribunal. The *junta de guerra de Indias* received all appeals from the military officials of the colonies and solved all questions of a judicial or administrative character that were carried to it.

The *junta de guerra* consisted of four ministers of the Supreme Council of War who were designated to sit with an equal number of ministers of the Council of the Indies.[13] It was, in fact, the executive committee and at the same time the special tribunal of military affairs for the Council of the Indies. It passed upon such military questions as were nominally referred to it by the president of the Council of the Indies, although these cases automatically came to this *junta* without the intervention of the president of the Council. It had jurisdiction over appeals in cases affecting soldiers tried in first or second instance in the colonies, over the administrative matters of armament and defense: the equipment of fleets and military operations, garrisons, military supplies, and munitions. It also tried appeals from the tribunal of the *Casa de Contratación*,

---

[13] *Ibid.*, 2–2–72, 74, 77; *Consulta de 18 de Febrero de 1673 sobre atribuciones de la Junta de Guerra de Indias*, A. I., 141–5–8.

and, in fact, it exercised general supervision over that institution in its various activities.

This was the machinery which existed for the adjudication of military cases during the greater part of the history of the Islands, the magistrates of the audiencia officiating as *auditores de guerra* when designated by the governor.[14] The royal decree of January 30, 1855, made a radical reform in this particular, adding two new magistrates, an *auditor de guerra* and an *auditor de marina* and to some extent relieving the ministers of the audiencia. These magistrates were appointed by the Minister of War and had original and secondary jurisdiction over cases involving soldiers and sailors of the fleet. These new magistrates served as ministers of the audiencia when their special duties permitted, and they were ordered to consult with the governor from time to time in regard to matters pertaining to their respective fields. Though the audiencia was forbidden to concern itself with cases which belonged to the military jurisdiction, the regent and two magistrates of the tribunal, acting with the *auditor de guerra* or the *auditor de marina,* could resolve themselves into a special court for the trial in second instance of cases pertaining to the respective fields of the last two officials.[15]

Two or three cases may be described here which illustrate the method of procedure in the trial of military cases by the tribunals. On January 22, 1787, a royal order was issued on the recommendation of the *junta de guerra de Indias,* approving of a sentence of death pronounced upon a soldier in the Philippines four years before. This soldier had been sentenced in first instance by the *castellán.* The captain-general, on ap-

---

14 *Auditor de guerra,* "the *juez letrado,* who has jurisdiction in first instance over cases under the military law, subordinate to the captain or commandant-general of an army or province" (Escriche, *Diccionario,* I, 369).

15 Royal order of January 30, 1855, *Colección legislativa de España,* LXIV, 105–147.

peal, affirmed the sentence, and the *junta de guerra* approved
the proceedings when the case was appealed a second time.[16]
Another case, and one which illustrates the slowness of the proceedings of this *junta,* as well as the nature of its jurisdiction,
was that of a soldier who had set fire to a powder magazine,
causing it to explode, thereby killing several persons. The
culprit was sentenced by the *consejo ordinario de guerra,* a sort
of local military and strategic committee, composed of local
military officers (in this case a kind of court-martial),[17] but
Governor Basco y Vargas, upon the advice of his *asesor,* suspended sentence, directing the case to the *junta de guerra.*
Nothing was done, however, and on December 10, 1788, Governor Marquina, successor to Basco y Vargas, wrote to the
president of the Council of the Indies, calling attention to the
fact that this soldier had been in prison for six years awaiting
the action of the Council of the Indies.[18] The matter was then
referred to the *junta* and the sentence was approved by that
tribunal.

As in all other departments and activities of government,
so in this, there were many opportunities for conflict between
the audiencia and the governor as to authority over cases
which by their nature bordered on the sphere of both the civil

---

[16] Royal order of January 22, 1787, A. I., 107–5–16.

[17] That the *consejo de guerra* was something more than a (tribunal
of) courtmartial and that it actually participated in the administration of military affairs may be seen in the *cédula* of June 22,
1599, which authorized the local *consejo* to act with the audiencia
and *cabildo* in restraining the military officials in the provinces
from imposing undue exactions on the natives, assessing them too
heavily or confiscating their property in the equipment of military
forces in time of threatened invasion *(Recopilación,* 3–4–3).

[18] On March 12, 1781, Governor Basco y Vargas complained to the
king against the inconvenience of having to appeal the decisions
of the local council of war to the Supreme Council in Madrid. This
was the practice followed in other parts, he said, but it was undesirable in the Philippines on account of the isolation and the
distance. He recommended instead that these cases should be appealed to a board consisting of the governor and two *asesores*—one
his own, and the other an *oidor* to be designated by him. This
recommendation was not accepted (A. I., 106–1–18).

and military jurisdictions. The governor who had the power to assign cases to whatever tribunal he chose, often took advantage of his position to bring the trial of civil cases within his own military sphere. Among these were suits involving the militiamen. These were subject to the military jurisdiction when they were under arms, and at other times, being civilians, they were subject to the civil authorities.[19] An instance of a case of this kind occurred in 1800. A militiaman, Josef Ruy, had killed an Indian, and the audiencia, on the basis of its authority over Indians, had sentenced the culprit to death. The governor, after sentence was passed, reopened the case on the ground that as a member of the militia, Ruy was subject to the military and not to the civil jurisdiction, although the militia was not at that time in active service. The judgment of the audiencia was therefore suspended. The case, meanwhile, had been appealed to the Council of the Indies, and that tribunal had approved the sentence of the audiencia, apparently without taking note of the fact that the case involved the military jurisdiction. A short time afterward the Council received a second report from the audiencia, stating that jurisdiction over the case had been surrendered to the governor on account of its military character. This procedure was accordingly approved by the Council. Soon after, report came of the receipt by the audiencia of the former judgment of the Council, relative to the action first taken by the audiencia, with the information that since the will of the Council was known, the governor had surrendered the prisoner again to the jurisdiction of the audiencia. Disgusted at the contradiction and cross-purposes at which the authorities in the Islands were working, the king decreed on March 27, 1802, that cases involving Indians should be tried in the audiencia, but that this poor wretch had been tried and re-

---

[19] Audiencia to Váldez, December 11, 1788, A. I., 107–5–16.

tried, condemned and condemned over again so often that he had already expatiated his crime. He was accordingly authorized to go free.[20]

The king administered a severe reprimand to the governor and *oidores* on this occasion for their insistence on these small points of personal dignity in which the real purpose of the law was entirely overlooked in the pompous insistence of these officials on what they imagined to be their own particular rights. The case just alluded to began in 1792, and was carried through ten years of petty strife. The blame for this cannot be ascribed entirely to the magistrates of the audiencia, or to the governor, who had to act in accordance with the law as he interpreted it. The real fault lay in the failure of the Spanish governmental system to place implicit confidence in the judgment and ability of its servants. Considering the final ends of justice, it made little difference whether sentence was pronounced upon this individual by the governor as military commander, or as president of the audiencia. It is true that the authorities might have compromised on many occasions; indeed, from the viewpoint of history it may be said that they should have done so, instead of so often wasting their energies on these petty battles. These incessant disputes were encouraged and facilitated by the ease with which appeals could be made to Spain, thus hindering the immediate execution of decisions. The Council of the Indies interfered in details which should have been left entirely to the colonial authorities. This interference encouraged appeal, and matters of no relative importance to Spain's colonial empire frequently occupied a large share of the attention of the sovereign tribunal. Colonial officials were not entrusted with the authority and responsibility which they should have had, and the central government

---

[20] Royal order of March 27, 1802, A. I., 107–5–16.

wasted its time attending to small affairs which should have been concluded by subordinates in the colonies.

The governor frequently claimed jurisdiction over cases involving retired soldiers on the grounds that they had once been under the *fuero militar*. He also claimed jurisdiction in suits affecting widows of soldiers, all of which, in accordance with the law of December 11, 1788, should have been tried by the audiencia.[21] Another abuse frequently perpetrated by the governor was the assumption of jurisdiction over suits for the payment by military officials of bonds which they had assumed for defaulted civil officials.[22] In doing this he was encroaching on the rights of the *oficiales reales*, and these were always supported by the audiencia in the contentions which arose over this question. Cases involving conflicts of jurisdiction between the civil and military authorities were appealed to the Council of the Indies, and there, after considerable delay, the proper sphere of authority was always determined.

While the audiencia as a tribunal was forbidden jurisdiction in the trial of cases involving war, we have already shown that the governor exercised the right of designating *oidores* to try cases of this nature on second appeal. The power of enforcing this right depended entirely on the governor. Frequently the efforts of the governor along these lines were attended with much difficulty as were those of Governor Marquina in 1789 when he sought to designate an *oidor* to assist in the trial of Antonio Callejo, naval artilleryman on a frigate of war. The case had first been tried before the proper military judge, but it was referred on appeal to a tribunal of which an *alcalde ordinario* of the city was a member. The governor designated Oidor Yuguanzo to act as a member of this tribunal for the trial of the case of Callejo on review. The magistrate

---

[21] Case of Don Diego Salvatierra, November 20, 1792, A. I., 105–2–10.

[22] Case of Don Josef de Áviles, November 2, 1792, A. I., 105–2–10.

begged to be excused on the ground that all his time was occupied with the trial of civil cases in the audiencia. The governor called on all the other *oidores* successively, and all declined to act. At last he peremptorily ordered Yuguanzo to serve, telling him that if he objected he might carry the matter to the king in the regular way, which, according to the laws of the Indies, was to comply with the governor's demands, under protest, while appealing the question of disagreement to the Council of the Indies.[23] This was accordingly done, the magistrate basing his claim to exemption on the law which prohibited the governor from sending *oidores* on commissions outside the audiencia.[24] The governor at the same time filed a memorial which forestalled all the arguments of the *oidor*.[25] He stated that the real cause of the disinclination of the magistrates of the audiencia to serve as *auditores de guerra* was their indolence, and not the pressure of their excessive duties. It was contrary to their ideas of dignity to be associated with the acting *auditor de guerra*, who was not a *letrado*, and it was therefore considered a sacrifice of their own personal dignity. The governor stated that no argument could justify such an attitude on the part of the *oidores*. The inconsistency of their position was further shown, he alleged, by the fact that they had served regularly on the tribunal of appeals of the *consulado*, in company with two merchants who were not

---

23 *Recopilación*, 2–16–12; 2–15–36.

24 *Ibid.*, 2–16–11.

25 The memorial which the governor sent in answer to the arguments of the *oidor* was an interesting exposition of his opinion of the audiencia. He said that the lack of time alleged by the *oidor* was a mere pretense, as the regular sessions of the audiencia did not exceed three hours a day. The governor stated that none of the *oidores* were occupied more than that length of time, excepting those who had special conservatorships of cockpits, tobacco, cards, betel, and wine. The suits of Spaniards and Indians were few, he alleged, since most of the questions involving commerce were tried in the tribunal of the *consulado* (Governor Marquina to the superintendent-general, July 10, 1789, A. I., 107–5–18); see Chapter III, note 88.

even lawyers. Hence there could be no reason for their refusal to serve with an *alcalde ordinario*.

The governor based his right to call upon the regular magistrates for this service on that section of the laws of the Indies applying to Española, Nuevo Reino, and Tierra Firme, which declared that jurisdiction over cases affecting soldiers belonged to the captain-general with inhibition of the audiencia, and that soldiers, during the time they were under arms, should not be tried on criminal charges.[26] The governor, according to this law, might call upon a magistrate to serve as special *auditor de guerra* for the determination of cases in second instance. Finally, by April 20, 1784, the king had extended this rule to all other colonies.[27] Although we have no record of the reply of the tribunal in Spain, the strength of the governor's position could not well be questioned, especially since he was resting his case on a law made in 1784, which was completely up-to-date, while the magistrate's contention was based on one promulgated in 1609.[28]

Aside from the duty of the *oidores* to try military cases when commissioned by the governor to do so, it will be seen that the tribunal itself exercised much more extensive authority in the actual administration of military affairs. Two factors may be said to have contributed to this. One was the fact that the audiencia was frequently consulted by the king or governor in regard to the defense of the colony. The other may be seen in the actual assumption of the government at various times by the audiencia, and the successful defense of the Islands by the military forces under the leadership of the *oidores*. Notwithstanding the fact that the governor's recognized sphere of action was military, and in spite of the re-

---

[26] *Recopilación*, 3–11–2.
[27] *Ibid.*, note 2.
[28] See citation of the *cédula* of January 24, 1773, applicable to Perú, wherein an *oidor* was permanently charged with the duty of serving as *auditor de guerra* (*ibid.*).

peated prohibitions against the interference of the tribunal in these matters, the audiencia received considerable official encouragement and authorization to interest itself in military affairs.

As the problems of general administration were too serious for the solution of one man without advisors, so the governor also found it frequently undesirable to assume sole responsibility for military affairs. The audiencia shared the *acuerdo* power in these matters to a lesser degree than it did in government. The hostility of the Japanese in the early years, the fear of the Chinese, the danger of native outbreaks, the raids of the Moro pirates, and the incursions of the Portuguese, Dutch, and English aroused the fears of the commonwealth to such an extent that defense was felt to be a matter of common concern. The governor, upon whom legally rested the obligations and responsibilities of defense, was glad to share these duties with any authority that could be of assistance. The history of the Philippines is replete with instances in which the audiencia either gave counsel in matters pertaining to defense, or took an active part in resistance. There were even occasions on which it advocated offensive warfare.[29]

We have seen in an earlier chapter that the audiencia manifested a keen interest in military affairs immediately upon its establishment. In the chapter on the establishment of the tribunal we noted the memorials of individual *oidores*, and of the audiencia as a tribunal, advising the governor and the king as to the necessity of conquering the Moros, and on the best way of putting down insurrections in the Islands. The question of defense against the Portuguese and the Dutch was

---

[29] Morga states that after the audiencia was established in May, 1584, "they (the *oidores)* began to attend to the affairs both of justice and of war and government" (Morga's Sucesos, Blair and Robertson, XV, 60).

also discussed in the letters of the *oidores*. In some cases their advice was considered, on other occasions the governor complained against them for exceeding their jurisdiction. One of the most noteworthy instances of the recognized intervention of the *oidores* in military matters was on April 19, 1586, when a council, called together by Governor Sande and consisting of the governor, the bishop, and the *oidores*, considered the immediate occupation of China. This was urged by Governor Sande, but he was overruled by the moderate counsels of the bishop and magistrates.[30]

No better illustration of the willingness of the governor to share his military responsibilities can be given than the reliance of Governor Dasmariñas on the religious authorities for advice in ·military affairs, after the suppression of the audiencia in 1589.[31] He consulted with them on ways and means of defending the colony against the Japanese, whose threatening attitude during his administration rendered precarious the continuance of Spanish power in the Islands. On one occasion he consulted the religious orders as to the advisability of expelling all Japanese and Chinese traders from

---

[30] Memorial of April 19, 1586, Blair and Robertson, VI, 197–233. The purpose of the proposed expedition was declared to be to "forestall the danger that the French and English, and other heretics and northern nations, will discover and navigate that strait which certainly lies opposite those regions—that of Labrador." A note suggests that this probably referred to the St. Lawrence River. Delgado says that Governor Sande called this council together on April 9, 1586, evidently meaning Santiago de Vera, as the latter became governor in 1584, and Sande left the Islands in 1580. De Vera's signature is affixed to this petition. Other letters of special importance, from the audiencia or individual *oidores* to the court, entirely or in part on military affairs, written during this period, may be noted in Blair and Robertson, VI, 56–65, 157–233, 254–264, 265–274, 311–321, XVII, 251–280, and throughout this series from Volumes VI to XXXV (1584–1650) especially. The general subject is covered in A. I., 67–6–6 to 26.

[31] Luzón Menaced, Blair and Robertson, VIII, 284–297. We shall see, in the next chapter, that Governor Bustamante, on a similar occasion, asked for the written advice of the various ecclesiastical authorities and corporations on the question of whether he had a right to remove and appoint *oidores* without express royal authorization.

Manila. The accumulation of provisions against a possible siege, the seizure of the persons and property of all Japanese residents, the establishment of a place of refuge for women, children, and sick persons in case of invasion, and the appropriation of the property of the natives as a pledge of their good behavior in the event of hostilities, were measures proposed by the governor to the religious for their consideration. Dasmariñas, on another occasion, asked the advice of the Augustinians, Dominicans, and Jesuits as to the best manner of dealing with an insurrection in Zambales, and the religious authorities, after quoting scholars, saints, and theologians, made lengthy recommendations.[32] These facts make clear the unwillingness of this governor to take the initiative in affairs pertaining to his own special province. He was content to ask and receive the advice of priests, monks, and magistrates, on military affairs. He was willing to seek the counsel of any and all available persons or authorities who could or would advise him. It is, of course, clear that the audiencia, when in existence, would be preferred as a source of advice and counsel to a community of religious.

Not only did the governor set a precedent of seeking the advice of the audiencia during this early period, but the king often sought the opinion of the magistrates in regard to military affairs. Various matters were referred by the sovereign to the *oidores* at different times: questions involving the building of walls and fortifications of Manila, and the number and size of cannon needed for the proper equipment of the latter; the audiencia was asked whether it would be better to bring gunpowder from New Spain or to manufacture it in the Islands; the magistrates were required on several occasions to furnish information as to the number of men needed for the defense of the Islands, and whether the

---

[32] Opinions of the religious communities on the war with the Zambales. January 19–20, 1592, Blair and Robertson, VIII, 199–233.

natives would make good soldiers. The audiencia furnished information to the king concerning the availability of the various Philippine woods for shipbuilding, and it furnished estimates as to the probable cost of ships both for commerce and war.[33] All these matters were supposed to come within the special military jurisdiction of the governor, yet, not only that official, but the king himself, required the advice of the magistrates on these questions.

The conquest of Mindanao and the war in the Moluccas were also subjects of correspondence between the court and the local audiencia.[34] The king, on various occasions, requested information of the *oidores* concerning the natives and their attitude towards law and order, whether the various tribes were quiet, by nature peaceful or warlike, and what measures, in the opinions of the magistrates, would be best in dealing with them. The audiencia was consulted on other occasions as to the best manner of fortifying the Visayan Islands against the attacks of the Moros, and northern Luzón against the Chinese and Japanese, the possible cost and most suitable locations of fortifications, and their availability and probable value in repelling invasions.

The reliance of the governor and the court upon the magistrates of the audiencia for advice in the matter of defense was not characteristic only of the early years of Philippine history. In 1744 Governor Torre submitted his scheme for the fortification of the city of Manila to the audiencia before he sent it to the king for final approval.[35] Torre was aided by a regular council of war (*consejo de guerra*) of which the *oidores* were members and he submitted questions relative to the defense of the Islands to this council. In 1746, this local council of war

---

[33] Audiencia to the King, January 7, 1597, A. I., 105-2-1.

[34] A. I., 105-2-1 to 10 are replete with documents illustrating this phase of the relation of the audiencia and the governor.

[35] Torre to the King, July 26, 1744, A. I., 108-2-21.

reported on the advisability and feasibility of manufacturing guns and powder in the colony.[36]   Governor Obando, writing in 1748 to the king, and commenting on the relationship of the previous governor with the audiencia in the matter of defense, divided between his predecessor and the audiencia the responsibility for the payment of ten thousand pesos to bribe the Dutch to keep away from the city, and not to reduce it.[37] In a subsequent chapter we shall discuss the important part played by the audiencia in the defense and surrender of the Islands to the British in 1762.   These incidents, taken at random from various governors' administrations, show that the audiencia was required to do all that it could to assist the governor and captain-general in the defense of the colony.   It was also called upon to advise the court on military affairs; thus it was frequently able to assist in formulating and guiding the policies of the home government with regard to defense and military administration.   In this way an indirect, but distinct check was placed upon the governor in his own field, and an incapable or radical executive was thus prevented from endangering the peace and security of the colony.

But the influence of the audiencia operated much more effectively in defense of the colony than through the advice which it rendered either to the king or to the governor.   From 1601 to 1625, during which period the residents of the colony were continually alarmed by the unceasing encroachments of

---

[36] Report of Council of War, June 18, 1746, A. I., 108–2–21.   See note 17 of this chapter, which deals with the local council of war. On the occasion referred to, it acted as a courtmartial.   It also had power to advise the governor, and even to prevent the military officials from taking steps which would inflict injustice on the natives in connection with military operations.   Here it may be seen that magistrates were actually members of this council, and in this capacity they advised the governor as to the best means of fortifying and defending the Islands.   The laws of the Indies are singularly lacking in definite statements as to the legal composition and membership of this council.

[37] Obando to the King, August 15, 1748, A. I., 108–2–21.

the Dutch, the audiencia was frequently obliged to assume responsibility for the defense of the colony. In 1600 and 1601, when Francisco Tello de Guzmán was governor, Antonio de Morga, the senior *oidor,* led an expedition against the Dutch pirate Van Noordt and defeated him in Manila Bay. In 1607, the audiencia, then in charge of the government, maintained the defense of Manila and Cavite against the Dutch.[38] While Governor Pedro de Acuña was absent in the Moluccas in 1605-1606 on a campaign of conquest, the audiencia entertained and responded to a petition from the king of Tidore for assistance in resisting the oppression of the king of Ternate. The war in the Moluccas was continued by the interim government of the audiencia (1606-1608).

The audiencia repeatedly assumed charge of the government during the frequent absences of Governor Juan de Silva (1609-1616) on expeditions of conquest; and it governed two years after his death (1616-1618). Under the leadership of Oidor Andrés de Alcaraz the military and naval forces of the Islands repeatedly repelled the invasions of the Dutch.[39] Of special merit was the work of this *oidor* in the preparation and equipment of a fleet of seven galleons which he led in the battle of Playa Honda, on April 14, 1617. In order to raise money with which to meet the expenses of this campaign, the audiencia was compelled to resort to the extraordinary recourse of seizing the money of Manila merchants on its arrival from Acapulco on the galleon. It also forced loans from residents and officials who were in the colony. The audiencia authorized the sale and the payment in advance for space on the galleon of the coming year. Alcaraz, in a report to the king, stated that the *oidores* had labored with diligence for the defense of the colony, personally concerning themselves with the casting of artillery, the drilling of soldiers, the obtaining of supplies, and

---

38 Morga's Sucesos, Blair and Robertson, XV, 205-237.
39 Martínez de Zúñiga, *An historical view,* I, 239-241.

in otherwise preparing the city for more adequate defense.[40]

Under the leadership of the able soldiers and captains-general, Juan Niño de Tavora (1626-1632), Sebastián Hurtado de Corcuera (1634–1635), and Diego Fajardo (1644–1653), the audiencia interfered but little with the notable military operations of that period. Exception to this statement must be made in the cases of the capture and relinquishment of the island of Formosa in 1629 and 1642, respectively. The audiencia was unreservedly opposed to the proposed conquest of the island by Governor Tavora, who, nevertheless, undertook the expedition and carried it to a successful conclusion. When Governor Corcuera decided that the position of the Spaniards in Formosa was untenable and resolved to withdraw the garrison, the audiencia was equally forceful in its remonstrances. It sent charges to the court against the governor, alleging that this loss, and that of the Moluccas the year before would assuredly lead to the greater disaster of the loss of the Philippines.[41]

The important part played by the audiencia in the defense of Manila against the British in 1762 will be discussed in another chapter. While Governor Rojo and the majority of the *oidores* were in the city, surrounded by the enemy, Oidor Anda y Salazar, who had been sent to the provinces as visitor, organized and maintained a defense against the enemy. When he was commanded by the governor to surrender, he refused, successfully maintaining the claim that as the sole, legally-appointed *oidor* who had not surrendered, he was both audiencia and governor, and as such his actions were legal. His

---

[40] In recommending the services of Licentiate Madrid y Luna, *oidor* of the Manila audiencia, Alcaraz wrote to the king as follows: "On that account, and for the good accomplished by his services in this Royal Audiencia, the said Licentiate Madrid claims that your Majesty should grant him as a reward permission to marry some of his seven daughters and three sons in Mexico" (Alcaraz to Felipe III, August 10, 1617, Blair and Robertson, XVIII, 52).

[41] Formosa lost to Spain, Blair and Robertson, XXXV, 128-162.

claims were recognized and approved by the king. This is perhaps the most peculiar and extraordinary example of the audiencia's assumption of military power.

The frequent assumption of the government by the audiencia, with responsibility for matters of defense and military administration may be cited as an additional reason for its reluctance to entirely abandon its interest in these affairs on the arrival of a governor. Notwithstanding this, and the additional fact that the king and governor frequently consulted the audiencia on military affairs, the tribunal did not always seek to retain preëminence in military affairs. This fact is shown by a letter which the audiencia wrote in 1598, acknowledging that "the only cases in which the governor is entitled to entire jurisdiction are those over soldiers—and these cases he may try independently, since he is captain-general."[42] There were numerous other occasions on which the audiencia unreservedly recognized the jurisdiction of the governor, often protesting against his excesses in military matters, but going no further than to register its protestations. For instance, it charged Governor Fajardo with carelessness in the outfitting of ships to resist the Dutch. One ship, it was said, was so poorly equipped that it sank before it left port. Fajardo was moreover accused of removing the commander of one of these ships, substituting his fifteen-year-old brother, Luís Fajardo, at a salary of 40,000 pesos. The audiencia contented itself with remonstrances against these wrongs, but it made no attempt to interfere.[43] Fajardo had his way in these matters, but he would have been compelled to answer for them personally in his *residencia* had he not died before that investigation took place.

The governor's accountability for the government of the Chinese was closely related to his jurisdiction over military

---

[42] Audiencia to the King, July 15, 1598, A. I., 67–6–18.

[43] Audiencia to Felipe III, August 8, 1620, Blair and Robertson, XIX, 77–89.

affairs. The Chinese were regarded with great suspicion by the residents of Manila, who lived in constant fear of an outbreak in the Parián, or of a descent upon the coast of Luzón by Chinese from without. The problem of the Chinese was therefore essentially one of defense, and as such it was entrusted to the governor and captain-general. Nevertheless, the audiencia claimed the right to intervene in many matters pertaining to the government of these people, and there was much dissension between the *oidores* and the governor over this question. The governor on some occasions rigidly resisted the claims of the audiencia to exercise jurisdiction over the Chinese, and on others he invited the participation of the tribunal. This state of affairs was brought about by the seeming conflict of the laws bearing upon this question.

The earliest legislation to be found in the laws of the Indies dealing with the government of the Chinese was enacted on April 15, 1603.[44] This law forbade the *alcaldes ordinarios* to exercise jurisdiction over suits of the Chinese in the Parián, but it ordered that all cases involving them should be tried by a special *alcalde* of the Parián with right of appeal to the audiencia. A special judge was thus created by this law, with jurisdiction over the Chinese.[45] The purpose of this enactment was to establish a system of judicial procedure for the Chinese, whereby the latter might be kept apart from the Spaniards and natives in judicial as well as in governmental administration. This necessity was pàrtly based on economic considera-

---

[44] *Recopilación*, 5-3-24; also A. I., 105-2-1.

[45] *Recopilación*, 2-15-55. Don Antonio de Morga, writing in his *Sucesos* in 1609, described the Chinese government of the Parián as follows: "The Chinese have a governor of their own race, a Christian, who has his officials and assistants. He hears their cases in affairs of justice, in their domestic and business affairs; appeals from him go to the alcalde-mayor of Tondo, or of the Parián, and from all these to the Audiencia, which also gives especial attention to this nation and whatever pertains to it" (Morga's Sucesos, Blair and Robertson, XVI, 197). See W. L. Schurz, "The Chinese in the Philippines," in *The Pacific Ocean in history*, 214–222.

tions, and partly on racial and religious reasons; it was designed essentially for the protection of the Spaniards.[46]

On the basis of the above law of April 15, 1603, the audiencia immediately proceeded to concern itself with the government of the Chinese. It claimed jurisdiction particularly over the right to issue licenses allowing Chinese to reside and trade in the Philippines. This authority was also claimed by the governor and captain-general, who was responsible for the defense of the Islands. The audiencia also proceeded to issue regulations for the Chinese trade, laying itself open to the charge of selfish interest in these commercial activities. Complaints against the audiencia's intervention reaching the court, new regulations were issued on November 4 and December 1, 1606, which forbade the audiencia to concern itself with anything relative to the government and administration of the Parián, or with the Chinese who might come to the Islands for the purpose of trade, except at the solicitation of the governor.[47] In the letter accompanying these orders, the king informed Governor Acuña that although the Chinese in the Parián were under his charge, he was to take no important steps for their government without first consulting the audiencia. The inference of this law is clear, therefore, that the audiencia might have other activities than the purely judicial. This implication gave rise later to a considerable difference of opinion, but in consequence of this law the governor was established as the fountain of authority in Chinese affairs, with the *oidores* in a secondary position.

---

[46] The Chinese were altogether too shrewd in business for the other residents of Manila. The desire to avoid trouble and to keep from provoking the Chinese to rebellion were also factors, and there were institutional and religious reasons. The Chinese were of different race and heritage and their practices and beliefs were regarded by the Catholic Spaniards as altogether heathenish and heretical, and, judging by almost any standard of morality and cleanliness it must be conceded that some of them at least were indecent and revolting.

[47] *Cédula* of December 1, 1606, A. I., 105–2–1.

On June 12, 1614, Philip III re-enacted the above law with some modifications. The *fiscal* was made legal protector of the Chinese. He was ordered to advise the *alcalde* of the Parián in legal matters pertaining to them, and the *alcalde* was to take no important steps without the advice and assistance of the *fiscal*.[48] The governor was ordered not to allow any ordinary or special judge, *alcalde del crimen,* or *oidor,* to exercise jurisdiction in first instance over civil suits or criminal cases of the Chinese, or to make inspections in the Parián. The last clause of this law, however, qualified and rendered dubious the effect and meaning of the entire enactment, by adding, "unless in a case so extraordinary, necessary and imperative that it may appear convenient to limit this rule."

It will not be extraneous to point out here that this was a common weakness of many laws, by which they were frequently rendered entirely inapplicable. In this case, for example, the evident object was to prevent the *oidores* from interfering in Chinese affairs, thus guaranteeing the government and administration by officials who were endowed with knowledge and understanding of their racial characteristics and peculiarities, while centering the ultimate responsibility for them in the governor. It was realized, however, that exceptional cases might arise in which some other procedure might be advisable, and accordingly a loophole was left whereby the entire law could be nullified. The audiencia was thus given a basis for intervention in the government of the Chinese whenever it suited the convenience of the magistrates. This defect is emphasized here because this particular exception justified the intervention of the audiencia on many occasions, and was a cause of continual contention between the governor and the audiencia in Chinese affairs.

Although it is difficult to settle conclusively the question

---

48 *Recopilación,* 6–18–6.

of the extent of jurisdiction which the governor and the audiencia, respectively, exercised over the Chinese in the Parián, a few cases may be presented in this connection to show that both the governor and the audiencia were justified by royal authority in advancing claims to control. On December 4, 1630, the king wrote a scathing arraignment of the audiencia for having entertained an appeal from the Chinese over the head of the governor, practically disregarding the latter, and for making recommendations relative to the Chinese and to military affairs, which questions were entirely outside its province.[49] One of the items of the report of the recent visitor-general to the Philippines, Licentiate Francisco de Rojas y Ornate in 1629, had been a charge that the audiencia had condemned and fined a Chinese merchant for smuggling munitions of war into the colony, after the latter had proved that he had been acting under the instructions of Governor Silva.[50] The visitor-general took the position that this case was entirely within the military sphere; therefore the governor's decision was final, and the audiencia was proceeding without jurisdiction in attempting to deal with it. The king called upon the tribunal to justify its action in the matter.[51] It is to be noted that in this case the point at issue was not that the audiencia was interfering with a Chinaman who should have been punished by another authority, but that in assuming jurisdiction the audiencia had infringed on the special prerogatives of the governor with regard to war and government. The frequency and seriousness of the Chinese insurrections in the early seventeenth century, and the fear of a hostile invasion from China, placed all questions of dealing

---

[49] King to the Audiencia, December 4, 1630, A. I., 105–2–10. The Chinese had asked the king on this occasion to remove Governor Tavora. The magistrates, jealous of the governor, and desiring to see him dispossessed of his office, forwarded this request to the king.

[50] Royal instructions to Gerónimo Ortiz y Capata, February 4, 1631, A. I., 105–2–1.

[51] King to the Audiencia, December 4, 1630, A. I., 105–2–10.

with the Chinese upon a military basis, hence the authority of the governor.

Much correspondence of various kinds might be cited to show that the governor was encouraged to consult the audiencia on Chinese affairs. Not only was the governor expected to do this, but the king himself directed many letters to the "governor and audiencia" and to the "governor and *oidores*," in which he asked for advice and information bearing upon Chinese affairs. As we have already seen, *cédulas* treating of these matters were frequently expedited to the "governor and audiencia." The audiencia was requested by the royal authority on August 8, 1609, to submit information as to the truth of various statements by persons in the Islands that the Chinese were carrying away vast quantities of silver. The audiencia was ordered to enact measures which would stop this abuse, which, if persisted in, would inevitably result in an impoverishment of the Philippine community and government. The *oidores* were asked to suggest a course of action which would result in the retention of the Chinese trade and at the same time prevent the Chinese from doing irreparable damage to the royal exchequer in the ways alluded to.[52]

In further illustration of the same subject, we may note the instructions of the king to Governor Silva, dated March 27, 1616. On this occasion the king prescribed a course of action for the governor to follow in case of the invasion of the Islands by the Chinese and Japanese. He was especially directed to prevent a union of the Chinese in the Parián with the forces of the expected invaders. Silva was ordered to take no steps without first consulting the *oidores*.[53] On July 25, 1619, having received news of the insubordination of the Chinese in Manila and of the danger of a revolt among them, the king wrote to the "president and *oidores*" expressing the belief that too

---

[52] King to the Audiencia, August 8, 1609, A. I., 105-2-1.
[53] King to Governor Silva, March 27, 1616, A. I., 105-2-1.

many Chinese had been admitted to the Islands and that thereafter only enough should be permitted to man the ships and
carry on trade.[54] The authorities to whom this letter was
directed were charged not to allow the royal will relative to
this matter to be disregarded, which, of course, implied the
exercise of an executive power on the part of the magistrates,
in addition to consultative authority.

Again, on December 31, 1630, the king wrote to the governor
and audiencia, stating that there had been received at the court
from the Chinese of the Parián, a series of memorials, letters
and petitions, complaining against the rigor of Spanish administration and requesting that they might be governed by mandarins, governors and *alcaldes mayores* of the "Chinese nation."
The king signified his unwillingness to comply with their request
at this time, and accordingly ordered the governor and audiencia
to permit no changes to be made.[55] On July 27, 1713, the tribunal, acting in a legislative capacity, decreed that within thirty
days "all Moros, Armenians, Malabars, Chinese and other
enemies of the Holy Faith" should be lodged in the Parián when
visiting Manila, or when living there temporarily for purposes of
visit or trade. Penalties were also prescribed for the infraction
of the above law.[56] This affords one illustration out of many
which could be cited of the legislation of the audiencia in Chinese affairs.[57]

On May 14, 1790, the king wrote to the "governor and president of the royal audiencia" and also to the tribunal, ordering
the re-establishment of the Parián. This Chinese quarter had
been abolished since 1756. It was agreed that the Chinese in

---

[54] King to the President and *oidores*, July 25, 1619, A. I., 105–2–1.
[55] King to the President and *oidores*, December 21, 1630, A. I.,
105–2–1.
[56] *Acuerdo* of July 27, 1713, A. I., 68–4–17.
[57] Attention was called in the last chapter to the *acuerdo* power
of the audiencia in Chinese affairs. It was seen there that the
audiencia passed ordinances regulating the Chinese trade, also their
organization and manner of living in the Islands.

this district should be ruled by an *alcalde*, who should also hear cases in first instance, with appeal to the audiencia. It was furthermore decreed that the Chinese population in the Islands should be fixed at 4000 and that each individual should be taxed at the rate of six pesos *per capita*.[58] This tax was to be collected by the *cabecilla* of the Chinese, a sort of local leader, subject to the *alcalde* of the Parián. This *cédula*, the king stated, was originally suggested by the *acuerdo* of the audiencia, and had been submitted for royal approval, which had been duly conceded. This correspondence, which shows the real operation of the government much more accurately than the citation of laws alone could do, makes it quite clear that throughout the history of the Islands, notwithstanding the existence of many *cédulas* to the contrary, the audiencia exercised advisory power in regard to the government of the Chinese. This authority was repeatedly recognized by the governor and by the king himself.

After the inauguration of the superintendency of *real hacienda* at Manila in 1787, the incumbent of that office was made largely responsible for the Chinese. This was probably so arranged because the care and administration of the Chinese at that time involved questions of finance rather than of war and defense. It will be remembered, too, that, during much of the time, the office of superintendent was combined with that of governor. A number of disputes arose between the governor and the intendant after the latter office was created in 1785,[59] but after the union of the governorship with the superintendency,

---

58 King to the President and *oidores*, May 14, 1790, A. I., 105-9-10. This tax was collected from the Chinese in 1852, when Jagor, the celebrated German traveller, visited the Islands. Chinese who were engaged in agriculture paid merely the tribute of twelve *reales*, which was collected from natives as well. In addition to the tax of six dollars (probably Mexican, which were equivalent to the silver peso) merchants paid an industrial tax of twelve, thirty, sixty, or one hundred dollars, according to the amount of business transacted (Blair and Robertson, LII, 57-58, note).

59 Consulta of June 28, 1786; Intendant Carvajal to King, December 31, 1787, and other letters; A. I., 107-5-15.

no further occasion of dispute arose. During the greater part of the nineteenth century, the peculiar nature of the office of intendant gave to the latter official the duty of collecting the licenses of the Chinese, subject to the superintendent.

There yet remains something to be said regarding the administration of justice among the Chinese, and we must note certain typical disputes and disagreements which arose in that connection. That the audiencia had authority to try cases in second instance involving the Chinese has already been stated. Likewise the *oidores* were liable to special delegation to try cases of an extraordinary character which arose among the Chinese, as, for example in 1786, when Oidor Bolívar y Meña was designated to try in first instance charges which had been made against Chinese bakers in the Parián, who were said to have put a quantity of powdered glass in bread which they had made for the Spaniards. This case was regarded as one of more than ordinary significance, as involving treason and insurrection, and it was accordingly tried by an *oidor* who had been especially delegated for the purpose by the governor.[60]

The question of Chinese jurisdiction is further illustrated by a dispute which arose in the colony between the audiencia and the governor, and which was carried to the king by the latter functionary on June 30, 1793. Oidor Moreno had ordered the arrest of the Chinese *cabecilla* of the Parián on a criminal charge.[61] The detention of the Chinaman, was conceded to be justifiable, but Governor Marquina alleged that Moreno had entirely disregarded the *cédula* of October 11, 1784, which had ordered that in case of the arrest of any royal official, notification should be served to the governor in sufficient time for him to take the proper precautions for the safeguarding of any óf

---

[60] *Testimonio de autos sobre sublevación de los sangleyes, substanciados y determinados por el oidor, Don Pedro Sebastián Bolívar y Meña, 1686–1690*, A. I., 68–1–27.

[61] Marquina to the King, June 30, 1793, A. I., 107–5–22.

His Majesty's property which might be in the care or under the protection of the official in question. He said that this particular arrest was typical of the petty interference of the *oidores* and illustrative of the slight pretexts upon which they frequently upset the whole system of government and caused untold annoyances. On account of the many difficulties in the collection of the tribute which had presented themselves as a consequence of the arrest of this particular Chinese official, and because the latter was especially efficient, the governor had asked the audiencia to permit the *cabecilla* to be excused on condition that he should bind himself to return to the custody of the audiencia after he had collected the taxes. This the tribunal had refused. The government, as a consequence, had been put to much inconvenience in finding a substitute, and the sum collected had been considerably less than was usually obtained, owing to the lack of experience of the new collector. After the *cabecilla* had been in prison over four months, he was brought to trial, and nothing being proved against him, he was freed. The audiencia, however, had won its point, and had manifested its right to the last word in judicial affairs relating to the Chinese.

The difference between the appellate jurisdiction of the audiencia in contentious cases involving Chinese and in administrative matters which it did not have is illustrated by a case which came up in 1794 and lasted through twelve years of litigation. In the year aforementioned, the *ayuntamiento* of Manila brought suit before an *alcalde ordinario* of the city against a Chinese, Augustín Chagisco, on a charge of the failure of the latter properly to fulfill a contract which he had made to supply the city with meat. The *alcalde ordinario*, before whom suit had been brought in first instance, cancelled the contract, and the Chinese appealed to the audiencia. The tribunal, after due consideration of the case, restored Chagisco to his status as provider of meats (*abastecedor de carne*) for the city. Instead of appealing the case as one of law, the *ayuntamiento* wrote to the king on January 19, 1796, alleging that the audiencia had interfered in behalf of a Chinese whose services the *ayuntamiento* had discontinued as provider of meats, over which matter the audiencia had no jurisdiction. The king immediately gave expression of his approval of the stand of the *ayuntamiento,* being of the impression that the question at stake was one of appointment only.[62] At the same time the king demanded a full explanation from the *oidores* as to why they had interfered in this matter which was so far removed from their jurisdiction. The audiencia, in reply, sent all the records and *testimonios* of the suit to the Council, and that tribunal called upon the *ayuntamiento* in due time to explain why it had misrepresented the case. After a long period of acrimonious correspondence between the Manila authorities, the case was concluded on February 19, 1806, by a reversal of the earlier decision, and His Majesty sent a letter of congratulation and approval to the audiencia in appreciation of its stand in the matter.[63] The king informed the tribunal that it had been entirely regular in its proceedings, having reversed the decision of the *alcalde ordinario* in a legal suit which had been appealed by the Chinese to the audiencia in protest against the adverse decision of the lower court.

Without carrying this discussion further, it is clear that the audiencia had general appellate jurisdiction in cases involving the Chinese. These cases, when they originated in the Parián, were tried in first instance by special judges for the Chinese, but suits brought against a Chinese who lived outside, or suits of a semi-public nature, as the one just noted, might be tried in first instance by the ordinary judges. It has also been noted that *oidores* were sometimes delegated to try cases in first instance involving treason or insurrection of Chinese. In regard

---

[62] King to the Audiencia, November 30, 1797, A. I., 105–2–18.
[63] King to the Audiencia, February 19, 1806, *ibid.*

to matters of government, it may be said that the governor was held responsible, but even in these the *oidores* participated in an advisory capacity.

CHAPTER VIII

THE AUDIENCIA AND THE GOVERNOR: CONFLICTS OF JURISDICTION

Although it may be said that the relations of the governor and the audiencia were comparatively peaceful and harmonious throughout the history of the Philippines, there were many conflicts of jurisdiction and these struggles for power assume great prominence on account of their bitterness. An investigation of the principles underlying them and the arguments advanced by the contending parties will go far towards explaining the relationship of the audiencia with the governor.

Certain factors and conditions were always prevalent in the colony to cause trouble and provoke enmity between the governor and the *oidores*. Chief among these were the rivalry between them for commercial profits, jealously of power and advancement, and the desire on the part of all, and particularly of the governors, to enrich themselves. Officials tended to regard their appointments as commissions to engage in profitable ventures and business undertakings—opportunities which were to be immediately improved. It is probable that the presence of the audiencia did more to check this tendency than any other agency, for the documents bearing on the history of the colony are replete with charges made by *oidores* and *fiscales* against governors. It is also true that the *oidores* did effective work in correcting the misdeeds of the provincial governors and justices on their official tours of inspection. That the audiencia should accomplish this result was to be expected, since the leading purpose of its establishment was to check the excesses of the governor. The other side of the question cannot be neglected, however, for charges were made in sufficient number against the *oidores*. It is with these charges and counter-charges, memorials, complaints, and arguments that the present chapter is concerned.

The method to be pursued in this chapter will be that of indicating in all fairness both sides of these conflicts, not with the purpose of seeing which side was right, but with the object of obtaining the respective viewpoints of the governors and magistrates. We shall first consider evidence which was submitted in behalf of the audiencia against the governor, and in turn, that of the governors against the *oidores*. This method of procedure is the only one feasible since the materials here utilized consist mostly of arguments for or against the governor or audiencia, respectively.

We have already seen that the first notorious disagreement in the colony arose between Bishop Salazar and Governor's Ronquillo de Peñalosa and Santiago de Vera. This occurred before the establishment of the audiencia. The audiencia was in fact established partly to have an impartial tribunal present to arbitrate such disputes, and partly to check the excesses of the governor.[1] We have also given attention to the charges made by Oidor Dávalos against his fellow-magistrates and the governor shortly after the audiencia was established. It has been noted that the incessant quarreling between the governor and the audiencia from 1584 to 1589 was one of the causes for abolishing the tribunal at the latter date. From 1590 to 1595 the governor was supreme in matters of government, war, and justice. It was clearly shown during this period that the dis-

---

[1] See Chapter II, notes 61 and 64 of this book. The study which Dr. David P. Barrows has recently made of the office of governor and captain-general is of value in showing the continuity, and at the same time the evolution of the office from Spanish times to the present. Dr. Barrows states that Miguel López de Legaspi became governor and captain-general of the Philippines when the office was created in 1567. The original *cédula* of establishment and appointment is in Blair and Robertson, III, 62–66, and bears the date of August 14, 1569. See Barrows, "The governor-general of the Philippines under Spain and the United States," in *The Pacific Ocean in history*, p. 239.

cord of a quarrelsome tribunal was eminently to be preferred to the unchecked abuses of an autocratic governor. In 1595 the audiencia was re-established by royal enactment; from that date onward it became a permanent part of the government, notwithstanding the fact that its relations with the other institutions of the colony were not harmonious.

There were two complaints most frequently made against governors. One of these was their commercial excesses and the other, their abuse of the power of appointment. The former consisted of the monopoly of galleon space for themselves, or their friends, the acceptance of bribes from merchants for various favors, or the manipulation of the Chinese trade in some way for their own advantage. The tendency of governors to appoint their friends and relatives to office, notwithstanding the royal prohibition, and the apparent inability of the audiencia to prevent this was a source of complaint, especially during the early years of the colony.[2] Dishonest proceedings in the sale of offices, including the retention of the money received and the disposal of offices to friends for nominal sums, were among the irregularities of the early governors. These abuses the magistrates often knowingly permitted in return for some favor allowed them by the governor. That the laws which forbade these abuses of the power of appointment had been openly and flagrantly violated was a charge brought up repeatedly in the *residencias* of governors and magistrates. An examination of the correspondence of the seventeenth and eighteenth centuries would almost lead to the belief that the home government despaired of ever righting these wrongs, and left them unpunished, rather directing efforts towards reform in other channels in the hope of remedying greater defects.

Perhaps no governor more flagrantly disregarded the audiencia and the royal authority which it represented, or more

---

[2] Fiscal to the King, July 21, 1599, Blair and Robertson, XI, 114, 115; Maldonado to the King, June 28, 1605, *ibid.*, XIII, 307–315.

frequently laid himself open to complaints on account of his violent conduct than Alonso Fajardo, who ruled from 1618 to 1624. Numerous charges were brought against him by the audiencia, some of which concerned itself, and some had to do with the general administration of the government. It was charged that Fajardo sought to usurp the judicial functions of the tribunal, and to assume control of the administration of justice. He had on one occasion broken up a session of the court during the trial of a certain person for murder, ordering a sergeant to take him out and hang him. Fajardo defended himself against this accusation by alleging that the criminal was a sailor from the royal fleet, whom he, as captain-general, had already condemned, and that the audiencia was acting illegally in entertaining the case. Fajardo was said to have released prisoners at his own pleasure, and to have abused the pardoning power. He had made threats of violence against the magistrates in the court-room.

The audiencia not only complained against this governor's interference with the exercise of its functions as a court, but it manifested a wider interest than the purely judicial by complaining against the excesses of the governor in his own administrative field. The charge was made that Fajardo had bought up due-bills and treasury certificates from the soldiers and other creditors of the government, at less than their face value, and had presented them to the *oficiales reales,* realizing the full amount on them, and retaining the proceeds. He was charged with exacting large sums from the Chinese in exchange for trading privileges, retaining the money himself instead of putting it into the treasury. He was said to have forced loans from the merchants in order to make up financial deficits, and to have taken money out of the treasury, secretly, at night. Another charge brought against him was that of allowing favorites to go out and meet the incoming ships of the Chinese, thereby obtaining for himself and for them the choice parts of the cargoes in advance of the merchants of Manila.[3] There is no evidence that the tribunal was able to put a stop to these abuses.

Oidor Álvaro Messa y Lugo, in a letter written to the king on July 20, 1622, continued the campaign which had been started by the audiencia against this governor. He claimed that Fajardo had sought to prevent officials and private citizens from sending complaints to Spain against him by examining all the outgoing mail before it left the colony. The *oidor* showed that wastefulness, private trade, bribery, carelessness in the administration of the exchequer, neglect of shipbuilding, corruption, and personal violence were among the misdeeds of this governor. Messa reported that he had tried unsuccessfully to authorize the auditing of the accounts of the galleon for two successive years, in accordance with the royal instructions which ordered that it should be done at the termination of each voyage by the *fiscal* and two *oidores*.[4] Messa said that the governor feared to have the colony's finances examined for it was well known that they were in a deplorable state.

One instance of the governor's financial ingenuity which was given by Messa, illustrates the limitations placed by the audiencia on the governor's appointing power. The audiencia relieved the secretary of government, Pedro Muñoz, of his office upon the expiration of his term, selling the place to Diego de Rueda for 8000 pesos. Fajardo dispossessed Rueda and restored the office to its former incumbent for 1500 pesos. The audiencia's action in disposing of this office without the consent of the governor was justified by a law promulgated on November 13, 1581, ordering that offices should be bestowed only upon persons of such qualities and attributes as met with the approval of the

---

[3] Audiencia to Felipe III, August 8, 1620, *ibid.*, XIX, 87–89; see also Messa y Lugo to King, July 30, 1622, *ibid.*, XX, 161–163.

[4] Messa y Lugo to the King, July 30, 1622, *ibid.*, XX, 162–163; see *Recopilación*, 9–45–3.

royal justices.[4a] The governor emerged triumphant in this contest, however, because it was generally recognized at that time that his word should be final in matters of appointment. Although we have seen in a former chapter that the governor consulted with the audiencia when an important appointment was to be made, the audiencia's intervention in matters of appointment depended largely on the strength of the tribunal and the relations existing between it and the governor. During this administration the audiencia was notoriously weak and harmony did not exist.

The memorial presented by Messa y Lugo was chiefly concerned with the story of his own arbitrary arrest and imprisonment at the instigation of Fajardo on trumped-up charges, as he alleged. The judicial inquiry lasted two months, and it furnishes an excellent example of the power of a governor over a weak audiencia. The occasion for the investigation had been a disagreement between the governor and the *oidor* over the latter's claim to act as administrator of the property of Oidor Alcaraz, who had died in office. The governor, by the appointment of a magistrate favorable to himself as *juez de difuntos,* had hoped to control the administration of the property, since Messa was under sentence of *residencia,* and the remaining magistrates of the audiencia were favorable to him. Moreover, Fajardo wished to forestall certain charges of misgovernment which he knew that Messa was prepared to make against him. Consequently the governor designated an *alcalde* of the city to conduct the *residencia.* Messa was given practically no opportunity to defend himself. His property was sequestrated, even to his wife's clothing. Seeing that he could not obtain justice, he escaped from prison and took refuge in a Dominican convent.

Messa, from the seclusion of the monastery, challenged the

[4a] *Recopilación,* 8–20–1.

legality of the governor's procedure. According to his contention, the previous law authorizing the governor to name an
alcalde ordinario to try an *oidor*, was now a dead-letter. Its
chief defect had been that an *alcalde*, who was the creature of
the governor, would always aim to render a decision pleasing
to his master. He urged that the law then in force authorized
the governor to proceed with the trial of an *oidor*, only upon
consulting the audiencia, and moreover that resulting condemnations, if they were personal or corporal, should be confirmed by the Council of the Indies.[5] Messa therefore claimed
that the governor had no authority to proceed with this case
alone, since "those nearest (your Majesty), as are the auditors
(*oidores*), cannot be imprisoned or proceeded against except
by your Majesty or the royal Council, or by your order."

The *oidor* then proceeded to show the extent to which, in
his opinion, the governor might intervene in the sessions and
proceedings of the audiencia. He wrote:

The president, in virtue of his superintendency over the Audiencia,
may ordain to the auditors what may be the just and reasonable in
matters that pertain to the government and its conservation; and even,
in the heated arguments that are wont to arise between the auditors,
has authority, in case the nature of the affair might require it, to
retire each auditor to his own house, until they make up the quarrel;
and, should he deem it advisable, he may inform your Majesty. For
the ordinance does not say that the president and alcaldes shall proceed, arrest, sentence and execute justice in criminal cases affecting the
auditors.[6]

This is the interpretation which Messa placed upon the law
giving authority over the trial of magistrates of the audiencia
to the governor.

Messa then proceeded to discuss other matters relative to
the respective spheres of the governor and audiencia. The governor had broken open the chest of the audiencia, extracting a
large sum and spending it without accounting for the expendi-

---

[5] *Recopilación*, 2–16–43 and 44.
[6] Messa y Lugo to the King, *op. cit.*, 186.

ture, and without any beneficial results. He was guilty of four murders, one of his victims being his wife. The audiencia should be empowered to try him for these crimes, but it lacked jurisdiction. During his term Fajardo had exercised such absolute power that justice had been paralyzed and litigants were holding back their suits from trial because justice could not be obtained in the audiencia. The governor had sent from the Islands more than a million pesos in goods and money, all of which he had obtained through fraudulent and illegitimate means.

The governor had quarreled finally with the *oidores* who had remained faithful to him; one of these had become incapacitated through sickness, while the other had taken refuge in a Jesuit convent. The audiencia was thus dissolved. The governor, feeling the need of a tribunal, withdrew the charges against Messa, and ordered the latter to come back and resume his office. The *oidor* complied, but his hostility toward the governor had in no way abated. Messa concluded his memorial with the request that a visitor should be sent to the colony to investigate the charges which had been made against the governor, and at the same time to restore the audiencia to its rightful position in the colony. He stated his conviction that the office of governor should be abolished, and that the audiencia should be empowered to act in his place. This belief he justified by the statement that the audiencia had already successfully acted in the capacity of governor and had administered affairs with great satisfaction.

The power which the governor had of imprisoning and chastising magistrates of the audiencia who dared to oppose him, enabled him to emerge victorious in his struggles with that body. He was even able to completely suppress the audiencia. Nevertheless he was obliged, through the need of the tribunal which he had vanquished, to restore it again, although it was opposed to him. In no less than three cases gov-

ernors, in order to comply with the law requiring that there
should be at least one *oidor* of royal appointment, were obliged
to restore to the audiencia magistrates who had formerly been
under arrest. Being in possession of all the powers of an
executive, the governor was usually able to reduce the audiencia
to subserviency, unless the dispositions of the opposing *oidores*
were such that they would not submit. On the whole, the
audiencia seemed unable to check the excesses of the governor,
by virtue of its authority, and the *oidores* were obliged to confine themselves to protests and appeals to the king; these, only
after years of delay, effected the removal or punishment of the
governor and the appointment of another to continue his
excesses.

The complaints which Messa made on this occasion resulted
in bringing to the Islands a visitor who conducted a lengthy,
though somewhat tardy, investigation. Fajardo was already
beyond the punishment of earthy kings and tribunals. But his
property was seized and his heirs were fined; aside, however,
from the removal of various of Fajardo's subordinates, the
government was but little better for the protestations and appeals made by the audiencia. The *oidores,* instead of obtaining
the desired reform measures, were usually rewarded for opposing a tyrannical governor and appealing to the court for support, by a reprimand for quarreling and an admonition to be
quiet and peaceful, to preserve harmony, to attend strictly to
their own affairs, and to abstain from interference with the
government. Indeed, judging from the many similar replies
which the *oidores* received in answer to their charges against
governors, it appears that the preservation of harmonious
relations between the officials of the colony was much more
important than good government. Usually, however, in these
struggles between the audiencia and the governor the contentions of one side or the other were based on law and justice.
The effectiveness of the Spanish colonial government would

have been greatly increased had the Council of the Indies taken advantage of these opportunities to investigate the principles at stake and support the right side, rather than by issuing impotent injunctions and remonstrances.

The most significant controversy which ever occurred in the Philippines between the governor and the audiencia arose in connection with the banishment of Archbishop Pardo in 1683. It is not the purpose here to give a detailed account of the Pardo controversy, which will be discussed again in connection with the relations of the audiencia and the church. However, since this episode involves certain incidents illustrating important phases of the relationship of the governor and the audiencia, it is desirable to refer to it here in considerable detail.

The real occasion for this conflict was the defiance of the laws of the royal ecclesiastical patronage by the archbishop, who insisted on making ecclesiastical appointments without consulting the governor. The governor appealed to the audiencia for support, and the tribunal exercised jurisdiction over the case on the basis of its right to try cases of *fuerza* and to prevent ecclesiastical judges from infringing on the civil jurisdiction. Juan Sánchez, the secretary of the audiencia, relates that, owing to the interference of the Dominicans and Jesuits, and their harsh public criticism from the pulpit of the audiencia and government, "the royal Audiencia felt obliged to advise its president, then Don Juan de Vargas, that he should apply a corrective to these acts."[7] This corrective was the banishment to Spain of certain individuals of the Dominican order to answer for their misdeeds and ultimately the exile of Archbishop Pardo from the city. It is enough to say that Governor Juan de Vargas Hurtado and the audiencia acted in harmony on this occasion, presenting a solid front to the ecclesiastical power. When the new governor, Curuzaelegui, arrived, how-

---

[7] Blair and Robertson, XXXIX, 177.

ever, he forced the audiencia to ask pardon and absolution from the archbishop, which the magistrates did on their knees. The new governor disgraced Vargas in the *residencia,* waiving for a time the *residencias* of the *oidores.* Pardo was recalled from exile, and the audiencia was forced to legalize his restoration to his see on October 25, 1684. Thus the new governor and the archbishop triumphed over the combined forces of the ex-governor and the audiencia.

It is clear that the power of the new governor was derived chiefly from his status as royal vicepatron, acting in conjunction with the archbishop. This power Vargas had formerly employed in co-operation with the audiencia, and thereby both had gained their victory over the prelate before the arrival of the new governor. Curuzaelegui used the same authority to recall Pardo; and in so doing he was probably the only governor in the history of the Islands who ever supported a prelate against the advice of the audiencia. The combination of a governor and an audiencia was much more frequent, as we shall see. The position of the governor was strengthened, also, by his commission to conduct the *residencia* of Vargas, and the respect which the audiencia had for him was increased by the fact that in judging the ex-governor's misdeeds he was also authorized to hold the *oidores* responsible for all their official opinions and acts in *acuerdo* with the disgraced governor.[8] Another source of the governor's strength was to be found in the royal instructions which he carried with him to stop the quarrels previously existing in the colony. The *oidores* very prudently submitted to the new governor, and therefore, for a time, they were patronized by the latter, who utilized their intimate knowledge of local affairs to aid him in obtaining control of the government and familiarizing himself with it. Meanwhile he literally held the *residencia* over their heads.

---

[8] In accordance with *Recopilación,* 5–15–2.

The attitude of the new governor toward the audiencia during the first six months may be described as conciliatory. That he did not act with entire independence of it is attested by the fact that when Vargas appealed to the tribunal against the ecclesiastical penalties imposed by the archbishop, the governor signed the act ordering the absolution of his predecessor. When the archbishop persisted in his intention to humiliate Vargas on the ground that the Inquisition demanded such action, the new governor threatened again to expel the prelate if he did not desist.[9] His pacificatory efforts also resulted in a temporary cessation of the hostility between the archbishop and the audiencia; he held private conferences with the *oidores,* manifesting repeatedly his determination to proceed harmoniously with them. As a result of this treatment, the magistrates were emboldened to urge that the return of the prelate was contrary to law, and inconsistent with all precedent.

Finally, unable to resist the pressure exerted by the archbishop, and obtaining advance information of the royal condemnation of the audiencia for its acts in the banishment of Pardo, the governor arrested, imprisoned, and exiled the magistrates, temporarily reconstituting the tribunal with local and more subservient members.[10] Curuzaelegui's proceedings were thenceforth as high-handed as they had formerly been conciliatory, and from that time onward the residents of the colony were subjected to the rule of an absolute governor, aided by an unscrupulous and vindictive prelate and a subservient audi-

---

[9] Foreman, *Philippine Islands,* 60; Blair and Robertson, XXXIX, 208–219.

[10] The governor arrested and imprisoned magistrates Zalaeta and Lezana before the arrival of Valdivia. Oidor Viga was exiled to Samar and Bolívar was sent to Mariveles. Both of these last-mentioned magistrates died in exile. By the time Valdivia arrived Fiscal Alanis was the only person connected with the former audiencia who was left to be punished. His *residencia* was taken and his property confiscated (Blair and Robertson, XXXIX, 135, 231–233, 277, 281–295).

encia. Just before his imprisonment, Magistrate Bolívar, in a letter to the Minister of the Indies, described the chaos existent in Manila as follows:

Here there is no will, save that of a governor, since he is absolute, we all had to acquiesce, under compulsion and pressure, in the restitution of the archbishop;[11] . . . to state the case in few words, the archbishop does whatever suits his whim, without there being anyone to restrain him.[12]

Fray Luís Pimentel, a Jesuit, in a letter which he wrote to a friend, stated that the arrest of the *oidores* by the governor had been inspired by personal spite and a desire for revenge. He had desired to punish magistrates Viga and Bolívar, particularly for their opposition to him in matters of administration and in his trading-schemes. The governor was also said to have been actuated by a suspicion that these *oidores* had formulated elaborate charges of misgovernment against him, and he desired to prevent these complaints from reaching the king.[13]

Pimentel proceeded to relate that the governor then found himself embarrassed without the aid of an audiencia, and had accordingly formed another of his own selection. This body was careful to execute the governor's will in every particular; consequently there was no check on his misrule. This new audiencia approved all the acts of the archbishop and refused to entertain the appeals of the ex-governor,

royal decrees were despatched against the preachers (Jesuits) who zealously proclaimed from the pulpits the arbitrary and malicious character of the recent acts, and the Dominicans alone had the privilege to utter whatever absurdities they pleased in the pulpits. . . . No

---

[11] Bolívar to Váldez, June 15, 1685, *ibid.*, 221.

[12] *Ibid.*, 223.

[13] Pimentel to Rodríguez, February 8, 1688. Blair and Robertson, XXXIX, 240. Pimentel accused the governor of scandalous conduct, "in the matter of chastity, not sparing any woman, whatever may be her rank or condition; and he keeps some worthless women who serve as procuresses for conveying to him those whose society will give him most pleasure." Pimentel stated that the archbishop and the friars of the city did nothing to check this conduct, but knowingly permitted it.

authentic statement of the evil deeds of these years can be sent to the court for the scriveners are intimidated and will not give official statements of what occurs, except what may be in favor of the governor and the archbishop. *Item*, (this) is written in much distrust and fear, on account of the numerous spies who go about prying into and noting everything that is done.[14]

Pimentel stated that the archbishop, who was a Dominican, had used this rupture between the governor and the audiencia, and the favor of the governor, particularly, as an occasion and pretext for imposing on the Jesuits and Franciscans. He had deprived them of their lands and parishes, and had obtained many favors for the Dominicans and Augustinians at the expense of the rival orders. "It seems as if the governor had come to the islands," Pimentel wrote, "for nothing else than to encourage the Dominicans in their rebellious acts, to trample on the laws, to abolish recourse to the royal Audiencia, to sow dissension, to be a tyrant, to disturb the peace, and to enable the archbishop to secure whatever he wishes, even though he imposes so grievous a captivity on the commonwealth."[15]

The Pardo controversy and its consequences show the extremes to which a weakened audiencia was reduced on occasion by a new governor who came to the Islands, armed with recent royal decrees instructing him to bring about peace and order. Curuzaelegui, assisted by the royal visitor, who bore instructions even more recent than those of the governor, imprisoned and exiled the *oidores*, confiscated their property and brought about their ruination and death. He then appointed another audiencia of his own choice. All these acts were strictly legal, and in accordance with his instructions. The governor's conduct before the appointment of the visitor was more lenient and tolerant than afterwards. This shows that he realized the necessity of fulfilling the royal will, the policies of which

---

[14] Pimentel to Rodríguez, February 8, 1688, XXXIX, 239–240.
[15] *Ibid.*, 242–243.

were entrusted to Valdivia for execution, even at the expense of harmony with the local tribunal. Had he not been assured of the support of the church on the one hand, and of the royal approval on the other, as shown by the commission of Valdivia, it is improbable that he would have broken with the audiencia, or would have attempted to use his power so extensively. The presence of an audiencia was necessary to the government of Curuzaelegui. This is shown by his conciliatory attitude toward the tribunal of Vargas, until he knew that it was under the condemnation of the king, also by his own act in forming a new one. This controversy clearly illustrates the extent to which a governor might use his power, and it shows, on the other hand, the indispensable character of the audiencia, even at a time when it was least powerful. Curuzaelegui, in the name of the king, completely obliterated the legally constituted audiencia, appointing another to serve until it could be legalized by regular appointment.

Chronologically speaking, the next great struggle which throws light on the subject which we are considering, occurred during the administration of Governor Bustamante (1717-1719). The audiencia was reduced to a deplorable state of helplessness and inefficiency on this occasion, and the circumstances surrounding its relationship with the governor were in many ways similar to those which have been described. For a period of two and a half years antecedent to the coming of Bustamante, the government of the Philippines had been nominally in the hands of the audiencia, but in reality, under the control of the senior magistrate, Torralba. One of the first acts of Bustamante, after his arrival in the Islands, was to take the *residencia* of Torralba, and this investigation led him to make serious charges against the other magistrates. In the *residencia* which followed, the finances of the colony were found to be in bad condition, and all the officials of the civil government, as well as many of the churchmen, were discovered to be deeply interested in private trade, to the neglect of their duties and to the detriment of the government. Large amounts of money were found to have been smuggled without permission into the colony on the galleon from Mexico. The accounts of the treasury department were discovered to have been loosely kept, and many of the officials, including magistrates of the audiencia, were found to be serving without financial guarantees.[16]

Bustamante immediately took steps to re-organize the government and to place the finances of the colony on a sound footing. He put a stop to the smuggling, forced the merchants to pay the authorized duties, and imposed fines on those who had been guilty of negligence and misconduct. At the end of six months the efforts of Bustamante had netted a sum of 293,000 pesos to the royal treasury. His successful efforts towards clearing up the finances of the colony, making every person pay his just dues without regard to position, rank, or affiliation, and the seeming harshness of his methods incurred general hostility and contributed largely to his downfall.[17]

His investigation of the finances was said to have revealed a shortage of over 700,000 pesos, for which he held Torralba and the other magistrates responsible, putting most of the blame, however, on Torralba. All but one of the magistrates were arrested and incarcerated in Fort Santiago. Before this was done, however, Bustamante asked the advice of the archbishop,

---

[16] Torralba to the King, June 23, 1718, A. I., 68–4–18. When Governor Bustamante arrived in Manila in 1717, Torralba's services as *oidor* and temporary governor, extending over a period of eight years, were investigated. Wholesale bribery was the leading charge against him. He had levied blackmail on *alcaldes mayores*, *encomenderos*, and Chinese and Spanish merchants. He was also charged with the misuse of government funds, and was held responsible for large deficits. It was said that he had sent his wife to Macao with most of this ill-gotten money. In his *residencia* he was fined 120,000 pesos, exiled forever from Madrid, Manila and New Spain, and was reduced subsequently to such poverty that he was compelled to beg. He died a pauper in the hospital of San Juan de Diós, in Cavite, in 1736.

[17] Government of Bustamante, Blair and Robertson, XLIV, 151; this account (pages 148–165) is a summary of Concepción, *Historia general*, IX, 183–424; see also Montero y Vidal, *Historia general*, I, 410–429.

the religious corporations, and the universities, as to what steps he should take in the matter. He recognized that he would be seriously embarrassed without an audiencia, but the investigations which he had made showed that all of the *oidores* were guilty of misappropriation of the government funds. Would he be justified in forming an audiencia of his own selection, composed of duly qualified lawyers, with one minister of royal designation remaining? It was his opinion that the presence of one regularly appointed magistrate would lend legality to the entire tribunal, so he asked advice as to which of the three *oidores* would be most suitable to retain. He cited as a precedent in favor of his reconstitution of the audiencia the action of Governor Curuzaelegui in 1687 and 1688 when he exiled and imprisoned the *oidores* and reformed the audiencia with his own appointees. Bustamante proposed to do exactly what Curuzaelegui had done, that is, to act as president himself, appointing the *fiscal* as *oidor*, and designating a duly qualified lawyer and an assistant *fiscal* to fill the other vacant places. Bustamante expressed an apparently sincere desire to do justice to all. He desired, particularly, that the administration of justice in the courts should be allowed to proceed without interruption and without that loss to the commonwealth which would come from the absence of a tribunal.[18]

The replies given by the orders on this occasion involve important laws and principles which underlie the nature of the audiencia and its relation to the governorship. The archbishop, in a subsequent report to the king on the government of Bustamante, stated that all the religious authorities in the colony advised the governor against the destruction of the audiencia, and questioned the authority of the prelate to constitute another.[19] It seems, however, from an investigation of

---

[18] *Consulta del gobierno de Filipinas sobre la formación de aquella audiencia, 2 de Mayo de 1718*, Zulueta Mss., Manila.

[19] Report of Archbishop de la Cuesta on the Bustamante Affair, June 28, 1720, Blair and Robertson, XLIV, 182–195.

the letters, that the Jesuits counseled the governor in favor of the proposed action. The reasoning of the Jesuit theologians was as follows: 'there should be retained in the Philippines, according to the *Recopilación de Indias*,[20] four *oidores* and a *fiscal* for the proper administration of justice, and if the *fiscal* were the only remaining member of the old audiencia he would become an *oidor* in case of a vacancy, by virtue of the recognized law.[21] Owing to the multitudinous duties of the *oidores* and to the great importance of the audiencia, great harm would arise if there were not enough magistrates. Since the governor's jurisdiction extended to all departments of government, it was the opinion of the Jesuits that it was incumbent on him to take such steps as might seem necessary for the preservation of the government. This was specially imperative since it was his duty to see that there was no delay or neglect in the administration of justice. Inasmuch as the audiencia was indispensable to him as vicepatron in its jurisdiction over ecclesiastical affairs, and because of its consultative powers in all affairs of government and finance, the governor should have the right to create an audiencia, if one did not exist, or if the members who were regularly constituted by royal appointment were incapacitated from service.[22]

The opinion of the Dominicans of the University of Santo Tomás differed widely from that advanced by the Jesuits. Their advice coincided with that of the archbishop, being to the effect that it would not be convenient to qualify one of the ministers alone, but that all of them should be restored to the audiencia. This meant that Bustamante should recede from his position, remove all the *oidores* from prison, and accept them as an audiencia. If the three *oidores* deserved punishment it would be unfair to the remaining two magistrates to exempt

20 *Recopilación*, 2–15–11.
21 *Ibid.*, 2–16–29.
22 *Contestación de la Compañía de Jesús, 6 de Mayo de 1718*, Zulueta Mss., Manila.

one, and such action would lay the governor open to charges
of inconsistency and favoritism. The Dominicans contended
that only the king in council could suspend or remove *oidores,*
and that such power was not given to any other authority, not
even to a viceroy.[23] Though

in Sicily and Naples this right is granted, in the Indies the contrary
is true, because only the king that appointed them may suspend them,
and it is commanded that the viceroys must not interfere with or impede their jurisdiction.[24]

The Dominicans were of the opinion that the governor had
authority to discipline the *oidores,* but in so doing he could not
go so far as to remove them from the tribunal unless commanded to do so by the Council of the Indies. Whatever disciplinary action the governor might decide on, it should not be
taken on his own authority, but in the execution of the orders
of the Council of the Indies.

This opinion, the Dominicans alleged, was in accordance
with the laws of the Indies.[25] They cited, in support of their
argument, an instance in which the king reproved Gálvez, the
Viceroy of New Spain, because, without the authority of the
Council, Gálvez had suspended a magistrate of the Audiencia
of Mexico, whom he should have honored and to "whom he
should have accorded the treatment of a colleague."[26] The
Dominicans expressed the opinion that the prosperity of the
Islands and the welfare of the government depended on the
audiencia, and though it might be desirable to remove the
oidores for personal guilt, it could not be done in this case
without wrecking the entire government. The king, himself,

---

23 *Recopilación,* 2–16–93.
24 *Opinión de la Universidad de Santo Tomás, 9 de Mayo de 1718,*
Zulueta Mss., Manila.
25 *Recopilación,* 2–16–44.
26 The legal phases of this question together with the opinions of the
royal *fiscal* and the leading councillors are set forth in the *consulta* of
the Council of the Indies of March 18, 1720, A. I., 68–2–8. In this *consulta* an effort is made to fix responsibility for the murder of the governor, and to determine the legality of his acts.

had shown respect for the inviolability of the audiencia when, in 1710, he had judged all the ministers to be equally guilty of not having fulfilled the laws and ordinances on the occasion of the coming to the Islands of the Patriarch of Antioch,[27] satisfying himself with the removal of the *decano* only and allowing the other magistrates to remain.

Disregarding the advice of this learned body, turning a deaf ear to the protestations of the archbishop, and heeding only the counsel of the Jesuits, which was more favorable· to his wishes, Bustamante proceeded to execute his. own will in a manner which proved distasteful even to the order whose advice he was following.[28] He arrested and imprisoned the guilty magistrates and created a new tribunal out of his own clientele, leaving only Villa, a former magistrate, in office. The latter protested against the action of the governor, and retired to the convent of Guadalupe, near Pásig. Informed that there was a conspiracy against his life and needing the counsel of some person, or persons, on whom he could rely, Bustamante was well-nigh desperate. His government, as it then stood, lacked the complexity of legality which the presence of one *oidor* of royal

---

[27] This refers to the reception of the French papal delegate, Tourón, who came to the Islands to inspect the archbishopric, and who was received by the audiencia without the authority of the Council of the Indies. This will be treated further in Chapter X of this book.

[28] Fr. Diego de Otazo, the Jesuit confessor of Bustamante, in a letter to his superior, described the power of the governor and his treatment of the audiencia as follows: "Here, my father," he wrote, "the governor takes away and establishes, gives, commands, unmakes and makes more despotically than does the king himself; . . . Royal decrees are not sufficient; for either he hides them, or he does not fulfill them as he ought. The Audiencia does not serve [as a check] on him, for he suppresses and he establishes it, when and how he pleases; nor do other bodies, whether chapters or [religious] communities (dare to oppose him), . . . for he does the same thing [with them]. And never do there lack pretexts for doing thus, even though such bodies are appointed by the king; and with the pretext that account of the matter has already been rendered to Madrid, what he has begun remains permanently done, or else he proceeds to change it, as seems good to him." (Letter of Diego de Otazo, S. J., November 19, 1719, Blair and Robertson, XLIV, 175.)

nomination would have given it. In order to remedy this defect he released Torralba, the guiltiest of the former magistrates, and the man under arrest for the defalcation of 700,000 pesos of the king's revenue. Torralba's crimes had been notorious, and the act of Bustamante in associating himself with a person of the unsavory reputation and the unpopularity of Torralba not only divorced him from whatever popular sympathy he might have had among the residents of the colony, but it aroused the hostility and antagonism of the Jesuits who had been heretofore the governor's friends. Aside from the unfortunate character of the act, it was also illegal, being contrary to the law which directed that in case an *oidor* were suspended from his place he should not be restored without the consent of the king and the Council of the Indies.[29]

The newly constituted audiencia busied itself at once with the task of government. Archbishop de la Cuesta, among others, questioned the legality of the tribunal's opposition to the excommunication of its members. He was arrested by the governor, and then arose the contest which culminated in the murder of Bustamante, in the suppression of his audiencia and in the first officially recognized government by a prelate in the Philippines. The archbishop reappointed all the former magistrates to office, with the exception of Torralba, and the misdeeds of the government of Bustamante were saddled upon the ex-magistrate.

Two noteworthy considerations stand out prominently in connection with this struggle; first, the influence of the governor over the audiencia, and his power to deprive regularly appointed magistrates of their positions and to constitute a new audiencia if he chose, notwithstanding the prohibition of the laws, and, second, the complete control by a governor over an audiencia which he had created. It is not necessary to state that the Madrid government discredited all the later acts

---

29 *Recopilación*, 2–16–93.

of Bustamante's administration, including the recall of Torralba, who was a self-confessed criminal under arrest, when restored by the governor. There is nothing to show, however, that the king disapproved of the acts of Bustamante in creating a new audiencia, unless it were the royal approval of Cuesta's act of reconstituting the old tribunal. Torralba, in his *residencia*, was made to suffer for all the misdeeds of his government (in reality that of the audiencia, Torralba being *decano*, 1715-1717), as well as for those of Bustamante (1717-1719).

The audiencia, after it had been reconstituted by the archbishop-governor, neglected to investigate the causes of the governor's death, alleging as a reason that

this proceeding will greatly disturb the community; that to proceed against these persons will be to cast odium on and grieve nearly all the citizens, since the commotion was so general; that all those who went out on that occasion did so "in defense of the ecclesiastical immunity, the preservation of this city, the self-defense of its inhabitants, and the reputation of the [Spanish] nation;" and that to carry out this plan would be likely to cause some disturbance of the public peace.[30]

In a word, the influence of the archbishop was sufficient to keep the audiencia from undertaking a formal investigation of the causes of the governor's death. It was quite generally recognized that the murder had been committed in the interests of the prelate, probably by an assassin who had been in his pay, or in that of his friends, the Jesuits. This is another illustration of the subserviency of the audiencia to the governing power, on this occasion a churchman, who had actively participated in the removal of his predecessor.

An interesting though ineffective protest was made by the audiencia against the appointment of José Basco y Vargas as Governor of the Philippines in 1778. A communication was

---

[30] Government of Bustamante (from Concepción), Blair and Robertson, XLIV, 161.

sent to the court describing the abject state into which the king had degraded the audiencia by subordinating it to a man whose title and rank as *Captain of Frigate* gave him only the right to be addressed as *You*, while each of the magistrates enjoyed the title of *Lordship*. The Council rejected the complaint as an absurdity, after which certain *oidores* conspired to bring charges against Basco y Vargas, to arrest him and to make Sarrio governor. The latter had been *ad interim* governor after the death of Anda, and he was at that time the beneficiary of the title and position of *segundo cabo*, or second in command of the king's forces in the Islands. Sarrio refused to join the magistrates in their revolt against the governor. Basco y Vargas was informed of their treason, and it is significant that he complied with the royal laws, not by attempting to punish the offenders himself, but by sending the recalcitrant magistrates to Spain where they were dealt with by the Council of the Indies.[31]

This was only a prelude to the discord which existed throughout the administration of this able governor. The king was obliged to issue special *cédulas* on various occasions, ordering a cessation of the perpetual discord.[32] Basco y Vargas formed a society for the advancement of the economic interests of the Islands,[33] and in that, as well as in his successful organization of the profitable tobacco monopoly, he was opposed by the audiencia. The tribunal claimed that the governor was limiting its sphere of authority in inaugurating these reforms.[34] Basco y Vargas recommended and brought about the separation of the superintendency of *real hacienda* from the rest of the government. This the audiencia also opposed, but in the con-

---

[31] *Recopilación*, 2–16–43, 44, 46.

[32] King to Basco y Vargas, December 10, 1783, A. I., 105–2–10.

[33] *Sociedad de los Amigos del País*, an economic, commercial, and agricultural society established in the Philippines by Governor Basco y Vargas in 1780.—Original *autos* and plans for society in A. I., 106–1–14.

[34] Audiencia to the King, December 17, 1788, A. I., 106–4–17.

test over jurisdiction which ensued between the governor and the intendant, the governor and the audiencia acted in complete harmony, because this new official threatened their mutual interests and prerogatives.[35]

Outlawry and highway robbery became so common throughout the Islands during the term of Basco y Vargas that the governor appointed prosecutors, sheriffs, and judges-extraordinary to assist in the preservation of order, which the *alcaldes mayores* were not able to accomplish by themselves. The audiencia, feeling that this was a grave intrusion upon its prerogatives, appealed to the king and succeeded in bringing the sovereign displeasure upon the head of the governor. The royal *cédula* stated that there was no need of these additional officials. The judicial machinery which had been provided for the Philippines from the beginning was sufficient. The governor was warned, furthermore, to abstain from meddling with the jurisdiction of the audiencia.[36] This case confirms the statement already made in this treatise that during this period and, in fact, after the establishment of the regency in 1776, the governor exercised a diminished authority in judicial affairs. When Basco y Vargas took his office as governor of the Philippine Islands, he was obliged to subscribe to two oaths, one as governor, and the other as president of the audiencia, but he was warned by a special decree of the king to keep from confusing these two functions as former governors had done.[37]

Many disagreements took place between the audiencia and Governor Marquina, who succeeded Basco y Vargas. Marquina quarreled with the audiencia over almost every act of government in which he had relations with the tribunal. Marquina was said to have repeatedly disregarded the *acuerdo* and to

35 *Expedientes sobre establecimiento de intendencias y subintendencias en Filipinas*, A. I., 105–1–17, 107–5–18, 105–3–5, 146–6–13.

36 King to the Audiencia, August 1, 1788, A. I., 105–2–10.

37 King to Basco y Vargas, October 9, 1777, A. I., 105–2–9.

have done as he pleased in matters wherein the audiencia had been or should have been consulted. There was a bitter contest in 1789, shortly after the arrival of this governor, because he had excused various officials of *real hacienda* from appearing when summoned to the audiencia to serve as witnesses. Marquina did this, he claimed, because they were needed in the provinces as financial agents, and because their absence from their posts of duty would entail a grave loss to the government. The audiencia solved the matter by forwarding all the correspondence relative to these cases to the Council of the Indies. It may be said that Marquina, in exempting these witnesses, was acting in his capacity as president of the audiencia, but in his solicitude that no loss should occur to the royal exchequer he was acting as superintendent of *real hacienda*, which was within his authority.[38]

In 1790 Marquina recommended the abolition of the audiencia on the grounds that its continued presence constituted an obstruction to the harmonious working of the machinery of government. He said that the tribunal was a powerful weapon in the hands of men who used it for their own personal advancement. In the place of an audiencia he suggested the substitution of three *asesores*, one for civil and criminal cases, one for *real hacienda*, and another for commerce and the *consulado*. These *asesores* would have jurisdiction over the cases which corresponded to these three departments. This scheme, he believed, would effectively provide for all the judicial cases arising in the Islands.[39] To this scheme, however, the Council paid no heed.

Considerable attention has been given in another chapter to the charges made by the audiencia against Marquina at the time of his *residencia*. These complaints show that a state of

---

[38] Audiencia to the King, December 23, 1789, A. I., 106-4-17.
[39] Montero y Vidal, *Historia general*, II, 324, note.

continual disagreement had existed between these two authorities throughout the entire term of the governor, and the bringing of these charges was instrumental in making Marquina undergo a very strict investigation. Personal jealousy was no small factor in these continual recriminations. At no subsequent date, however, were the large issues at stake which were characteristic of the struggle between the audiencia and the governor at the time of Fajardo, Curuzaelegui, and Bustamante. Those were death-struggles on the issue of whether the audiencia should be an independent tribunal or whether it should be subservient and subject to the governor. During those struggles the tribunal was momentarily suppressed, or converted into an instrument in the hands of the governor. But these were exceptional cases, and during the greater part of the long period of three hundred years the relations between the audiencia and the executive were not so discordant as they would seem to have been, judging by the instances cited in this chapter. The audiencia, on all occasions of dispute with the governor, was able to offer a formidable resistance to his so-called encroachments on the prerogatives of the tribunal. Although the governor, on most of the occasions noted above, occupied the stronger position, owing to his more recent instructions, the support given to him by the church, and his control of the *residencias* of the magistrates, nevertheless it may be said that either authority was sufficiently powerful and independent to be respected as an antagonist by the other, and each was indispensable to the other.

These disagreements have been discussed in the foregoing pages largely from the view-point of the audiencia. Practically all the charges and complaints which have been cited were made in behalf of the audiencia, and these show the magistrates in almost all cases to have been acting in defense of their rights against usurpation and tyranny. Fairness demands, however, that the other side should be presented in the same manner.[40] Reference will now be made to a few of the many memorials heretofore unquoted, which were sent by various governors in protest against the alleged excesses of the audiencia.

As a first instance we may note the criticisms which Governor Gómez Pérez Dasmariñas made of the first audiencia which served from 1584 to 1589. We shall also consider the complaints which Dasmariñas made against Pedro de Rojas, former *oidor* and later *teniente* and *asesor* of that governor (1589-1593). Dasmariñas came to the colony shortly after the first audiencia had been suppressed and from his correspondence one may estimate the prevailing opinion of the tribunal which had been recently removed. The governor wrote as follows:

As the royal Audiencia was here so haughty and domineering, he (Pedro de Rojas) retains that authority and harshness, with which he tries to reduce all others as his vassals. In the matters of justice that he discusses, he is unable to be impartial, but is in many matters very biased. This is because of his trading and trafficking, which the president and all the auditors (*oidores*) carried on from the time of their arrival—and with so great avidity, trying to secure it all to themselves, that I find no rich men here beside them. This is the reason why Rojas . . . and the auditors opposed the pancada in order that the consignments of money sent by them to China might not be known —which, at last, have come to light.[41]

The governor charged the audiencia, moreover, with having opposed the three per cent tax levied for the construction of the city wall. Indeed, he accused the magistrates of having influenced the friars to oppose all his acts as governor. He referred to the commercial excesses of the *oidores,* saying: "If the matter of inspection and the residencia held here had fallen to my order and commission, as it fell to that of the Vice-

---

40 For further testimony bearing upon the formative period of the audiencia's history, see Chapter II of this volume, wherein are described the conflicts attendant on the establishment of the audiencia in the Philippines.

41 Dasmariñas to Felipe II, June 6, 1592, Blair and Robertson, VIII, 253.

roy of Nueva España, I would have proved to your Majesty the investments of past years.'' He concluded with the statement that Rojas had been so busy with gain that he had been unable to attend to his other duties; he was ''puffed up with the authority and name of auditor'' (*i. e., oidor*). He protested against the transfer of Rojas to an office in Mexico, ''for,'' he wrote, ''such men go delighted with their interests and gains from trade here, they are fettered and biased by their relations with the trade of this country.''

Thus we see that even this early in the history of the Islands, the *oidores* as well as the governors were accused of a predominating interest in commercial affairs.

Governor Pedro de Acuña recommended the suppression of the audiencia in 1604, although he said that he had had no serious trouble with that tribunal. His chief reason in favoring its removal was that an appreciable saving would be realized thereby. The audiencia was, moreover, very unpopular in Manila. He alleged that the name of *oidor* was so odious that it was in itself an offense. He stated that affairs had come to such a pass that

because I, in conformity to what your Majesty has ordered, have attempted to maintain and have maintained amicable relations with the auditors; and have shown, on various occasions, more patience and endurance than the people considered right; and more than seemed fitting to my situation, in order not to give rise to scandal; some have conceived hatred for me, publicly saying that . . . I was neglecting to look after them, and that I could correct the evil which the Audiencia was doing. But as I cannot do that, it has seemed to me the best means to let the public see that there was good feeling between me and the Audiencia.[42]

Here we have the case of a governor, who, in order to get along in harmony with a quarrelsome and unpopular audiencia, gave way to it on many occasions, and even incurred the displeasure of the residents of the colony on account of what

---

[42] Acuña to Felipe III, July 15, 1604, Blair and Robertson, XIII, 232.

seemed to them to be the governor's easy-going attitude. His zeal for the king's service, as he expressed it, moved him to recommend the abolition of the tribunal. He said that the audiencia would not be missed if it were removed, since there were only twelve hundred residents in the colony and there were few cases to be tried. Most of the suits arising in the Islands could be adjudicated by the *alcaldes ordinarios* and appeals could be sent to Mexico. The *acuerdo*, or administrative session, Acuña alleged, existed in name only.

Acuña made practically the same charges that have been so often repeated already in this chapter. The magistrates had interfered in the appointment of officials, which the governor claimed as his sole prerogative. Each magistrate was accompanied on his journey to the Islands by a vast company of relatives and dependents, who came to get rich. These persons ultimately monopolized all the offices. Notwithstanding the king's orders which forbade that offices should be held by relatives of *oidores*, the governor was placed in such a position that if he did not allow these persons to hold office, the magistrates would take revenge by opposing him at every turn, thus ruining the success of his administration.[43] The same was true of trade, for these relatives had to live, and if the government could not support them, they had to be assigned privileges and advantages in trade, which the *oidores* by virtue of their official positions could guarantee.[44]

---

[43] Acuña continued as follows: "If the governors do not consent to this (the appointment of the relatives and dependents of *oidores*), the auditors dislike them, and seek means and expedients whereby the worthy persons to whom the said offices and livings are given shall not be received therein. Accordingly the governors, in order not to displease the auditors, give up their claims and dare not insist upon them" (*ibid.*, 234).

[44] Acuña further commented on their commercial abuses: "The said creatures and connections of the said auditors trade and traffic a great deal in merchandise from China; and the citizens complain that it is with the auditors' money (their own or borrowed), and that with the favor they receive they cause great injury to the commonwealth, for they take up the whole cargo. They desire to be preferred

In view of all these abuses and evils which, directly or indirectly, proceeded from the audiencia, Acuña maintained that all the powers of government, war and justice, should be concentrated in the office of governor and captain-general. The country, he said, was more at war than at peace. It was essentially military, by virtue of its location and isolation. Acuña contended that all authorities and departments of the government should therefore be dependent on a miliary chief rather than on a high court of justice which was out of sympathy with the spirit and needs of the colony. In a government so new as that of the Philippines, the same laws and punishments should not be enforced so rigidly as in more settled parts, yet the magistrates of the audiencia had failed to understand that their functions in a colony of this character should be in any way different than those of a similar tribunal in Spain. Acuña stated that there had been occasions in which the audiencia, in possession of partial evidence in regard to a military matter, had interfered with an action which the governor had wished to take. He had thus been rendered powerless to exercise sovereignty which rightfully belonged to him,

---

therein, and in buying the cloth and in every other way, try to take advantage. If the president wishes to remedy this they do not cease to offer him little annoyances; for the auditors know how to magnify themselves, in such a manner that they give one to understand that any one of them is greater than he; and they attain this by saying that what the president or governor does they can cancel, and that what the auditors decree has no appeal, recourse, or redress" (*ibid.*, 234–5).

Acuña testified that the magistrates had rendered life unpleasant for the residents of the colony, because of their selfishness. He continued: "the resources of this land are scanty, but if there is anything good the auditors also say that they want it for themselves; and when there is a Chinese embroiderer, tailor, carver, or other workman, they proceed to take him. . . . Such benefits do not extend to the citizens; but rather, if any of these things are available, the said auditors demand them and by entreaty and intimidation get possession of them. It is the same thing in regard to jewels, slave men and women, articles of dress, and other things. . . . We are compelled to overlook these things, and others of more importance, that we may not experience worse trouble; . . . as your Majesty is five thousand leguas from here and redress comes so slowly" (*ibid.*, 235–236).

and which, if put into effect, would no doubt have been for the best interests of the colony.

In addition to the above representations, the governor laid great stress on the financial advantages which would be derived from a suppression of the tribunal. He stated that the colony was short of money, a condition of which the magistrates were well aware, yet they always insisted on being the first to collect their own salaries, to the exclusion, if necessary, of all other officials in the colony.[45] With the money saved from the abolition of the audiencia, an armed fleet could be provided for the defense of the Islands. This was badly needed, and there was no other way of obtaining the necessary ships. The Chinese rebellion of the year before[46] had caused a diminution of 46,000 pesos in the commercial duties collected,[47] and the

[45] Their salaries must be preferred, he wrote, "even if it be from the stated fund for the religious orders, bishops, ministers of instruction, and for the military forces, who are before them in order,—they have difficulties and misunderstandings with the royal officials (*ibid.*, 236) . . . as the treasury is always straitened (*sic*), and, on account of the great care which the auditors take to collect their salaries, as it cannot be so prompt as they would wish, they seek borrowed money from the citizens—who give it to them, willingly or unwillingly, each one according to his means or designs. From this follow difficulties, to which they pay no heed; as some of them demand these loans from persons who are parties to suits at the time, who grant these to the auditors in order to place them under obligations, and profit by them" (*ibid.*, 239).

[46] The rebellion referred to here occurred in 1603. It was said to have been instigated by two mysterious mandarins who came to Manila for the alleged purpose of searching for a mountain of silver, which was located near Cavite. On the Eve of St. Francis the Chinese made their attack with great success, owing, the ecclesiastical element claimed, to the personal intervention of St. Francis, who appeared on the walls and led his followers to victory. In this revolt 24,000 Chinese were hunted down and slain. In 1639 another rebellion occurred. A third insurrection of the Chinese took place in 1660. In 1763 the Chinese joined with the British in their attack on the city. It is estimated that Anda, in his campaign in the provinces, put an end to 6,000 Chinese. Another massacre, and the last in the history of the Islands, took place in 1820. This was an uprising of the natives against all foreigners who were thought to be responsible for the plague of cholera then raging (Foreman, *Philippine Islands*, 108–119; A. I., 105–1 to 10 and 68–1–27).

[47] The entire dependence of the colony on the Chinese trade is attested by Concepción (*Historia general*, IV, 53). He states that: "With-

consequent shortage of money in the treasury of the colony furnished further reasons for the dismissal of this useless and burdensome tribunal. Acuña admitted that the institution of the audiencia might be successful in larger dependencies of Spain, where the people were prosperous and where the government had an assured income, but in the Philippines, where the citizens were poor, with scarcely any means of support, and harassed by many magistrates and their dependents, the audiencia had been a failure and a serious burden.

Acuña's concluding statement very aptly sizes up the situation and voices his demand for the abolition of the tribunal. He wrote:

The difficulty which presents itself to me in this matter is that, if the Audiencia is abolished and everything left in charge of the governor, there will be but slow and poor remedy for the grievances and disorders which may occur. For they must be taken to the Audiencia of Mexico, which is so far away that the aggrieved ones would consume both life and property before the business was settled. . . . all say that they consider government by one person the best, when he governs justly. These men (who believe in the above) know what the governor can do without the Audiencia, and with it; and they believe that it is better when there are not so many to command them, for they have never seen the audiencias redress illegal acts by the governors . . . Although there is no doubt that much of what this paper recounts occurs in other regions where there are audiencias, it must be remembered that in this country, which is the newest of all and more engaged in war than any of the others; and where the hardships of conquest and maintenance are so omnipresent; and your Majesty has little profit or advantage, except the cargo of cloth which goes to Nueva Hespaña (*sic*), and which is divided among all; and as the resources of the country are so scant that there is no place to go in order to seek a livelihood outside of Manila: there is much criticism in this matter, and the people are much aggrieved at seeing themselves in the utmost part of the world, harassed and troubled by so many magistrates and officers and their dependents, and at having so many to satisfy; and

---

out the trade and commerce of the Chinese these dominions could not have subsisted." Morga, in his *Sucesos* (349), further testifies: "It is true the town cannot exist without the Chinese, as they are the workers in all trades and business, and are very industrious, working for small wages."

that matters are in such a state that he who has an auditor for a protector may, it appears, go wherever he wishes and with as much as he wishes, and he who has not must be ruined.[48]

This brings us to the administration of Governor Alonso Fajardo (1618-1624), whose relations with the audiencia we have already shown to have been very unpleasant. Fully as many charges were brought against the *oidores* by that governor as were put forward by the magistrates against him. According to Fajardo, the *oidores* had so used their power of appointment that it amounted to virtual dictation. Fajardo, like Acuña, found his control over the filling of offices greatly diminished. He energetically protested against the proposition which had been made to increase the size of the court from four to five magistrates. He stated that the amount of legal business which came before the tribunal did not justify an augmentation of the number of *oidores;* he recommended that the magistrates should spend their time more advantageously, and waste less in quarreling among themselves and in wreaking their passions on their rivals. Like Acuña, Fajardo complained against the presence of so large a number of relatives and personal followers of the *oidores,* whose lust for office had to be satisfied.[49] The magistrates had engaged in trade through intermediaries, and had spent the time which should have been devoted to the administration of justice in devising schemes whereby they and their agents could get the most out of forbidden commercial transactions, and at the same time be protected in their illicit activities. Fajardo claimed that the magis-

---

[48] Acuña to Felipe III, July 15, 1604, Blair and Robertson, XIII, 239–241.

[49] Fajardo described "the oppression caused by the multitude of relatives and followers (of the auditors); their appropriation of the offices and emoluments, to the injury of the meritorious; their hatred and hostility to those who unfortunately fall out with them; their trading and trafficking, although it be by an intermediary, since they, being men of influence, buy the goods at wholesale and protect their agents." He stated that this caused him great embarrassment and made good government almost an impossibility (Fajardo to Felipe III, August 10, 1618, Blair and Robertson, XVIII, 126).

trates had abused their positions to such an extent that they had become an intolerable incumbrance to the colony.

Strife and discord between the audiencia and the governor were perhaps more bitter during the administration of Fajardo than at any other time in the history of the Islands. This governor accused the magistrates of deliberately attempting in all petty and inconsequential ways to harass him into compliance with its desires. He wrote that he had done everything possible to keep peace with the *oidores*, even at a sacrifice of the respect of the other elements of the colony.[50]   This testimony is practically identical with that submitted by Governor Acuña in 1604. The influence of the tribunal in the matter of appointments, judging by this and by other statements and allegations already quoted, and by the laws themselves, must have been great.

The tendency to fill offices with friends and relatives was characteristic not only of the magistrates, but of the viceroys and governors as well. More laws are to be found in the *Recopilación* which guard against such abuses by governors and viceroys than by the magistrates of the audiencia.[51]   Bearing in mind, of course, that there are two sides to the question, it is at least clear that the audiencia was successful in one of the purposes for which it was created—namely, that of preventing the governor from exercising entire control over appointments. We have the confession of Governor Fajardo here and of Governor Acuña in the preceding paragraphs that those governors were unable to prevent the *oidores* from filling offices

---

50 "The auditors," Fajardo wrote, "have few important matters that oblige them to close application, (and) they must apply the greater part of their time to devising petty tricks on the president in order to vex and weary him, until [as they hope] not only will he allow them to live according to their own inclination but also their relatives and followers shall, in whatever posts they desire, be employed and profited. And since harmony has never been seen here without this expedient, one would think it easy to believe such a supposition" (Fajardo to the King, August 15, 1620, Blair and Robertson, XIX, 120–121).
51 *Recopilación*, 8–20, 21, 22.

with their own friends. Although we have been following the
governor's side of the question in these last few pages, we
have noted in the preceding chapter that the laws of the Indies
gave to the audiencia the right of participating in *acuerdo*
with the governor in matters of appointment.

Governor Fajardo's method of referring matters to the
audiencia for advice is interesting. Instead of submitting questions to the *acuerdo* for the general advice and opinion of all
the *oidores,* he was said to have sought to escape the obligation
of acting in accordance with the advice given him, by asking
the *oidores* for their individual .opinions concerning matters
on which he desired advice. The audiencia took exception to
this method of procedure, alleging that he was thus escaping
the responsibilities of the *acuerdo.* Fajardo defended himself
against the accusation by the statement that the *oidores* met
together so seldom that he had been unable to submit questions
to the magistrates collectively in accordance with the law.

Fajardo also complained against the failure of the *oidores*
to comply with his instructions in regard to the inspection of
the provinces. He stated that the magistrates disliked to
bestir themselves from their inactive and indolent lives amid
the comforts of Manila, and no inspections had been made during the three years prior to the date of this letter. Philip III,
without raising his voice in indignation or decreeing any punishment upon those officials who had refused to execute his
decrees, mildly solicited that they should devote their care and
attention to the matter in the future. He remonstrated that
this was the only way in which the facts relating to the
country and to the interests and needs of its people could be
ascertained.

These inspections are very essential, since they are based on the
relief of miserable persons, and in no way can the condition of affairs
be fully ascertained unless by means of these inspections; and the
most advisable measures can hardly be well understood, if the condition and facts of what ought to be remedied and can be bettered are

not known. Hence I again charge you to pay especial attention to these inspections. The Audiencia is commanded to observe the orders that you shall give in your capacity as president so that each auditor, when it concerns him, may observe his obligations and go out on the inspections.[52]

In reply to these observations, the Council ordered Fajardo to make recommendations for the reform of the government, stating that such suggestions as he would make would be duly considered and observed.[53]

On his arrival in the Islands, Fajardo, as yet unfamiliar with the duties and conditions of his office, expressed his unwillingness to recommend the entire abolition of the audiencia, preferring to have present a council which he could consult regarding the problems of his new office. The tribunal in the Philippines was probably not so important as were those in Spain, under the immediate supervision of the king, "where," as he expressed it,

one obtains strict justice, administered by upright and holy men—the people here considering that those who are farthest from meriting that name are those who are farthest from the presence of your Majesty and your royal counselors. . . . In what pertains to me, I do not petition you for anything in this matter, since in no respect can it be ill for me to have someone to consult, and who will relieve me in matters of justice.[54]

Fajardo's act in forming a new audiencia after he had suppressed the real one shows that the audiencia was essential to him in the two particulars mentioned by him in the above letter.

That his attitude towards this question was somewhat altered by three years' experience as governor of the Philippines is shown in his memorial of July 21, 1621. On this occasion Fajardo argued against the continuation of the tribunal,

---

[52] Decree written on margin of letter: Fajardo to the King, August 15, 1620, Blair and Robertson, XIX, 136.

[53] *Ibid.*, 122.

[54] Fajardo to Felipe III, August 10, 1618, Blair and Robertson, XVIII, 126.

showing himself to be of the same opinion as Acuña, who, it
will be remembered, contended that because the colony was
military in character, there should be one person to control
affairs, without any interference whatsoever. He wrote:

> I beg your Majesty that while it shall last (the war) you may be
> pleased to discontinue the Audiencia here, as it is this that most
> hinders and opposes the administration and the government, . . .
> This is the enemy which most afflicts this commonwealth, and most
> causes dissensions, parties, factions, and hatred between the citizens—
> each auditor persecuting those citizens who are not wholly of his own
> faction, especially those who extend aid and good-will toward the
> governor, against whom, as it seems, they show themselves always in
> league. They always make declarations of grievances [against him]
> because they are not each one given, as used to be and is the custom
> here, whatever they may ask for their sons, relatives and servants;
> and they habitually discredit the governor by launching through secret
> channels false and malicious reports, and afterward securing witnesses
> of their publicity. They even, as I have written to your Majesty, man-
> age to have religious and preachers publish these reports to which end,
> and for his own security, each one of the auditors has formed an alli-
> ance with the religious order which receives him best.[55]

He summarized as follows:

> I consider this government much more difficult, with the auditors
> of this Audiencia, than it is or would be even if there were more war,
> for that war which they cause within its boundaries appears beyond
> remedy, on account of their abilities and rank.[56]

An abundance of evidence exists on both sides of this controversy; letters of complaint against the governor and charges
against the *oidores* by the governor. The vividness and appar-

---

[55] Fajardo to the King, July 21, 1621, Blair and Robertson, XX, 53.

[56] *Ibid.*, 54. Fajardo continued as follows: "To such a point has it
(the dissension) gone that if this country were not involved in the
perils of war as it has been, and as they are still threatening it, I should
beseech your Majesty to place it in charge of some other person, who
would be more interested in documents. But may God not choose that
I should be relieved from the service of your Majesty, in which from the
age of fifteen years I have been engaged; . . . It would be no little
pleasure to me to be employed in naval and military affairs and other
things in which, with my counsel and my personal aid, I might be able
to help; and to know that the matter of auditors and their demands,
their rivalries, and their faultfinding, should concern another."—*Ibid.*,
55–56.

ent directness of the charges and the apparent sincerity of both the governor and the *oidores* make it extremely difficult, and, in fact, quite impossible to decide on the basis of the evidence presented, who was right or wrong, which charges, true or untrue, and who was really responsible for the difficulties. It would appear that the king was prone to sympathize with the governor rather than with the audiencia, for in practically all cases the decision of the sovereign was adverse to the tribunal. The fact that the governor was the royal representative was probably a large factor in securing him the support of the home government. Yet, on the other hand, the audiencia was in the same sense the royal tribunal.

Governor Fajardo affords an example of a successful military man who, having won fame for himself in the wars of the continent, but without legal knowledge or administrative experience, was called to the government of a distant and isolated colony, with the responsibilty of continuing in harmonious relations with a hostile civil and judicial tribunal on the one hand, with whose powers and functions he was not familiar, and an equally hostile religious institution on the other. Men of military training usually had great contempt for the abilities and good intentions of priests and lawyers in those days, and it was frequently evident, both by their actions and by their own confessions, that *conquistadores* of the stamp of Fajardo, Acuña, and Corcuera were little fitted for the exercise of administrative and governmental functions, however useful they might be in adding to the domain of the Spanish empire.

Thus, there being present in the colony a tribunal of trained lawyers who were at the same time capable and experienced administrators, the governors became accustomed to rely on them for advice and assistance, in compliance with the commands of the laws of the Indies. As one governor of military tastes and training succeeded another, each lacking administrative ability and experience, the audiencia came to assume an increased share in the governmental activity of the colony. This tendency was accentuated by the fact that the governor was absent from the capital city on campaigns of conquest and defense a large share of his time. Ability as a soldier and commander was always the chief criterion for the selection of a governor and captain-general, and military affairs were given more attention by far than matters of administration. Spain's policy of selecting soldiers instead of administrators for the post of governor went far towards making the audiencia more than a court of justice, and towards giving it a share in the executive functions of government. This tendency was also furthered by the fact that the audiencia came to assume the entire administration on the death or absence of the governor, a power which it did not always exercise well, but which it always relinquished with reluctance.

The Salcedo affair in 1668-1670 emphasizes other differences than those of the audiencia and the governor, yet reference should be made to it in this connection, because, after all, the *oidores* were concerned indirectly in the struggle. An examination of the data at our command will reveal the fact that the refusal or failure of the *oidores* to intervene in behalf of the governor led to his defeat and humiliation by the commissary of the Inquisition. The audiencia might have prevented that disaster had the magistrates been so inclined.

Before Governor Salcedo was arrested, imprisoned and sent to Mexico in 1668 by the commissary of the Inquisition on charges of a purely ecclesiastical character, the two *oidores,* Bónifaz and Montemayor, were consulted by the enemies of the governor as to the legality of the proposed action. There is every reason to believe that the entire plot was worked out beforehand with the fore-knowledge and consent of the *oidores.* Inharmonious relations had existed before the arrest of the governor between Salcedo and his associates, because of his independence and his unwillingness to provide offices and opportunities for commercial profit for their relatives. The exact part which the audiencia played in the arrest of Salcedo is not known, since the entire plot was schemed and executed under the cloak of the Inquisition; but the fact remains that Oidores Montemayor and Bónifaz each hoped to assume the management of governmental affairs upon the exile of Salcedo. Indeed, the ambitions of Bónifaz were realized. The removal of Salcedo culminated in the usurpation of the government by Bónifaz, in the exile of Montemayor, his rival, to the provinces, and in the complete suppression of the audiencia for a year. It is said that Bónifaz, through a usurper, ruled beneficently and well; and that he little deserved the sentence of death which was pronounced on him by the Council of the Indies. The authority for the assertion that his rule was meritorious was ecclesiastical and hence, in this case, possibly questionable.[57] It is certain, at least, that Bónifaz and his government were under the complete domination of the church.[58]

It has been frequently stated in this chapter, that jealousy and rivalry were always determining factors in the relationship of the audiencia and the governor. A new executive, until familiar with the duties of his station, was always glad to seek the advice and assistance of the *oidores*, meanwhile permitting the audiencia to assume many functions which belonged to him as governor. A new governor was gracious and agreeable to all, and we find that most of the favorable comments made concerning governors by magistrates, prelates, and officials were pronounced when the environment was new to them or to the governor. When the routine of official duties became irksome

---

[57] Concepción, *Historia general*, VII, 168 *et seq.;* see Lea, *Inquisition in the Spanish dependencies*, 299–318, and Cunningham, "The inquisition in the Spanish colonies; the Salcedo affair," in the *Catholic historical review*, III, 417–445. The Salcedo affair will be more fully discussed in Chapter XI, of this book, which treats of the relations of the audiencia and the church; citations 60–72, Chapter XI.

[58] See Augustinians in Philippines, in Blair and Robertson, XXXVII, 235, 239, 269–273.

and opportunities for private profit presented themselves, as always happened in the course of time, friction arose, and jealousy and discord took the place of the goodwill and harmony which at first seemed so promising.

The most contaminating influence in the colony was the commercial spirit. Governors and magistrates engaged in trade on a large scale, and .the churchmen also yielded to the commercial instinct. The latter assertion will be enlarged upon in its proper place; proof of the commercial activities of governors and magistrates has already been given. The resentment of the *oidores* always led them to place every .conceivable opposition in the way of the governor when it was seen that he was obtaining more than his fair share of profit from trade, appointments, or indulgences to the Chinese. This led to a refusal to ratify his appointments in many cases, to oppose him in the *acuerdo,* to incite the residents of the colony against him, and to do everything possible to make a failure of his administration. Governors on the other hand might employ one of two methods in dealing with the magistrates. That most commonly pursued was to allow them a liberal share of the booty, commercial or political, the latter obtained by permitting them to disregard the law by giving offices to their relatives and followers, thereby purchasing their favor. The other method was to meet their charges with counter-charges, which were probably as truthful, though usually not so serious as those which the magistrates made against them. The administrations of those governors who openly opposed the audiencia and sought to keep it within the limits of its jurisdiction as a judicial tribunal, were most notable for their conflicts.

The Court of Madrid was unable to remedy these defects in colonial administration. It could and did discipline the officials by sending an occasional visitor, or by forcing them to give vigorous *residencias,* but these punishments only led to greater abuses in order to reimburse themselves for the fines which they had to pay. Officials were able to send away large sums of money and consignments of merchandise, and then, after having paid liberal penalties, they returned to Spain and lived in comfortable retirement. Acceptance of the office of governor, *oidor*, *corregidor*, or *alcalde mayor* was made with a foreknowledge that disputes would arise, enemies would bring accusations, and punishments would be meted out, whether deserved or not. This condition led to the abuses which have been noted, and the recriminations and struggles between authorities. From the view-point of these officials the Philippines were neither governed for the good of the natives nor for the residents, nor for the honor of Spain, nor for the propagation of the Catholic religion, but merely for the profit and advancement of those who were on the ground to take advantage of their opportunities. They were struggles for profit; pure and simple contests between the officials either to get all the proceeds possible from their offices or to keep other officials from getting all, and thus to get a share for themselves. There were exceptions, of course, to the conditions and circumstances just noted. Some able and well-intentioned men came to the Islands, as came to all of Spain's colonies, among whom may be mentioned Oidor Antonio de Morga, the *fiscal*, Francisco Leandro de Viana, and Governors Anda y Salazar, Basco y Vargas, Aguilar, Enrile, and others of the nineteenth century when opportunities for gain were somewhat diminished. Some of these officials erred on the side of overstrictness, and their efforts to restrain the avarice of their colleagues and to infuse the spirit of honestly into their administrations united the opposition and led to battles as violent and unrelenting as those which were fought when all parties were dishonest.

In a chapter which deals alone with the conflicts of jurisdiction which occurred between the governor and the audiencia, it would be possible to arrive at an entirely mistaken conclusion. Disagreements and differences were frequent as well as pronounced, yet the history of the Philippines throughout the three hundred years of Spanish rule is not a record of perpetual strife. It is, of course, understood that no effort has been made in this chapter to describe all the struggles which occurred in the Islands between the audiencia and the governor. Those which have been reviewed were selected for the purpose because they illustrate, in a general way, the subjects over which disagreements arose, and the principles underlying them.

We have noted, in general, that the audiencia exercised functions and prerogatives which were not conferred upon it by the laws of the Indies. The type of men who were appointed to the office of governor and captain-general made inevitable the accretion of power in the hands of the magistrates. The audiencia gradually came to assume more attributes than the solely judicial ones. Necessity compelled the governor in many instances to entrust the tribunal with many of his own functions because of his lack of skill and experience as an administrator or on account of his devotion to military affairs. In these ways the *acuerdo* came to be legislative as well as advisory; the frequent absence of the governor, or his death, led to the audiencia's assumption of the governorship and the tribunal was always reluctant to surrender the administrative powers once gained.

Jealousy between officials and the resultant conflicts of authority may be classified together as a cause of strife. These difficulties resulted in part from the fact that the sphere of authority of each official was not defined with exactness in the laws of the Indies, and also because those laws were often countermanded by later *cédulas* of whose existence the colonial officials were not always aware. Spanish laws were frequently repealed and subsequently put in force without notice; this was always a source of confusion. Then again the exceptional opportunities for trade offered by the transfer of the rich oriental cargoes at Manila tempted *oidores* and governors alike. The trading privileges conceded by the government did not always end when the limit of permission was reached. Some officials, and particularly governors, could command more than their rightful share of galleon space; this led to disputes and recriminations which often interfered seriously with the government. We have noted that the appointing power which belonged nominally to the governor and which was shared by the *oidores* was also a source of much trouble. The knowledge that the *residencia* would ultimately bring about the punishment of guilty officials and enemies, the distance and isolation of the colony, and the length of time necessary for communication—all these factors made it possible for officials to commit excesses. Another cause of discord was what might be termed the reaction of the executive against the increased power and authority of the audiencia. This accretion of power was due to the complete dependence of the governor on the tribunal in administrative matters, especially at the begining of his term, the increasing power of the *acuerdo,* the superiority of the audiencia as a court of appeals from the decisions of the governor, and the fact that the latter always needed the presence of the audiencia to lend legality to his government.

It may be stated, nevertheless, that the governor actually held the more powerful position in the colony, and that he most frequently emerged victor in the various struggles with the audiencia. Various reasons may be assigned for this. The governor was the personal representative of the king, and in this capacity he had the backing of the home government. He commanded the military forces in the colony. The authority of the royal patronage was vested in the governor; he was thus often able to command the support of the church and clergy in his struggles with the audiencia. The authority over the disposal of offices, either by sale or appointment belonged legally to the governor, although this power was effectively disputed and often shared by the audiencia. The governor employed the last-mentioned power on some occasions to the extent of reforming and reconstituting the audiencia, thus making the government entirely dependent on him. A new governor always carried with him a more recent appointment than those of the *oidores* whom he found in the colony, and aside from this he usually possessed definite instructions embodying the royal will on all current issues. The control of the *residencias* of the *oidores* was usually in the hands of the governor, and lastly, the *laissez faire* attitude of the Spanish government, its extreme conservatism, and its apparent reluctance to correct the evils and abuses which were reported to it—all these were potent factors in leaving the balance of power as it had been, in the hands of the governor, notwithstanding the presence of the audiencia.

A previously quoted statement made by a famous British historian in his description of the relative powers of the viceroys of New Spain, and Perú, and their respective audiencias, may be used here, with equal effect, to characterize the situation in the Philippines, and to summarize this part of our discussion: "They (the magistrates of the audiencia) may advise, they may remonstrate; but in the event of a direct collision between their opinion and the will of the viceroy (governor), what he determines must be brought into execution, and nothing remains for them but to lay the matter before the king and the Council of the Indies."[59]

---

[59] Robertson, *History of America*, IV, 20. See Chapter VI, note 54, of this book.

CHAPTER IX

THE AUDIENCIA AND THE GOVERNOR: THE AD INTERIM RULE

The most extensive non-judicial activity in which the audiencia participated at any time was its assumption of the provisional government of the colony during vacancies in the governorship. Aside from the ten different occasions on which this was done, the audiencia very frequently assumed control of the government when the exigencies of defense and foreign conquest rendered necessary the temporary absence of the governor. This was true at irregular intervals during the administrations of Governors Pedro Bravo de Acuña (1602-1606), Juan de Silva (1609-1616), Juan Niño de Tavora (1626-1632), Sebastián Hurtado de Corcuera (1635-1644) and Diego Fajardo (1644-1653). The administrations of these several governors were characterized by extensive military operations, largely in a foreign field, and the audiencia not only took over governmental affairs but it assumed the obligations of defense during their absence. On such occasions, of course, the tribunal retained its exercise of judicial functions.

Since the audiencias in Perú and New Spain assumed the government much earlier than did the audiencia in the Philippines, and as the laws authorizing the rule of the audiencia were promulgated first to meet conditions in those viceroyalties, it seems advisable to inquire into the circumstances surrounding the establishment and development of this practice there. Having done this, we shall proceed to a study of the *ad interim* rule of the Audiencia of Manila, noting particularly the causes of the success or failure of its administration and the effect of this practice upon the subsequent relations of the audiencia and the governor.

The first law in the *Recopilación* authorizing the assumption of the government by an audiencia was promulgated as early as March 19, 1550. This law provided that in case of a vacancy in the office of Viceroy of Perú, the audiencia there should succeed to the governments of Perú, Charcas, Quito and Tierra Firme, and that the three last-named subordinate audiencias should obey the mandates of the Audiencia of Lima until a permanent successor to the viceroy was named.[1] This law was proclaimed again on November 20, 1606.

Even before the promulgation of the above law the audiencias of Lima and Mexico had assumed control of the government in their respective viceroyalties. Shortly after the death of Francisco Pizarro, the conqueror, an audiencia was sent to Perú, arriving at Lima in January, 1544, in company with Blasco Núñez Vela, the first viceroy. The rigidity and thoroughness with which this new executive enforced the New Laws which were entrusted to him met with the opposition of the residents of the colony, and the audiencia accordingly removed him from his position as viceroy and suspended the operation of the code referred to, assuming charge of affairs itself.[2] Its rule was brief, however, for on October 28, 1544,

---

[1] *Recopilación*, 2-15-46.

[2] Moses, *The Spanish dependencies in South America*, 1, 221. The Council of the Indies manifested its disapproval of the acts of the audiencia and of Pizarro by commissioning Pedro de Gasca as president of the Audiencia of Lima. Gasca was ordered to restore that viceroyalty to the sovereignty of Spain, and to do whatever the king would do under like circumstances. This was in May, 1546. "He (Gasca) was at the head of every department of the administration," writes Professor Moses; "he might raise troops, appoint and remove officers, and declare war; he might exercise the royal prerogative of pardoning offenses; and was especially commissioned to grant an amnesty to all who had been engaged in the rebellion. He was authorized to revoke the ordinances which had caused the popular uprising and the overthrow of Blasco Núñez; and, returning to the earlier practice, he might make repartimientos, or confirm those which had been previously made. In accordance with his expressed wish, he was granted no specific salary, but he

it invited Gonzalo Pizarro, the brother of the conqueror, into
the city and turned the government over to him, proclaiming
him Governor and Captain-General of Perú.

During the period from 1544 to 1551, until the arrival in
Perú of Viceroy Mendoza, the audiencia exercised control of
governmental affairs. It made and unmade captains-general
and viceroys, irrespective of royal appointments. It suspended
the New Laws of 1542 and its commands were obeyed. From 1550
to 1551 it governed alone. In these incidents we note that the
audiencia actually assumed the government *ad interim* prior to
the time of the promulgation of the law of March 19, 1550,
exercising administrative as well as judicial powers, thirty-five
years before the Audiencia of Manila was created. "To it
(the audiencia) were confided in the beginning and later in
the absence of the viceroy," writes Moses, "all matters with
which governmental authority might properly deal."[3] He
further states that "the audiencia in its executive capacity,
failed to justify the expectations of the king, and a new order
of things was introduced by the appointment of a viceroy"
(Mendoza, April 17, 1535) for New Spain.[4]

These powers were not only exercised by the Audiencia of
Lima, but also by a second tribunal which was created in 1549
at Santa Fé de Bogotá. The latter body was endowed permanently with both judicial and administrative powers, appealing
important cases to the superior government at Lima. This
audiencia had the status of a presidency. Its president was
often captain-general, *visitador*, and senior magistrate, and in
exercising the functions of these various offices he was in all
respects the most powerful official in New Granada, always
being able to enforce his will over the other magistrates. At
times this official acted with entire independence of the Viceroy

---

might make any demands on the treasuries of Panama and Peru."
Ibid., I, 225.
  3 *Ibid.*, I, 264.
  4 *Ibid.*, I, 267.

of Perú.[5] The exercise of military functions by this president
and audiencia is especially to be noticed in the part they played
in putting down the Pijáo Indian revolt in 1565.[6] On the
whole, however, judging by the strife prevailing in the colony,
the various struggles between the *oidores* and the president,
and between the audiencia or president and the archbishop,
the government could never have been considered successful.
The official corruption which became apparent as a result of
the *pesquisas* and *residencias* held during the rule of the Audiencia of Santa Fé could scarcely have encouraged the home
government to entrust that tribunal with the administration of
affairs in the future.

The defects referred to above in connection with the government of the Audiencia of Santa Fé did not deter the Spanish
crown from founding the Audiencia of Charcas in 1559.
This tribunal, "like the audiencias established elsewhere, exercised not only judicial, but also administrative powers."[7] It had
jurisdiction over the neighboring city of Potosí. Again we may
note the case of the Audiencia of Santiago de Chile, which was
established on August 27, 1565. Its members arrived in 1567
and the audiencia was installed at Concepción "as the supreme
court of the colony, and, at the same time, in accordance with
the royal decree, it became the administrative head of the
government. In this latter capacity it undertook to reorganize
the military forces." Later, in 1568, Melchoir Bravo de Sar-
avia assumed the office and functions of the governorship of
Chile (1568-1575) and the audiencia became a judicial tribunal,
without other attributes.[8]

We may gather from these various citations taken from the
early history of the audiencias of South America that these
tribunals not only exercised the authority of governing *ad*

---

[5] *Ibid.*, I, 276–301. See *Recopilación*, 2–15–8.
[6] *Ibid.*, II, 82.
[7] *Ibid.*, II, 16.
[8] *Ibid.*, I, 361.

interim, but that they had permanent governmental and administrative powers as well. It would seem, as Professor Moses has suggested, that the original purpose of the Spanish government had been to entrust the executive and administrative functions in the dependencies to the audiencia, and that the endowment of the viceroys and captains-general with extensive executive powers was an expedient to which Spain was obliged to turn after the breakdown of the audiencia as an administrative agency. The main fact to be emphasized in this connection is that during the period of the promulgation of the laws which we are now studying, the minor audiencias were exercising regular governmental powers.

The Audiencia of Mexico, which was created in 1527 to check the excesses of Hernán Cortés, had participated in governmental affairs even before the events described above. This tribunal, which was composed of four magistrates, with the notorious Guzmán as president, conducted the *residencias* of Cortés and his followers, and after obtaining control of the government, administered affairs to suit its own convenience.[9] It was at this time, and as a result of these abuses, Bancroft tells us, that the Spanish government decided to establish a viceroyalty in New Spain, with a semiregal court and regal pretensions. A new tribunal was left in charge of governmental affairs while this reform was being inaugurated. This second audiencia governed with great satisfaction, correcting the abuses of its predecessor and devoting itself to various improvements.[10]

Although the audiencia of 1528-1535 exercised the administrative functions above mentioned, Bancroft brings forth no evidence in support of the theory that it was ever the royal intention to entrust the institution of the audiencia permanently with administrative authority. He states that as early

---

[9] Bancroft, *History of Mexico,* II, 273–295.
[10] *Ibid.,* II, 318–340; 367–381.

as 1530, three years after the establishment of the first tribunal in Mexico, the sovereigns had already decided to establish a viceroyalty. Although the audiencia was entrusted with the government for a few years, the above facts would seem to indicate that this was only a temporary arrangement. The audiencia's chief attributes were judicial, and we have repeatedly noted that the principal object of its establishment, aside from the administration of justice, was to check the abuses of the captain-general.

Cortés retained his rank as captain-general after the audiencia was established. The conqueror was in reality reduced to a secondary position, and he was compelled repeatedly to acknowledge the supremacy of the audiencia. His commission was recognized by the tribunal on its arrival, but soon after its establishment the *oidores* exhibited a royal order requiring that ''Cortés, in all his operations, should consult the president and *oidores* and act only on their approval.''[11] Even in his field, as commander of the military forces, Cortés was subordinated to the tribunal, and the audiencia and the conqueror quarrelled bitterly over practically all matters which presented themselves for solution. The audiencia had been created to meet extraordinary and unusual conditions. It was the business of the tribunal to correct the abuses which had previously been inflicted on the colony by Cortés, and it did so. On the arrival of Mendoza in 1535, however, the audiencia surrendered the control of administrative affairs, and it did not assume them again, except in the regular way in conjunction with the viceroy, until it next served to administer the *ad interim* government.[12]

---

11 *Ibid.*, II, 410.

12 An audiencia was created at Compostela, Nueva Galicia, in 1548. This tribunal bore the same relation to the audiencia and viceroy in Mexico as did that of Santa Fé de Bogotá to those in Lima. The Audiencia of Nueva Galicia had both judicial and administrative functions, exercising its jurisdiction over the *partidos* and *corregimientos*, with their respective *alcaldes* and *corregidores*. It concerned itself,

The first legal provision for the succession of the audiencia in Mexico, according to Bancroft, was contained in the royal instructions to Visitor Valderrama, who arrived in Mexico in 1563. These instructions, says Bancroft, provided that in the event of the death or inability of the viceroy to discharge his duties, the audiencia should rule temporarily.[13] This was indeed timely, in view of the death of Viceroy Velasco on July 31, 1564. The audiencia, which was legally authorized to take charge of the government, was under investigation when the death of the viceroy occurred, and the tribunal was dominated during the first half of its rule by the visitor, who, Bancroft tells us, was virtually viceroy.[14] Valderrama dismissed two of the *oidores,* and sent them to Spain. The audiencia was even less able to administer justice during the early part of its *ad interim* government than it had been when the viceroy was alive. After the departure of the visitor, however, the audiencia inaugurated a season of proscription and reprisal which bade fair to include every opponent of the *oidores* in the colony. Matters had reached a very unsatisfactory state, indeed, when the new viceroy, the Marqués de Falcés, arrived at Mexico on October 14, 1566.[15]

---

moreover, with projects of conquest, discovery, the development of mines, and internal improvement. Subsequently this audiencia was transferred to Guadalajara and given that name. See *Recopilación,* 2–15–7.

[13] Bancroft, *History of Mexico,* II, 586.

[14] *Ibid.,* II, 602–7.

[15] It is interesting to note that in 1564, while the Audiencia of Mexico was governing *ad interim,* the voyage of Legaspi and Urdaneta was undertaken, and the first permanent settlement was made in the Philippines by authorization of that tribunal. Bancroft (*History of Mexico,* II, 599–600) is both indefinite and inaccurate in his account of the expedition of Legaspi and Urdaneta to the Philippines. He says: "Finally on the 21st of November, 1564, the squadron sailed, and after a prosperous voyage, reached Luzón, where Legaspi founded the city of Manila." It is well known that Legaspi did not sail directly to Luzón, as Bancroft implies, but he visited a number of islands in the Archipelago before he settled at Cebú on April 27, 1565. Manila was not formally claimed until May 19, 1571 (Montero y Vidal, *Historia general,* I, 39; Martínez de Zúñiga, *An historical view,* 113–119). Bancroft (*op. cit.,*

In view of the fact that the next important law dealing with the question of the succession was not promulgated until 1600, a continuance of this survey of affairs in New Spain will not be necessary. The audiencia there did not again assume the government until 1612, and then only for a very short period. We have already noticed the conditions under which the Audiencia of Mexico was created, and the various occasions on which it assumed charge of the government. Though entrusted with the government upon its establishment, the example set by three years of its unsatisfactory rule convinced the Spanish monarch of the unwisdom of entrusting such governmental authority to the audiencia permanently. Therefore, a viceroy was sent out in 1535, and it was not until 1563 that the first law was promulgated which provided for the temporary government by the audiencia when there was a vacancy in the office of viceroy. This was thirteen years after such a law had been promulgated for Perú, and fourteen years after an audiencia had been created, with all the functions of government, at Santa Fé de Bogotá.

The *cédula* of February 12, 1569, following in sequence that of March 5, 1550, provided that the faculty of filling vacancies among the *oficiales reales,* in case of death or removal from office, should rest with the viceroy, president, or the audiencia, if the latter body were governing.[16] This, of course, was a recognition of the principle of the assumption of the government by the audiencia. This law was not confined in its application to any particular territory, but was general in its

---

II, 743) states that Manila was founded in 1564 by Miguel de Legaspi. Manila was a prosperous commercial center before the Spaniards came to the Islands. Dr. James A. Robertson in his article entitled "Legaspi and Philippine colonization" (see American Historical Association, *Annual report, 1907,* I, 154), states on the basis of original documents that "this well-situated and busy trade center was erected into a Spanish city on June 3, 1571, and on the 24th the necessary officials were appointed." Dr. Robertson states in a note (p. 154) that "possession was taken of Luzon, June 6, 1570."

16 *Recopilación,* 8-4-24.

scope and applicable wherever an audiencia existed. It was later confirmed by the *cédula* of August 24, 1619.[17]

The next law dealing with the subject of succession was promulgated on January 3, 1600. It applied especially to New Spain, and it provided that in case of a vacancy in the office of viceroy, either by death or by promotion, the audiencia should assume charge of the government of the provinces there, and it should execute the duties which ordinarily devolved upon the viceroy, performing them "as he could, would and ought to do." It furthermore ordered the subordinate Audiencia of Guadalajara, under such circumstances, to obey and fulfill the orders which the Audiencia of Mexico might give or send, in the same manner as it would do, were those orders issued by the viceroy.[18] Under a separate title on this same date the assumption of the government of the minor dependencies of Perú and New Spain by the respective audiencias was authorized in case of the illness or absence of the viceroy. In other words, this law authorized in New Spain the same procedure in case of the death or absence of the viceroy as had already prevailed in South America for half a century.

The above laws form a precedent for the subsequent authorization of the Audiencia of Manila to assume charge of the government on the death of the governor. This authorization was given on April 12, 1664, but the Audiencia of Manila, like those of Mexico and Lima, had already assumed the functions of the executive on four earlier occasions, and the king, in the *cédula* of 1664, merely recognized, with some qualifications, a practice which had been followed in the Philippines for half a century. A *cédula* dated as early as September 13, 1608, had authorized the nomination in advance by the Viceroy of New Spain of a resident of the Islands to assume the governorship

---

17 *Ibid.*, 3–2–47.
18 *Ibid.*, 2–15–47 and 48.

on the death of the regular governor.[19] The intention of this law seems to have been to guard against the ills incident to a vacancy in the governorship by an arrangement whereby some person should be appointed in advance and thus be ready to assume the command without delay. Whatever the royal intentions may have been, this law was never effective in bringing about the benefits for which it was designed. In fact, this particular provision met with general dissatisfaction in the Philippines, and the audiencia, acting in accordance with the custom observed in other parts of Spain's dominions, continued to govern on the demise of the governor, ruling two or three years on some occasions, until the arrival of a temporary governor, sent from New Spain. So flagrantly was the prescribed method of procedure violated in the Philippines that in 1630, Visitor Francisco de Rojas y Ornate reminded the Council of the Indies of the existing law (that of 1608) and recommended that henceforth on the death of a governor the audiencia should have nothing to do with administration, but that one of three persons secretly designated by the viceroy should take over the government at once, thus eliminating all possibility of the interference of the tribunal.[20]

The irregularities and inconveniences arising from the inefficacy of the law of 1608 led to the promulgation of the *cédulas* of January 30, 1635, and of April 2, 1664, and to the enactment of the *consulta* of September 9, 1669. These regulations applied exclusively to the Philippines, and they legalized the intervention of the audiencia in governmental affairs on the death of the governor. The first of these admitted the right of the audiencia to administer political affairs, but ordered that military defense should be in the hands of a person

---

[19] King to the Audiencia, November 23, 1774, quotes the *cédula* of September 13, 1608, as *testimonio;* A. I., 105–2–9. A copy of this *cédula* also exists in A. I., 67–6–3.

[20] *Testimonio al acuerdo de 19 de Julio de 1654, Audiencia de Manila,* A. I., 67–6–3. See *Recopilación,* 2–15–58.

appointed in advance by the Viceroy of New Spain. The *cédula* of April 2, 1664, ordered that the audiencia should serve temporarily during vacancies in the governorship until the temporary appointee of the viceroy should arrive. This law further prescribed that the audiencia should assume charge of political affairs while the senior magistrate should take over the military command. He was to see that the forces and defenses of the Islands were adequately kept up, and that the soldiers were disciplined; he was authorized to command them in case of insurrection or invasion. The *consulta* of September 9, 1669, above referred to, re-enacted the *cédula* of April 2, 1664, but in addition it specifically ordered that the viceroy should not designate a temporary governor until news of the death of the regular incumbent was received, and then that no resident or native of the Philippines should be appointed.[21]

The Council of the Indies, by the law of September 29, 1623, had already sought to guard against any undue assumption of power on the part of the audiencia by ordering that when the viceroy was absent from the capital city, but within his own district, he should still retain his status as governor, and neither the audiencia nor any of the *oidores* should interfere in governmental affairs.[22] This law was not applicable to the Philippines alone, but it was of general validity, throughout Spain's dominions. The control of the audiencia in governmental affairs was only to become effective when the governor was absent from the colony, or incapacitated through sickness or death. Otherwise the governor's sphere of authority was to be recognized by the tribunal.

A variety of laws exist in the *Recopilación* prescribing the duties and conduct of the audiencia when it had charge of

---

21 Copies of the *cédula* of January 30, 1635, and of April 2, 1664, and of the *consulta* of September 9, 1669, exist in A. I., 67–6–3.

22 *Recopilación*, 2–15–45. It will be seen that this law was slightly modified by laws promulgated in the eighteenth century.

governmental affairs, and defining the relationship which should exist between the *oidores* under such conditions. The magistrates were ordered to proceed harmoniously and moderately both in the execution of governmental affairs and in the administration of justice, not erring either on the side of excessive severity, or of undue moderation. They were to devote special attention to the increase and care of the royal revenue during these times.[23] The right to grant *encomiendas*, essentially the function of the governing authority, was conceded to the audiencia when it acted in the capacity of governor. All such concessions ultimately had to be confirmed by the king. On these occasions, also, the audiencia filled vacancies and made appointments. However, the *oidores* were warned against discharging officials and vacating offices in order to fill them with their dependents and friends.[24] All appointments made by the audiencia were to become void after the arrival of a regular governor, unless they had subsequently received the royal confirmation. When a vacancy arose, it was the duty of the senior magistrate to propose a candidate, but the actual filling of the place was to be effected by the *acuerdo* vote of the entire audiencia.[25]

The laws provided that the audiencia, as a body, should exercise two distinct types or classes of powers when in charge of the government. These were designated as governmental and military. The exercise of these functions was assigned respectively to the audiencia as a body, and to the senior magistrate, individually. While an effort was made to insure the fair and equal participation of all in government in case of a vacancy, the senior magistrate assumed the position and honors of the executive, though not granted all the governor's powers.[26] In the functions and duties of administration all the magistrates were to participate. As noted above, each was

---

23 *Ibid.*, 60.
24 *Ibid.*, 56; 3–2–12, 13, 53, 28–33.

25 *Ibid.*, 9–11.
26 *Ibid.*, 10.

to have a share in the exercise of the appointing power, the administration of colonial finances, participation in the *acuerdo,* and in every other function except defense, which was entrusted to the senior *oidor.* In this capacity, the *oidor* was always the most prominent figure in the government. Among those who distinguished themselves through the exercise of this power were Rojas, Morga, Alcaraz, Bónifaz, Coloma, Montemayor, and above all, Anda. Although these men were assisted and supported by their colleagues of the audiencia, and the parts played by the latter were not without importance, the periods of rule of the audiencia are always identified with the names of the senior *oidores,* while those of the ordinary magistrates are forgotten.

A complete understanding of the governmental functions and authority of the audiencia, and the relation of the latter to the other departments of government under these conditions may best be obtained by a review of the circumstances and conditions of the audiencia's rule during vacancies in the Philippines. The first occasion which in any way approached the temporary rule of an audiencia in the Philippines was in 1593, after the murder of Governor Gómez Pérez Dasmariñas. Pedro de Rojas, who had been a magistrate of the audiencia when it was suppressed in 1589, was at that time sole judge, with the additional rank of lieutenant-governor and *asesor,* standing next to the governor in authority.[27] After the death of Gómez Pérez Dasmariñas, Rojas had occupied the governor's chair less than a year when he was succeeded by the deceased governor's son, Luís Pérez Dasmariñas, who became governor on the authority of a royal order found among the papers of his father, whereby he was given the power to name his successor.[28] His tenure seems to have been only temporary, however, for as

27 Montero y Vidal, *Historia general,* I, 94; Martínez de Zúñiga, *An historical view,* I, 184–192.
28 *Ibid.,* I, 192.

soon as news reached the court of the death of the elder Dasmariñas, Francisco Tello de Guzmán was appointed permanent governor and an audiencia was sent to the Islands, arriving at Manila in 1596.[29] Meanwhile Rojas was succeeded as lieutenant-governor and *asesor* by Antonio de Morga. According to Montero y Vidal, Dasmariñas turned over the government to Morga in 1595, but it is more probable that Morga assumed the temporary governorship when Dasmariñas was in Cambodia and elsewhere fighting against the Dutch. In fact, this conclusion is confirmed by Zúñiga.[30] At any rate, Morga administered both governmental and military affairs on several occasions when the various governors were absent from the Islands, engaged in expeditions of conquest.

On the suppression of the audiencia in 1589, the administration of justice remained entirely in the hands of the lieutenant-governor and *asesor*. This position was first occupied by Rojas, and later by Morga, who succeeded to the same judicial duties and enjoyed the same prerogatives as had formerly belonged to the audiencia. In the absence of the tribunal, therefore, they assumed functions which elsewhere were carried out by the audiencia on the death of the governor or viceroy, partly because they had taken the place of the audiencia, and partly because they were lieutenants-governor. After the audiencia was re-established in 1598, Morga continued in charge of military affairs when the governor was absent or dead, while the audiencia administered the government, not by virtue of any laws relating especially to the Philippines, but seemingly because this was the general practice in all of Spain's colonies. Morga's defense of Manila against the Dutch in 1600 has been referred to in an earlier chapter.

---

[29] *Ibid.*, I, 199.
[30] Montero y Vidal, *op. cit.*, I, 106–107; Martínez de Zúñiga, *op. cit.*, I, 195.

Not only did the audiencia do much in defense against outside enemies at this time, but it carried on offensive operations against them in the Moluccas after the deaths of Governors Tello and Acuña. The Japanese who were residing in the city also caused trouble, and the audiencia was under the necessity of taking repressive measures against them.[31] In 1606, while Governor Acuña was absent from the colony, the fortification of Cavite, the equipment of a fleet and the defense of the city were undertaken and carried out successfully by Oidor Almansa.[32] Then on the death of Governor Acuña the audiencia succeeded to the government and it managed affairs from June 24, 1606, to June 15, 1608, with Almansa in charge of military affairs.

The various governmental matters with which the audiencia concerned itself during this period are shown in a memorial which it sent to the king on July 6, 1606. After reporting the death of Governor Acuña, and its succession to the government, the audiencia took up questions of finance and commerce. It stated that the money in the treasury was insufficient for the necessary expenses of the colony, owing to the extraordinary outlays which had been necessary to defray the costs of the wars and expeditions which had been undertaken at this time. The audiencia suggested that the galleon returns be increased from 500,000 to 1,000,000 pesos a year. It was pointed out in this connection that the total cost of transport-

---

31 Morga's Sucesos, Blair and Robertson, XVI, 61.

32 Acuña designated Almansa to supervise military affairs instead of Oidor Maldonado, who was in reality senior magistrate, and as such should have assumed the direction of military affairs in accordance with the practice elsewhere, and in compliance with the laws of the Indies. The *fiscal* objected to this illegal procedure, as he termed it, alleging that the governor was not authorized by law to choose his own successor. He pointed out that, according to the existing laws, the senior magistrate should succeed to the military command by his own right, without the interference either of the governor or the audiencia. Notwithstanding this protest, Almansa continued to hold the post of acting captain-general, for which it was said that he was better fitted than Maldonado.

ing goods from Manila to Acapulco, including freight and
duty, aggregated thirty per cent of their value, leaving to the
merchants a profit of only 350,000 pesos. The *oidores* admitted
that this arrangement might have been ample and satisfactory
when the colony was small or when there was peace, but at
that time, when the inhabitants of the colony had been forced
to expend so much of their revenue for defense, a larger return
was necessary.[33] Further recommendations were made regarding commerce and the management of the galleons. It was said
that their great size encouraged smuggling; in order to avoid
this, and at the same time to contribute to the revenues of the
colony, it was urged that the ships should carry cargo to the
limit of their capacity, instead of being restricted to an insufficient amount. Large reductions of salaries of ships' officers, soldiers, and sailors were urged. The *oidores* did not
think it advisable to forbid the crews and officers of the galleons to trade, however, since their interest in the cargo would
encourage them to be obedient and loyal.[34] The audiencia

[33] Audiencia to Felipe III, July 6, 1606, Blair and Robertson, XIV,
140–148. These demands were ultimately met by a subsidy from the
treasury of New Spain. It may be remarked in this connection that the
oidores were probably interested in somewhat more than increased
revenue for defense, since they were known to have been absorbed in
commercial ventures. This episode marks the beginning of a struggle
on the part of the Manila merchants for increased trading privileges—
a battle which continued until the close of the eighteenth century.
They were opposed by the merchants of Cádiz and Seville, and it was
in the interest of these last-mentioned cities that the Manila trade was
restricted (Royal order of November 10, 1605, and King to the Audiencia, February 6, 1606, A. I., 105–2–1).
[34] Although the laws of the Indies forbade the *oidores* from trading
(*Recopilación, 2–16–59, 60, 62, 64, 66*), and the correspondence of the
period shows that the *oidores* were at first denied trading privileges,
(King to Conde de Monterrey, April 14, 1597; A. I., 105–2–1), they
were allowed to send to Spain sufficient cloth, silk and other dress
materials for their own use and for that of their families (*Recopilación, 2–16–63*). This last-mentioned privilege was abused, however,
until the right of each official to send only a limited amount of cargo
on the galleon was generally recognized. For example, the cargo list of
the galleon "Trinidad" in 1753, shows that ministers were assigned six
boletas, or bales, of the nominal value of 125 pesos each—that being
only half the amount usually allowed. This reduction, effected by

concluded its memorial with an appeal for the reform of the freight and customs charges on the galleon. The abolition of all fixed duties was .recommended; instead, it was suggested that these duties be graduated to meet the regular expenses of the colony as they were incurred year by year. This recommendation was made on the basis of the theory that duties should not be levied for the benefit of the king's exchequer, but only for the support and maintenance of the merchants and inhabitants of the colony.[35] This memorial would seem to indicate that the audiencia, when acting in the capacity of governor, exercised considerable authority and assumed entire responsibility for the commercial and financial affairs of the colony.

Zúñiga, after describing the success of Oidor Almansa in putting down an insurrection of the Japanese, characterized the administration of affairs by the audiencia during this period as follows:

The Royal Audience conducted themselves with great approbation in the civil administration, until the year 1608, when Don Rodrigo Vivero of Laredo, who was named by the Viceroy as Governor *ad interim*, arrived at Manila, and having had great experience in the management of the Indians in New Spain, he availed himself of it on this occasion, giving instructions to that effect to the chief judges, and other ministers of justice. He governed with much satisfaction

---

Governor Arandía, caused much opposition on the part of the audiencia (*Expediente* of January 30, 1754; A. I., 108–3–11). The officials having first claim on the right to send goods in the galleon were those of the municipal *cabildo* of Manila. On March 27, 1714, they were conceded the right to ship 132 *fardillos*, the specifications of which were not given. It was mentioned, however, in the *consulta* which recommended this bestowal that this was a re-enactment of the grant of 1699, and that it was the policy of the king to be generous to the *regidores* in this matter because they were not given salaries (A. I., 68–2–8). The royal order of June 30, 1786, bestowed on the *regidores* the right to ship one ton of goods. This right was confirmed by the *consulta* of October 7, 1789 (A. I., 105–3–5). The *cédula* of April 25, 1803, conceded five *boletas*, each valued at one hundred pesos, to each *regidor*. The *oidores* were each allowed ten *boletas* by this *cédula* (A. I., 106–2–15).

35 Audiencia to Felipe III, July 6, 1606, Blair and Robertson, XIV, 147.

for one year, when he delivered up the insignia of his office, and returned to Mexico.[36]

Vivero arrived in the colony on June 15, 1608. Vivero was the first of the military governors appointed from New Spain. Under this and succeeding arrangements, these governors exercised absolute control of military affairs, while the audiencia concerned itself solely with matters of government, the senior magistrate, of course, not participating in military affairs.

Vivero was relieved in 1609 by Governor Juan de Silva, who had a permanent appointment and served for seven years. Silva's administration was characterized by his military exploits, chief among which was his defense of the colony against the attacks of the Dutch pirate, Wittert, and subsequently of Spielberg. These frequent expeditions gave the audiencia many opportunities to assume charge of affairs, and after Silva's death in the Moluccas the tribunal ruled from April 19, 1616, to June 8, 1619. During a part of this time Andrés de Alcaraz, the senior magistrate, exercised the duties of captain-general, successfully defending the city against the Dutch. On September 30, 1617, the office of military governor devolved on Gerónimo de Silva, who was especially designated for the post by the royal order of March 20, 1616.[37] He was not an *oidor*, however, but had served as governor of Ternate, having recently returned from the Moluccas.[38]

While the post of captain-general devolved upon Silva, the audiencia retained control of administrative affairs in the colony until Alonso Fajardo y Tenza, the next royal appointee, arrived on June 8, 1618, to enter upon the duties of governor and captain-general. As we have already seen, Alcaraz was relieved of his military responsibilities on September 30, 1617,

---

[36] Martínez de Zúñiga, *An historical view*, I, 230–331.

[37] *Ibid.*, I, 239, *et seq.;* Montero y Vidal, *Historia general*, I, 162, *et seq.*

[38] Martínez de Zúñiga, *op. cit.*, I, 241; Montero y Vidal, *op. cit.*, I, 166.

and was at once obliged to submit to *residencia*. In this trial he was compelled to answer for his failure to warn the Chinese traders, who usually approached the Islands at that time of the year, of the presence of the Dutch. As a result of his oversight in this matter, a large quantity of merchandise, including provisions for the city, had fallen into the hands of the enemy. He was also held accountable for the disaster which had occurred to a portion of the Spanish fleet in the battle of Playa Honda through the appointment of the son of one of the *oidores* to its command.[39] Alcaraz, senior *oidor*, who was legally responsible for defense, was compelled to answer for the failure of this inefficient commander. The choice of a relative of one of the *oidores* was a violation of the laws of the Indies.[40] Although Oidor Alcaraz seems to have acquitted himself well of his duties as commander of the military forces, seven galleons were lost in an expedition to the Moluccas during the rule of the audiencia, and considerable difficulty was experienced in fixing responsibility for this disaster. Alcaraz claimed that Silva was answerable; the latter maintained that the audiencia was to blame, and the audiencia disclaimed responsibility because, it alleged, "the audiencia was entrusted with government and not war." In an investigation ultimately made in 1625, Silva was deprived of his office and was prevented from leaving the Islands.

Governor Fajardo has left us a number of comments and criticisms of the work of the audiencia as governor. His observations are timely and appropriate, since the tribunal had been in charge of the government for two years preceding his rule, and he was brought intimately in touch with the deeds and mistakes of the previous administration.[41] Fajardo's comments relate to the abuse of the appointing power by the

---

39 *Inventario de Residencias*, A. I. *op. cit.*
40 King to the Audiencia, August 9, 1609, A. I., 105–2–1.
41 See Chapter VII, notes 49 to 56.

audiencia, and the failure of that body to provide adequately
for the defense of the colony.   In support of the former
charge, Fajardo said that the magistrates had appointed several
officials for life, which was forbidden by the laws, since the
audiencia was only permitted to fill offices for the period of its
rule.[42]   The audiencia had also infringed upon the prerogatives
of the governor by the permanent bestowal of *encomiendas.*
Fajardo stated that when he arrived in the Islands he found
all the offices and *encomiendas* filled with friends and dependents of the *oidores.*   Thus as a direct consequence the success
of his administration was impaired by the presence of officials
who regarded him, their chief, with hostility.   He cited an instance in which similar infringements upon the rights of the
viceroy by the Audiencia of Mexico had been nullified by the
royal veto, and he urged that some definite *cédula* or law
should be promulgated relative to these matters in the Philippines.[43]

The difficulty of fixing responsibility for the loss of the
galleons in the expedition to the Moluccas led Fajardo to
criticise the practice of allowing the audiencia to assume control of affairs during vacancies.   He regarded it as a cumbrous
proceeding which could only result in chaotic and incompetent
government.   No better results could be expected when a body
of magistrates and lawyers undertook to rule an isolated colony,
and especially when one of them assumed responsibility for
military affairs, which could not be successfully carried out by
any but a military man.   He emphasized the necessity of locat-

---

[42] *Recopilación*, 2–15–56; 3–2–47; 3–2–11 and 12.

[43] Fajardo to Felipe III, August 10, 1618, Blair and Robertson, XVIII,
127.   In regard to the points covered in the above letter of Fajardo,
the audiencia legally lacked the power of granting *encomiendas* at this
time, although it undoubtedly bestowed them, nevertheless.   The power
to grant *encomiendas* for the period of its temporary rule was granted
October 24, 1655.   Moreover, by *cédulas* of May 25, 1596, August 24,
1619, and September 5, 1620, the audiencia was conceded authority to
make temporary appointments to offices when it assumed the government *ad interim* (*Recopilación*, 2–15–56; 3–2–47; 3–2–11 and 12).

ing responsibility for every department of government in a central authority. He recommended the designaticn of "two military men of such standing and ability that, when the governor and captain-general is absent, they might succeed to those duties."[44] He considered it advisable that during vacancies, as well as when the regular governor was present, authority should rest with one person and not be scattered or divided among a number of magistrates.

Gerónimo de Silva had been given a commission from the viceroy to assume the post of captain-general, and upon the demise of Fajardo in 1624, he took charge of military affairs, while the audiencia retained the government. Silva's responsibility for the loss of the ships in 1617, already referred to, as well as for other disasters in 1624, caused him to be removed from the command and confined in Fort Santiago where he remained until released by the new temporary governor, Fernando de Silva, who arrived in 1625. The latter commanded the military forces, while the audiencia administered the government.[45]

Of far-reaching importance was the action of the audiencia in 1624, in nullifying the action taken by the former governor, Alonso Fajardo, relative to the construction of a seminary for Japanese priests and students. This edifice had been par-

---

[44] Fajardo to Felipe III, August 10, 1618, Blair and Robertson, XVIII, 124–125.

[45] Martínez de Zúñiga, *An historical view*, I, 250–251. The latter Silva was a relative of the viceroy, the Marqués de Cerralbo. He was well known in the Philippines, where he had formerly resided and married the daughter of an influential resident. He held the temporary governorship about a year. It was during his administration, and through his efforts, that the first Spanish expedition was made to Formosa, Silva having ordered the *alcalde mayor* of Cagayán to land there with a military force and establish fortifications. This was done; thereupon a large number of Dominican friars sought and obtained permission for the spiritual conquest of the Island. Zúñiga says that the latter "exerted themselves with such zeal, that in a short time they built several towns, and were able to number the greater part of the natives among the professors of our faith" (*ibid.*, I, 252–253; Montero y Vidal, *Historia general*, I, 180-181).

tially constructed when the audiencia took over the government. It is interesting to note that the *oidores*, although not collectively responsible for the defense of the colony, took a stand on this occasion in a matter which had to do with the common security. The objections of the *oidores* were significant. The location of the seminary within three hundred feet of the wall was thought to be unwise in view of the danger of a Japanese revolt. The Japanese emperor had signified his disapproval of Christianity on many occasions by banishing and torturing numerous friars who had gone to Japan from the Islands. He had forbidden the worship and propagation of Christianity in his empire. There were at that time rumors of an impending conquest of China and the Philippines by the Japanese, consequently the audiencia did not wish to invite the emperor's wrath upon the colony by attempting to proselyte his subjects. The audiencia thought best to stop this before the displeasure and enmity of the Japanese were incurred. Fear of the loss of trade with China, dread of an alliance of the Japanese with the Dutch, making probable a concerted attack on the Philippines, and the danger of an outbreak of the Japanese already within the colony in conjunction with an attack by those without, were all considerations which induced the audiencia to take responsibility upon itself in this matter.[46]

The official correspondence of the governor following immediately upon the administration of an audiencia is always valuable as showing the state of affairs under the preceding rule. That of Fernando de Silva coincides closely with the correspondence of Governor Fajardo in charging the audiencia with many misdeeds, chief among which were the abuse of the appointing power and the concession of *encomiendas* without authorization. Silva, on his accession to the governorship, also found the finances of the colony in a bad condition, great waste

---

[46] Audiencia to the King, July 24 and August 15, 1624, Blair and Robertson, XXI, 84-97.

having been incurred in their administration. There had been neither peace nor order; the *oidores* had quarreled among themselves, and residents were leaving the city as a consequence of this turmoil. The *oidores* had, without cause, dismissed all the officials appointed by Fajardo, filling their places with their friends.[47] The following account of the excesses of the audiencia was given by Silva:

Under pretext of the arrest and removal of Don Geronimo de Silva, Licentiate Legaspi, . . . exercised the office of captain-general, carrying the staff of office and making them lower the banners to him, and address him as "your Lordship," and his wife as "my lady." He immediately appointed his elder son to the post of sargento-mayor of this camp, and his younger son to a company, while another company was assigned to a relative of Auditor Matias Flores y Cassila (also an *oidor*). Others were assigned to brothers of the said Don Matias, the fiscal, and other auditors, except Don Albaro (Messa y Lugo), who refused to have anything given to his household. Upon seeing the illegality of these appointments, I issued an act declaring them vacant and restoring those posts to those who had held them before.[48]

That the king had not entirely lost confidence in the audiencia, notwithstanding the above complaints, is attested by the instruction issued by the Council of the Indies to Francisco de Rojas y Ornate, royal visitor to the Philippines.[49] This communication, which was dated August 17, 1628, approved the stand which the audiencia had taken in insisting that all money

---

[47] Silva to Felipe IV, August 4, 1625, Blair and Robertson, XXII, 62–78.

[48] *Ibid.*, XXII, 66. The governor estimated the services of the magistrates in a special report to the king on July 30, 1626. He stated that Messa was "an upright judge, and zealous in the service of your Majesty." His comments on the other three were as follows: "Geronimo de Lagaspi does what his two sons wish, whom, on account of their reckless lives, the governors cannot employ, and thus they are unable to satisfy their father, who is not contented except with favors. Don Juan de Valderrama does as his wife says; and Don Matias Flores, although a young man, is less harmful; . . . He makes all the profit he can from the office, and on the whole is not acceptable to the community, which is always disturbed by him" (Silva to Felipe IV, July 30, 1626, Blair and Robertson, XXII, 102).

[49] Instructions to Francisco de Rojas y Ornate, August 17, 1628, A. I., 105–2–1.

obtained from Chinese trading-licenses should be put into the royal treasury and accounted for by the *oficiales reales* before it was spent. It appears that the governor had hitherto used this money as an extra fund upon which to draw for the expenses of the colony. The king also approved the attitude of the audiencia in denying to persons in New Spain the right of using the Manila galleon for the shipment of their goods, and in refusing to allow money sent by them to the Islands to be invested in the Chinese trade. Silva contended that the audiencia had no right to intervene in either of the above matters, but in this Silva was not sustained, Rojas y Ornate being instructed to see that Governor Tavora respected the action of the audiencia in the two particulars referred to.[50]

The audiencia assumed management of political affairs in 1632, on the death of Governor Juan Niño de Tavora, but neither the audiencia as a body, nor the senior *oidor* personally were entrusted with the military command. This responsibility devolved on Lorenzo de Olazo, the *maestre de campo*, who had been designated by the viceroy of New Spain to assume temporary charge of military affairs. He was succeeded the following year by Juan Cerezo de Salamanca, who had been sent from Mexico by the viceroy as soon as the death of Tavora was announced in that city. Cerezo served *ad interim* for three years, and during his administration the audiencia acted solely as a judicial body, not attempting to interfere in governmental or military affairs.[51] It was under the rule of this gov-

---

[50] See Royal Instructions to Rojas y Ornate and Tavora (duplicates), June 4, 1627, A. I., 105-2-1.

[51] Martínez de Zúñiga, *An historical view*, I, 264–266, Montero y Vidal, *Historia general*, I, 189–200. The method of filling vacancies in the governorship during this period was described in a letter from Governor Corcuera, Cerezo's successor, to the king, dated June 30, 1636. He wrote: "Your Majesty has conceded to your viceroys of Nueva España authority, in case of deaths and vacancies in this government, to send commissions to those who are to have charge of military matters; and until the arrival of the regularly appointed governor you order them to send another governor from Mexico" (Corcuera to Felipe IV, June 30, 1636, Blair and Robertson, XXVI, 150).

ernor that important expeditions were undertaken against the
Moros in the South, and the first fort and settlement were
made at Zamboanga.

It is to be especially noted that in the appointment of
Olazo and Cerezo in 1632 and 1633 respectively, the senior
oidor was deprived of the control of military affairs. This had
been done also in 1617 and in 1624 when Gerónimo de Silva,
governor of Ternate, had taken charge of military affairs during vacancies in the regular governorship. Temporary appointments had been made on two different occasions by the
Marqués de Cerralbo, Viceroy of New Spain, once in the sending of Fernando de Silva after the death of Governor Fajardo,
and on this occasion, when Cerezo de Salamanca took the place
of Governor Juan Niño de Tavora, after the audiencia had
governed a year. Experience had shown that the assumption
of the military command by the senior *oidor* was not productive of the most satisfactory results. It was not to be expected, of course, that a magistrate would administer military
affairs with the skill of a captain-general, and we have seen
that various governors recommended that the practice should
no longer be continued. So it came about that the law of 1608
was revived, and the viceroy appointed a temporary governor
to assume control of military affairs, the audiencia being restricted to judicial and administrative functions. In 1633, on
the accession of Cerezo de Salamanca, the audiencia was deprived of the right of intervention in the last mentioned
activity, and was confined to its judicial duties alone. This was
confirmed by the *cédula* of January 30, 1635, which relieved the
Audiencia of Manila of all jurisdiction over military affairs
during vacancies, ordering that they were to be administered
by a temporary appointee of the viceroy.[52]

Nevertheless, considerable opposition to this method of fill-

---

[52] *Cédula* of January 30, 1635, A. I., 67–6–3.

ing vacancies in the governorship had developed within the
colony. This is shown in various protests which came from the
Islands from time to time. These are set forth with great
clarity in the correspondence of the governors. Corcuera, in
a letter written to Philip IV on June 30, 1636, stated that
these temporary governors had allowed persons in Mexico to
make large fortunes out of the Philippine trade, and that the
governors had devoted most of their time when in Manila to
serving as agents of the residents of Mexico. Corcuera, however, seemed to regard the audiencia as incapable of government, for he claimed that in the brief term of a year in which
the tribunal had ruled, three years prior to his accession, it had
run the colony into debt from 80,000 to 100,000 pesos. He
charged the *oidores* with the same dishonest practice as
had been alleged against Governor Fajardo, namely, that they
had issued duebills in payment of debts and had bought them
up later at less than their face value, realizing the full amount
on them upon their presentation to the treasury later. He
stated that these warrants were not only bought by the *oidores*,
but by practically all the officials of the government. During
Cerezo's term a sum in excess of 100,000 pesos was said to
have been paid out to officials as usury.[53]

Corcuera presented a scheme of reform designed to remedy
the evils resulting from the succession either of the audiencia
or of an irresponsible military commander to the *ad interim*
governorship. He recommended that the regularly appointed
governor should be assisted by five commissioners, who should
be military men, holding the respective commands of Fort
Santiago, Cavite, the Port of Manila, Formosa, and the *Parián*.
These were to be eligible in the order named in case of a
vacancy. This plan, like so many of the schemes of the soldier
governors, only took cognizance of the military side of the gov-

---

[53] Corcuera to Felipe IV, June 30, 1636, Blair and Robertson, XXVI,
150 *ct seq.*

ernor's office. The marked tendency of these commanders was to continually underestimate the administrative and political phases of their positions. The plan of Corcuera was not adopted, however, and the viceroy continued to appoint temporary governors to succeed the audiencia when it assumed the government *ad interim.*

Governor Diego Fajardo, on July 10, 1651, wrote a letter to the king protesting against the policy of appointment which was then in force. He said:

> I should be unfaithful to Your Majesty if I did not advise you of the inconveniences arising from the appointment of governors by the Viceroy of New Spain; the practice of sending money from Mexico for investment in this colony has continued and increased, to the exclusion and deprivation of the merchants of these Islands. . . . Investments have been made by the viceroys through the agency of others.[54]

Fajardo urged that the audiencia should be permitted to retain the government as it had done formerly. He showed the advantages accruing to the colony from a continuity of policy which would result from the rule of the *oidores.* He showed that the incursions of the viceroys and residents of Mexico upon the galleon trade would more likely be checked by the *oidores* than by any other agency, adding moreover that this particular matter should be attended to at once since the life and prosperity of the colony depended on the control of the Acapulco and Chinese commerce by the merchants of Manila.[55] A similar argument was presented by Governor Manrique de Lara in a letter written July 19, 1654. This governor urged that a commission of magistrates, familiar with the needs of the colony through experience and long residence, was better fitted to rule for the common good than a stranger, appointed by a distant viceroy, coming to the Islands as most of the temporary governors had done, with the sole purpose of exploitation.[56]

---

[54] Fajardo to the King, July 10, 1651, A. I., 67–6–9.
[55] *Ibid.*
[56] Governor Lara to the King, July 19, 1654, A. I., 67–6–9.

Probably the sentiments of the residents and officials of the Philippines were best and most effectively expressed on this subject in the letter written by the audiencia to the king on July 19, 1654.[57] The audiencia, on this occasion, described the inconveniences resulting from the appointment of a resident of the Islands by the Viceroy of New Spain. It was alleged that these appointees, being already established in the Islands as merchants, officials, lawyers, and even as soldiers, spent all their time in the service of their own special interests. The commercial abuses of these appointees were said to be notorious. The presence of so many relatives, friends, and business connections made it impossible for these temporary rulers to officiate properly as presidents of the audiencia, or to administer the affairs of the government with diligence and impartiality.

As a result of the general dissatisfaction in the colony, which was reflected in the above letters, and in compliance with the repeated requests previously made for reform, the law of April 2, 1664, was proclaimed, and followed by the *consulta* of September 9, 1669, which has been already referred to. These laws still recognized the right of the Viceroy of New Spain to appoint governors temporarily, but these were no longer to be designated in advance from the residents of the Islands. While the senior magistrate was to have charge of military affairs, he was to seek the advice of such military officials as were stationed in the colony, "exercising very particular care and vigilance in all that pertains to military affairs, endeavoring to keep the *presidios* well stocked and provided with all the defenses necessary for whatever occasion may arise." This, then, was a return to the practice which had prevailed prior to September 13, 1608, when the Viceroy of New Spain was first authorized to appoint a temporary gov-

---

[57] *Cédula* of April 2, 1664, with *testimonios* of former *cédulas* and correspondence on succession, A. I., 67–6–3.

ernor in advance of the death of the incumbent. Although
the audiencia assumed the government with partial legal justification from 1593 onward, the period from 1664 to 1719 may
rightly be said to constitute the era of the audiencia's authorized rule.

An occasion for the exercise of the new law occurred in
1668, when Governor Diego de Salcedo was arrested and imprisoned by the commissary of the Inquisition. In accordance
with the law of April 2, 1664, just referred to, the audiencia
was entitled to assume the government until the arrival of
the provisional governor from New Spain. A dispute arose
between the two most eligible *oidores*, Francisco de Coloma and
Francisco Montemayor y Mansilla, for the honors of the military command. Coloma had been commissioned as magistrate
of the Audiencia of Manila before Montemayor, who maintained his claim to the headship of military affairs on the
grounds that he had arrived in the Philippines earlier than
Coloma.[58] These two officials were unable to agree as to their
respective rights, and Juan Manuel de la Peña Bónifaz, junior
magistrate of the audiencia, took advantage of the discord to
further his own interests. Put forward by the commissary of the
Inquisition and by the ecclesiastical element of the colony as arbiter in the contention between his two colleagues, he solidified his
own power until he was able to usurp the entire government. He
issued orders to the soldiers, compromised with Coloma, exiled
Montemayor, enacted financial and governmental measures, appointed his friends to office, and in general acted the part of a
dictator, combining in his own person all the functions of the
military, judicial and executive departments.[59] The audiencia,

---

[58] These two magistrates had come to the Islands on the same ship;
Montemayor had disembarked at Cagayán and had come to the city by
land, arriving a few days earlier than Coloma (Montero y Vidal,
Historia general, I, 336).

[59] Events in Filipinas, 1668, Blair and Robertson, XXXVII, 23–63;
also correspondence of Governor Manuel de León, and *consultas* of the

of course, was entirely suppressed. Certain ecclesiastical authorities state that he governed with greater consideration and fairness than many of his predecessors, and that his rule was more just than that of the audiencia had been.[60] The spirit of his administration was particularly favorable to the churchmen, by whose favor he gained office, and by whose aid he was able to retain his position. His successor, Manuel de León, was appointed regular governor as soon as news of the arrest of Salcedo reached Spain. Bónifaz was apprehended and sentenced to pay the customary penalty for treason, but death intervened and defrauded the king's justice. It may be considered, in a sense, that Bónifaz conferred a service upon the colony by forcibly putting an end to the disputes which had been prevalent between the rival *oidores* whose claims could not have been settled for three years at least—the time necessary for the Council of the Indies to transmit to the distant colony a ruling on the points at issue.

The audiencia next took over the government in April, 1679, on the death of Governor León, and it retained control of affairs until the arrival of Governor Juan de Vargas Hurtado in September, 1678. The rule of the tribunal on this occasion was without sensational features. Oidor Francisco de Coloma, in whose favor the Council of the Indies had declared in the dispute described above, assumed charge of military affairs, serving as captain-general until his death. His seniority was acknowledged by Montemayor, who was called back from exile to a place in the audiencia.[61]

The inefficiency of the audiencia as a governing agency as

Council of the Indies on Salcedo Affair, 1670–1673, A. I., 67–6–9, 10, 11; 67–6–3. For a more extended account of this episode, see Cunningham, "The inquisition in the Philippines; the Salcedo affair," in the *Catholic historical review*, III, 417–445.

[60] Augustinians in the Philippines, 1641–70, Blair and Robertson, XXXVII, 273–275; also *Consulta* of Council of the Indies, July 16, 1674, A. I., 67–6–3.

[61] Montero y Vidal, *Historia general*, I, 354–361.

shown in the episode just described was surpassed by the state
of utter impotency to which the tribunal was reduced during
the Pardo controversy in 1684. Though at first successful in
exiling the archbishop, the audiencia and Governor Vargas
were later completely undone by the intriguing of the new governor, Curuzaelegui, with the prelate to discredit the previous
administration. The struggle ended in the restoration of the
prelate, the *residencia* of Vargas and the appointment of a
new tribunal which was calculated to be more subservient to
the commands of the new governor and the prelate. This
audiencia assumed the government after the death of Curuzaelegui on April 17, 1689, with Alonzo de Ávila as chief
executive.[62]

The events of the Pardo controversy prepared the way for
a period of rule by an audiencia in which the entire government was dominated by the ecclesiastics. Archbishop Pardo
and his successors were the real governors and the victory of
the church over the various officials of civil administration
lowered the moral tone of the entire government. Corruption
flourished and the vigor of the administration decayed.[63] It is
clear that the depravity of the civil government proceeded
largely from the weakness of the audiencia and its submission
to the governor. The latter was under orders from no less an
authority than the king, himself, to put an end to the disputes
between church and state in the colony and to bring about
peace; it also happened that the situation in the colony at that
time caused the governor to lean towards the side of Pardo and
his supporters. The audiencia was entirely disregarded both

---

[62] *Ibid.*, I, 375. See Chapters X and XI of this book.

[63] There is no question of the harmful effects of the intervention of
the church in the government on this occasion. For a general survey
of this subject throughout the history of the Philippines, see the author's article entitled "The ecclesiastical influence in the Philippines"
(1565–1850) in *The American journal of theology*, XXII, 161–186, and
Robertson, "Catholicism in the Philippine Islands," in *The Catholic
historical review*, III, 375–391.

by Governor Curuzaelegui and by the court, which may be attributed in some measure to that policy of the Spanish government previously alluded to—that of sacrificing principle in order to preserve harmony. There is no doubt but that the weakness and inefficiency of the audiencia during these two controversies contributed largely to the subsequent decision of the court to deprive the audiencia of the right of governing *ad interim*.

The last occasion on which the audiencia regularly assumed the government of the Islands, and one which demonstrated still more conclusively the inefficiency of the audiencia as governor, occurred in 1715, after the death of Governor Lizarraga. His rule had been uncommonly quiet and peaceful, and the period of extortion and strife which succeeded it furnished a marked contrast to that governor's administration. The audiencia ruled from February 4, 1715, to August 9, 1717, with Oidor José Torralba as senior magistrate. The reports sent by Torralba to the court during the two years of his service as military commander show that the audiencia as a body played a very small part in the government. This was again the rule of a dictator. We have seen in a former chapter that Torralba was held accountable in his *residencia* for a deficit of 700,000 pesos which developed during this period;[64] it is difficult to

---

[64] See Chapter VIII, note 16. On June 30, 1716, Torralba forwarded an elaborate memorial to the king, showing that the finances were in an excellent state, a net gain of 38,554 pesos having accrued to the treasury since the beginning of the audiencia's rule. On the day that this report was filed there existed in the treasury, according to Torralba's figures, a favorable balance of 294,000 pesos. This report contains the following interesting data: Income from the subsidy, 250,000 pesos; betel monopoly, 13,167 pesos; tributes, 109,152 pesos; royal auctions, 20,377 pesos; *medias anatas*, 16,373 pesos; *almojarifazgo*, 20,377 pesos; wine monopoly, 14,000 pesos (Report of Torralba on Financial Affairs, June 30, 1716, A. I., 68-4-18). In a letter dated July 8, 1716, Torralba reported his compliance with the *cédula* of October 10, 1713,. by means of which the king had appealed for a "free gift or contribution on the part of the inhabitants of the Islands to assist in putting down a Catalonian conspiracy." Torralba stated that the audiencia had seen to the fulfillment of this command and had

understand how this could have been possible had the senior magistrate concerned himself solely with military affairs. Concepción states that Torralba, inflated by his position, and ambitious of getting absolute control of the government, drove from office the *oidores* who dared to oppose him.[65] He refused to honor the royal *cédula* of April 15, 1713, which ordered the reinstatement of Oidor Pavón to his place as senior *oidor* since the fulfillment of this order would have deprived Torralba of his command.

Torralba reported great progress in the repair and restoration of royal and municipal warehouses, hospitals, convents, and churches during his administration. The wall of Manila was re-built and new bronze guns were cast and placed thereon. As acting captain-general, Torralba inspected Fort Santiago, and, "noting grave needs both in construction and in the morale of troops," made the necessary repairs, reforms and corrections.[66] He concerned himself also with the promotion and appointment of military officials. These latter acts were vigorously resisted by the *maestre de campo,* and by other military officials, as encroachments on their authority. They ultimately sought to bring about the nullification of all Torralba's "unjustifiable acts of interference within the military sphere."[67] Whether animated by a sincere desire to see the natives justly treated, or rather by his natural dislike of the friars, Torralba intervened on various occasions for the protection of the Indians against the encroachments and abuses of the churchmen on the

---

collected the sum of 7,042 pesos (Torralba to King, July 8, 1716, A. I., 68–4–18).

[65] Concepción, *Historia general*, IX, 44, *et seq.* Pavón, it will be remembered, had been removed for advising Governor Zabalburú to receive the French papal delegate, Tourón. In 1718 all of Torralba's acts against Tourón and Villa were nullified by the Council of the Indies, and those officials were restored to office, while Torralba was condemned to perpetual exile (A. I., 68–2–8).

[66] Torralba to the King, July 15, 1715, A. I., 68–4–18; another report of Torralba on the same subject, dated September 1, 1717, exists in A. I., 68–2–8.

[67] Royal Fiscal to the Council, August 21, 1719, A. I., 68–4–18.

encomiendas and in the native towns. These acts were carried out in the name of the audiencia, and in accordance with the law, ultimately meeting with the approval of the Council of the Indies.[68]

A great deal of dissatisfaction, both at the court and in the colony, had resulted from the audiencia's assumption of the government at various times since 1664. We have already noted that the restoration of this authority to the audiencia was attended by the disgraceful quarrel between Coloma and Montemayor and the usurpation of Bónifaz in 1668. The Pardo controversy did not produce a favorable impression of the activities of the audiencia. Torralba's dictatorship in the name of the audiencia from 1715 to 1717, conspicuous for the huge deficit in which it culminated, demonstrated the unfitness of the audiencia to be entrusted with the rule of the Islands.

Indeed, it may be said that the various experiments made by the monarchs during the seventeenth and early eighteenth centuries for the purpose of perfecting a system whereby the governorship could be satisfactorily filled *ad interim* had failed to demonstrate or develop any authority capable of maintaining harmony or decent government. Co-operation among the authorities of the colony was practically unknown. The royal disapproval was passed upon practically all the official acts of these interim administrations. The thirst for personal glory, and the desire for private gain invariably induced some official who was stronger than his contemporaries to assume control of affairs; thus the government of the colony was made repeatedly to subserve personal ends, and civil and political life was characterized by its strife and discord. The probabilities that the temporary administration of the audiencia would not be entirely successful had been recognized from the beginning, and in order to guard against its misrule the king had authorized the ap-

---

[68] Torralba to the King, June 15, 1716 [with approval of Council indicated on margin], A. I., 68–4–18; *Recopilación*, 6–8, 6–9, 6–10.

pointment of a temporary governor by the Viceroy of New Spain. It was unavoidable, however, that the audiencia should govern until the arrival of this official. For a time the alternative was tried of allowing the *maestre de campo* to assume the military command, but this resulted in such an incompetent rule that the former prerogatives of the audiencia were restored. Whether the audiencia was capable of governing successfully or not, it certainly had the power to make or mar the government of any other person or authority, whether he was regularly appointed by the king, or chosen temporarily by the viceroy.

The church, as represented by a succession of triumphant archbishops, had exercised the preponderance of power and authority throughout the forty years of strife, ending with the death of Governor Bustamante. We need not be concerned here with the various struggles and disagreements with governors and audiencias, but the fact remains that the church was the only institution existing during this period which was able to present a solid and united front to its enemies, or which manifested any symptoms of power, unity or royal approbation. The culmination of ecclesiastical power was virtually reached on October 11, 1719, when Governor Bustamante was murdered by emissaries of the church and Fray Francisco de la Cuesta, Archbishop of Manila, assumed the vacant governorship.

Zúñiga, the Dominican historian, says that the archbishop declined the governorship on this occasion, but was subsequently prevailed upon to accept it.[69] It is certain that the tribunal was in no state or condition to take charge of affairs; its administration had been discredited by the murder of its protector, its senior magistrate had been proved an embezzler in his *residencia,* and the remaining members of the

---

[69] Martínez de Zúñiga, *An historical view,* II, 37–40.

tribunal were not qualified to remain in office. Oidores Villa and Pavón, removed by Torralba and Bustamante, were restored by the archbishop, and were content to recognize him as president of the audiencia. Each of them had his own claims to the position of acting-governor and had Cuesta not occupied the governorship with their consent, these *oidores* would either have been languishing in banishment as punishment for having resisted the prelate, or they would have been struggling for the honors of a position occupied by a pretended mediator, as on former occasions. So there can be no doubt that it was best for all concerned that the church ·was powerful at this time; the colony had had enough of strife and murder and there was urgent need of some authority with sufficient power to bring about peace. It is sufficient to say that the audiencia renounced its claims to the government, and, according to Zúñiga, who devotes an unusual amount of space to this important epoch in the ecclesiastical history of the Islands, the people were very content with the archbishop's rule after the injustice and oppression of Bustamante.[70] It may be noted that the archbishop exercised complete authority over the audiencia, even to the extent of restoring *oidores* who had been unlawfully dismissed, and of acting as an intermediary between magistrates. He was master of the situation and his interim rule was preferred by the sovereign and by the people to that of the audiencia.

The royal order of September 8, 1720, legalizing the gov-

---

[70] Zúñiga, who was favorable to the rule of the churchmen, writes: "There never appeared less confusion at an insurrection than on the present occasion, every individual seeming satisfied with his lot in being relieved from unjust oppression and violence. The archbishop, who had assumed the reins of government, was the only person whose mind was not at ease; but in a short time he was restored to tranquillity by the arrival of a royal order, enjoining him to suspend the Governor from his office, and imprison him; replace the Royal Audience on the same footing as before; set at liberty Señor Velasco (an *oidor* who had been imprisoned by Torralba), and assume the reins of government himself, which was exactly what had been effected by the late disturbance."—Martínez de Zúñiga, *op. cit.*, II, 39–40.

ernment of the prelates, applied not only to the administration of Cuesta, but it established a precedent for the temporary rule of four prelates.[71] In compliance with this decree, three sealed envelopes (*pliegos de providencia*) were sent to the audiencia to be placed unopened in the archives of that tribunal, and the seals were to be broken only on the death of the governor. These envelopes were accompanied by an order from the king, directing that the person mentioned in the first envelope should be recognized as temporary governor. In case of his absence or incapacity to serve, the second envelope was to be opened and the directions contained therein were to be followed, and if these could not be complied with, the third envelope was to be opened.

No further necessity for the observance of this law of succession arose until after the death of Governor Gaspar de la Torre, when, on August 15, 1745, the first envelope was opened in the presence of the audiencia. The post of archbishop being vacant at this time it became necessary to follow the directions prescribed by the second envelope. It was found that Fray Juan de Arrechedera, Bishop of Nueva Segovia, had been designated as the governor's successor. The audiencia relinquished the control of affairs into his hands and he governed for a period of five years.

It would seem that the ecclesiastical calling of this governor in no way incapacitated or hindered him in the execution of his duties. His administration was characterized especially by

---

[71] Royal order of September 8, 1720, A. I., 106–4–16. *Testimonio* of *cédula* of November 23, 1774, A. I., 105–2–9. Two years later, the home government showed its disapprobation of the rigorous acts of Cuesta by demoting him from his place as Archbishop of the Philippines to the minor post of Bishop of Mechoacán in New Spain (Montero y Vidal, *Historia general*, I, 432). The assumption of the government by Cuesta invited the suspicion that he had been a party to the murder of the governor. Seven archbishops had already ruled on various occasions in New Spain (Bolton, *Guide*, 469–470). It is surprising that such an attempt to solve this problem was not made earlier in the history of the Philippines.

various measures taken for the defense and fortification of the Islands. He suppressed several insurrections in Ilocos and Cagayán, dispatching military forces under the command of *alcaldes mayores* against the revolting natives. He repelled several Moro raids and made treaties of peace with the Sultan of Sulu.[72] There is no evidence of discord between the governor and the audiencia during this period. Although Archbishop Trinidad arrived and took possession of his see on August 27, 1747, he made no attempt to take charge of political affairs.[73] He permitted Arrechedera to continue as governor for three years, handing over to him

a royal mandate, for the absolute expulsion of the Chinese [which was never] . . . carried into execution, the interest of the Governor being too deeply involved in the suspension of it, the Chinese paying him a contribution for his forbearance. The Archbishop found that Arrechedera was strongly attached to this nation, and he became so far a convert to his sentiments on this subject that he did not put the royal order in force. . . . This seems to have been the only error committed by this illustrious prelate during the time he held the government. In all other respects his conduct reflected the highest honour on him.[74]

The third time the government was taken over by a prelate was in 1759 on the death of Governor Arandía. On this occasion it became necessary to open the third *pliego de providencia*. The metropolitan see of Manila and the diocese of Nueva Segovia being vacant, Bishop Espeleta of Cebú was the senior prelate of the Islands. Shortly after the accession of Espeleta, Manuel Rojo, the new archbishop, arrived, commanding Espeleta to vacate the governorship at once. Rojo refused,

---

[72] Martínez de Zúñiga, *op. cit.*, II, 84–95; Montero y Vidal, *Historia general*, I, 480–495.

[73] Martínez de Zúñiga says he carried a special government commission as governor *ad interim*, and his refusal to accept the office was later used as a precedent by Bishop Espeleta in his refusal to turn over the governorship to Archbishop Rojo (Zúñiga, *An historical view*, II, 89). Evidently he had all the qualifications necessary to fill the office of governor, for he had been a member of the Audiencia of Quito for seventeen years, and had been also a member of the Council of the Indies (Blair and Robertson, XLVIII, 145–146).

[74] Martínez de Zúñiga, *An historical view*, II, 89–90.

citing the precedent established by Bishop Arrechedera. Espeleta appealed to the audiencia for support, but the *oidores* were unable to agree on the question, two of them, Calderón and Galbán supporting Rojo, and the other two remaining in favor of the retention of the governorship by Espeleta. The question was left to the *fiscal*, Francisco Leandro de Viana, who advised that the matter should be carried to the Council of the Indies for final settlement.[75] It transpired, therefore, that Espeleta retained the governorship from 1759 until 1761, and he did very effective work in repelling the raids of the Moros, who had been ravaging the provinces with impunity for some time.

The prosecution of Dr. Santiago Orendaín occupied a large share of Espeleta's attention during his administration. This controversy should be noted here because it illustrates the relations between the audiencia and an ecclesiastical governor. Orendaín had been the advisor (*asesor*) of Governor Arandía, and was held responsible for the repressive measures taken against the church during the administration of the latter. The rule of an unscrupulous prelate presented an excellent opportunity for revenge and Orendaín's prosecution was unanimously demanded by the ecclesiastical element of the colony. The magistrates also welcomed the opportunity to retaliate upon a hitherto successful, but unpopular, rival. The *fiscal* brought action against Orendaín, who sought refuge in an Augustinian convent, whereupon the civil authorities forced an entrance into the asylum, seizing Orendaín and imprisoning him in Fort Santiago. The *provisor* of the ecclesiastical court excommunicated Magistrate Villacorta, who had exculpated Orendaín in his trial, but the ban was disregarded by the audiencia. A division over the question arose in the tribunal,

---

[75] Opinion of Pedro Calderón Enríquez, July 26, 1759, Opinion of Francisco Leandro Viana, July 31, 1759, *Autos* of Appeal, August 3, 1759, A. I., 106–4–16. Montero y Vidal (*Historia general*, II, 8) states that Espeleta used intimidation to secure the office.

and matters were assuming a threatening aspect, when the authorized appointment of Governor Rojo arrived. Espeleta gave up his office, and the first act of the new governor was to restore Orendaín to full favor as his counsellor. The affair of Dr. Orendaín illustrates a phase of Spanish colonial administration which is too characteristic to be left unnoticed here. Aside from the influence which Orendaín exercised over Governor Arandía, his persecution shows the measure of personal rancour which even a prelate might put into his administration, spending practically two years in the pursuit of revenge. In this he was supported by the audiencia. In this affair neither the church nor the audiencia were animated so much by motives of right and justice as they were influenced by personal feelings.

The rule of Archbishop Rojo from 1761 to 1764 was a notable one in the history of the Philippines. The principal event during his administration was the capture of Manila by the British. This furnished the occasion for the resistance of Oidor Simón de Anda y Salazar, in the name of the audiencia, both to the English and to the archbishop who had ordered his surrender. These events show the complete incapacity of an ecclesiastical governor of Rojo's type and personality to fulfill the military requirements of his position. In the operations of Anda we note how a man of decisive action, energy, courage, and loyalty was able to force the issue and deprive the archbishop-governor of the executive functions which he had assumed legally, but which he was unable to dispense. This episode illustrates, furthermore, the general disregard of the laws which placed the governorship in the hands of a man who was unfit for its exercise, showing again that in the selection of a person to carry out the duties of governor the military side of the situation could not be disregarded.

Anda, at the time of the accession of Rojo, was a junior magistrate in the audiencia, having arrived in Manila on July

21, 1761.[76] The British squadron entered Manila Bay on September 22, 1762. The British subsequently attacked the city, the fall of which seemed imminent on account of the neglectful state into which the defense had fallen.[77] The proposition was made to the archbishop-governor by Fiscal Francisco Leandro de Viana and the audiencia that Oidor Anda should be dispatched to the provinces with the title of Governor and Captain-general of the Islands for the purpose of maintaining and defending them under the sovereignty of the Spanish monarch,[78] and "in order that he might keep the natives quiet in their Christian instruction and in their obedience to the king."[79] The archbishop refused to accede to this proposition on the grounds that "neither he nor the Audiencia had any authority to create a governor and captain-general, which was the proper privilege of his Majesty; and that it was enough to give him the title of visitor of the land . . . and . . . of lieutenant of the captain-general."[80] This was done, therefore, and Anda left on the night of October 3, 1762, with these titles and powers.

It is important to note that Anda was not given the title of governor and captain-general, but that as *oidor* he was commissioned *visitador de tierras* and *teniente de gobernador y capitán general*.[81] The authority to designate *oidores* as visitors of the provinces was a function regularly exercised by the president of the audiencia and authorized by the laws of the Indies.[82] It appears from the above that Anda was sent to the

---

[76] Anda was sixty-two years of age when he left Manila to undertake the defense of the provinces (Blair and Robertson, XLIX, 211).

[77] *Relación de la conquista de Manila por los Ingleses y presa del galeón de Santísima Trinidad en el mes de Octubre de 1762*, A. I., 107–1–15.

[78] Manifiesto of Viana, March 8, 1762, A. I., 107–3–2.

[79] Rojo's Narrative, Blair and Robertson, XLIX, 210.

[80] *Ibid.*, 210–211.

[81] *Testimonio del Secretario de Cámara, 13 de Noviembre, 1762*, A. I., 107–3–2.

[82] *Recopilación*, 2–31–1 to 14.

provinces to defend them against the English. This was the main object as stated in the original proposition of the audiencia. Zúñiga states the purpose of the departure of Anda to have been "to maintain the islands in obedience to the King of Spain,"[83] and this is corroborated by the testimonies of Anda,[84] Viana[85] and of Rojo,[86] himself. In view of these facts, Rojo's failure to co-operate with Anda, his proneness to listen to those who counseled surrender, his complete reversal of tactics in repeatedly summoning Anda to abdicate, and his willingness even to betray Anda into the hands of the British are almost inexplicable.[87]

---

[83] Martínez de Zúñiga, *An historical view*, II, 180.

[84] *Testimonio del Secretario de Cámara* (authorized and sworn to by Anda), *13 de Noviembre, 1762*, A. I., 107–3–2.

[85] *Testimonio del fiscal, Francisco Leandro de Viana, 8 de Marzo, 1763*, A. I., 107–3–2.

[86] Rojo's Narrative, *op. cit.*, *Testimonio de D. Antonio Díaz, (ayudante de Rojo)* . . . *28 de Noviembre de 1762*, A. I., 107–3–4.

[87] Montero y Vidal (*Historia general*, II, 67; see, also, note 114, Blair and Robertson, XLIX, 176) summarizes the life and character of Archbishop Rojo as follows: "This prelate was more imbecile than traitor. . . . His obstinacy in submitting the Islands to the dominion of the English; his struggles against Anda . . . his absolute ignorance of his powers . . . his pardonable ignorance of whatever concerned the military defense of the archipelago, his calm submission to whatever the English advised, even in matters clearly opposed to the integrity and interests of Spain . . . give an exact idea of the capacity and character of the unfortunate one who had the misfortune in such an anxious time to exercise a command for which he was lacking in intelligence, valor and in all other attributes necessary to its successful accomplishment."
Le Gentil (*Voyage*, II, 252) characterizes him as follows: "Archbishop Rojo was a capable man for the management of finances; he was clever in business and very zealous for the service of the king; but he did not understand anything of military affairs; . . . he was between two fires, and being of an irresolute disposition, he did not know which way to turn, . . . besieged on one side by *oidores*, on the other side by monks, he would not (otherwise) have waited till the English were on the assault."
Charges of indecent living and riotous conduct were made by Anda in his various letters to the Archbishop. While the English were at the gates of the city, the prelate was passing his hours with indecent women. Anda stated that Rojo alternated between the dance-hall and the pulpit, leaving to others the question of defense. Anda stated that Rojo had allowed himself to be influenced by the traitorous Santiago

Anda organized a provisional government in his capacity as lieutenant-governor. He disregarded the repeated summons of the archbishop to return to the city and surrender to the British. In a letter to the archbishop, dated October 21, 1762, Anda justified his position and made clear that he was not acting on the basis of any delegation of power as captain-general, which authority, he acknowledged, still rested with Rojo. He stated that he had been appointed visitor-general of the provinces "with the real mission of protecting them if the English captured Manila;" in case this happened he was to solicit the aid of prelates, religious and *alcaldes mayores* in defending the Islands. He complained that Rojo had already "endeavored to influence the prelates, religious and natives to submit to the British."[88] He urged that Rojo should desist from his opposition to his efforts, pointing out the great desirability of their co-operation.

When Anda became convinced of the infirmity of Rojo and the uselessness of further attempts at co-operation with him he completely changed his attitude towards his own position and towards the question of the defense and government of the Islands. While he had hitherto recognized Rojo as governor and captain-general, he now assumed the position that the archbishop was a prisoner in the city and he therefore refused

---

de Orendaín, refusing to listen to the more loyal counsel of the king's ministers (Blair and Robertson, XLIX, 132–160).

Francisco Leandro de Viana, the *fiscal*, believed that the archbishop neither wished to be a traitor to the king nor to his country, but he asserted that he (Viana) was the only person in the colony who was so charitable in his opinion. He felt that Rojo's stand was a result of his incapacity, timorousness, irresolution and ignorance. Viana, like Anda, commented on the archbishop's lasciviousness and immorality (Viana to Rojo, March 1, 1763, A. I., 107–3–2).

Zúñiga, the ecclesiastical historian, seeing through priestly eyes, affirmed that Rojo was guilty of only one error during his rule. This was his engagement to pay four millions of pesos to the English and to deliver up the Islands to them (Martínez de Zúñiga, *An historical view*, II, 239).

[88] Anda to Rojo, October 20, 1762, Blair and Robertson, XLIX, 153–154.

to recognize the orders of the latter. Anda issued a call to all loyal inhabitants to defend the honor of Spain. He ordered the *alcaldes mayores* to pay no heed to the dispatches and commands issued by the archbishop or the British in the city. He set himself up as governor and captain-general of the Islands, subsequently moving his capital to Bacolor, Pampanga. He obtained possession of the funds of the royal treasury, which had been sent to the province of Laguna when the English had appeared, and he turned a deaf ear to the demands of the archbishop that the money should be returned to the city in order that it might be applied on the payment of the four million-peso war indemnity imposed by the victorious British. Anda enlisted a military force aggregating eight thousand men, and he successfully prevented the enemy from doing more than capture Cavite, Pásig, and a few other places of minor importance. Notwithstanding the demands of the British, who had placed a price of four thousand pesos on his head, and the entreaties of the archbishop, Anda resisted until he was assured that peace was definitely arranged between Spain and Great Britain.[89]

The justification which Anda offered for his conduct was as follows: the regular governor and the audiencia (excepting himself) were prisoners in the city of Manila; their positions and places were therefore vacant, and Anda, as the sole *oidor* who was not incapacitated, should accordingly succeed and had succeeded to the management of political affairs and defense. He was both audiencia and governor. In support of his contention that he himself was the legally constituted audiencia, he cited the law promulgated by Philip III on August 14, 1620, declaring that ''in some of the audiencias of the Indies it has

---

[89] When news of the temporary suspension of hostilities reached him in July, 1763, Anda refused to place confidence in the assurances either of the British or of the archbishop. He held out until the arrival of the new governor, Francisco Xavier de la Torre. See Anda to Rojo, July 29, 1763, A. I., 107–3–4.

happened, and it might happen still that the *oidores* being absent and . . . only one remaining, . . . in such cases the audiencia is to be conserved and continued with only one *oidor.*"[90] Anda had been a legally appointed *oidor* on special delegation to the provinces when the city fell into the hands of the British; the governor and the remaining *oidores* had become prisoners and were civilly dead; being the only magistrate of the audiencia yet on duty, he was at once audiencia and governor. He stated that he would surrender his office to the archbishop and audiencia when both had regained their liberty, but he warned the archbishop that if he went to the extreme of surrendering the Islands, he (Anda) "would in no wise obey so unjust and absurd a treaty," and furthermore stated that if the British wished to rule the country, they would have to conquer it first. He expressed the conviction that neither the archbishop nor any other authority except the king had the power to surrender the Islands.[91] In these arguments and sentiments Anda was supported by the *fiscal*, Francisco Leandro de Viana, and by Oidores Galbán and Villacorta, who subsequently escaped from the city and joined him in the provinces, aiding him in his resistance to the invaders.

Although the British had agreed in their terms of capitulation that the audiencia should continue in the exercise of its normal powers in Manila,[92] that tribunal and the archbishop

---

[90] *Recopilación*, 2–15–180.

[91] Anda to Rojo, October 30, 1762 (with *testimonios* of witnesses), A. I., 107–3–3; *Recopilación*, 2–15–57 and 58. On October 20, 1762, Anda wrote as follows: "I said and I repeat that the presidency and government fell to the royal Audiencia; and I add that the latter is conserved and continued in me, that I am the sole and only minister, that by my absence from that capital because of the commissions confided to me at a convenient time, I remained free from the enemies . . . so that in my person is met the prescriptions of law clxxx of the above-cited book and título, since my associates are lacking and have been imprisoned with your Excellency in the fatal loss of that capital." (Blair and Robertson, XLIX, 136).

[92] *Relación de la conquista de Manila por los Ingleses*, . . . 1761–1764, A. I., 107–1–15.

were virtually prisoners; the idea of their recognition therefore appears almost an absurdity. The *oidores* acted as members of the council of war which considered the proposition
made by the British for the surrender of the city, but if we may
trust the testimony of Viana, the archbishop, influenced by his
favorites, Monroy and Orendaín, forced the magistrates to sign
the articles of capitulation. Viana says that in the various
matters which came up for solution after the city had surrendered, the *oidores* were formally consulted, but the archbishop
followed his own counsel, or that of his favorites.[93]

The position of Rojo after the escape of the *fiscal* and the
oidores was an exceedingly unpleasant one. The English commander complained that the prelate and the audiencia had
failed to keep the agreement which had been made between
them; in escaping, the *fiscal* and the *oidores* had violated their
oaths; the indemnity had not been paid; the provinces had not
surrendered and Anda was still continuing his resistance. The
sack of the city was threatened. These conditions made Rojo
redouble his efforts to betray Anda and to get possession of the
treasure which had come on the *patache*, ''Filipino''. The
British offered remission of tribute to all natives then in insurrection who would surrender. Anda was charged with responsibility for the danger with which the city was threatened.
He was said to have prevented the fulfillment of the treaty
between Rojo and the British. To this Anda replied that he
had not been a party to the treaty. The state of perpetual
worry in which Rojo was kept brought about his death on
January 30, 1764. Even before this he had practically lost his
status as governor and the British were treating with Anda for
the surrender of the Islands.[94] This continued until the legiti-

---

93 Memorial of Viana, March 8, 1763, A. I., 107–3–2.
94 Blair and Robertson, XLIX, 172–175.

macy of the position of Anda was recognized by Governor
Torre.[95]

A statement of the above facts aids in clarifying our view
of Anda's position. It certainly can be said that there was
neither an audiencia nor a governor with sovereign powers in
Manila; this lack furnished a reasonable basis for Anda's
claims. However clearly it was established that a vacancy
existed in the governorship, his position would have been sufficiently tenable had it been based solely on the grounds that
the archbishop had delegated him as lieutenant of the captain-
general, with military powers. The archbishop-governor had
granted him that title and those powers for the very purpose
for which he had utilized them, namely, for the defense of the
Islands against the British. In view of the support which was
extended to Anda in his contention that he was governor and
captain-general as long as the archbishop and the regularly
constituted audiencia were prisoners, it is not easy to understand why it was necessary for him to justify himself by advancing the claim, first, that he was the audiencia, and, second,
that he was the governor because he had the authority of the
audiencia. The only accountable reason for this was probably
the necessity of nullifying the commands of the archbishop
which were being issued from the captured city. He may have
felt that such measures were imperative in order to gain and
retain the respect of the natives and provincial officials who
were not under his immediate influence and who were consequently more independent and inclined to be insurrectionary
and riotous. Yet, it is hardly possible that the legal arguments advanced in support of his claims were understood by
this class.

It does not appear, moreover, that Anda was entirely justified in his argument by the laws. No doubt he was right in

---

[95] Report of Governor Francisco Xavier de la Torre on the Negotiations for the Evacuation of the City of Manila, 1764, A. I., 107–1–15.

regarding himself as the audiencia, on the basis of the laws cited by him. However, the law did not at that time authorize the succession of the audiencia to a vacancy in the governorship. The *cédulas* of September 8, 1720, and of August 15, 1731, were still in force in the Philippines, and by virtue of these and by the special *cédula* promulgated in 1761 in favor of Rojo, an ecclesiastic was authorized to act as governor in case of a vacancy. According to law and precedent, the post vacated by the archbishop-governor should have been filled by the bishop of Nueva Segovia, and by the bishop of Cebú, respectively. It is true that neither of these ecclesiastics put forth any effort to maintain their legal rights, probably for the reason that they realized their incapacity to organize and conduct the defense of the Islands as well as Anda had done. The audiencia had not succeeded to the government since 1715; it had been forbidden to do so in 1720 and subsequently. It is therefore difficult to understand how Anda could have seriously advanced the claim that in his capacity as sole *oidor* he should succeed to the government.

Aside from the opposition of the archbishop, there does not seem to have been any great difference of opinion on the question of whether Anda could rightfully claim the prerogatives of the audiencia and governorship at the same time. Rojo paid no attention to the legal arguments advanced by Anda, but contended that both the governor and the audiencia were still in full possession of their powers and in complete enjoyment of their liberties within the city. No comment is to be found on Anda's contention in the royal dispatches which were sent in answer to his reports. It is important to note, however, that after the death of the archbishop, and after the restoration of peace, the *fiscal* was of the opinion that the government should go to Fray Ustáriz, bishop of Nueva Segovia.[96] In this opinion he was seconded by Oidor Galbán.

---

[96] Martínez de Zúñiga, *An historical view*, II, 234.

It would seem that Anda was supported in his resistance to Archbishop Rojo and the British largely on grounds of expediency. This is clearly brought out in a letter which Fiscal Viana wrote to the king on October 30, 1762, stating his opinion that:

> Since the Audiencia and governor are unable to exercise their duties, Anda, as the only active and unembarrassed minister who is able to retain his place under the authority of Your Majesty, has declared himself governor, royal audiencia and captain-general. It is evident that, being a prisoner, the archbishop cannot be governor and captain-general, and it is equally certain that the government and office of captain-general falls back on the audiencia and the oldest *oidor*.[97]

This argument savors of expediency and sound practicability rather than of interest in the legal quibble. Had Viana been convinced of the legality of Anda's claims he would not subsequently have supported Ustáriz. Viana contended that neither the archbishop nor the audiencia enjoyed sovereign powers when they were prisoners. Anda, on the other hand, was in such a position that he could utilize his legal powers; he used them to good advantage and effectively, therefore he was entitled to recognition.

Aside from the question of legality, it is important to note that Anda was the only person who was able to exercise sovereign powers during this time. It is certain, moreover, that he prevented the Islands from falling into the hands of the British and that he maintained the continuity of the sovereignty of Spain in the Islands from 1762 to 1764. During his rule in the provinces he exercised practically all the functions of a normal government. Aside from the management of military affairs he administered the finances and levied tribute. As noted above, he contrived to obtain possession of the royal treasure which had been sent to Laguna; he was consequently better equipped financially than he would have been otherwise, and better than his rivals in the city. His

---

[97] Viana to the King, October 30, 1762, A. I., 107–3–2.

finances were also augmented by the favorable circumstance of his capture of the "Filipino" which was returning from Acapulco with the proceeds of the sale of her former cargo.[98]

Other functions of a semi-military and governmental character were exercised by Anda in his capacity as acting governor. In some of these matters he was assisted by the *fiscal* and audiencia in the latter part of his administration. He regulated the prices of provisions in order to prevent them from attaining prohibitive proportions. He did all that he could to further and encourage interprovincial trade. He issued orders in regulation of wages. In order to discourage drunkenness he forbade the sale of *nipa* wine except in small quantities. He discouraged the importation of wine from Laguna. He took measures to prevent the Chinese from counterfeiting or chipping coins, and he declared what should be legal tender. He forbade the shipment of provisions to the beleaguered city and refused to permit the natives under his jurisdiction to shelter or otherwise assist an Englishman. He prevented secular priests from communicating with the archbishop. In order to encourage service in the army he exempted natives from the *polo*, or labor tax, and he also made certain exceptions to the general rule for the payment of tribute to offset the decree of the British who had offered wholesale exemption from the payment of tribute in order to attract the natives. Anda issued very severe orders to prevent looting and

---

[98] By this seizure the sum of 2,253,111 pesos was realized in the interests of his government and at the same time, of course, it was kept from falling into the hands of the British. Anda subsequently reported to Governor Torre that the capture of the treasure of the "Filipino" made possible the conservation of the Islands, "and that the English did not leave them completely desolate, since without this aid, the subsistence of the state would have been impossible" (Anda to Carlos III, June and July, 1764, Blair and Robertson, XLIX, 299).

The fact that the galleon carried a cargo of over two million pesos affords no small insight into the way in which the merchants and officials obeyed the law which forbade an annual return exceeding 1,000,-000 pesos. See Martínez de Zúñiga, *Estadismo*, I, 266–270.

extortion on the part of his soldiers. Because of the alliance between the Chinese and the British, Anda was obliged to take repressive measures against the former. He forbade games of dice, cock-fighting and card-playing so as to raise the morale of the natives, to prevent thefts and to encourage law and order. He prescribed the death penalty for theft. Anda's rule was little less than a dictatorship, with all the powers of government centered in himself and in his immediate advisors.[99]

It has already been pointed out that when Anda's resistance gave certain assurances of success, the *fiscal*, Viana, and the *oidores*, Galbán and Villacorta, escaped to his capital, attached themselves to his cause and assumed a share in his government. Anda was willing to recognize them as magistrates of the audiencia, and as such they officiated. Villacorta made some trouble for Anda, however, by claiming the right to act as governor on the ground that he was Anda's senior in the audiencia. This was generally recognized, but Anda refused to accede to his demands, and the matter was dropped for a time.[100] Anda found that his colleagues, Viana and Galbán, were of the opinion that Bishop Ustáriz was legally entitled to the office of governor, but there was some doubt in their minds whether he should be invited at that time to act as governor. Anda consulted the Bishop of Camarines and that prelate expressed his willingness to submit to the decision of the audiencia. The Augustinians and Dominicans were of the same opinion, but the Jesuits and Franciscans

told him, that in the then (*sic*) situation of the islands he alone could preserve the public tranquillity, and on that account he ought to retain the supreme authority. This diversity of opinion was not very gratifying to Señor Anda, and although the troops were in his favour, he was by no means desirous of having recourse to violence.[101]

---

[99] Anda to Carlos III, June 22, 1764, Blair and Robertson, XLIX, 262–268.

[100] Martínez de Zúñiga, *An historical view*. II, 234–235.

[101] *Ibid.*, II, 235; see Montero y Vidal, *Historia general*. II. 65–66.

Shortly after the death of Archbishop Rojo, Anda received dispatches informing him that peace had been restored between Spain and England;[102] at the same time the British received orders to evacuate the city. Now that Anda's presence in the field as military commander was no longer absolutely required, a three-cornered fight arose among the supporters of Villacorta, Ustáriz and Anda. Each of these contenders was able to advance a reasonable claim. Villacorta was certainly the senior magistrate, and thus he had a better right legally to the office than Anda. Ustáriz was bishop of Nueva Segovia and as such, was entitled to the governorship according to the most recent law. "Anda had in his favor the circumstance of having defended the islands, and of having prevented the English from advancing to the northern provinces; and, above all, he commanded the troops, who were attached to him, and this served to check the pretensions of the others."[103]

The arrival of the interim governor, Francisco Xavier de la Torre, put an end to these disputes. He had been dispatched to the Islands by the Viceroy of New Spain with the title of *teniente del rey* (king's lieutenant), and in accordance with his instructions he assumed the temporary government on March 17, 1764, which he retained until the arrival of Governor Raón in July, 1765. Anda's *residencia* was taken by his successor, and it was found that the finances of the colony had been faithfully and honestly administered during his administration.

---

[102] Montero y Vidal, *op. cit.*, II, 68–70. The treaty of peace between England and Spain was signed on February 10, 1763. Notice had been served on Anda several times that suspensions of military operations had been authorized, but the *oidor-gobernador* was suspicious, and would not respond to the overtures of the British. The Spanish troops under Anda's command entered Manila on June 10, 1764, and the British forces evacuated the same day. Montero y Vidal (*op. cit.*, II, 71) states that the new governor, Torre, feigned illness on the day of the transfer of sovereignty that Anda might be enabled to receive the keys of the city and thus not be deprived of the honors which he had so faithfully earned.

[103] Martínez de Zúñiga, *An historical view*, II, 241.

He was able to account for all of the money taken from the "Filipino", turning over two million pesos of these funds to the new governor, accounting for the balance. Anda was recalled to Spain, where he was presented at court, receiving the personal thanks of the sovereign.[104]

Torre's accession to the governorship marks the discontinuance in the Philippines of the practice of allowing the archbishop to take charge of the government during vacancies. On no subsequent occasion in the history of the Islands did an ecclesiastic take over the rule of the Islands.[105] It would seem that this plan of succession was abandoned quite generally throughout Spain's dominions, though there is no instance in which the rule of a prelate ever resulted quite so disastrously as in the Philippines from 1762 to 1764. Torre's accession marks the return to the practice introduced in 1608 and followed from time to time throughout the history of the Islands.

The audiencia, as a tribunal, concerned itself no further with the temporary government of the Islands. On September 30, 1762, a new *cédula* authorized the appointment of a *teniente del rey* by the viceroy of New Spain, and the succession of this official was ordered in case of a vacancy. This law was repromulgated on two subsequent occasions, the first time on November 23, 1774, and again on July 2, 1779.[106] The plan of succession which it authorized was followed quite generally in the subsequent history of the Islands, until the separation of New Spain in 1821 rendered impossible the appointment of a *teniente* by the viceroy. Anda's government was the last occasion on which the audiencia, in reality or in theory, ever attempted to rule by its own right, except by association with

---

[104] Anda was made Councillor of Castile on November 6, 1767. A life's pension was bestowed on him on November 19, 1769. He remained in Spain until 1770 when he returned to the Philippines as governor (A. I., 106–4–4).

[105] In Mexico two prelates governed *ad interim* after this time— Peralta in 1787 and Beaumont in 1809. Bolton, *Guide*, 469–470.

[106] *Cédulas* of November 23, 1774, and July 2, 1779, A. I., 102–2–9.

the *teniente del rey,* with whom it acted in the usual advisory capacity, as authorized in the above-mentioned laws.

By the Royal Instruction of Regents of 1776, the regent was authorized to act as president of the audiencia during the absence of the governor, and in case there were no regent, the senior magistrate of the audiencia was to take his place.[107] This law was confirmed by the *cédula* of August 2, 1789, which ordered that viceroys and presidents, on going outside of their capitals, "should assign to the regents the faculties for the dispatch of the most important and immediate affairs."[108] A subsequent law, dated July 30, 1779, stated that "these important and immediate affairs" did not include "the duties and functions of the captain-general." Again, the royal order of October 23, 1806,[109] commanded that the audiencia should in no case take control of the government when there was a vacancy, but that the name of the temporary governor should be contained in an envelope which was to be opened on the death of the governor, or on his absence from the district. In case provision had not been made in this way, it was ordered that the government should be taken over by the ranking military officer of the colony, if he were higher than the grade of colonel; if not, the regent or *decano* should be temporary president, governor and captain-general, without ceding the exercise of any of the functions of this office to the audiencia.[110] This law was suspended by the royal order of July 12, 1812, and by the decree of November 2, 1834, which ordered that the *segundo cabo,* or lieutenant-commander of the king's forces should suc-

---

[107] Articles 61 and 63, Royal Instruction of Regents, Rodríguez San Pedro, *Legislación ultramarina,* VII, 22–28. This Instruction trans- belonged to the senior magistrates of the audiencias. These are deferred to the regent all the powers and prerogatives which formerly fined in *Recopilación,* 2–15–57 and 58.

[108] *Recopilación,* 2–15, note 16.

[109] *Ibid.;* also A. I., 102–2–9.

[110] Royal order of October 25, 1806, *Recopilación* (1841), II, *Apéndice.*

ceed the governor and captain-general.[111] It is important to note that these laws were applicable throughout the Spanish colonial empire. Subsequent vacancies in the Philippines were filled by military men, and the audiencia refrained from interference with the government.

Considering the question in its broadest phases, it cannot be said that the audiencia administered the *ad interim* rule with a great degree of success. This method of filling vacancies in the governorship failed for a number of reasons. Owing to the divided composition of the tribunal, the rivalry and personal jealously of the magistrates and the perpetual quarrels and struggles which arose as a consequence, the periods of its rule became wild scrambles for power in which the strongest survived and reaped all the benefits of office. By their example, the *oidores* stimulated others to wrong-doing, and in their efforts to secure advantages for themselves they oppressed the residents, Spanish and native, with the burden of their misrule. They did not scruple to indulge in dishonest practices whenever occasion offered; indeed, they went out of their way to seek such opportunities.

Perhaps the gravest defect of the rule of the audiencia lay in its failure as an executive, owing to the divided character of its composition. There was much jealousy, but neither unity nor centralized responsibility. In their governmental capacity the *oidores* frequently enacted measures and made recommendations of a statesmanlike character, although they did not always succeed in enforcing them. The magistrates were neither experienced legislators nor trained soldiers, and the latter defect seems to have been a cause of considerable dissatisfaction, especially among the military classes. These were naturally jealous of an assumption of military power by lawyers, whose commands they refused to obey. Nevertheless it must be con-

---

[111] Rogdríguez San Pedro, *Legislación ultramarina*, I, 90–91.

ceded that such individual *oidores* as Morga, Alcaraz, Almansa and Anda acquitted themselves of their military duties with great credit when called upon.

The reform which gave the government to the churchmen was designed to obviate the defects expressed above. It was believed that a prelate would not be open to so many ventures of a questionable and mainly commercial character. Moreover, the archbishops in Mexico and elsewhere had fulfilled the duties of the executive on former occasions with a fair degree of success. The church was the most powerful, highly centralized and unified institution in the Philippines at the time when both the audiencia and the governorship were weakest. The ecclesiastical authority had repeatedly triumphed over the civil government, and the former gave promise of being able to control matters more effectively in the future than the audiencia had done in the past. The rule of the churchmen did not remedy matters, however, except that it produced harmony through the exercise of force. During the rule of the archbishops, with the exception of that of Rojo, the audiencia was so completely dominated by the ecclesiastical power that the tribunal could scarcely be considered a factor in the government.

There were various defects in the rule of the ecclesiastics. Of these, perhaps the most prominent was their failure to meet the military requirements of the position. Because of the natural incongruity existing between ecclesiastical and military duties, they were obliged to delegate the command of the troops to military leaders, who thus exercised an influence never realized by them during the rule of the audiencia. Archbishop Rojo was unwilling to trust the problem of defense to any other person, though unable to cope with the situation himself. Hence Anda forced his way to the front because he was fitted to command and Rojo was not. As administrators and executives the prelates were as efficient as any others, but they were never able to reconcile successfully the opposition of the civil, political, and commercial elements, who were displeased with the rule of an ecclesiastic. Surprising as it may seem, the government of a prelate was usually most unsatisfactory to the churchmen and religious authorities. If the prelate-governor were a friar, his rule was resented by the members of all the rival orders. If he were a secular priest, he was opposed by the friars of all the orders.

The failure of Rojo was enough to condemn the practice of permitting ecclesiastics to assume the government, but aside from that, there was a more significant and fundamental reason. The increasing political authority of the church at tnat time, both in the colonies and in the mother country, its widespread and almost irresistible dominance over temporal affairs, demanded a radical change of policy whereby this dangerous ecclesiastical power could be checked. The rule of Anda, though technically based on that law which gave the succession to the tribunal, was not a typical instance of the government of the audiencia, nor did that period present all the features of such a rule. The influence of the audiencia as a body was practically *nil*. Anda governed because he was a strong man, not because he was sole *oidor* or because he was lieutenant-governor. His government was virtually a dictatorship, based on military power, but, nevertheless, just and benevolent. His extra-judicial actions met with the king's approval, because they were efficient.

History will show that the Audiencia of Manila assumed temporary charge of the government because the distance and isolation of the colony rendered such a course necessary and because it was thought that the audiencia was best fitted to assume control. The government by the audiencia in the Philippines was not an isolated incident, but was typical of the entire Spanish colonial empire. Owing to the conditions which we have noted, and judged by the standards which constitute good government, the rule of the audiencia was neither successful nor satisfactory. Its most far-reaching defect, as far as the relations of the audiencia and the governor were concerned, lay in the wholesale exercise of administrative and military functions by the magistrates of the audiencia. This impaired the quality of their services as impartial magistrates and contributed in most cases to an insatiable thirst for power. The magistrates were loath to surrender the exercise of these governmental activities on the accession of the succeeding governor, the audiencia displaying a marked tendency to continue in the exercise of administrative control. This, then, was a decided cause of strife and dissension between the audiencia and the governor.

CHAPTER X

THE AUDIENCIA AND THE CHURCH: THE ROYAL PATRONAGE

The audiencia was frequently brought into contact with the powerful ecclesiastical organization in the Philippines. We have already referred in this book to some of the notable occasions of this relationship. Before the establishment of the audiencia the church exercised an extensive authority in governmental affairs. The ecclesiastics aided the civil government by administering justice in the provinces when there were no civil courts. The prelates of the Islands, the provincials of the religious orders and even the friars advised the governors and provincial officials on Indian affairs and the administration of the *encomiendas*. When the advice of the church was solicited by the home government as to the advisability of removing the audiencia, the suggestions of Fray Alonso Sánchez and Bishop Salazar went far toward bringing about a final solution of the problem of government in the Philippines.[1] These were some of the ways in which the influence of the church was impressed upon the audiencia.

The creation of an audiencia, with judicial and advisory functions, put an end to the exercise of these extraordinary powers by the church and tended to confine its activities to the ecclesiastical field. Nevertheless, the prelates continued to advise the governors in administrative matters throughout the entire history of the Islands. Their influence was especially strong in matters relating to the natives, their government and protection, and the archbishops even went so far at times as to

---

[1] Concepción, *Historia general*, III, 336, *et seq.* This is discussed in Chapter II of this volume. Original materials exist in A. I., 68–1–32.

give advice on questions of foreign policy. Most of the time this counsel was solicited and was well received. From 1650 onwards, as we noted in the last chapter, the church waxed exceedingly strong in the Philippines and the prelates not only advised, but dominated governors and audiencias. In 1668, Governor Diego Salcedo was unseated, imprisoned and exiled by the commissary of the Inquisition, while a pliant magistrate of the audiencia took over the government and administered affairs in a manner entirely satisfactory to his ecclesiastical supporters. The period from 1684 to 1690 showed the weakness of the audiencia when opposed by a powerful prelate allied to a hostile governor. And in 1719 the church reached the climax of its power by bringing about the murder of a governor, and then succeeding him, overcoming every opposing element in the colony, including the audiencia. From that time onward the prelates governed during vacancies in the governorship—something which the audiencia had failed to do. Finally, in 1762, Simón de Anda y Salazar assumed the reigns of government and the obligations of defense, an act which was sanctioned technically because he was an *oidor* but really because he was an able man, capable of accomplishing what the church had failed to do.

In this chapter it is not our purpose to review the historical facts of the relations of the audiencia and the church or the growth of clerical influence over the audiencia. These matters have been referred to in earlier chapters. It is rather the design to study here the influence which the audiencia, in its turn, exercised in ecclesiastical affairs, noting whence it derived its authority and what was the nature of its powers.

The audiencia was established as the ultimate local authority, co-ordinate with the governor (or the viceroy in New Spain or Perú). for enforcing the laws of the royal patronage.[2]

---

[2] The royal patronage in the Indies was based on the bulls of Alexander VI, dated May 4, 1493, and November 16, 1501, and on that of

Not only was it authorized to act as a tribunal in these matters, but also to officiate as an active executive agent. It is clear that although the governor was the royal vicepatron, he was not expected to act alone and unsupported in dealing with the powerful and often hostile ecclesiastical authority. In former

---

Julius II, dated July 28, 1508. By the first two bulls the temporal and spiritual jurisdiction of the Indies was conceded to the monarchs of Spain and by the last one the universal *patronato* was given. Aside from the responsibilities of government, this concession involved the duty of christianizing the natives and the right of collecting tithes from them. By virtue of these papal bulls the Spanish rulers were granted the right of nominating prelates for the Indies, the assignment of benefices and provinces to the different orders, the confirmation of minor ecclesiastical appointments, and, in fact, general supervision and control over the regular and secular clergy in the colonies (*Recopilación*, 1–6–1 to 7). By these acts the pope was relieved of all direct responsibility for the spiritual government of Spain's over-sea dominions, his authority being limited to the approval of prelates nominated by the Spanish king and to other ecclesiastical duties of a nominal character.

The *patronato real* in Spain furnished a precedent for that of her colonial empire. Although the royal patronage in Spain and in the colonies were closely associated, the beginning of this relationship may be found in the early years of Spanish history, when concessions were granted by the king to nobles, cities, and similarly, to churchmen, in exchange for fealty of some sort. For example, the vast tracts of land in Spain were received by the church as a gift from the state, wherefore the state reserved the right to declare who should hold these lands and enjoy these privileges and also the power to dictate the conditions under which they were to be held. The right of appointment by the crown to vacant benefices and to all the higher church offices were applications of this principle. (See Cunningham, "The institutional background of Latin American history," in the *Hispanic American historical review*, Vol. I, pp. 24–39.)

The concession of 1501 by Alexander VI was only one of a number of privileges of the sort accorded by the popes to the Spanish crown. The emperor, Charles V, obtained from Pope Hadrian VI the perpetual right to nominate prelates and abbots to vacant benefices. In 1543 the Spanish government further demanded and received the concession that all posts within the church in Spain and her colonies should be held by Spaniards. In 1538 the right of the church to issue bulls and briefs affecting the colonies was limited. In 1574 Philip II declared that the right of patronage belonged privately to the king. As a result of this, says Professor Altamira, "the Spanish clergy considered itself more closely bound to the king than to the pope, . . . more dependent on the court than on the *curia*, . . . more eager for the privileges of the crown than for the rights of the church, . . . the bishops were obliged to obey the monarch more than the archbishop." (Altamira y Crevea, *História*, III, 418–19.)

The laws of the royal patronage centralized the supervision and

chapters of this treatise attention has been given to the considerations which forced him to share the duties and responsibilities of government, finance, commercial supervision, and even military affairs with the audiencia; the support of that body was even more necessary in dealing with the powerful ecclesiastical organization.

The authority which the audiencia exercised jointly with the royal vicepatron was based upon the law ordering

our viceroys, presidents, *oidores* and governors of the Indies to see, guard, and fulfill (the laws), and in the provinces, towns, and churches (in the Indies) to see that all laws and pre-eminences which pertain to our royal patronage are guarded and fulfilled, . . . which they will do by the best means that may appear to them convenient, giving all the orders and instructions necessary to the end that all (the instructions) that we may give shall be carried out in due form; and we *pray and charge*[3] our bishops and archbishops, deans, and ecclesiastical chapters of the metropolitan and cathedral churches and cathedrals and all the curates and occupants of benefices, clerics, sacristans and other ecclesiastical persons, and the provincials, guardians, priors and other religious of the orders, in so far as it is incumbent upon them, to guard and fulfill them (the laws and preëminences of the king) and see them fulfilled and obeyed, conforming with our viceroys,

---

control of the clergy of the Philippines in the person of the governor of the Islands. The latter was vicepatron and representative of the king in ecclesiastical matters. He was the responsible head of church affairs in the Islands so far as these matters concerned the government. He was legally authorized and required to receive and assign prelates, to confirm minor appointments by the prelates to parishes and curacies, to make removals from the same when necessary, to make temporary assignments of provinces to the regulars and to support the prelates in the exercise of episcopal visitation. His consent was necessary to the suppression, division, or union of districts, curacies and parishes, and no priest could leave the Islands without his consent. The king was patron, but the exercise of his authority in the colonies was delegated to the respective viceroys and governors. See entire title of *Recopilación*, 1–6; for general observations on the royal patronage see Gómez Zamora, *Regio patronato;* Parrás, *El gobierno de los regulares de la América*, I, 2–16; Mendieta, *Historia eclesiástica*, 20–21, 186–196; Hernáez, *Colección de bulas*, 12–28.

[3] This is a translation of *ruego y encargo*, which form civil officials were required to employ on all occasions in addressing ecclesiastical officials. The king himself observed this rule and his act was supposed to form a precedent for general use within the Spanish colonial empire.

presidents, audiencias and governors as much as may be appropriate and necessary.[4]

In accordance with this law the audiencia exercised the right of intervention in practically all matters to which the authority of the vicepatron extended. Foremost among these were the supervision and administration of ecclesiastical revenues, the administration of vacant benefices, the extension of missionary influences and the construction of churches and monasteries. The audiencia, moreover, had authority over the reception and installation of prelates, parish priests, and regulars, and their removal for cause. In all these matters the audiencia was responsible directly to the king and made reports thereon; in fact, it may be said that the tribunal, in co-ordination with the vicepatron, served as a connecting link between the church in the Islands and the royal council in Spain.

An analysis of the relations between the audiencia and the church will show that the tribunal exercised two kinds of ecclesiastical powers. These may be regarded respectively as executive and judicial. Although it was in their union that the audiencia exercised its most extensive and far-reaching power of ecclesiastical control, it is advisable for several reasons that these powers should be considered as distinct from one another. They will therefore be discussed separately in this treatise. In this chapter we shall consider only the first of these powers—the one which was most directly concerned with the maintenance of the royal patronage—namely, the authority which the audiencia exercised co-ordinately with the governor in the supervision and control of the church in the colony.

Although there appears to have been no conflict of authority between the governor and the audiencia over their mutual relations under the laws of the royal patronage, it is advisable at the outset to settle one difficulty which may present itself in

---

4 *Recopilación*, 1–6–47.

this connection. Many of these powers which the audiencia exercised were conferred upon the vicepatron exclusively. Indeed, a study of the laws alone would suggest the possibility of a conflict of jurisdiction between the governor and the audiencia in matters relating to the royal patronage. In actual practice, however, the governor shared the powers of ecclesiastical supervision with the audiencia, and their relations were harmonious in all matters appertaining thereto. Indeed, there is record of fewer conflicts between the audiencia and the governor in this field of activity than in any other.

It would seem that the intervention of the audiencia in ecclesiastical matters developed in the same manner and for the same reason as it came to have authority in matters of government, finance and military administration. The manifest impossibility of the successful administration of the many affairs of civil and ecclesiastical government by the governor (or viceroy in New Spain and Perú) made inevitable the division of power, which, though real, was not always formally recognized by the laws. The audiencia was the only body available with which the governor (or viceroy) might share these responsibilities. Its judicial character, and the talent, training, and administrative ability and experience (wider than that of the governor himself) of its members made it the logical institution to which the executive should naturally turn for advice and assistance. Not only did he require counsel, but the moral and physical support of a tribunal of weight and authority was invaluable in dealing with the united forces of a powerful ecclesiastical hierarchy. This is the best possible explanation of that gradual assumption of authority by the audiencia which seems to have been so indefinitely, yet freely conceded, and which apparently grew up neither in conflict with the law nor yet entirely in accord with it, but which, now recognized, and now ignored, was never denied or prohibited.

The *cédula* of October 6, 1578, in explanation of the various forms of address in the expedition of royal *cédulas,* was designed to make clear the respective jurisdictions of the vice-patron and the audiencia in ecclesiastical as well as in other governmental affairs. It ordered that

when our royal *cédulas* refer in particular to the viceroys, they alone shall attend to their fulfillment without other intervention; if they designate the viceroy, or president or audiencia, they shall all attend to their execution in accordance with the opinion of the greater part of them that are in the audiencia, and the viceroy or president shall not have more than one vote like the rest that may be present, provided that this do not contravene the superior government which we regularly commit to our viceroys and presidents.[5]

While more than a joint authority with the vicepatron cannot be claimed for the audiencia, and that authority not necessarily coequal, this *cédula* established beyond question the royal intention of recognizing the audiencia as a support and an aid to the governor. This law applied to all the affairs of government, not pertaining any more extensively to the ecclesiastical than to the administrative sphere, but this *cédula,* together with what actually happened, may be taken as evidence that the audiencia was meant to have jurisdiction in ecclesiastical affairs when royal *cédulas* granting or assuming the exercise of such jurisdiction were addressed to it.

The right of the officials of the civil government to interfere in questions of patronage was seldom seriously questioned by the churchmen, although there were some notable instances in which religious authorities objected to this exercise of power. Bishop Salazar, in his opposition to the plan of Fray Alonso

---

[5] *Ibid.,* 2–1–10. Laws 11 and 12 of the same title did not in any way diminish the authority of the royal audienca. Law 11, dated May 16, 1571, antedating the one above quoted, declared that although *cédulas* on governmental subjects were occasionally addressed to the "president and *oidores,*" the viceroys and presidents might have private jurisdiction over these matters. Law 12, dated April 6, 1638, recognized the fact that ministers of justice were frequently addressed on (governmental) subjects, which, it declared, should not be construed to prejudice the viceroy's pre-eminence in these matters.

Sánchez at the court of Madrid (1593-1595), expressed his disapproval of the interference of the governor and audiencia in questions of patronage. His opposition is further attested by several of his letters and declarations enunciated previous to that time.[6] He admitted that the civil government, by virtue of the bulls of Alexander VI and Julius II, should act as the defender and champion of the church, but he opposed any further participation in ecclesiastical affairs by the civil power. Salazar's arguments are worth noting because they were advanced during the formative period of the Islands' history. It was during his prelacy that the basis of all future relations of church and state was established. The arguments of Bishop Salazar were repeated with little variation by Archbishop Poblete in his controversy with Governor Solcedo in 1665 and later by Archbishop Pardo in 1686.[7]

---

[6] Concepción, as cited in note 1 of this chapter. Salazar's arguments are outlined in Chapter II of this treatise.

[7] Archbishop Pardo's well known opposition to the exercise of governmental control on the basis of the royal patronage and his resistance to the pretensions of ultimate superiority over the church which the temporal government claimed and assumed are referred to in another part of this treatise. In a letter written by the archbishop relative to the ecclesiastical controversy bearing his name, Pardo made the assertion that no person was more zealous to encourage or conform to the royal authority than he, for he realized the necessity of complete temporal jurisdiction over all things secular. He stated that he had always encouraged the ecclesiastics to comply with the just demands of the civil government, "for it is just," he wrote to the king, "to observe the temporal things over which Your Majesty has providence, since the secular power must be obeyed, . . . yet I cannot offend the royal person by allowing him or his servants to transgress the rules or authority of God without interposing my influence against it, even at the risk of being disgraced; . . . while I am allied to the civil authority in things secular, I am the superior in spiritual matters." He continued: "God has placed side by side the ecclesiastical and temporal authorities and the latter were intended to be subject to the former, and therefore, the temporal ministers ought to cede to the spiritual, according to the rules of the Holy Catholic Church. It is manifestly unjust, therefore, that a governor, *maestre de campo*, or other royal official should command or summon to justice a prelate who is charged with the welfare of the souls of the people of his commonwealth" (Pardo to King, September 7, 1686, A. I., 68–1–44).

A violent, though ineffective resistance was maintained by the church when Governor Simón de Anda y Salazar sought to abolish

In considering this question, the calm and impartial judgment of a scholar is eminently preferable to the passionate arguments of a prelate deeply concerned in the outcome of the dispute. Let us turn from the field of original research to a modern Spanish writer on church history and law. Fray Matias Gómez Zamora, writing from the vantage ground of the modern day, characterizes the acts of the government officials of the earlier era as excessive and unjustified by papal bull or ecclesiastical canon. He even goes a step farther when he declares that "many royal decrees and *cédulas* were wrongfully issued, without proper basis." He cites examples to prove his contention and among these he points to the founda-

---

certain practices observed in the chanting of mass. Anda based his action on his authority as vicepatron. In his stand he was supported by the archbishop and by two suffragan bishops. However, Bishop de Luna, of Camarines, who was also papal delegate, violently opposed "sending [a copy of] this scandalous mandate to the royal Audiencia— a body consisting of three magistrates, to whom an appeal may lie against the governor" (Letter of a Franciscan Friar, December 13, 1771, Blair and Robertson, L, 318–319.) That a soldier should be the final arbiter in a question belonging so pre-eminently to the ecclesiastical sphere, seemed to this bishop to be entirely subversive of the interests of religion and he turned to the audiencia for protection and support. The governor sent a squad of soldiers to arrest the prelate, and the latter was forced to leave the Islands.

In 1770, Governor Anda was vehemently opposed by the ecclesiastical authorities of the colony in his efforts, as the churchmen described it, "to interfere in the governmental and judicial rights and pre-eminences of the church." This was during the struggle over the question of episcopal visitation; in this matter the governor supported the archbishop. The former had gone so far as to declare that the friars had neither the right nor the authority to administer the sacraments. The replies of Fray Sebastián de Asunción, a Recollect, and of Antonio de San Próspero, of the Augustinians, attacked the whole foundation of the royal patronage, claiming that the church should be given entire control in ecclesiastical matters. According to their views the attention of the governor should be confined to administrative affairs (*Expediente de los provinciales de Filipinas, 15 de Julio, 1772*, A. I., 107-7-6). As these friars were the provincials of their orders, their opinions are of value in reflecting the ideas of the religious in the Islands on the subject of episcopal visitation. These opinions were contrary to the accepted practices and to the ideas of men of higher standing in Spain's colonial empire.

Archbishop Pardo's well-known opposition to the exercise of governmental control on the basis of the royal patronage gave him pre-eminence in these same matters.

tion of churches and monasteries by civil authorities without the confirmation of the prelate, alleging that such practices were entirely illegal.[8] In like manner, he criticises the *cédulas* of October 19, 1756, and of June 24, 1762, which bestowed upon the governor jurisdiction as vicepatron,[9] with the right of settling whatever questions might arise. "But," he writes, "it is clear that the viceroys, the audiencias and the governors did not have, nor could they have spiritual jurisdiction over the persons or property of the ecclesiastics, because in no case can power which is delegated be greater than he to whom it is delegated."[10] Thus does this distinguished writer attack the foundation of the entire institution whereby Spain controlled the church in her colonies during a period of three hundred years.

Notwithstanding the fact that the governor was the civil head of the church in the colony, it would be possible to fill this chapter completely with quotations of laws which were addressed to the audiencia in recognition of its right of intervention in ecclesiastical matters. The necessity of reserving space for specific cases illustrative of history and practice permits only a scanty summary of the most important of these laws. In practically all these cases the audiencia participated conjointly with the vicepatron. The interposition of the audiencia was authorized in the calling of provincial councils and synods, and the resolutions of these bodies had to be examined by the viceroys, presidents, and *oidores* to see that they were in accordance with the laws of the royal patronage.[11] The audi-

---

8 Gómez Zamora, *Regio patronato*, 330 *et seq.*
9 *Ibid.*, 330–354.
10 *Ibid.*, 378.
11 *Recopilación*, 1–8–2, 3, 6. A dispute concerning the jurisdiction of the audiencia over the findings of synods arose in 1773 and again in 1776, when the Bishop of Nueva Segovia protested against the ruling of the audiencia that all the deliberations of a provincial synod which had been held in that bishopric should be submitted for its approval. The bishop appealed to the Council of the Indies and that body approved the action of the audiencia (King to the Audencia, October 19, 1776, A. I., 105–2–9).

encia was empowered to examine all papal bulls and briefs and to suspend those which had not been properly authorized by the Council of the Indies. Disputes between prelates and arguments of churchmen based on bulls and briefs were to be referred by the audiencia to the Council of the Indies. The audiencia was authorized to enforce all properly authorized bulls and briefs and to exercise care that the ecclesiastical courts were granted their proper jurisdiction in accordance with canon law.[12]

The audiencia was authorized to enforce the law which forbade laymen to trade with priests. Punishment in the latter case was not meted out by that tribunal, but the offending churchmen were handed over to the prelates.[13] The audiencia, viceroy, and governors were commanded to exercise supervision over the prelates and provincials, receiving from the latter annual reports on the state, membership, and progress of the religious orders and the work performed by them, which information in turn was forwarded to the Council of the Indies.[14] All possible assistance was to be furnished by the audiencia and governor to missionaries remaining in the Philippines or going to Japan.[15] The governor and audiencia were ordered to supervise closely the work of ecclesiastical visitors in the provinces, exercising special care that the natives were not imposed on or abused. The *oidores* were prohibited from interference with the internal government of the religious orders.[16] Members of orders could not usually be removed by their provincials without the consent of the vicepatron and the audiencia, the authority of the latter extending to the removal and exile of offending priests.[17] The audiencia was ordered to make

---

[12] *Recopilación*, 1–9–2, 7, 10.
[13] *Recopilación*, 1–13–23.
[14] *Ibid.*, 1–14–1, 20, 42; 3–14–3.
[15] *Ibid.*, 1–14–34, 38.
[16] *Ibid.*, 44, 67.
[17] This law was nullified by the *cédula* of August 1, 1795, which forbade the intervention of the vicepatron and audiencia in these matters. See *Recopilación*, 1–6, note 17, also 1–14–37.

every possible effort to preserve harmony among the religious and to adjust all differences arising between the orders, or within them.[18] The tribunal was authorized to keep prelates from exceeding their authority in passing judgment on erring priests, especially to see that no punishments were imposed such as would interfere with the prerogatives of the civil government.[19]

The following brief summary of laws of the early period, although possibly repeating data already given, shows the extent of the participation of the audiencia in the regulation of ecclesiastical affairs:[20]

All ecclesiastics holding office were first to gain the recognition of the viceroy, president, audiencia or whatever authority might be in charge of the province.

A list of the members of each order was to be furnished by their provincial to the governing authority. Any changes subsequently made in the membership of the orders had to be reported in the same way.

The names of all religious teachers were to be submitted to the audiencia, governor or other authority in control, for inspection and approval.

The audiencia was instructed to inform itself relative to the efficiency of the clergy and of religious teachers working among the Indians, and to see that those lacking in educational qualifications or in general capacity were not permitted to enter the Islands.[21]

Notices of removals or of new appointments made among the clergy were to be sent to the governor, audiencia, and to the bishop.[22]

The jurisdiction of the audiencia under the royal patronage extended to practically all classes of churchmen and church affairs.[23] By the *cédulas* of August 4, 1574, and of October 25, 1667, the audiencia acquired the right of passing on the credentials of prelates who came to the Islands. That tribunal

---

[18] *Ibid.*, 68.
[19] *Ibid.*, 71, 75.
[20] *Cédula* of June 1, 1574, Blair and Robertson, XXI, 27–31.
[21] *Cédula* of November 14, 1603, Blair and Robertson, XXI, 50–52, note.
[22] Royal order of April 6, 1609, A. I., 105–2–1.
[23] *Recopilación*, 1–14; 1–7–54.

was entrusted with the duty of seeing that bishops and archbishops carried with them the duly attested confirmation of the
Council of the Indies, and no prelate was allowed to leave the
Islands unless he had the permission of the governor or audiencia.[24] The tribunal exercised a check on the governor in this
particular and saw to it that in granting this permission he
did not show favoritism or otherwise violate the laws of the
royal patronage.

Two striking illustrations of the audiencia's jurisdiction
over the inspection of the credentials of the prelates and higher
churchmen occur in the history of the Phillipines. In 1674,
Francisco de Palóu, a French bishop who had been engaged in
missionary work in China, was cast upon the shores of the
Philippines. The audiencia immediately dispatched orders for
his detention, and he was not permitted to return to his district on the ground that his presence and jurisdiction in China
constituted an encroachment on the rights of Spain. China had
been conceded to Spain by Alexander VI, and by virtue of the
royal patronage, the right of making ecclesiastical appointments
and the exercise of jurisdiction there were prerogatives belonging to the Spanish crown.[25]

A similar case occurred in 1704, when Archbishop Tourón,

---

24 *Ibid.*, 1–7–1, 36.

25 Montero y Vidal, *Historia general*, I, 357–358. Illustrative of this
same authority on the part of the audiencia and the Council of the
Indies was the *consulta* of the latter tribunal, enacted January 22, 1781.
The Audiencia of Manila had called the attention of the home government to the fact that the nomination of Fray Manuel de Obelar, a
Dominican, to the post of apostolic vicar of the province of Fukien,
China, had been irregular because it had lacked the formality of presentation by the Spanish monarch. Other nominations, namely, those
of 1753 and 1759, were cited as examples wherein this formality had
not been lacking. The Council of the Indies recommended to the King
that the nomination should be accepted and that an *ayuda de costa*
should be voted, but that His Holiness should be notified through the
Spanish ambassador in Rome that in the future the requirements of
the royal patronage should be observed, and that no appointments in
China, Spain, or in the Spanish colonies should be made without the
consent of the Spanish monarch (A. I., 105–3–2).

a French delegate destined for China, arrived in Manila. He was received by the governor and audiencia, as he bore a legally executed commission from the pope for the visitation of all the churches in the Orient, and for the settlement of all ecclesiastical controversies which had arisen there. The royal *acuerdo* considered that the dispatches and credentials which he carried were in accordance with the law. Tourón was accordingly permitted to set up an ecclesiastical court. He suspended Archbishop Camacho from his office and freed from prison some of the worst criminals in the Islands. He ordered the regulars to submit to diocesan visitation; but they refused to obey him since they had already rejected the efforts of the archbishop to enforce the principle. The Council of the Indies ultimately disapproved of the admission of this foreign ecclesiastic without the authorization of the Spanish government[26] and as a consequence ordered the removal of the governor and senior *oidor*, heavily fined the remaining magistrates and reduced Archbishop Camacho to the position of Bishop of Guadalajara.[27]

In its joint capacity as assistant to the vicepatron and as a high court with jurisdiction over ecclesiastical cases, the audiencia settled disputes between rival claimants to positions of authority in the church, particularly to the position of archbishop. The law which had been in force up to 1619 pre-

---

[26] *Recopilación*, 1–6–31 and 1–14–12, treat of the admission of foreign prelates and visitors to ecclesiastical posts within the Spanish colonial empire. The latter law stipulates, in addition, that all bulls must be confirmed by the Council of the Indies before their introduction into the Indies.

[27] Tourón proceeded to China, where he continued his inspection. He revoked many of the privileges of the Spanish friars there and forced their retirement to Manila (*consulta* of the Council of the Indies on the report of the proceedings of Cardinal Tourón in China, February 24, 1710, A. I., 68–2–8). That his proceedings were recognized by the Spanish government is shown by the *consulta* of April 21, 1708, whereby 4000 pesos were voted to defray the expenses of Tourón in the Philippines and China. This money was added to the Philippine subsidy in Mexico (*ibid.*).

scribed that the ecclesiastical chapter should fill the vacancy
with a temporary incumbent, but some effort had already been
made to have the senior bishop succeed to the post. Bishop Arce
of Cebú was opposed to this plan on the ground that each prelate had more than he could do in the proper administration of
his own bishopric.[28] Nevertheless it may be noted that on
January 22, 1630, Arce was made acting archbishop of the
metropolitan see of Manila by virtue of the *acuerdo* of the
audiencia and the vicepatron.[29] Arce's accession to the post was
in accordance with a papal bull which had been promulgated
with the king's approval at some date between 1619 and 1630.
There had been a three-cornered fight between the ecclesiastical chapter, the Bishop of Cebú, and the Bishop of Nueva
Segovia, and this conflict had been settled by the *acuerdo* in
favor of Arce, while the chapter appealed to the Council of
the Indies. When Guerrero, the new appointee, arrived, he
immediately laid claim to the office, which Arce refused to surrender on account of an irregularity in the archbishop's appointment. Arce appealed to the audiencia, but the tribunal
refused to authorize any innovations.[30] In a statement to the
king, dated October 17, 1655, he related that in 1629 the governor and audiencia had solicited that he come to Manila and
take the place vacated through the death of Archbishop
Serrano. This would seem to indicate that the audiencia had
acted solely on the basis of its authority derived from the royal
patronage, but in settling the dispute among the various ecclesiastical authorities it also acted judicially. Guerrero's credentials finally came, apparently executed in the proper form and
they were referred to the audiencia by the governor. The

28 Arce to Philip III, July 30, 1619, Blair and Robertson, XVIII,
238–239.

29 Díaz, *Conquistas*, II, 267, *et seq.;* Martínez de Zúñiga, *An historical view*, I, 259.

30 Tavora to Philip IV, July 8, 1632, Blair and Robertson, XXIV,
224–228.

tribunal, when it had satisfied itself that the commission was valid, placed thereon the stamp of its approval and accepted Guerrero as archbishop. Then the latter, in the words of Governor Corcuera, presented himself ''in the royal court of justice (the audiencia) before which he appeared to be presented [to his see], he swore upon the gospels not to interfere with your Majesty's jurisdiction, to respect your royal patronage, and to be always your royal vassal.''[31] In other words, he took his oath of office as archbishop in the audiencia.

The above may be considered as a typical case of the temporary designation of a prelate for the archbishopric of Manila by the audiencia. To cite further instances of a similar nature would be unnecessary. The tribunal continued to inspect the credentials of bishops and archbishops before they were admitted to their posts throughout the history of the Islands. This practice was followed even during the period from 1660 to 1762 when the church counted for more as a political institution than either the audiencia or the governor.[32]

The audiencia exercised intervention in the removal of curates from their parishes.[33] As noted already, these removals were made by the vicepatron upon the recommendation of the prelate concerned. Of course, when the audiencia was governing *ad interim* it made these removals itself. It also intervened when the vicepatron was present on occasions when he re-

---

[31] Corcuera to Philip IV, June 30, 1636, Blair and Robertson, XXVII, 21.

[32] The *cédula* of December 15, 1797, authorized the installation of the Bishop of Nueva Segovia as archbishop in the vacant see of Manila, on the death of the incumbent, in accordance with the requirements of the royal patronage. On September 8, 1800, the Bishop of Cebú was designated as archbishop in the same manner. The installations were made by the vicepatron on the strength of these *cédulas*, with the understanding that the latter were to be followed by the proper papal bulls, executed in due form. *Cédulas* of December 15, 1797, and of September 9, 1800, A. I., 105–2–18.

[33] The vicepatron had a right to do this in conjunction with the prelate until August 1, 1795, when authority was bestowed upon the latter without the interference of the civil government. *Recopilación*, 1–6–38, note 17.

quested the support of the tribunal or failed to act himself. The judicial authority of the audiencia, exercised through its entertainment of appeals from curates who had been removed, will be considered in the next chapter.

A great many reasons for removals were purely ecclesiastical, such as questions of the private lives and conduct of priests and friars and their insubordination and non-compliance with ecclesiastical or monastic rules. With these matters the audiencia did not concern itself unless deportation was involved, or the offenses of the priests constituted crimes against the civil government. There is record of many removals from curacies because of infractions of the marriage laws by priests, such, for instance, as uniting heathen Chinese with Christian women, which was a violation of the pragmatic law of March 23, 1776. Such cases, and indeed all which had to do with removals from curacies after 1795, were settled by ecclesiastical tribunals with appeal to the papal delegate, without the intervention of the audiencia.[34]

The operation of the removal of regulars for cause was slightly different. Unless the regular was the holder of a parish and subject to episcopal visitation, the prelate had no jurisdiction over him, and neither the governor nor the audiencia could interfere in the matter, unless such intervention was requested by the provincial.[35] When the deportation of

---

[34] *Cédula* of August 1, 1795, and of September 16, 1803, A. I., 105–2–10; *Recopilación*, 1–6, note 17.

[35] *Recopilación*, 1–14–71 to 75; the entire title (14) of this book deals with the general subject of the religious orders. The method of procedure in such cases may be illustrated by the efforts of the government to correct the abuses of Fray Alonso Zamudio, an Augustinian, who was in charge of a parish, and who therefore was subject to episcopal visitation. He was charged with immoral and vicious conduct. The provincial of his order made an investigation and reported that the evidence brought against him would warrant his prosecution. He recommended the removal of the friar, which, he stated, he could not himself bring about because Zamudio was acting as a parish priest. The *provisor* of the archbishopric recommended the banishment of Zamudio, which act was carried out by the governor in

regulars not holding curacies was decreed, the consent of the vicepatron or audiencia, acting for him, was necessary. This was usually given on the recommendation of the provincial, and the exile accordingly became an act of the civil government. The formal consent of the Council of the Indies was necessary for all deportations of this character, but the complete exercise of this prerogative gradually devolved upon the vicepatron, who notified the Council of the act.[36]

The crimes of priests or ecclesiastics against the law and order of the realm were punishable in the same manner and by the same agency as the simpler violations of ordinary subjects. Attention has already been given in another part of this treatise to a case in which the audiencia, in 1617, tried and punished six Augustinian friars who had been convicted of murder.[37] Their guilt was first ascertained by a preliminary investigation within the order, after which they were handed over to the audiencia.

The statement has been made above that the audiencia was not allowed to interfere in the internal régime of the convents or monasteries.[38] However, when the provincials of the orders were unable to keep the friars in subordination they frequently called upon the civil government for support and assistance.

---

acuerdo with the audiencia. A *ruego y encargo* was dispatched by the tribunal, soliciting the surrender of the friar. He was accordingly handed over to the civil authorities and was incarcerated in Fort Santiago until the sentence could be executed (*Información del juez-provisor, y testimonio de los abusos del fraile Alonso Zamudio, May 27, 1650,* A. I., 67-6-9).

[36] *Recopilación,* 1-14-71, 72. An illustration of the operation of this sort of banishment may be noted in the case of three Augustinian friars whose deportation was requested by their provincial. The request was ignored by Governor Anda, whereupon the provincial wrote directly to the court; consequently on April 13, 1777, the king ordered the audiencia to see that these three friars were returned to Spain; Anda was advised to give more attention in the future to matters pertaining to the royal patronage (King to the Audiencia, April 13, 1777, A. I., 105-2-9).

[37] This has been discussed in Chapter III of this treatise.

[38] *Recopilación,* 1-14-67.

This was done in 1715 when the Castilian Recollects rebelled against their provincial, incorporated themselves into a separate chapter, and entrenched themselves in the convent at Bagumbayan, outside the Manila wall. Oidor Torralba, then acting as governor and vicepatron, came to the support of the provincial upon appeal. He cannonaded the recalcitrants, arresting and imprisoning them on their surrender, and finally banished their leaders.[39] On this same occasion, it may be noted, the provincial solicited the aid of the archbishop, whose interference the rebellious friars had resisted as an attempt at episcopal visitation.

The disciplinary jurisdiction over priests and friars referred to above suggests a similar authority which the audiencia exercised over the prelates. Within the period of one year after the installation of Archbishop Guerrero at Manila in 1636, the governor, with the support of the audiencia, had banished this same prelate and his ecclesiastical provisor,[40] condemning the former to pay a fine of 2000 ducats. The governor contrived also to influence the judge-conservator[41] to pronounce a ban of excommunication upon them both, in return for a like censure that had already been passed on the governor by the prelate.[42] The banishment of Archbishop Poblete by Governor Salcedo and the audiencia prior to the arrest of that governor by the commissary of the Inquisition, the exile of Archbishop ·Pardo in 1684, and the imprisonment of Archbishop de la Cuesta by Governor Bustamante and the audiencia in 1719, are incidents

---

[39] Concepción, *Historia general*, IX, 190; Montero y Vidal, *Historia general*, I, 400–401.

[40] "*Provisores* and *vicarios generales* exercise the ordinary ecclesiastical jurisdiction throughout the entire territory of the diocese and reside in the head city of the bishopric or archbishopric" (Escriche, *Diccionario*, II, 453). The magistrates and other judicial functionaries of the ecclesiastical jurisdiction will be described at greater length in the succeeding chapter.

[41] *Juez-conservador*, an ecclesiastical or secular (not civil) judge named by the pope with jurisdiction or power to defend a particular church, monastery or convent. (Escriche, *Diccionario*, II, 260).

[42] Nuns of St. Clare to King, Blair and Robertson, XXVI, 24.

in the history of the Islands which serve well as illustrations of the disciplinary and coercive jurisdiction of the vicepatron and audiencia over the churchmen. These events need only be referred to here, as they have already been discussed in relation to other phases of the history of the audiencia.

As visitors of the provinces, the *oidores* were required to inspect the ecclesiastical work of the parish priests and to note their care and treatment of the Indians.[43] In the exercise of these duties they were protected by a law which forbade prelates to proceed against them with censures while they were carrying on such investigations. Le Gentil, the noted French traveller, who visited the Islands during the middle of the eighteenth century, testified that the *oidores* did not fulfill their duty with great faithfulness. Le Gentil stated that on account of their dependence on the hospitality of the priests when travelling from place to place in the provinces, the visitors' inspections were merely perfunctory and of little value.[44]

The above testimony is not corroborated, however, by the report of Oidor Francisco Guerela, who was sent to Camarines in 1702 to take account of tribute and to inquire into the state of the *encomiendas*. He reported that in the curacies which were administered by the Franciscans there was an entire absence of religious instruction, the natives were mistreated, and they were permitted to continue in idolatry, drunkenness, and superstition. Neither the priests nor the *alcaldes mayores* exerted any uplifting or civilizing influence. The *alcaldes mayores*, it was alleged, connived with the priests to defraud the natives by the imposition of excessive tribute and by the exaction of all sorts of fraudulent ecclesiastical tithes. The *oidor* in this case sought to remedy this state of affairs by dispatching reformatory edicts against the friars, and by posting notices and copies of royal decrees and *cédulas* designed to

---

[43] *Recopilación*, 2–31–1, 8; 6–10–8, 9.
[44] Le Gentil, in Blair and Robertson. XXVIII, 218.

inform the natives of their rights under the law and to warn them against the imposture of the friars. Whereupon the Franciscans appealed to the Bishop of Camarines and persuaded him to excommunicate the *oidor* on the grounds that he had usurped the ecclesiastical jurisdiction. This appeal to the papal delegate was in direct violation of the *cédula* mentioned above, protecting such visitations against ecclesiastical censure. The *oidor* appealed to the audiencia and that body solicited the prelate by *ruego y encargo* to remove his censures. The audiencia would go no further, however, as two of the magistrates were personally hostile to Guerela, hence the *oidor* was obliged to remain in the provinces at the mercy of the friars. After six months of isolation, Guerela, who was broken in health, sent an appeal for aid to the king on June 20, 1702. This memorial embodied a full account of his attempts to make necessary reforms in the provinces subject to his visitation.[45] It was presented to the Council of the Indies on October 14, 1706.[46] Three observations might be made from this incident. First, there was little vigor, promptitude, or effectiveness in the Spanish judicial system as therein exemplified. It took four years for this petition to be presented to the Council and considerably more time for an answer to be made. Secondly, this affair shows to what extent petty spite and private quarrels interfered with good government and efficient administration. Thirdly, it illustrates the fact that the entire civil government, including the audiencia, was very much under the domination and influence of the ecclesiastics.

An inspection which was similar to that just described was made by Oidor José Torralba, in 1713, in the provinces of Albay and Cebú. Torralba was unable to complete his work, owing to his recall to Manila, where he was obliged to resume his place in the audiencia on account of the insufficient number

---

[45] *Recopilación*, 3–14–28.
[46] Guerela to the Council, June 20, 1702, A. I., 68–4–12.

of magistrates present in the tribunal. It seems that in the provinces subject to his visitation, the former charges of the Franciscans had been turned over to the seculars, most of whom were natives. Torralba reported that under the careless and incompetent administration of the parish priests, the churches had gone to ruin and all Indian instruction had been abandoned. In his report he commented unfavorably on the stupidity and immorality of the native clergy, alleging that in them lay one of the causes of the poverty and degradation of the people. He recommended the restoration of the regulars.[47] Torralba's recommendations were not followed. Either because of his hurried departure from the provinces where he left his work unfinished, or because of the disinclination or lack of authority of the audiencia and vicepatron, no definite steps were taken at this time for the amelioration of the condition of the people or for the reform of the clergy.

That the interests of the friars were vigorously and effectively championed at the court is evidenced by the royal decree of June 14, 1714, which was dispatched not alone to the Philippines, but which was made general in Perú and New Spain.[48] It forbade the governors and audiencias using their authority as vicepatrons to justify their interference with the interior administration of the convents and monasteries of the orders, which it was complained they were doing without authorization. This decree particularly emphasized the principle which has already been set forth in this treatise that the vicepatrons and audiencias should not concern themselves with the discipline and punishment of friars not holding curacies. The promulgation of this decree was brought about

---

[47] Report of Torralba, July 20, 1713, A. I., 68-4-16. Torralba was charged in his *residencia* with having received bribes from the Franciscans for making this report, which was favorable to them and which was designed to bring about the restoration of the curacies to the friars of that order.

[48] Royal decree of February 14, 1713, A. I., 68-4-18.

as a result of the efforts of the commissary of the Franciscan order in Madrid.

Not only were the *oidores* required to inspect the work of the parish priests, but the audiencia, in the exercise of the royal patronage, was authorized to receive, assist, and supervise the ecclesiastical visitors who came from Spain or Mexico, or were designated from the ranks of the local clergy to inspect the orders.[49]   These visitors were also authorized to inspect friars who were in charge of parishes,[50] and when on these tours of inspection they might be accompanied by the prelate in charge of the curacies retained by the friars under inspection.   The audiencia was to co-operate in all possible ways with these visitors, and should any question arise between them and a prelate over jurisdiction, the tribunal was to do everything possible to bring about a harmonious adjustment of the points of difference.   This is illustrated by a case which arose in 1776, when Fray Joseph Pereyra was given a royal commission to make a general investigation of the Augustinian order in the Philippines.   Fiscal Andrade of the audiencia demanded that Pereyra should submit all his documents for inspection on the basis of the royal patronage and other laws.[51] but the audiencia, under the presidency of Governor Anda, refused to support the *fiscal*.   The king, on April 6, 1778, rebuked the audiencia for its failure to support the royal patronage, citing two *cédulas*, those of July 2 and of October 14, 1773, respectively, in which he had already admonished the vicepatron in that particular.[52]   The failure of the audiencia and governor to exercise all their prerogatives in support of the royal patronage on these various occasions can probably be attributed to dissensions within the tribunal and to the corrupting influence of the church.

---

49 *Recopilación*, 1–14–42 to 46; 1–7–21 to 31; 1–6–49; 2–15–146 and 147.
50 Royal decree of December 31, 1622, Blair and Robertson, XX, 253.
51 *Recopilación*, 2–18–18.
52 King to the Audiencia, April 6, 1778, A. I., 105–2–9.

The statement has frequently been made in this treatise that the audiencia served as a connecting link between the court and the colony. It constituted a channel through which a large amount of correspondence was carried on, and one of the duties most frequently required was that of furnishing special and regular reports and *informaciones*[53] on various subjects connected with the church.[54] Notwithstanding the vast number of ecclesiastics present in the colony, who could and did make special and regular reports, and were indeed required to make them, the audiencia was frequently called upon to render reports on precisely the same subjects as those covered by the churchmen. In this way points of view other than the ecclesiastical were obtained. Thus the advice of magistrates, lawyers and men in active touch with the government served to temper ecclesiastical opinion in the same way that the advice of prelates exercised an influence on matters purely governmental. Taking into consideration their position in the colony, the *oidores* were better qualified to obtain and impart information concerning the church than most authorities.

To indicate the vast field of special subjects in which the *oidores* were required to report, various instances may be mentioned. On July 1, 1598, the king desired information concerning the alleged need of a greater amount of space on the galleon for the support of the bishopric of Nueva Segovia. The archbishop and the bishop of that diocese had both recommended that more cargo-space be given to the church. The king

---

[53] *Información*, a legally-attested document establishing proof of some act or crime (Escriche, *Diccionario*, II, 156). In the broader sense an *información* was an opinion or a body of evidence on a special topic drawn up and legally attested by the proper authority. These *informaciones* appear to have been submitted by the audiencia, or by individual *oidores, contadores, oficiales reales* and others, but in all cases they were legally drawn up and sworn to. An *información* was always a special report, drawn up in compliance with a request or command and is thus to be distinguished from a regular yearly or semi-annual report.

[54] *Recopilación*, 2–23–13, 12, 15.

desired to know whether, in the opinion of the *oidores,* the privilege of shipping two hundred tons would be sufficient for the needs of the bishopric in question.[55]   Again, on December 7, 1610, the audiencia was called upon to forward to the Council of the Indies evidence bearing upon a dispute between the natives of Quiapo and the Jesuits over lands claimed by the latter society.[56]   On another occasion the king requested of the audiencia a report concerning the work, deserts, and financial condition of the convent of Santa Clara, which had asked for royal aid.[57]   Frequently the audiencia was called upon to take a census of the number of priests, secular and regular, in the Islands and to report on the size of each order, the number of friars holding secular curacies in each, and the number of missionaries.[58]   It came to be its regular duty to furnish these reports at stated intervals, and when, for some reason, it failed to render them, a royal reprimand was forthcoming. A yearly report was also made on the number of friars entering the Islands, how many had gone to China, the number of souls ministered to by each order, how large was each province, and how many people there were in each curacy.[59]

It is interesting to know that the churchmen were also held responsible for this information and that reports on these same subjects were required of the prelates and provincials.[60]   It is evident that the report of the audiencia was utilized as a check to prevent misrepresentation on the part of the friars, especially since it was always the object of each order to prove that it was over-worked and in urgent need of more members.   As

---

55 King to the Audiencia, July 1, 1598, A. I., 105–2–1.

56 King to the Audiencia, December 7, 1610, Blair and Robertson, XVII, 151–152.

57 King to the Audiencia, August 17, 1628, A. I., 105–2–1.

58 *Recopilación,* 1–14–1.

59 *Ibid.,* 1–14–31 to 34, 38, 40, 91, 92; 2–33–11 to 15.   Hundreds of these reports appear in A. I., 105–2–1 to 10.

60 *Recopilación,* 1–14–2, 3, 4.

friars were sent to the Islands at the royal expense,[61] and as they were supported after their arrival by the royal treasury, the exercise of economy was always desirable. On the other hand, it was to the interest of an order to make its requirements and accomplishments appear as great as possible.

Another function which the audiencia came to exercise by virtue of its authority in behalf of the royal patronage was that of general supervision over the colleges and universities. In the laws of the Indies this duty was imposed upon the viceroys and governors,[62] and nothing was said of the authority of the audiencia in that particular. According to the laws of the Indies, in fact, the audiencia had little jurisdiction or authority over colleges, universities and seminaries, but as the administration of these was entirely in the hands of the church, the audiencia came to exercise much the same authority over education that it did over other church activities.[63] *Oidores* and *fiscales* were forbidden to act as rectors, but they might participate in the law examinations to satisfy themselves whether the standard of instruction in the royal universities and colleges was sufficiently high, and whether the education, training and ability of candidates for the licentiate's degree gave evidence of their fitness.[64] According to the royal decree of November 27, 1623, the University of Santo Tomás was founded in the Philippines with the advice of the governor and *acuerdo* of the audiencia.[65] Here again that tribunal may be seen in the act

---

[61] *Ibid.*, 1–14–90, 91, 20. Missionaries were so badly needed in the colonies in the sixteenth century that they were sent free of expense. The governors and' viceroys were commanded to pay particular attention to them, assisting and providing for them in all possible ways. "Until the members of the different orders were enabled, by their sufficient numbers and increased prosperity, to establish themselves in communities . . . both king and pope extended privileges and protection to them in order to facilitate the labors of their calling." (Bancroft, *History of Mexico*, III, 702.)

[62] *Recopilación*, 3–14–4.

[63] *Ibid.*, 1–22–7.

[64] *Ibid.*, 19.

[65] *Ibid.*, 1–22–53.

of assuming non-judicial functions which primarily belonged to the governor through the unwillingness or inability of that official to act alone.

The audiencia early exercised advisory powers in educational affairs. The Jesuits as early as 1585 had requested permission to found and establish a college or seminary in Manila, and the king, on January 11, 1587, requested of the audiencia a report on the general conduct, progress and accomplishments of the Jesuit order, asking in particular what benefit would accrue from the establishment of a Jesuit college in Manila. The audiencia, in its report of June 25, 1588, characterized their work as very effective, the learning and ability of their personnel remarkable, but in the opinion of the *oidores* there was scarcely any need of a college in Manila at that time, and there were no means of supporting one.[66]

When Santo Tomás became a royal university in 1648, the Jesuits were obliged to sue in the audiencia for the right to continue the bestowal of academic degrees. Their request was denied by the tribunal, but the decision was reversed by the Council of the Indies in 1653.[67] On May 3, 1722, San José was made a royal college and was subjected to the visitation and patronage of the audiencia. In 1769, when the Jesuits were suppressed, an attempt was made to continue San José as a secular institution under the supervision of the audiencia. This brought forth such determined opposition from the Dominicans

---

[66] Audiencia to Felipe II, June 25, 1588, Blair and Robertson, VI, 318. The Jesuits, on July 8, 1598, again requested permission to bestow the degrees of licentiate and doctor, urging that the distance from Europe was so great that the universities there were inaccessible to students of the Philippines. At that time the petition of the Jesuits was not granted, but that order succeeded in getting permission to establish the college of San José in 1601. This institution was enabled to maintain itself without royal aid until 1767. Its chief support was derived from the immense wealth of the society and from the large donations of individuals.

[67] Montero y Vidal, *Historia general*, I, 283–294; Pastel-Colín, *Labor evangélica*, III, 414–418.

and from the friends and supporters of Santo Tomás that on
June 30, 1778, a *cédula* was issued ordering the audiencia to
close San José and hand over all students in attendance there
to the archbishop, so that they might be placed in secular colleges and seminaries.[68] This was done, and the audiencia rendered to the Council of the Indies a report on the administration of the finances pertaining to the transaction. The revenues
derived from all unsold properties belonging to the Jesuits
were included in the temporalities, and the income from these
were transmitted to the royal treasury. Subsequently the
archbishop attempted to assume jurisdiction over these Jesuit
properties and funds, and to this the audiencia objected. In
1784 the matter was finally settled by the decree of the king
in answer to an appeal which had been carried by the prelate
from the audiencia to the Council of the Indies. He sustained
the audiencia and forbade the prelate from interfering with
these temporalities.

The Dominicans were more successful in the maintenance of
an educational institution.[69] On the occasion of the extension
of the charter of the Universty of Santo Tomás on May 17,
1680, the king ordered ''my president and the auditors of my
Audiencia of that city, and request and charge the archbishop
of the city, the bishops of the said islands, the ecclesiastical
and secular cabildos, the superiors of the orders, and any other
of my judges and justices,'' . . . to acknowledge the University of Santo Tomás as a beneficiary of the royal patronage.
Its title was formally extended on June 21, 1681, by act of the
audiencia.[70] The tribunal not only exercised the right of

---

[68] *Cédula* of June 30, 1778, A. I., 105–2–9.
[69] The college of Santo Tomás was founded on August 15, 1619,
eighteen years after the foundation of the rival college of the Jesuits.
Due largely to the guiding influence and paternal care of a number of
Dominican archbishops it grew and prospered. It became a royal university in 1645 and its title was extended at various times subsequently (Montero y Vidal, *Historia general*, I, 169 [note], 283).
[70] Blair and Robertson, XXXVIII, 78–80.

patronage over the Dominican university, but also over the College of San Juan de Letrán, a seminary for boys which was founded in 1640 and maintained by the Dominicans as an adjunct to Santo Tomás.

Reports, recommendations, and *informaciones* exist in abundance to prove that the audiencia exercised considerable influence in the life and history of these institutions. The tribunal celebrated *acuerdos* to improve the instruction in mathematics, physics, law and medicine. It provided for the examination of students, passed on their credentials, made regulations for the bestowal of degrees and decided upon the fitness of prospective teachers.[71] It supervised the records of these institutions, audited their finances and sent reports to the king and Council concerning the work of the universities and colleges. In its jurisdiction and authority over these educational institutions the audiencia served in behalf of the sovereign as his royal tribunal. These were royal universities, endowed with special royal charters and privileges and it was fitting that they should be controlled by the royal audiencia in the king's name. In addition to this, as they were administered by the church, the audiencia and the vicepatron exercised joint control over them, in the name of the royal patronage in the same manner that they supervised other ecclesiastical activities.

---

[71] A number of *testimonios* exist in A. I., 105–2–6 bearing on suits of natives and Chinese *mestizos* who aspired to enter the royal university. In later years they were admitted, but these institutions were primarily intended for the children of Spaniards. Of especial interest was the suit brought in the audiencia by the Chinese *mestizo*, Francisco de Borja, against the University of Santo Tomás for the degree of master of arts, which the educational institution refused to grant on account of the nationality of the plaintiff. The suit was carried to the Council of the Indies, and that tribunal, after requiring the opinion of the royal *fiscal*, declared in its *consulta* of July 17, 1780, that the laws of the Indies (*Recopilación*, 1–22–57) denied to *mestizos*, Chinese, and mulattoes the right of studying in the royal universities, but once having qualified, however, there was nothing in the origin or nature of an infidel that should prevent his receiving his degree (A. I., 105–3–1). Another question which was deliberated with much care was whether illegitimate children should be admitted as students or qualified as licentiates.

As we have already noted, the audiencia exercised jurisdiction over matters of church finance. The most notable examples of its control may be seen in the administration of
tithes,[72] the funds of temporalities, *obras pias,* funds of the
Crusade, and *espolios* of the prelates.

---

[72] Ecclesiastical tithes (*diezmos*), according to Martínez Alcubilla,
were "taxes upon the products of the earth which the producers paid
from the entire product of their labor, without deduction of the expenses to which they were put, or consideration of the capital invested"
(Martínez Alcubilla, *Diccionario,* V, 412). Escriche defines the ecclesiastical tithe as "the part which is paid by the faithful for the maintenance of the ministers of the church," usually consisting of a tenth of
their products, although at times it was less, varying with the use and
custom of the locality (Escriche, *Diccionario,* I, 638). This payment
was required from merchants, farmers and *encomenderos* (*Recopilación,*
1–16–1 to 10). In 1537 Viceroy Mendoza was directed to exact tithes
from the natives (Bancroft, *History of Mexico,* III, 666). This was
again ordered by the *cédulas* of July 12, 1778, and January 20, 1786
(A. I., 105–2–9). Subsequently the agricultural estates of friars were
made liable to the payment of tithes. As early as 1655 the Jesuits in
New Spain were obliged to pay tithes on all crops and productions of
their estates (Bancroft, *History of Mexico,* III, 668).

The purpose to which these funds were theoretically devoted was the
support and maintenance of the church. The right of collecting and
administering them was conceded to the crown by Pope Alexander VI
in the bull of November 16, 1501, in "full, absolute and irrevocable
ownership, with the condition that the crown should assist the church
with a sum sufficient for the decent support of divine worship, its prelates and ministers" (*Recopilación,* 1–16–1 and 23). The *cédula* of
April 29, 1648 reaffirmed and amplified this bull, ordering in addition
that one-third of all money arising from vacant benefices should be set
aside for the support of the church, while the residue should be sent
to Spain (*ibid.,* 1–7–41; see also 1–16–28 and Article 8, *Real Ordenanza
de Intendentes de Buenos Ayres;* Robertson, *History of America,* IV
[Bk. viii], note XXXII).

On February 3, 1541, Charles V prescribed that the tithes should be
divided into four equal parts, two of which were to go to the prelate
and chapter of the diocese, wnile the remaining two parts were to be
further separated into ninths (*novenos*), of which two were to be
reserved for the crown, three for the construction of churches and hospitals, two for salaries of curates, and the remaining two portions
were to be set aside to pay the dignitaries and subalterns of the
diocese (*Recopilación,* 1–16–23).

In case the portion reserved for the salaries of curates proved insufficient, the royal treasury guaranteed a yearly stipend of from one
hundred to a hundred and twenty pesos to each priest. This *cédula*
was amended by the regulation of March 28, 1620, which provided that
the royal ninths should be taken from the gross amount of tithes paid
in (*Recopilación,* 1–16–25). So it developed that the crown came to
assume entire jurisdiction over the administration of the tithes, retain-

The audiencia was authorized to guard the royal interest in the matter of the collection and the administration of tithes, particularly with a view to seeing that over-ambitious churchmen did not obtain more than their share, and that in the collection of the tithes they did not oppress the natives. The special care of the *oidores* was to see that tithes be not paid directly to the prelates.[73] In fact, these funds were to be administered by the civil government, and prelates were not to be allowed to interfere with their collection. No changes were to be made in the authorized manner of collecting these funds on the responsibility of colonial officials. Recommendations for reform should be made to the Council of the Indies either by the prelate or by the audiencia.[74] The audiencia was ordered to see that the proper division and distribution of tithes were made, and that the two-ninths of the gross sum collected was duly set aside for the crown, in accordance with the law.[75]

Further evidence that the audiencia was regarded as the instrument of the royal will in these matters is afforded by the circumstances leading up to the reforms of 1768 and 1786; and it should be noted particularly that the king and Council relied

---

ing a portion of these episcopal rents for non-ecclesiastical purposes. The royal share was placed in the treasury and was administered by the *oficiales reales*, leaving only seven-ninths of the money actually obtained to be expended for the support of the church. These funds were collected in the provinces by the provincial revenue officials, subject to the supervision of the *alcaldes mayores*, who were responsible in turn for this particular matter to an *oidor* and a royal treasury official of the central government (*Ibid.*, 1–16–1, 30).

These *novenos* were not infrequently farmed out in New Spain, and at the auctions thereof frauds were as repeatedly committed as at the sales of other royalties. Instructions were issued ordering the Audiencia of Mexico to investigate the nature of these transactions. In March, 1728, the royal *novenos* were leased for a period of nine years at $19,000 annually. When this lease expired they were let again for a similar period at $20,000 a year (Bancroft, *History of Mexico*. III, 666–668 and note 57); see Priestley, *José de Gálvez*, 249–253, for data on the administration of tithes in New Spain.

73 *Recopilación*, 1–16–11, 3.
74 *Ibid.*, 13.
75 *Ibid.*, 24; also *Real Ordenanza de Intendentes de Nueva España*, Art., 193.

on that tribunal for advice and assistance in the drafting and execution of these measures. A number of tentative laws and proposals for changes in the system of collection and administration of the tithes was sent to the audiencia, from time to time, prior to 1768, and the magistrates were required to submit opinions as to the availability and applicability of the proposed measures. In 1768 a decree was issued fixing the tithe at ten *reales* per Indian. Previous to that year a number of religious orders owning large tracts of agricultural land had refused to pay these taxes, and the audiencia, by virtue of the royal order of September 25, 1768, was ordered to enforce the law, which it did, even proceeding to the seizure of the chattels of the recalcitrant friars.[76] On December 11, 1775, the audiencia passed an ordinance diminishing the tithes to be paid by natives, *mestizos*, Chinese and Japanese by one-half *real* per person.[77] On July 12, 1778, the king asked the audiencia to submit evidence on the question of whether the law worked any hardship on the inhabitants of the colony, and whether *encomenderos* and friars were paying their share.[78] At the same time, and on the same date, the royal approval was given to the *auto* which the audiencia had enacted on December 11, 1775. The recommendations of the audiencia were also largely followed in the decree of January 20, 1786, which was merely a repromulgation of an earlier *auto* of the audiencia, which ordered that tithes should not be collected directly from the Indians unless the latter were owners of lands. Otherwise they were to be collected from the landlords.[79]

---

[76] Royal order of September 25, 1768, A. I., 107–5–23; see also Royal decree of July 9, 1785, A. I., 106–2–15.

[77] *Testimonios* accompanying *auto* of December 11, 1775, A. I., 105–2–9.

[78] King to the Audiencia, July 12, 1778, A. I., 105–2–9.

[79] Decree of January 20, 1786, repromulgated December 16, 1796, A. I., 105–2–10. While the laws of the Indies make no mention of the requirement that the natives should pay tithes, the above *cédulas* expressly order it. This is interesting, in view of the fact that Gómez Zamora, in his *Regio Patronato* (381 *et seq.*) says that in the Philip-

By subsequent laws the audiencia was temporarily deprived of its jurisdiction over tithes. When the Philippine government was reorganized in 1787 by the Ordinance of Intendants, many of the special commissions which had been previously retained by the magistrates were ceded to the superintendent of *real hacienda*. The actual collection of tithes was made the duty of the superintendent by *cédula* of October 6, 1792,[80] but because of its relation to the royal patronage the audiencia, in practice, found it convenient to retain control. Governor Aguilar, who was also superintendent of *real hacienda*, wrote to the king on July 31, 1799,[81] alleging that there was no reason why the audiencia should exercise this authority, when, by virtue of its financial nature, this duty belonged to the superintendent. He stated that the audiencia had been given this jurisdiction when there had been no other authority for the collection of tithes, but that as it was not a controversial matter, there was no reason for the continuance of this condition. In the letter referred to Aguilar stated that he had attempted to put his interpretation of the law into execution, but in so doing had been opposed by the audiencia. The answer to this appeal does not appear in connection with the original, but the royal *cédula* of April 21, 1803, restored to the audiencia jurisdiction over the collection of tithes.[82]

It may be said, however, that with the creation of the superintendency the audiencia was shorn of many of the miscellaneous functions with which it had been formerly endowed.

---

pines the natives were not called upon for tithes. Montero y Vidal (*Historia general*, III, 179) cites the *cédula* of May 23, 1801, which exempted Indians from the payment of tithes.

[80] Montero y Vidal, *Historia general*, III, 179; also King to the Audiencia, October 6, 1792, A. I., 105–2–10.

[81] Aguilar to Soler, July 31, 1799, A. I., 107–5–23.

[82] On August 17, 1853, the superintendent of *real hacienda* of Manila made an effort to revive the payment of tithes, which practice had become extinct. He ordered the religious provincials to present in the *administración general de tributos* lists of all taxable property under their jurisdiction (Montero y Vidal, *Historia general*, III, 178).

The funds of the temporalities, however, did not come under this category. They were greatly augmented in 1767 when the Jesuits were suppressed, and as was usual with such miscellaneous and unclassified duties, as well as on account of the audiencia's relation to the royal patronage, the administration of these funds came under the charge of an *oidor* whose official title was "administrator of the funds of the temporalities."[83]

Nevertheless, the audiencia's share of direct control over these funds was still considerable. On January 23, 1803, a *cédula* was issued ordering that the money of the temporalities and *obras pias* should be put at the disposal of the *acuerdo* of the audiencia.[84] A report was submitted to that tribunal by Superintendent Aguilar on July 20, 1804, in accordance with this *cédula*. The report of Aguilar showed a balance on hand of 151,625 pesos waiting to be sent to Spain by the first transportation. In 1809, the jurisdiction of these funds was completely restored to the audiencia, with the provision that the *oidores* who acted as their administrators should receive a three per cent commission. As the funds were constantly drawn upon, and there were no further confiscations of property of this sort, they can be accounted as of little importance, yielding practically no revenue from that date. Owing to the continual appeals of the government for money with which to defray the expenses of putting down the various insurrections from 1808 to 1814 and subsequently, the funds of the temporalities, like every other peso that came into the treasuries

---

83 While the temporalities were originally the endowments of the sovereign for the support of the clergy, in the Philippines at this time they were chiefly derived from the sale of jewels, lands, live-stock, and other chattel properties of the Jesuit order, which had been suppressed in 1769. Property to the value of 2,000,000 pesos fell into the hands of the government on this occasion. The temporalities did not include convents, school buildings, colleges, churches and church furnishings. The latter were turned over to the archbishop and the secular church.

84 *Cédula* of January 22, 1803, A. I. 107–5–29.

of the colonies, were sent to Spain as rapidly as they were collected.[85]

The audiencia also audited the accounts of the *obras pías*, though its jurisdiction over these funds was often opposed.[86]

---

[85] A very instructive and hitherto unexplored field of investigation lies in the reports of the different officials and bodies in the colonies which were entrusted with the duty of collecting and forwarding money to help Spain in putting down the various revolts of the late eighteenth and early nineteenth centuries. We may note the letter of Governor Aguilar, dated July 20, 1804, in which he reported compliance with the royal order of June 20, 1798, relative to the raising of money for the purposes indicated. He had opened two public subscriptions for "voluntary offerings" to aid in putting down the Catalonian revolt of 1798. In the first subscription, 80,946 pesos were raised and in the second, 15,397 pesos. The Dominicans alone gave 5000 pesos, the magistrates of the audiencia, the members of the *consulado*, the *contadores, oficiales, reales, obras pias*, prelates, temporalties, the *Compañía de Filipinas*, the *monte pio militar*, the veteran soldiers, religious orders and other organizations and individuals each contributing their share. Aguilar reported that subscriptions had been opened in all the provinces by the *corregidores, alcaldes mayores* and *intendentes*. The various provinces and districts contributed on this occasion as follows: Tondo, 11,059 pesos; Laguna, 2768 pesos; Cebú, 300 pesos; Albay, 85 pesos; Cápiz, 318 pesos; Leyte, 21 pesos; Antique, 4 pesos; Samar, 1090 pesos; Zambales, 41 pesos; Calamianes, 1607 pesos; Mindoro, 221 pesos. This money was sent to the Viceroy of New Spain, and was forwarded to Spain by him together with the remittances collected for the same purposes in that viceroyalty. Reports of *alcaldes mayores* show that these assessments (*contribuciones voluntarias* or *directas*, or *donativos voluntarios*) varied from half a *real* from the poorest Indian to five hundred pesos from the wealthier landlords and merchants. In many cases these assessments practically amounted to confiscations (Aguilar to the King, July 20, 1804, A. I., 105–3–23).

On June 18, 1806, the king acknowledged receipt of money which had been confiscated from the common funds of the village communities (King to Aguilar, June 18, 1806, A. I., 105–2–18).

Hume, in his *Modern Spain* (158), says that in 1809 the colonies contributed 3,000,000 pounds sterling for the relief of the home government. Priestley, *José de Gálvez*, 370–71, sheds some light on the matter of these forced contributions in New Spain.

[86] Martínez Alcubilla, *Diccionario*, X, 719. The *obras pías* were charitable associations or corporations, usually under ecclesiastical control, which were founded and supported by persons who contributed or willed their money for beneficent objects. In Manila there were two leading societies of this character, the Santa Misericordia and San Juan de Diós. The former was a branch of a larger organization of the same name, which had originated in Portugal, and was quite generally established throughout Spain, Portugal and their colonies. A branch was founded in Manila in 1596, with the object, as stated in the articles of establishment, of erecting and maintaining a college for orphan children, the support of the poor, and particularly of the orphans and

The chief foundations of the *obras pías* in Manila were the Santa Misericordia and San Juan de Diós. The wealth and power of the Misericordia became so great,[87] and so well did it profit by the various immunities extended to it, that by the early part of the eighteenth century it had become the object of the distrust and envy of all classes of Manila society. It was chiefly disliked because it had been permitted to utilize so much free space on the galleon. Other inconveniences had arisen from its participation in trade, wherein, possessed of so many advantages, it was enabled to derive profits and benefits that were denied to competing merchants in the colony. Complaints were made against it by certain religious orders, merchants, treasury officials, *oidores*, and the governor, himself. It

---

widows of soldiers. This society flourished from the beginning under the favor of certain governors and *oidores* and by their assistance and by that of other friends, and through the endowment by the government of a large amount of free space on the galleon, it became a wealthy and powerful institution. San Juan de Dios, which was organized as a brotherhood, was established in the Philippines in 1617 with avowed charitable purposes. In the *cédula* of February 10, 1617, the king ordered the audiencia at Manila to place the hospitals under the care of this brotherhood (Blair and Robertson, XLVII, 164–165). Though it did not attain the wealth or importance of the Misericordia and it never had the extensive relations with the government of the other society, it did exceedingly valuable work in the Islands, going far toward accomplishing the purposes for which it was founded.

[87] By 1660, the Misericordia had received in contributions the sum of 356,363 pesos. In 1619, the treasury at Manila had become so exhausted by the expenses involved in resisting the Dutch that Governor Fajardo borrowed from the society the sum of 39,599 pesos. Later Governor Corcuera exacted a loan of 104,609 pesos. In all, up to 1670, an aggregate of 441,909 pesos had been borrowed from this wealthy society for the current expenses of the government. In 1762–3 the Misericordia contributed the sum of 195,588 pesos as tribute money to the British and was, according to its own accounts, despoiled of 301,597 pesos, making a total of 506,184 pesos, and leaving a balance of 193,246 pesos (*Procurador de la Misericordia de Manila al Rey, 23 de Julio, 1764*, A. I., 106–5–8).

The capital of the Misericordia of Manila on January 31, 1755, was estimated at 701,477 pesos (*Informe del Contador de Cuentas, 31 de Enero, 1755*, A. I., 106–5–8). In the occupation of Manila by the British and in the loss and despoliation of property suffered thereby, the Misericordia received a blow from which it never entirely recovered. By July 20, 1804, the capital of the society had dwindled to 151,625 pesos (Aguilar to the King, July 20, 1804, A. I., 107–5–29).

was the consensus of opinion among these that the accounts of this society should be inspected by the government, and, in accordance with these recommendations, a *cédula* was expedited, ordering the society to submit its accounts to the audiencia for inspection and approval.[88]

The suspicions of the general public were confirmed, and the popular distrust increased when the inspection of Oidor Calderón revealed that the finances of the society had been carelessly kept, and that the books contained numerous discrepancies. The scrutiny of the *oidor* showed the existence of a deficit of 383,437 pesos; that is, the records called for property in the hands of the society to the value of that sum which could not be found. The Misericordia, in a series of protests, accounted for the discrepancies by alleging that the audiencia had declared many of its debtors bankrupt. Relief from the inspection was requested on the grounds that the local feeling and the prejudice of the *oidores* would cause them to be unfair to the society. It pleaded that the inspection should be made by the chief accountant of the Council of the Indies (*contador de cuentas*) once in five years. In this request it was supported by the recommendation of this official.[89]

On April 19, 1755, the *cédula* of November 9, 1747, was modified on the basis of these protests, and in lieu of the annual inspection of the *oidor* was substituted the requirement that once in three years the Misericordia should submit its own accounts.[90] This brought forth a storm of protest from the residents of Manila, headed by Governor Arandía, who went to some length to describe the abuses which had arisen in the past from the unrestricted liberty which the Misericordia had enjoyed. He accused the society of dishonest political practices,

---

[88] *Cédula* of November 8, 1747, with *testimonios* of previous correspondence, A. I., 106–5–8.

[89] *Informe del Contador de Cuentas del Consejo de Indias, 31 de Enero de 1755*, A. I., 106–5–8.

[90] *Cédula* of April 19, 1755, A. I., 106–5–8.

interference with the government, bribery and corruption. He said that behind its commercial operations there existed a veiled scheme by which the church was seeking to monopolize the trade of the Islands.[91] The opposition of the governor and residents bore fruit to the extent that a compromise was made in the royal *cédula* of February 21, 1759, which restored the practice of having *oidores* inspect the accounts of the Misericordia, though the examination was to be held only once in five years. This, of course, was sufficiently lenient to defeat the entire scheme. *Oidores* were forbidden to interfere with the property of the society at any other time and in any other manner.[92]

The Misericordia maintained a stubborn and vigorous resistance to the principle of visitation by the audiencia, but as far as may be judged by the data at hand, the law was not changed again, and the audiencia continued to exercise supervision. That the audiencia was prone to overstep its authority in the matter of these inspections is shown by an incident which occurred in 1776–1777. In the regular quinquennial inspection of the records of the Misericordia a number of abuses were uncovered. The funds were found to have been carelessly administered, and the books inaccurately kept, owing to the negligence, incapacity, and corruption of the members to whom the funds had been entrusted. Governor Sarrio, as .vicepatron, appointed Oidor Calderón as receiver and administrator of the funds, with the charge that the *oidor* should suspend all payments until the accounts were straightened out. The Misericordia protested and on April 25, 1778, the king ordered the governor and audiencia to desist from further interference with the funds of the society, the royal disapproval being based on the *cédula* of February 21, 1759, which, while authorizing the inspection of the books of the society, forbade any minister

---

91 Arandía to the King, July 24, 1757, A. I., 106–5–8.
92 *Cédula* of February 21, 1759, A. I., 106–5–8.

"to interfere with or interrupt said House in the administration or distribution of its funds."[93]

The *cédula* of February 21, 1759, was reaffirmed on repeated occasions when the Misericordia refused to submit its books to the audiencia. The last law touching upon this particular question was promulgated on August 2, 1787, when it was decreed that the accounts, books, records, and work of the Misericordia and its officials should be subject to the inspection of the audiencia.[94]

Not only was the opposition of the Misericordia a source of dispute between that society and the audiencia, but the matter of financial inspection caused disputes between the audiencia and other officials and departments of the government. The reforms of 1787 made trouble between the superintendent and the audiencia. Since this was a financial matter, the former claimed the right of auditing these accounts, which the audiencia refused to concede for the reason that it had always had supervision over these funds (when the right was exercised by any secular authority). The question was definitely settled by the *cédula* of January 22, 1803, which ordered that "the money of temporalities, pious funds, and charitable societies should be put at the disposal of the *acuerdo,* and that if any matters relative to those branches were then pending before the superintendent, they should be remitted at once to the audiencia."[95] This was accordingly done by Governor (and Superintendent) Aguilar,[96] and after that time the jurisdiction of the audiencia was no longer questioned.

Shortly after the establishment of the *consulado* of Manila in 1769, a bitter dispute arose between that body and the audiencia for jurisdiction over cases involving the commerce of

---

[93] King to the Audiencia, April 25, 1778, A. I., 105–2–9.
[94] *Cédula* of August 2, 1787, A. I., 105–2–10.
[95] Aguilar to the King, July 20, 1804, A. I., 107–5–29.
[96] The capital of the society was at that time estimated at 151,625 pesos.

the Misericordia. On the basis of the *cédula* of July 8, 1774, the *consulado* claimed exclusive jurisdiction over all disputes involving trade which arose between merchants. It advanced the contention that in all suits involving losses of galleons the society should be considered in the case of an individual merchant. The audiencia, basing its claims on the royal patronage, declared the *consulado* to have exceeded its powers, in assuming the jurisdiction described above, and fined several of its members. The *consulado* appealed the case, and in reply the king promulgated a *cédula* on June 7, 1775, declaring that neither to the audiencia nor to the *consulado* belonged the jurisdiction over such cases, but that they should be tried in first instance by the Council of the Indies.[97] The reasons assigned for this decision were that the *consulado* could not try such cases because merchants constituted its membership and because the *fiscal* and two *oidores* also belonged to its tribunal. Neither the audiencia nor the *consulado,* accordingly, could impartially try commercial suits between merchants and the Misericordia; accordingly thereafter all evidence should be submitted to the Council for special action.

The audiencia and the governor had supervision over *espolios* and vacant benefices.[98] When a prelate entered into office it was his duty to file with the *fiscal* an inventory of all properties belonging to him at the time of his advent to the diocese.[99] On the occasion of his death a treasury official was

---

97 King to the Audiencia and *Consulado,* June 7, 1775, A. I., 105–2–9.

89 The term *espolio* was applied to the properties which archbishops and bishops left at the time of their death, such property having accumulated when they were in office. All possessions of deceased prelates reverted to the crown in accordance with the *cédula* of March 25, 1620. The rents from vacant benefices accumulated from the time of the death of a prelate to the appointment of another to succeed him (Escriche, *Diccionario,* I, 735; Bancroft, *History of Mexico,* III, 699). The money derived from *espolios* and vacant benefices was aggregated to the royal treasury for such subsequent distribution as appeared necessary for the relief of cathedrals, parishes, colleges, asylums, and charitable institutions.

99 *Recopilación,* 1–7–38, 39.

designated to estimate and administer the property left, pay the debts of the deceased churchman, execute his will with regard to his property in accordance with the law, and turn over the residue to the royal treasury. This process was known as taking the *espolio.*

The *espolio* of a deceased prelate was taken, according to the early laws, by an official of the royal treasury, who was designated by the president for the purpose, and who officiated under the supervision of the audiencia. The tribunal verified the *autos* and substantiated the proceedings of the agent.[100] Whether any modifications in the manner of collecting, distributing or accounting for the funds or properties derived from these *espolios* were made elsewhere is not clear, but in the Philippines the abuses which arose in the settling of these ecclesiastical estates and benefices made the personal intervention of the *oidores* necessary on a number of occasions. By royal *cédula* of June 23, 1712, it was ordered that in all the audiencias of the Indies the magistrate next in rank to the senior *oidor* should be constituted as the

private judge, who, with the concurrence of the *oficiales reales,* should have jurisdiction over and should proceed against, receive and collect all the products and rents of the vacant archbishoprics and bishoprics until the day on which the new prelates should take possession of their offices, proceeding with full cognizance . . . to the collection . . . of whatever might be due, . . . with the assistance of the *oficiales reales* who in this matter are subject to the royal audiencia.[101]

By this same law the audiencias, viceroys, presidents and tribunals were forbidden to interfere with this judge in the execution of his duties, or to impede the execution or the law in any manner whatsoever. The estates of prelates were thus placed on a basis similar to that occupied by the properties of civilians, which, we have noted, were administered by a special magistrate of the audiencia. This *cédula* also provided that all

---

100 *Ibid.,* 37, 40.
101 *Cédula* of June 24, 1712, A. I., 68–4–17; *Recopilación,* 1–7, note 8.

money left as a residue, after the debts of the prelates were paid, should be sent to the king for distribution.

In view of the above-mentioned law, the practice followed in 1715, on the death of Bishop Gorospe of Nueva Segovia, seems to have been a direct violation of the royal command, and somewhat different from the usual method of settling the estates of prelates. As soon as Gorospe died at Magaldán, Pangasinán, the *alcalde mayor* of the province sent immediate notification to the governor and audiencia. The tribunal, in *acuerdo*, on the motion of the *fiscal*, authorized the *alcalde mayor* and the treasury officials to take the *espolio* of that prelate, which order was duly complied with.[102] The audiencia also dispatched a formal notification to Archbishop de la Cuesta and the metropolitan chapter, designating the former as the ecclesiastical governor of the bishopric.[103]

The significant feature of this *espolio* is that it was taken by an official as inferior in rank as an *alcalde mayor* through the express authorization of the audiencia, instead of being conducted by the second magistrate of the audiencia as the law directed. It is possible that the arrival of the *cédula* of June 24, 1712, had been delayed, or that this may have been a case, so frequent in the Spanish colonies, of compliance without obedience. Certain it is that the conditions of life and travel in the provinces were of such a character that an *oidor* would have found it more comfortable to remain in the capital and delegate the disagreeable duties of the *espolio* in a far-distant province to the resident *alcalde mayor*. Attention has already been called to various complaints made by governors and others against the disinclination of the magistrates to sub-

---

[102] *Auto de Espolio* of Bishop Gorospe, May 28, 1715, A. I. 68–4–18.
[103] In the colonial bishoprics the temporary successor of a deceased prelate was usually designated by the local diocesan chapter. If, as was the case in the Philippines, the latter body were lacking, the archbishop, by virtue of his position, became temporary ecclesiastical governor, with jurisdiction over the revenues of the diocese. The benefice was considered vacant until the appointment of a regular bishop.

mit to the inconveniences of provincial inspections. Again, it is very probable that the time and attention of the magistrate whose duty it should have been to take this *espolio* were occupied with more important judicial duties.[104]

The citation or further multiplication of data relative to *espolios* would be monotonous and unprofitable. Sufficient has been said already to show the extensive participation of the audiencia in the administration and settlement of the estates of prelates and the assignment and care of vacant benefices. It may be noted, however, that the audiencia suffered little if any diminution of its authority over the *espolio* through the Ordinance of Intendants. That code deprived the *oficiales reales* and *oidores* of the duty, formerly incumbent on them, of taking *espolios* and conferred it upon the intendants and corregidor-intendants of provinces. However, it was still required that the papers relative to the proceedings should be submitted

---

[104] A fairly typical example of an *espolio* was that of Bishop Arévalo of Nueva Cáceres, rendered by the audiencia on July 19, 1759. The total sum left by that prelate was 19,000 pesos. The leading items of the *espolio* were: costs, 1919 pesos; bequest to College of Santo Tomás, 2000 pesos; bequest to the cathedral of Nueva Cáceres, 400 pesos; bequest to the brother of the deceased, the Marquis of Monte Castro, 1000 pesos. The remaining portion was paid to creditors in sums varying from 20 to 300 pesos, leaving something over 6000 pesos for the crown (*Auto de Espolio, 20 de Julio, 1759, Audiencia de Manila*, A. I., 106–4–16).

On June 14, 1774, the audiencia reviewed the *autos* of *espolio* of the Bishop of Cebú, the total of which aggregated 11,210 pesos. The papers were duly forwarded to the *Contaduría General*, at Madrid, and were approved by that tribunal on June 20, 1778 (A. I., 105–2–9).

Owing to the anarchical conditions prevailing at the time of the death of Archbishop Rojo, his *espolio* had to be postponed until June 26, 1777, and the royal treasury received 3078 pesos therefrom. The prelate left a valuable library to the College of San Ildefonso in the city of Mexico, and 13,617 pesos in money to be distributed among his personal creditors and heirs (*Consultas del Consejo, 20 de Marzo, 1778*, A. I., 108–7–1 and 2; 105–3–2).

The large sum of 12,000 pesos was netted to the royal treasury by the *espolio* of Bishop Espeleta of Cebú on May 6, 1783 (A. I., 105–2–10). By way of contrast, the fact may be noted that the *espolio* of Archbishop Santos y Rufina yielded 92 pesos. (*Auto de Espolio del Arzobispo Santos y Rufina, 20 de Octubre, 1792*, A. I., 105–2–10.)

afterward to the audiencia for legalization and approval.[105]
Appeals and cases of litigation arising from them were to be
settled in the audiencia. This decree made little difference in
the procedure in the Philippines, as the corregidor-intendants
were never instituted there, and the *oidores* continued in the
settlement of these matters, subject to the designation of the
superintendent, who, it will be remembered, was also governor
and president of the audiencia. The tribunal passed, as always,
on all acts of *espolio* and heard cases affecting them on appeal.
In this manner the properties of the prelates were administered in a conservative and legal manner and the interests of
the crown were safeguarded.

The audiencia exercised joint authority with the vicepatron
over questions relating to the construction of churches and the
conservation of ecclesiastical property. No monastery, convent,
college, hospital, or other religious institution could be founded
without the consent of the king, and this permission was obtained through the viceroy, governor, or audiencia upon the
recommendation of the prelate of the diocese.[106] The laws of
the Indies conceded that matters which did not admit of delay
could be settled by the president and audiencia.[107] In fact, as
early as August 15, 1620, Governor Fajardo acknowledged
receipt of a letter from the king in which occurred the statement that "no church or convent, not even a chapel, ought to
be, or can be, founded unless concurrent with your permission,
and that of the Audiencia."[108] It was provided that all petitions of religious orders for permission to construct convents
and monasteries should be referred to the council, with the
recommendations of the audiencia, but in actual practice, when

---

[105] *Real Ordenanza de Intendentes de Nueva España, Artículos* 227,
228, 229.
[106] *Recopilación*, 1–3–1; 1–4–25.
[107] *Ibid.*, 1–2–14.
[108] Fajardo to the King, August 15, 1620, Blair and Robertson, XIX,
163.

the advice of the audiencia was in the affirmative, the vice-patron gave the desired consent, reporting on his action to the Council of the Indies. Thus we see that the governor and audiencia in reality exercised complete authority in uncontested cases.

A large number of communications written to the audiencia by the royal authorities exist, illustrating the nature and extent of the influence of the audiencia in these matters. In 1604, the king learned that the Augustinians of Cavite had founded a convent with no other authority than that of the governor. This was contrary to the laws of the royal patronage and the audiencia was ordered to correct the abuse, and to see that the royal orders were obeyed in the future.[109] On another occasion the audiencia was ordered to correct certain abuses of the Jesuits, who had dispossessed the natives of their lands and had built various structures thereon. The lands were ordered to be returned to their rightful owners and the buildings destroyed.[110]

The ambitions of the friars to construct monasteries, convents and hospitals, and otherwise to manifest their powers and add to their increasing strength had to be checked frequently. The audiencia was called upon to do this throughout the history of the Islands. Possibly the best illustration of the authority of the audiencia in these matters may be noted in the part which it played in restraining the Augustinians from the further extension of their influence during the period from 1762 to 1778. The entire matter was summarized in the *consulta* of the Council of the Indies dated December 10, 1777, and the *cédula* of April 6, 1778, with unfavorable results for the Augustinians.

On November 17, 1770, the provincial of this order applied for permission to construct a convent in Cavite and solicited an appropriation of four thousand pesos for this purpose. It was

---

109 King to the Audiencia, June (?) 1604, A. I., 105–2–1.
110 King to the Audiencia, October 30, 1634, A. I., 105–2–1.

suggested that the money should be supplied either by the income from vacant benefices or from the profits of the sale of betel to the natives. The provincial laid special claim to royal aid on the extraordinary justification that the convent of his order at Imús, Cavite, had been bombarded and destroyed by the British in 1763. On August 16, 1772, the Council of the Indies referred the matter to the Audiencia of Manila and the tribunal, after an exhaustive investigation of the subject, recommended non-compliance with the provincial's request. In its report, the audiencia reviewed the former attempts of this order to extend its power and influence. On December 2, 1765, it had tried to obtain permission to construct a convent at Nagtaján, which the audiencia and Fiscal Viana frustrated. The Augustinians tried again on February 20, 1766, asking for permission to build at Bagumbayan. This plan the audiencia was also able to defeat. On August 16, 1772, this same order, impatient at the delay of the Council in answering its petition of November 17, 1770, and still persistent, solicited permission from the governor alone, not alluding to the fact that a petition of this sort was at that time pending before the Council of the Indies. This request was considered in the *acuerdo* with unfavorable consequences for the Augustinians.

The report of the audiencia was forwarded to the court and was there reviewed by Francisco Leandro de Viana, formerly *fiscal* of the Audiencia of Manila and at that time a member of the Council. Viana recommended that not only should the desired permission be refused but a rigid investigation of the legitimacy of titles to properties held by the Augustinians should be made. He regarded as especially reprehensible the deliberate effort on the part of the provincial to obtain this permission from the governor in view of the unfavorable attitude of the Council of the Indies and of the laws ordering that licenses for the construction of convents should be given only by the Council of the Indies, after consultation with the prelate of the ecclesiastical district and with the audiencia, governor, or viceroy.[111] In this way, due very largely to the influence of the audiencia, the efforts of this order to extend its authority were checkmated. This may be considered as a typical case of the intervention of the audiencia in behalf of the royal patronage.

It will be noted in another connection that the audiencia was called upon, from 1680 to 1720, partly as a tribunal of justice and partly as an agent of the royal patron, to investigate the titles of the lands of the friars, and, by this proceeding, the tribunal deprived the orders of much of the property which they had usurped.[112] It may also be noted that an *oidor* regularly inspected the royal hospital at Manila,[113] and when prelates and curates were transferred from one district or parish to another, property left by them was inventoried and taken under the direction of the audiencia.[114] These measures were designed to insure the security and conservation of royal property.

In summary, it may be said that the audiencia possessed joint authority with, but not equal to the vicepatron in the regulation and supervision of religious affairs. As a tribunal, and as an agent of the civil government, the audiencia supported and assisted the vicepatron. At times, indeed, it acted in his stead. We have seen that the audiencia labored in the interests of the royal authority when it passed on the acts of provincial synods and councils, and it inspected bulls and briefs before they were allowed to become operative in the colony. It sought always to bring about a peaceful settlement

---

[111] *Recopilación*, 1–3–1, 1–6–2. The *expediente* covering this case is in A. I., 105–3–1. The *cédula* of April 6, 1778, and *testimonios* are in A. I., 105–2–1.

[112] See Cunningham, "Origin of the friar lands question in the Philippines," in *The American political science review*, X (August, 1916) pp. 465–480.

[113] *Recopilación*, 1–4–20.

[114] *Ibid.*, 1–2–20.

of disputes between prelates, curates, and religious orders. Acting in the interests of the civil government, the *oidores* made inspections in the provinces, noting the work of the friars and parish priests in their particular fields, giving special attention to the treatment afforded to the Indians by their ecclesiastical protectors. The tribunal acted as the patron of the royal colleges and universities. It regulated the administration of ecclesiastical finances, devoting especial attention to tithes, *obras pías* and *espolios*. And finally, as we have just noted, it was endowed with considerable authority in determining the advisability of authorizing the construction of churches, monasteries, and convents, or of permitting the orders to extend their influence in various parts of the colony. The intervention of the audiencia in these matters was recognized by the court at Madrid and by the ecclesiastics of the Philippines.

CHAPTER XI

THE AUDIENCIA AND THE CHURCH: THE ECCLESIASTICAL JURISDICTION

In the same manner that the audiencia performed the functions of a civil court, so did it exercise jurisdiction as a superior tribunal or court of appeal over prelates, church tribunals, and ecclesiastical judges. It will be our purpose in this chapter to determine the relations of the audiencia with the various ecclesiastical tribunals and to direct attention to the occasions on which it acted as a court, either with original or appellate jurisdiction in ecclesiastical cases.

In this particular phase of the investigation an effort will be made to distinguish between the ecclesiastical jurisdiction of the audiencia and its acts relative to the royal patronage. Not only may this distinction be made for conveniences of discussion, but it will be readily seen that the character of the powers and jurisdiction exercised was widely different. When acting as a tribunal of appeal over prelates, provincials, and ecclesiastical courts the chief concern of the audiencia was the administration of justice. When acting in defense of the royal patronage, as noted in the preceding chapter, its authority was primarily executive and administrative, designed always to safeguard the interests of the civil government.

It is, of course, true that all the power exercised by the civil government over the church proceeded from authority invested in the former by the laws of the royal patronage.[1] Nevertheless, it must be observed that there were times when the audiencia exercised the function of an impartial, disinterested court, with no aim or object other than that of maintaining simple

---

[1] See Note 2 of the preceding chapter.

justice. It may be conceded, for example, that the authority
which the audiencia exercised in the settlement of disputes between religious orders and between the prelates and the regulars partook of the same judicial character as the jurisdiction
which it had in settling disputes between civil corporations and
individuals. The intervention of the audiencia for the protection of the Indians from the abuses of the churchmen,[2] its
entertainment of the *recurso de fuerza*[3] and its function as a
court of appeals for the protection of the natives against
ecclesiastical tribunals may be said to have constituted acts in
defense of the royal interests as well as in securing the ends of
common justice. In restraining church authorities from the in-
temperate use of the interdict,[4] or from a too liberal extension
of the right of asylum,[5] the audiencia was not seeking the ends

----

[2] *Recopilación*, 2–16–138.

[3] See Note by A. P. Cushing, in Blair and Robertson, V, 292. Escriche
(*Diccionario*, I, 838–9) defines *fuerza* as "the wrong which an ecclesiastical judge does to a party when he assumes jurisdiction over a
case which does not belong to him, or when he fails to observe the rules
prescribed by the laws and canons, or when he unjustly denies appeal."
Recurso de fuerza is defined as the reclamation to a civil judge, made
by a person believing himself aggrieved by an ecclesiastical judge,
imploring the protection of the former in order that the *fuerza* or
violence may be terminated or undone. There are three ways mentioned by Alcubilla in which an ecclesiastical judge may commit
fuerza: 1. When he assumes jurisdiction in a purely temporal case,
which by its very nature is not rightfully subject to his authority.
2. When, by trying a case whose jurisdiction belongs to him, he fails
to observe the method and form prescribed by the laws and canons.
3. When he refuses to allow appeals which should be rightfully allowed (Martínez Alcubilla, *Diccionario*. V, 807).

[4] *Recopilación*, 2–15–148, 149. The interdict, as defined by Escriche
(*Diccionario*, I, 712), is a prohibition, mandate, or censure, pronounced
by an ecclesiastical authority by which is prohibited the use of certain spiritual privileges which are common to all. The effect of the
interdict may be to prohibit Christian burial, the administration of the
sacraments or the celebration of divine services. Exception may be
made in rare cases of baptisms, confirmation and confession for the
dying. Even though the interdict may be pronounced it does not prohibit the saying of mass in a low voice behind closed doors and without the ringing of bells. A priest who violates the interdict may be
pronounced "irregular", but a layman who does so may incur the penalty of excommunication (see *Catholic Encyclopedia*, under "Interdict").

[5] This refers to the privilege extended by the church to offenders
against the laws of the realm, who were allowed to take refuge from

of justice (though judicial proceedings were instituted) so much as it was defending the royal prerogative and protecting the officials of the civil government. This may also be said of its efforts to prevent the abuse of power by the commissary of the Inquisition. In these last-mentioned activities, therefore, the audiencia may be said to have acted in defense of the royal patronage, though in all these cases its method of procedure was that of a court of justice.

The church in the Spanish colonies had its own judicial tribunals for the trial and settlement of cases arising within it which did not concern the civil government.[6] The division of

---

the civil authorities in a church or convent. This practice was recognized by the government. By a bull of Clement XIV, the right of extending asylum was limited to a few churches only, the number of these depending on the population of the town or city. Those guilty of certain specified crimes of the most heinous character were denied the privilege of sanctuary. The act of sheltering oneself under the protection of God was supposed to be spontaneous and not premeditated. The privilege was often abused by individual churchmen (Escriche, *Diccionario*, I, 353).

[6] A clarifying description of the ecclesiastical jurisdiction has been given by Escriche. He defines it as "the power of the Church for the trial and adjudication of civil and criminal affairs exercised either by its own right or by concession of princes." This jurisdiction, says Escriche, is of two kinds, inherent (spiritual) and privileged (temporal). After classifying the different cases which fall naturally under each category, he describes the tribunals for the interpretation of canon law. "The ecclesiastical jurisdiction,' he writes, "the inherent, as well as the privileged, is exercised, in first instance, by the bishops and archbishops in their respective dioceses, in the second, by the metropolitan with respect to the suffragans, and in the third, by the papal delegate. The bishops and archbishops do not exercise the jurisdiction by themselves but by means of their *provisores* or *vicarios*. These latter may be either *generales* or *foráneos.* . . . The term *provisor* or vicar-general is used to designate him who exercises the ordinary ecclesiastical jurisdiction in the entire territory of the diocese and resides in the episcopal city situated therein; . . . *foráneos* are the others established as delegates in certain parts of the diocese in order to facilitate the administration of justice; no appointments to these offices may be made without the royal approbation. The authority of the *provisores* and *vicarios* cease by death of the prelate from whom they obtained the nomination, and is reassumed by the *cabildo* or chapter, *sede vacante*, which selects persons to succeed them" (Escriche, *Diccionario*, II, 453).

Escriche further describes this hierarchy of ecclesiastical judges: "The metropolitans, then, are the ordinary judges of first instance with

authority between the civil and ecclesiastical courts and the respective jurisdictions of each are described by Professor Moses, who writes:

The courts of the civil government and not the ecclesiastical authorities considered . . . all questions involving the limits of bishoprics, the rights and prerogatives of the holders of benefices, controversies between ecclesiastical councils and their bishops and archbishops concerning the administration of the Church, all disputes between parish priests and their parishes, in a word, all cases that in any manner touched the royal patronage. Even matters spiritual and cases between persons of a privileged tribunal were not excepted from the civil jurisdiction; but certain cases might be brought before the viceroy, and, if desired, an appeal might be taken from the viceroy's decision to the audiencia.[7]

regard to the archbishoprics and at the same time they are the judges of appeal from the suffragans, and, accordingly, they are accustomed to appoint, aside from the *provisores* or *vicarios, ordinarios* who discharge the functions of judges of first instance. As the *obispos exentos* are not subject to a metropolitan, but directly to the holy see, recourses of appeals from their decisions go to the papal delegate." The cases of appeal from the metropolitans and other ecclesiastical judges were heard in third and last instance by the tribunal known as the *rota* of the papal delegate, which was composed of the *nuncio* of the pope, and the ecclesiastical auditors appointed by the crown.

The ecclesiastical courts of the Philippines conformed generally, in organization and limits of jurisdiction, to the scheme outlined in the preceding paragraphs. The three bishops of Nueva Segovia, Camarines, and Cebú had their courts in the chief towns of their respective dioceses. They were assisted by the customary *provisores*. Appeals were carried from them to the court of the metropolitan which was located in Manila; this latter tribunal consisted of the archbishop, the vicar-general, and a notary. Above this court was that of the papal delegate who tried cases of appeal from the lower tribunal in accordance with canon law. In conformity with a bull of Gregory XIII, dated May 15, 1572, the authority of the papal delegate in appeal cases was final; "he might overrule and even supersede the metropolitan, as being the judge in final appeal." The Bishop of Camarines most frequently acted as papal delegate (Blair and Robertson, XLII, 27, Note 4). Aside from these courts there was that of the commissary of the Inquisition whose jurisdiction will be subsequently noted.

Each order, also, had its own judicial machinery for the settlement of cases arising within it. The courts of the orders were presided over by their provincials, generals and commissaries, and were composed of those dignitaries and other magistrates selected in accordance with their own rules. Special investigators or visitors were also delegated to try cases arising within the orders, and to make inspections, ascertaining the general character of the work of the orders, the conduct of their dignitaries and the regularity of their administration.

[7] Moses, *South America on the eve of emancipation*, 126.

It will be our function in this chapter to determine the participation of the civil courts in these matters.

The power of intervention in ecclesiastical matters which
was exercised by the civil tribunals was always a source of discord in the Philippines. The attitude of the churchmen on this
question is well shown by a letter written January 20, 1688, by
Fray Alonso Laudín, procurator in Madrid for the Franciscans
of the Philippines, in protest against the encroachments of
civil government. He wrote that

the principal causes of trouble in the Philippines are the disagreements which continually exist between the royal audiencia and the
ecclesiastical judges; . . . the ministers of the royal audiencia, by
virtue of the royal patronage of Your Majesty whom they represent,
. . . hold . . . that the audiencia has ecclesiastical jurisdiction over
the Church and over purely ecclesiastical persons, over spiritual
cases and the administration of the Holy Sacrament, . . . and spiritual
and territorial jurisdiction in regular and secular parishes.[8]

Laudín described the helplessness of the ecclesiastical judges
and the ineffectiveness of their jurisdiction, circumscribed as
it was by that of the civil magistrates. He stated that all the
judicial acts of the ecclesiastical ordinaries were rendered null
by the magistrates of the audiencia and that the ecclesiastical
authorities were reduced to such a condition that they did not
know where to turn for relief or remedy, as even the papal
decrees were rendered ineffectual by the encroachments of the
civil jurisdiction. He stated that "the ecclesiastical judges
see in all this a meddling and interference with the ecclesiastical jurisdiction, which has always been allowed, but they
cannot hereafter give fulfillment to the provisions of the audiencia, even at the risk of expulsion from their districts."
Laudín was of the opinion that the laws had been misinter-
preted by the civil officials and that the king had never intended that the churchmen should be so entirely shorn of their
powers. He concluded his appeal with the solicitation that

---

[8] *Carta de Fr. Francisco de Laudín . . . al Consejo de Indias,
20 de Enero, 1668,* A. I., 68–1–44.

such laws should be made as would determine the questions at issue and bring about harmony between church and state in the Islands. This should be done, he said, ''in order that each may be caused to see clearly the duties and jurisdiction which belongs to him and that each may freely make use of his own powers and prerogatives, and thus avoid suits and other disagreements.''

The laws of the Indies prescribed that the most harmonious relations should prevail between the ecclesiastical and civil magistrates. The audiencia was commanded to aid the prelates and ecclesiastical magistrates in the exercise of their jurisdiction, neither interfering with them nor permitting them to be molested by other civil authorities.[9] These laws, like those of the royal patronage, not only gave to the civil government a commanding position with relation to the church, but they established the magistrates as the supervisors and guardians of the church courts.

It was the duty of the audiencia, on the other hand, to guard strictly the prerogatives of the civil magistrates, and, in fact, those of all officials of the government, and not to allow the ecclesiastics to infringe on their jurisdiction through acts of *fuerza*, interdicts, or by any other illegal means.[10] The ecclesiastical courts were forbidden to try laymen or those subject in first instance to the jurisdiction of the civil courts. They were forbidden to imprison private subjects, or embargo or sell their property without first seeking the consent and co-operation of the secular arm.[11] They were forbidden to try any cases except those involving the church, and they could not, without the aid of the civil authorities, impose fines or condemn persons to labor.[12] In general, they were solicited to

---

9 *Recopilación*, 1–7–54; 2–15–150; 3–1–4; Escriche, *Diccionario*, II, 453.
10 *Recopilación*, 1–10–1, 2.
11 Escriche, *Diccionario*, II, 453.
12 *Recopilación*, 1–10–4, 6, 7, 12; 1–7–12.

work in harmony with the audiencia, and to give all possible assistance to that body.[13] Wherein doubt existed or where there was reason to believe that an action might constitute an interference with the civil prerogative, the ecclesiastical judges were ordered to ask the advice of the secular authorities. The ecclesiastical and secular magistrates were enjoined to aid each other actively when occasion demanded, the prelates supporting the audiencia, and the latter dispatching provisions to its magistrates and subdelegates in support of the ecclesiastical judges and tribunals.[14]

The laws cited above did not become effective suddenly, but were evolved through a long period of dissension and dispute between the ecclesiastical and the civil authorities. Before the audiencia was established in the Islands, the parish priests, friars, and ecclesiastical ordinaries in many cases exercised the duties of local judges in both the spiritual and temporal spheres. There can be no question but that the church rendered very efficient service in this particular, especially under the leadership of Bishop Salazar.[15]

The surrender of their prerogatives by the ecclesiastics was gradually though reluctantly made as the civil courts became more firmly established in the Islands. At first, the entire clergy, with few exceptions, from the bishop to the most isolated parish priest, opposed the change, and regarded the assumption of their former powers by the civil authorities as unauthorized usurpation.[16] It was with great difficulty that

---

13 *Ibid.*, 11.

14 *Ibid.*, 2–15–153; 1–10–13; 3–1–3.

15 As an example of this we may refer to the work of the Augustinians in bringing to the light of judicial scrutiny the abuses of certain *encomenderos* against the Indians of Mindanao. This was in 1581, before the audiencia was established. The offending *encomenderos* were brought to Manila and tried by Bishop Salazar, who temporarily deprived them of their holdings and sentenced them to imprisonment and fines (Governor to the King [day and month not given], A. I., 67–6–6).

16 The opposition of Salazar to what he termed the encroachment of the civil jurisdiction was based on the assumption that the royal

the churchmen were able to adjust themselves to the new conditions. They were required frequently to aid the civil authorities in the apprehension of criminals and in the obtaining of testimony, thus co-operating generally in the administration of justice.[17] A noteworthy conflict arose when the audiencia summoned Bishop Salazar before it to testify as an ordinary witness, and to explain his own actions on various occasions, in retarding the work of the civil courts. These summonses he regarded as detracting from his ecclesiastical immunity. Subsequently, the audiencia was admonished that on no occasion should churchmen be called to act as witnesses.[18] So it came about that although the intervention of the audiencia was prescribed by the laws of the Indies and admitted elsewhere in the Philippines, owing to the strength of the ecclesiastical organization, and its former prominence in affairs of government, the assumption of its legal power by the audiencia was necessarily gradual. Nevertheless, the tribunal ultimately attained extensive authority in ecclesiastical affairs, an analysis of which will now be made.

---

patronage did not extend to tribes which lived in an uncivilized and savage state. He contended that the pope had not conceded this, consequently, as bishop, he had entire jurisdiction without interference from the audiencia or governor over the Mohammedans (as he termed all non-Christians) and the Chinese (A. I., 1–1–3/25).

[17] *Cabildo de Manila* to the King, A. I., 68–1–35.

[18] Fajardo to Felipe III, August 15, 1620, Blair and Robertson, XIX, 155. The pendulum seems, however, to have swung in the other direction at times. In 1604, the audiencia was charged with having tried members of religious orders *in absentia* without giving them a chance to summon witnesses or otherwise to defend themselves (King to Audiencia, October 30, 1604, A. I., 105–2–1). That the audiencia did not always have power to discipline the friars for infractions of the royal laws in 1626, is attested by the case of an Augustinian who led an assault on an *alcalde mayor* in Batangas, destroyed his house, maltreated his person, and, in the presence of the natives, publicly accomplished his disgrace. The king demanded from the audiencia a statement of all the facts of the case so that he and the Council might take proper steps for the punishment of the offending religious and the protection of His Majesty's servants in the future (King to Audiencia, May 21, 1623, A. I., 105–2–1). The audiencia conducted an investigation and forwarded the papers relative to the case to the court for final action. See Chapter X, note 35.

The audiencia exercised jurisdiction as a high court of appeal over suits to which the religious orders were parties. Most of these cases originated in misunderstandings or contentions over jurisdiction, titles to land, and over the claims relating to occupation of provinces under the royal patronage, which the various orders advanced. Most frequent of all were the suits between the orders, as to jurisdiction over provinces. An example of this is furnished by the contention which arose in 1736 between the Jesuits and the Recollects for the exclusive right to minister in Mindanao. Another case of a similar nature was the adjudication of a dispute between the Recollects and the Dominicans for spiritual jurisdiction in the province of Zambales, as a result of which the Recollects were finally ordered to confine their missionary activities to Mindoro.[19] Another case was the dispute between the Franciscans and the Observant friars. A large number of the latter arrived in the Islands in 1648 with letters from the Viceroy of New Spain. They were at once given territory which had been previously assigned to the Franciscans. On the basis of a brief of Urban VIII, prohibiting the occupation of the same province by two different orders, the Franciscans brought suit in the audiencia with the result that the newcomers were not only dispossessed of the province that had been assigned to them, but their patents and briefs were cancelled on the grounds that they were not properly authorized by the Council of the Indies.[20]

Reference was made in the last chapter to the suits which occurred between the Jesuits and Dominicans, the two orders most extensively interested in higher education, for the right to maintain universities in Manila. The greater number of these disputes, in fact all of them, seem to have been based on the rivalry of their two colleges and on their zeal for royal

---

19 Blair and Robertson, XXVIII, 314–15; see XLI, 22–25, 134, 231–4, 239, 255.

20. Montero y Vidal, *Historia general*, 283–284.

favor and patronage. When Santo Tomás became a royal university in 1648, and was empowered to grant degrees as such, the Jesuits brought suit in the audiencia for the right to confer honors of a like character in their college of San José. The audiencia denied their petition; the case was appealed to the Council of the Indies, and the higher authority decided that both institutions should enjoy equally the privilege of conferring scholastic honors.[21] The rivalry and bitter feeling between these two orders did not cease with this settlement, but in 1683 the Dominicans again brought suit in the audiencia, seeking to limit the educational activities of the Jesuits. The matter was again carried to the Council of the Indies. Although the decision was made in favor of the Jesuits, the disagreements between the two orders, the charges and countercharges, and the influence of Archbishop Pardo, a Dominican, in behalf of his own order, went far beyond the authority of the audiencia, whose efforts to restrain them were entirely ineffectual.[22]

Even the natives themselves, at times, went so far as to sue the religious orders in the audiencia. This was done in 1738 when the *mestizos* of Santa Cruz brought suit against the Jesuits, because the latter had sought to make the residents of Santa Cruz pay for certain improvements in the parishes of that district. These improvements had been authorized by the Jesuits, and from them the society had derived great benefit, while the residents had derived no particular good from them.[23] In 1737, on complaint of the natives, an investigation was conducted by Oidor Calderón which put a check upon certain transactions of the Jesuits in the province of Batangas. It was proved that

[21] Letter of Fray Miguel de Solano, May 7, 1753, A. I., 67–6–4.
[22] Orellana to Carlos II, February 24, 1683, Blair and Robertson, XXXVIII, 81–85.
[23] Concepción, *Historia general*, IX, 107. There are records of many suits of this character throughout the history of Juan de la Concepción. The original documents relating thereto are to be found in A. I., 105–3–1 to 10. See also A. I., 67–6–3, 67–6–9 to 11.

they had collected rents repeatedly from the Indians for lands to which they had no title.

The most significant and decisive judicial authority which the audiencia exercised in ecclesiastical matters, and that which was productive of more conflicts and opposition on the part of the church than any other cause, was the jurisdiction of the tribunal over the secular church courts, at the head of which was the metropolitan tribunal of the archbishop. The method of intervention most frequently followed in cases appealed from the archbishop was by the entertainment of the *recurso de fuerza*.[24] In this way the civil jurisdiction, acting through the audiencia, could intervene for its own protection, and by means of this special procedure that tribunal actually did restrain the ecclesiastical judges more frequently and effectively in important cases than in any other way. It was on the grounds of *fuerza* that the audiencia justified its action in practically all cases of interference with the jurisdiction of the church courts.

Cases of *fuerza* were those which came to the audiencia through the abuse of their judicial powers by prelates or ecclesiastical judges; cases, literally, in which the latter had usurped or trespassed the authority of the civil courts or government.[25] The execution of the decision of an ecclesiastical judge could be suspended by an edict of the audiencia on the grounds of *fuerza*, while the case was being investigated by that tribunal.[26] The civil government usually took the initiative in these appeals, but there were occasions in the history of the Islands in which ecclesiastical authorities and tribunals interposed *recursos de fuerza* against the archbishop. In dealing with these cases the audiencia first ascertained whether *fuerza* had been committed and then, if the results

---

24 See note 3 of this chapter.
25 Martínez Alcubilla, *Diccionario*, V, 807.
26 *Recopilación*, 1–10–10; 2–15–136.

of the investigation were affirmative, the tribunal was empowered to raise the *fuerza* (*alzar* or *quitar la fuerza*)[27] and place limitations upon the ecclesiastical authority in order to prevent future abuse of power.[28] The audiencia was without authority to fine prelates, bishops, or ecclesiastical judges, but it had sufficient jurisdiction to remedy excesses and restore conditions to their former state. The tribunal was urged to use the utmost discretion in dispossessing offending prelates and judges of their benefices or positions,[29] as a punishment for *fuerza*, and not to proceed to such lengths except in exceptional cases, wherein the strictest measures were necessary. On such occasions the audiencia might exile the offending ecclesiastic, giving account of its act to the Council of the Indies.[30] All proceedings of this nature had to be carried on secretly and with the greatest possible dispatch and brevity,[31] and all churchmen who were deprived of their benefices through the *recurso de fuerza* had the privilege of an appeal to the Council of the Indies.[32]

In the treatment of cases of *fuerza* an informal judicial hearing was given; the spirit of the proceeding was supposed to be that of a harmonious investigation, in which both sides, ecclesiastical and civil, were mutually and equally concerned in the solution of a given problem, and in ascertaining wherein error had been committed. The object of this proceeding was said to be the furtherance of the interests of the crown, the salvation of souls and the spread of the benevolent influence of the church. That the spirit of peace and harmony failed to manifest itself at many of these investigations, is shown by the

---

[27] *Alzar* or *quitar la fuerza* was the act on the part of a royal tribunal of abrogating, annulling, or reforming the effects of violence committed by an ecclesiastical judge.—Escriche, *Diccionario*, I, 839.

[28] *Recopilación*, 2–15–134, 135.

[29] *Ibid.*, 2–15–143.

[30] *Ibid.*, 144.

[31] *Ibid.*, 152 and 142.

[32] *Ibid.*, 2–2–4.

bitter contests which arose between the civil and ecclesiastical judges as results of the entertainment of the *recurso de fuerza*. The spiritual authorities alleged on these occasions that they regarded the restraining action of the government as presumption, unauthorized by ecclesiastical canons.

In the well-known Pardo controversy (1683-1689), references to which may be found in any history of the Philippines, there occurred many occasions on which the audiencia was obliged to avail itself of the *recurso de fuerza*. By this means the audiencia sought to restrain Archbishop Pardo from usurping the civil jurisdiction and that of the religious orders and of the metropolitan chapter. Interference with these orders was in violation of the royal patronage, the ultimate authority over them being the patron and not the archbishop. Such action, therefore, became a civil offense, punishable by the civil tribunals, the highest of which and the one properly equipped to deal with such cases, was the audiencia. It will be noted that Pardo paid the penalty of exile for repeatedly ignoring the audiencia and its right of interposition through the *recurso de fuerza,* and the subsequent ineffectiveness of the audiencia was due to reasons and conditions other than the decline of the authority and importance of the *recurso de fuerza*. This controversy which is more fully described in preceding chapters affords the best example extant of the operation of the *recurso de fuerza,* its nature and effects, hence the citation of minor cases is rendered unnecessary.

Closely related to the question of *fuerza* as illustrating the jurisdiction of the audiencia over the church courts, occurs that of the interdict. A price which the civil authorities frequently had to pay for the entertainment of the *recurso de fuerza,* or any other opposition, in fact, to the unrestricted authority of the ecclesiastics, was the penalty which usually accompanied the interdict, of being forbidden to participate in religious rites and ceremonies, or to continue receiving the customary spiritual consolations and benefits of the church.[33] The authority of the audiencia to restrain the excessive use of this weapon by the ecclesiastics may be considered to have been judicial in its nature, since the prelates, by undue use of the episcopal censure, went beyond their ecclesiastical jurisdiction and encroached upon the royal prerogative. A form of judicial inquiry was instituted to ascertain the act and degree of encroachment; indeed, the excessive use of the interdict was interpreted to constitute *fuerza,* and the method just described was employed by the tribunal to combat it.

We may turn again to the Pardo controversy for an example of the intervention of the audiencia to restrain a prelate from excessive use of the interdict. Pardo, after his return from exile, fulminated censures against ex-Governor Juan de Vargas and the entire audiencia which had supported him against the archbishop. The ban against the *oidores* was quickly removed, technically on the grounds that the magistrates were still royal officials, but in reality for the sake of expediency. Vargas, however, was not absolved. The audiencia, according to the existing laws, had the right to force the prelate to remove the ban,[34] but owing to dissensions within the tribunal, the opposition of the new governor, the increasing power of the archbishop, the certainty that the royal authority had already disapproved of its acts, and the impending visitation of a royal commissioner (Valdivia), who had instructions to settle the discord and strife at Manila at any cost, the *oidores* thought it best not to take this step. The archbishop refused to absolve Vargas because of the technical reason that his case came under the jurisdiction of the Inquisition.

The audiencia was expected to restrain the interdict whenever this ecclesiastical prohibition interfered with the govern-

---

[33] Escriche, *Diccionario,* I, 712.
[34] *Recopilación,* 2–15–148: See *expediente* on affairs in the Philippines, 1690, A. I., 67–6–3.

ment or incapacitated the officials thereof from executing their duties. The interdict was not to interfere with the royal prerogative, nor was it to be imposed for insignificant causes, or personal reasons.[35] The audiencia was given the special injunction not to interfere with censures generally, but to permit them to be applied in needful cases, the *oidores* bearing in mind only the requirement that these ecclesiastical measures should not be allowed to interfere with the civil government.[36]

It had frequently been the practice of the prelates to pronounce censures against *oidores* and *alcaldes,* who, in proceeding with their duties as inspectors of the provinces, encroached upon what the churchmen regarded as their own particular and private jurisdicton. This, of course, was forbidden, and the audiencia, by way of *fuerza,* usually entertained appeals from these officials of the civil government and set aside all such acts on the part of the representatives of the church. Reference was made in the last chapter to the circumstances surrounding the effort of Oidor Guerela to inspect the province of Camarines. This magistrate was excommunicated by the bishop of that diocese and was compelled to remain in banishment five months, the audiencia refusing to set aside the censure on account of the personal animosity of the magistrates toward Guerela. Nevertheless, prelates were enjoined to obey the audiencia when that tribunal ordered the cancellation or suspension of an episcopal censure or prohibition.[37] When an appeal was made to the audiencia from such an act by an *alcalde, oidor,* visitor, or other official at some distance from the capital, the prelate was expected, upon the judicial summons of the audiencia, to suspend his censure until the facts of the case had been ascertained, and the decision of the tribunal had been rendered.[38] This was the law, but occasionally, as in

---

35 *Ibid.,* 1–7–47.
36 *Ibid.,* 2–15–149.
37 *Ibid.,* 1–10–9.·
38 *Ibid.,* 10; 2–15–136.

the case of Guerela, local circumstances rendered impossible or undesirable the fulfillment of the law.

It has been shown in the preceding chapter that before the coming of the audiencia, the church had utilized the weapon of excommunication on very slight pretext, and it had been partly for the purpose of restraining this abuse that the audiencia was established.[39] The early governors, especially, had many difficulties with this phase of ecclesiastical high-handedness and the letters of such executives as De Vera, Tello, Dasmariñas, and Morga complained continually against this particular abuse of power by the prelates,[40] regretting the lack of any authority to set aside these excessive acts on the part of the churchmen. All the above-mentioned governors had been excommunicated for various acts in opposition to the ecclesiastical power. Governor Ronquillo, in the characteristic letter which is quoted in another part of this treatise, reported that the audiencia, after its establishment, had effectively restrained the excesses of excommunication on the part of the church.[41] Indeed, during the twenty-five years succeeding Ronquillo's term as governor, the audiencia had so frequently set aside ecclesiastical censures, and so completely terminated the abuses of the privilege of sanctuary by friars and priests, in fact so generally held at naught the principle of ecclesiastical immunity, that the king, on November 13, 1626, was obliged to issue a special *cédula* in restraint of his Manila tribunal and for the protection of the ecclesiastical jurisdiction.[42]

Examination of a large number of cases shows that the method by which the audiencia set aside excommunication was

---

[39] This is discussed in the preceding chapter.
[40] A. I., 1–1–3/25; Blair and Robertson, VIII, 275–281; X, 79, 245–275.
[41] Ronquillo to the King, July 12, 1599, A. I., 67–6–6, cited in the preceding chapter.
[42] *Cédula* of November 13, 1626, A. I., 105–2–1; for cases of the excommunication of viceroys and *oidores* and other matters relating to the Inquisition in Perú and in New Spain see Lea, *The inquisition in the Spanish dependencies*, 191–298, 319–451.

usually through an ultimate reliance on force. Nevertheless, taking three hundred years of the history of the Philippines into consideration, there were relatively few cases in which matters went so far that the audiencia actually had to use force, the case being usually that the judicial protest of the tribunal against an abuse of this kind was sufficient. Theoretically, any act of excommunication or interdict was suspended, *ipso facto*, by the intervention of the audiencia pending further investigation, and the prelate was required to abide by the decision of the tribunal.

The following typical cases may be cited to show that the audiencia frequently did rely on the civil power, as a last resort, for the enforcement of its injunctions. In 1623, an *oidor* was excommunicated for having violated the ecclesiastical sanctuary in seizing Juan Soto de Vega, a fugitive from justice, who had taken refuge in the cathedral. The audiencia, finding itself opposed by the metropolitan court, sent a constable to arrest the *provisor* who had fulminated the excommunication, threatening the latter with a fine of two thousand pesos and banishment if he did not desist and cancel the censure. The archbishop, who at first supported the *provisor*, was put under military guard at the behest of the audiencia. The Jesuits then used their good offices in behalf of the government, as a result of which the matter was arbitrated and peace was brought about.[43] In 1636, however, the archbishop and *provisor* were banished and fined heavily, because they persisted in a censure which the audiencia had restrained. Their continual refusal to harken to the commands of the vice-patron and the royal tribunal and their insistence on the censure were adjudged to constitute *fuerza*. This case originated in the violation of the right of asylum by the governor and the arrest of a murderer who had taken refuge in the Augus-

---

[43] Corcuera to Felipe IV, September 25, 1623, Blair and Robertson, XXVI, 104–107.

tinian convent. So open was the defiance of the civil government that the criminal was executed in the courtyard, under the very windows of the convent wherein were congregated the prelate and his supporters who were commanded not to touch the body for three days.[44] The archbishop was removed from his convent by soldiers at the command of the *acuerdo* and banished to the island of Corregidor, where he remained twenty-six days, after which mediation was effected and the weak old prelate, tottering with age, was restored to his metropolitan capital.[45] Montero y Vidal states that this case is interesting and important as a test of the power of the governor; for many persons, he alleges, did not believe that the governor could raise an interdict.[46] That he was enabled to do so, with the support of the audiencia and with the aid of his military forces there can be no question.

Some reference should be made at this time to the abuses of the interdict by Archbishop Pardo. This prelate went so far as to place a ban upon the church of the Jesuits because it contained the dead body of an offending *oidor*. For reasons other than the lack of legal authority, the audiencia was powerless to restrain his censures at that time. On another occasion the audiencia and governor, by placing armed guards at the doors of the Dominican church and preventing the celebration of services therein, suppressed an interdict which had been issued through the influence of that order on behalf of Archbishop Pardo. Governor Bustamante claimed that he was acting in accordance with his own properly constituted authority in 1719, when he appointed his own audiencia, set aside repeated interdicts, penetrated the asylum of the church, arrested the archbishop and defied the entire ecclesiastical organization.

---

44 Martínez de Zúñiga, *An historical view,* I, 268.

45 Relation of 1635–1636, Blair and Robertson, XXVI, 39–40; see also Corcuera to Felipe IV, Blair and Robertson, XXVI, 60–127; Montero y Vidal, *Historia general,* I, 195–196.

46 Montero y Vidal, *op. cit.,* I, 193–197.

He seems to have exceeded his powers no more flagrantly than did some of his predecessors under like circumstances; yet, for personal and political reasons, he was unable to count on the support of the other elements of the colony in this struggle with the ecclesiastical power and the battle ended disastrously for him. Acting-Governor Anda, relying on armed force alone, defended Manila against the British, achieved victory for his cause and secured the approbation of the king in the face of repeated ecclesiastical censures from Archbishop Rojo. These incidents, which occupy a prominent place in the history of the Philippines, illustrate the usual method by which ecclesiastical censures were set aside in actual practice, either by the audiencia or by the vicepatron, who was supported by the tribunal.

A department of the church over which the audiencia did not have such complete authority, either judicially or administratively, was the Inquisition. Properly speaking, there was no tribunal of the Holy Office in the Philippines, the Inquisition being represented in Manila by a commissary.[47] This representative was sufficiently powerful, however, to constitute a worthy opponent for the civil power and one who, on account

---

[47] The Inquisition, as represented by one commissary and three alternates (who were usually bishops) was established in the Philippines on March 1, 1583. The commissary of the Inquisition had for his special field all questions of faith and heresy, clearing away the errors and superstitions against the dogma and the lax opinions which pervert Christian morals (Pérez y López, *Teatro*, XXVIII, 208). The Inquisitor of the Philippines was instructed, on his arrival, to present his papers "to the ecclesiastical and lay chapters in order that they might receive him and recognize him in so high and holy an office." The Inquisition was represented continuously in the Philippines until 1813. With the introduction of this dignitary may be noted the presence in the Philippines of at least five authorities with ecclesiastical jurisdiction. The ordinary ecclesiastical tribunals dealt with contentions within the Church. The papal delegate tried cases which had been appealed from these ecclesiastical courts. The regular orders had their own particular tribunals for the rule and discipline of their members and the audiencia exercised such ecclesiastical jurisdiction as we have noted in this chapter. There may be slight wonder, therefore, in view of the presence of so many ecclesiastical tribunals with similar powers, that there were frequent conflicts of authority.

of the immunities which he enjoyed and because of the secret
methods which he was able to employ, kept all the tribunals
and authorities of the civil government at a respectful distance.
Although the laws of the Indies directed that the inquisitors who were sent to the colonies should present their titles
to the audiencias and viceroys, this did not give the civil
authorities any advantage over them. The audiencia was expected to formally receive the inquisitors and to pay them all
due respect.[48] At the time of the establishment of the Inquisition in Manila, no audiencia as yet existed. From the very beginning, however, the dignitaries of the Inquisition were placed
under special royal protection, with complete power over their
own sphere. Officials of the government and all other persons
were warned and enjoined not to interfere with or oppose
them in any way. As early as May 22, 1610, the Council of
the Indies placed itself and all subordinate audiencias and governors in a position inferior to that of the Inquisition. The
interference of civil magistrates with the inquisitors in behalf
of the government was forbidden,[49] even the ordinary means of
protection were denied them. The *recurso de fuerza* could
not be employed, nor could the interdicts of the inquisitors be
raised, even in notorious cases of their infringement upon the
royal jurisdiction.[50] Little change was made in these laws until the latter part of the eighteenth century. The *oidores* were
ordered to lend such secular aid as might be required, and were
originally instructed to obey the mandates and carry out the
orders of the inquisitors without inquiries into the religious
reason for any action the latter might take. Each judge,
ecclesiastical or royal, was to limit himself strictly to his own

---

[48] *Recopilación*, 1–19–1.
[49] Law of May 22, 1610, *Recopilación*, 1–19–2.
[50] The authorized proceeding in such a case was to appeal to the
General Council of the Inquisition, which held its sessions at the court.
This tribunal was authorized to nullify or reverse any harmful act or
decision which the ordinary inquisitors might resolve upon. (*Cédula*
of March 10, 1553, *Recopilación*, 1–19–4).

particular field and thus conflicts of authority were to be avoided.

The laws of the Indies prescribed many regulations which were designed to induce harmony and co-operation between the officials of the Inquisition and those of the civil government. Viceroys, audiencias and governors were authorized to execute the sentences of the representatives of the Inquisition and to extend to them every facility and assistance.[51] *Oidores* and executives were forbidden to open the mail or tamper with the correspondence or legal documents of the inquisitors.[52] *Oidores* and *fiscales* were authorized to give legal advice to the judges of the Inquisition when counsel of this kind was required.[53] The inquisitors were to be given precedence over the officials of the civil government in everything pertaining to the official duties of the former, but in questions of civil administration and in matters of ceremony, the *oidores* took precedence over inquisitors, unless the latter enjoyed higher rank by virtue of some other office.[54]

The tendency of the laws, however, through a period of two hundred years, was to delimit and circumscribe the authority of the Inquisition in matters bordering on the jurisdiction of the civil government. This is seen, especially, in the offense of polygamy, which, up to 1754, was dealt with solely by the Inquisition. By the *cédula* of March 19th of that year, polygamy was brought under the *fuero mixto;*[55] the same law ordered that prisoners, after punishment by the inquisitorial tribunal for heresy, should be dealt with by civil judges for an offense against the laws of the realm. On September 7,

---

[51] *Recopilación*, 1–19–18, 19.
[52] *Ibid.*, 16.
[53] *Ibid.*, 21 and 22.
[54] *Ibid.*, 3–15–78.
[55] "When a case may be tried indistinctly either by an ecclesiastical or lay judge it is said that the case is of the *fuero mixto* and then either of the two judges may take up the case, but the judge who begins it must be the last to try it" (Escriche, *Diccionario*, I, 832–833).

1766, this crime was again made punishable solely by the Inquisition, but on August 10, 1788, jurisdiction over cases of polygamy was taken entirely from the Inquisition and given to the royal justices.[56] This may be considered as indicative of the decline of the authority of the Inquisition in the eighteenth century. The inquisitors, of course, were not permitted to exercise jurisdiction over the Chinese, or over the aboriginal inhabitants of the Islands.[57]

In its relations with the civil power in the Philippines, and particularly with the audiencia, two charges have been brought against the Inquisition. The first was that in the early years of the Islands' history, it was utilized by the prelates for the more complete usurpation of powers belonging to the civil government and the audiencia. The tribunal, of course, was left entirely without recourse, by virtue of the exemptions and immunities of the Inquisition mentioned above. On July 20, 1585, the audiencia, in a letter to the king, cited several instances in which Bishop Salazar, unwilling to cede his claims to jurisdiction over certain civil offenders, handed them over to the commissary of the Inquisition, instead of surrendering them to the audiencia, to which jurisdiction over such cases belonged. The audiencia, appealing to the king for aid, alleged that the prelate had taken undue advantage of the civil power, "by sheltering himself behind the Inquisition, . . . where the audiencia has no jurisdiction."[58] This charge

---

[56] See note to *Recopilación*, 1-19-4.

[57] Le Gentil, II, 172. *Recopilación*, 6-1-35.

[58] Audiencia to the King, July 20, 1585, A. I., 67-6-18. On June 26, 1586, the audiencia recommended the discontinuance of the Inquisition in the Philippines on the ground that it had been utilized "as a citadel for the shelter of those desirous of resisting the royal authority" (Audiencia to the King, A. I., 68-1-33). Archbishop Santibañez, on the other hand, was desirous of converting the inquisitorial authority into a tribunal to consist of two ecclesiastics and one *oidor*. He argued that the distance from Mexico made procedure cumbersome, and it was manifestly unjust that residents of the Philippines should be judged by a foreign court (referring to the tribunal in Mexico.— Santibañez to Philip II, June 24, 1598, Blair and Robertson, X, 151).

was also brought against Salazar by the Jesuit, Sánchez, in his memorial of 1591.[59] It is significant that no decree was issued during the earlier era which authorized the audiencia to repair the abuses of the inquisitors, although on many occasions the audiencia and the local court of the Inquisition were respectively enjoined to confine themselves to their own particular fields of authority.[60]

The second charge made against the Inquisition was that it allowed itself to be influenced, utilized, and possessed by individuals and private interests for their own selfish ends. Under these conditions the audiencia was powerless; the Inquisition openly fought the government and vanquished it entirely on various notable occasions. There may be found no better illustration of this than the Salcedo affair in 1667 and 1668, during which the commissary of the Inquisition was the instrument of the governor's enemies, proceeding to such excesses in his zeal that he ultimately proved to be the agent of his own downfall.[61]

These same sentiments were expressed sixty years later by Francisco Bello, procurator at Madrid for the religious orders. The Council of the Indies returned the petition which had been submitted by this last-named ecclesiastic, to the Viceroy of New Spain, and to the Audiencia and Archbishop of Manila, respectively, for their advice. The consensus of opinion was against the idea of creating a tribunal in Manila, partially on account of the expense. It was also shown that such a reform would have meant a loss of power to the viceroyalty of New Spain, and by the adoption of such a suggestion there would be created a powerful tribunal which would seriously inconvenience the authority and supremacy of the audiencia and the archbishop at Manila (*Consulta* of the Council of the Indies, March 15, 1659, A. I., 67–6–22).

[59] Cited already in various connections, particularly in Chapters II and X of this treatise.

[60] In the Philippines, archbishops were frequently able to combine the functions and offices of metropolitan prelate and commissary of the Inquisition. This gave greater pre-eminence to the archbishop and made the situation more difficult for the civil authorities. We have already noted an illustration of this in the case of Archbishop Pardo (1683–1689). Being also commissary of the Inquisition, he refused to grant absolution to ex-Governor Vargas, claiming that his authority as sole inquisitor was not sufficient to justify such action on his part without first receiving advice from the tribunal in Mexico.

[61] Lea, in his well-known work on *The inquisition in the Spanish*

The various sacerdotal historians of the Philippines, in treating of the Salcedo affair, agree that the failure of the audiencia to do its duty in checking the so-called excesses of the governor led the prelate and the ecclesiastical dignitaries of the colony to turn to the Inquisition for relief.[62] Among the acts of treason

dependencies says that "while this branch of the Inquisition (referring to that in the Philippines) accomplished so little for the faith, it was eminently successful in the function of contributing to the disorder and confusion which so disastrously affected Spanish colonial administration" (p. 308). For a more detailed account of this episode see Cunningham, "The inquisition in the Philippines: the Salcedo affair," in *The Catholic historical review*, III, 417–445.

[62] The leading church historians of the Philippines—Martínez de Zúñiga, Salazar, Fonseca and Concepción—were naturally unfavorable to Salcedo in their accounts of the events of his administration. All agree, however, that Salcedo was a man of energy and precision, who, at the beginning of his rule, gave promise of universal satisfaction. The correspondence of the civil officials who were contemporaneous with the governor, and the letters of Salcedo himself show that his chief concern was the enforcement of the laws and the elimination of the ecclesiastical and commercial graft with which the administration of the government of the Philippines was permeated on his arrival in the Islands (Letters of Coloma, Bónifaz, Montemayor, León, and the Municipal Cabildo, 1670–1, A. I., 67–6–3; see also note to Ventura del Arco Mss., in Blair and Robertson, XXXVII, 262).

Zúñiga, however, states that Salcedo's commercial reforms were only intended for the benefit of himself and his friends, and that he reserved the chief articles of trade for himself, leaving only second-rate and spoiled goods for the merchants. This same historian states that the governor arranged for the early departure of the galleon on one occasion, with his goods on board, leaving those of the majority of the merchants unshipped (Martínez de Zúñiga, *An historical view*, I, 307–308). Fonseca charges him with avarice, maintaining that all classes of society in Manila were disgusted with the governor's commercial transactions and were shocked at his exile of the archbishop. This historian relates that "the magistracy, the army, the merchants, arts and industries, . . . all raised their voices against the badly directed government of Salcedo, determining to over-turn him; representative citizens of Manila petitioned the audiencia, asking that it deprive him of the government, . . . and the royal *acuerdo* determined to do so, but at the last moment the judges disagreed over the question of whose signature should precede the others; this question remained in litigation, and blocked the action of the royal *acuerdo*" (Fonseca, *Historia de la provincia de santissimo Rosario*, Libro V, Capítulo VIII, quoted in *Sobre una reseña histórica*, 92). Concepción, the Augustinian historian, confirms the above, and gives a more clarifying reason for the failure of the audiencia to oust the governor—namely, that the latter was sharing his commercial profits with the magistrates, thereby purchasing their favors; the *oidores* were therefore reluctant to take action against the governor (Concepción, *Historia general*, VII, 137–138, 162–200).

and heresy of which Governor Salcedo was said to have been
guilty, the most conspicuous were his negotiations with the Dutch
at Batavia for the conquest by them of the city of Manila.[63] This
was the leading pretext for his arrest. We have already mentioned in a former chapter that the conduct of the *oidores* was
not above reproach on this occasion. Immediately after the removal of the governor, a dispute arose between magistrates
Coloma and Montemayor for the control of affairs, only to be
settled by the usurpation of the government by the ecclesiastical
candidate, Bónifaz. With Salcedo out of the way and the audiencia intimidated and powerless, the Inquisition and the ecclesiastics ruled with a high hand for a period of three years, until
the arrival of the new governor, Manuel de León, in 1671.[64]

---

[63] Salcedo was charged with plotting to sell the Islands to the Dutch
and with surrounding himself with Flemings, one of whom was a
Calvinist. It was alleged that he had already sent large sums of money
to Macao, including a large part of the funds in the Manila treasury,
and.that he was preparing to depart in person. It was said moreover
that he intended to return in command of a Dutch squadron and capture the colony for Holland. It is evident that there was no lack of
charges against Salcedo (The original correspondence and *consultas* of
the various tribunals which considered the charges against Salcedo may
be noted in A. I., 67–6–3. See Blair and Robertson, XXXVII, 37–60,
Lea, *The inquisition in the Spanish dependencies*, 299–318, and the
ecclesiastical authorities mentioned in the preceding note).

Dr. Pardo de Tavera, in his account of the arrest of Governor Salcedo, says that "in 1668, Governor Salcedo had some difference with
(the friars) . . . and the archbishop and as a result, the latter decided
to avenge themselves, plotting with the military officials, *regidores* and
merchants to bring him before the Inquisition. They made a conspiracy and, one night while the governor slept, the conspirators,
among whom were the provincial of the Franciscans, the *guardián* of
the convent of that order in Manila, and various other ecclesiastics,
entered his room, surprising him while he slept, and placed him in
irons. He was thus taken to the convent of the Franciscans, but considering the latter insecure, they carried him to that of San Augustín,
loading him with a heavy chain" (Pardo de Tavera, *Reseña Histórica*,
37). After a period of imprisonment in Manila, Salcedo was ordered
to Mexico for trial by the tribunal of the Inquisition, as the local
authority was without authority to take further action in the matter.
Salcedo never reached his destination, however, as he died at sea.
This was subsequently the fate of Paternina, the inquisitor who was
responsible for his disgrace.

[64] That Governor León had a trying position to fill may be believed
by his description of affairs as he found them in Manila, and of his

The audiencia, after it had been reconstructed by Governor León, gave some account to the king of the excesses of "Fray Joseph de Paternina, religious of the order of San Agustín, and commissary of the Holy Inquisition, who has been so vain and haughty since the imprisonment of Governor Salcedo, a thing very unfortunate for these Islands."[65] The most harmful result of the affair, in the estimation of the audiencia, was the growing feeling on the part of the people of the Philippines "that the Inquisition (was) the most powerful agency there, and that every person in the colony was subject to it." The effrontery of the commissary was said to have gone so far on one occasion that he entered the *acuerdo* session of the audiencia and violently interfered with its proceedings, forcibly arresting and carrying away persons attendant thereupon. This defiant and insolent act was the greatest offense that could be offered to the royal authority, and the audiencia felt that if a continuance of these excesses were tolerated the royal tribunal would be despised and held at naught by the very citizens who should regard it with the most veneration.

A list of the acts of aggression on the part of the commissary was submitted by the audiencia at this time. He had commuted a sentence pronounced by the tribunal and had excused various fines imposed by the tribunal, declaring publicly that it was not necessary to obey the acts of this body of lawyers. He had excommunicated all the magistrates of the audiencia,

---

struggles to restore the royal authority to its proper status. He gave a full account of "the excessive presumption of the commissary of the Inquisition in the arrest of Don Diego Salcedo, my (his) predecessor, and his interference in matters wherein he had no real jurisdiction." León reported having prevailed upon the royal audiencia to order the commissary to refrain from meddling in affairs which did not concern the Inquisition. The ways of the Inquisition he described as "dark and secret;" it was "a danger and a fearful power," a "monster, feared by all," working, not in the light of day, but insidiously, constituting a sinister power whose strength was not fully realized (León to Council, June 10, 1671, and July 4, 1672; *Consulta* of the Council of the Indies, July 16, 1674, A. I., 67–6–3).

[65] Audiencia to the King, June 15, 1671, A. I., 67–6–10.

who remained for a long period without recourse and without the privileges of religious communion. He had interfered on behalf of an *encomendero* who was on trial before the audiencia. He had produced such a state of affairs that the impotence of the civil government was a subject of common jest, even in the mouths of the natives. The supporters of the government had been reduced to a panic of fear, not knowing where the wrath of the Inquisition would fall next. The commissary, on the other hand, had fortified himself with claims of immunity and had acted in defiance of royal and ecclesiastical law by erecting a tribunal of which he was the head, notwithstanding the fact that such an institution was forbidden in the Philippines. The audiencia presented this picture of affairs in its memorial, admitting its incapacity to cope with this powerful institution, whose acts were prepared and executed in secrecy. The evil situation for which he was responsible could only be repaired by an appeal to Mexico. Meanwhile the government and people in the Philippines were compelled to suffer the consequences of his assumption of authority.

There was no tribunal or any other agency in the Philippines able to place an effective check on the triumphant inquisitor. The only relief that could come was furnished on June 4, 1671, in the appointment of a new commissary, who was ordered to arrest Paternina and send him back to New Spain. This timely relief emanated from the tribunal of the Inquisition of Mexico, which by this act manifested its disapproval of all that had been done by its ambitious agent. On August 12, 1672, the Council of the Indies also disapproved of Paternina's acts in connection with the establishment of a Philippine tribunal.[66] The new commissary did nothing toward the continuance of the tribunal which his predecessor had established illegally.

---

[66] *Consulta* of the Council, August 12, 1672, A. I., 67–6–10.

With these manifestations of the royal support, the audiencia, which had been reconstituted on the arrival of Governor León, regained its authority and proceeded ably to second the executive in his struggle with the powerful ecclesiastical organization. The new commissary, who had lost his papers in a shipwreck, appealed to the tribunal for recognition and support in a struggle which he had undertaken against the Franciscans. Through the aid given him by the audiencia, he imprisoned the provincial and definitor of that order. Then the audiencia reconsidered its decision and effected the liberation of the two prisoners on the ground that the title of the commissary did not authorize him to act at this time.[67] In interfering with and actually cancelling the acts of the commissary, the audiencia was exceeding its authority, for the laws prescribed that his decisions could be reversed only by his immediate superior, the tribunal of Mexico. However, the audiencia maintained that it was acting in accordance with the law which authorized it to receive and recognize inquisitors. On this occasion it was merely deciding that the commissary was acting without proper authority since his credentials had never arrived.[68] At this time, the moral standing of the Philippine agent of the Inquisition was at a very low ebb, both in Manila and Madrid, which, of course, influenced the decision of the audiencia.

The Salcedo affair and the succeeding events make it clear that neither the authority of the audiencia nor of the Inquisition was unlimited. The fear and respect with which the latter institution was regarded contributed to its momentary triumph. The audiencia did not interfere with or seek to restrain the acts of the commissary; indeed, the tribunal connived at the exile of the vicepatron since the *oidores* expected to profit from the act. During these three years the Inquisition allied itself

---

67 Montero y Vidal, I, 356.
68 *Acuerdo* of August 24, 1672, A. I., 67–6–10.

practically to every interest in the colony which had been opposed to the governor. The royal interests were for a time forgotten and wholly unchampioned, owing to the weakness of the audiencia, the removal of the governor, and the united front presented by the ecclesiastical element. This condition was altered by the arrival of a new governor who bore evidence of the disapprobation of the superior government. The tribunal of Mexico discountenanced the acts of its former representative, and that disapproval was further emphasized by .the adverse attitude of the Council of the Indies. The audiencia was restored to its proper position, and, in conjunction with the vicepatron, it resumed its status as the agent of the royal will. So it may be asserted that the supremacy of both authorities was relative, recognition depending partially on local circumstances and ultimately on the attitude of the superior government. In fact, it may be said that the latter was the deciding factor. In the struggle itself, before the decision of the home authorities was rendered, the preponderance of power was enjoyed by the Inquisition. This was owing to the advantages which law and precedent had given to it as a privileged ecclesiastical tribunal, although the efficacy of the Inquisition lay for the most part in the immunities which were extended to it and in its swift, unexpected and secret methods. Its ultimate defeat on this occasion, and the continued abuse of its power, did much to detract from its prestige and authority in the Philippines.[69]

---

[69] While the Salcedo affair accurately depicts the power which the Inquisition assumed on a particular occasion, the episode cannot be said to illustrate its power and influence throughout the history of the Islands. Indeed, never on any former or subsequent occasion did the Inquisition constitute such a menace to the state. It was generally prevented from exercising too much power in the Philippines by its own isolation. Represented by a single agent, who was not always on good terms with the other ecclesiastical authorities there, and who was thousands of miles from his immediate superior, the tribunal of Mexico, he was confronted and opposed by the combined civil, secular and monastic powers. Owing to these circumstances, the commissary of the Inquisition in the Philippines could not, single-handed and unaided, constitute a long-continued danger to the commonwealth.

During the eighteenth century considerable authority over the Inquisition was given to the civil courts. The former position of supremacy, wherein its authority could not be so much as questioned by a secular tribunal, was gone forever.. On August 2, 1748, a decree was promulgated whereby chanceries, audiencias, and *corregidores* were authorized to restrain any inquisitorial tribunal from maltreating its own prisoners.[70] This same law provided for the punishment by the civil courts of inquisitors who contravened this law. This was the first regulation which really gave to the audiencia the power necessary to restrain the acts of the Inquisition. We find no indication of any such liberal legislation in the sixteenth and seventeenth centuries, but by the time this law was promulgated, the power of the church in Spain was considerably reduced and that of the Inquisition was already on the decline. By a number of subsequent laws the Inquisition was gradually but surely limited in power and authority. We have already noted that on August 10, 1788, jurisdiction over the crime of polygamy and over cases involving the infraction of the marriage relation was taken from the Inquisition and given to the civil courts.[71] By the *cédula* of December 12, 1807, authority was given to the royal justices to receive inquisitors, inspect their titles and to assign them to their districts, assisting them in all possible ways. The civil authorities were ordered to guard against an excessive number of these functionaries. The magistrates were especially instructed to act as guardians of the royal prerogative in dealing with the representative of the Inquisition and to report to the superior government on their relations with them. By this *cédula* the authority of the inquisitorial agents was distinctly limited to matters of faith, with appeal to the tribunal of the Inquisition. The magistrates

---

70 *Reales resoluciones no recopiladas*, Pérez y López, *Teatro*, XXVIII, 207.
71 *Recopilación*, 1–19, note 2.

were ordered to see that these instructions were followed.[72] In this way the civil authorities, and particularly the magistrates of the audiencias, became the guardians of the royal prerogative against the agents of the Inquisition, who were kept within the proper bounds of a purely religious jurisdiction.

It would be desirable, did time and space allow it, to illustrate further the jurisdiction of the audiencia over ecclesiastical affairs by showing in detail the part which the tribunal played in the friar lands litigation[73] and in the disputes over ecclesiastical visitation in the seventeenth and eighteenth centuries in the Philippines. It will be sufficient here to state that the government sought at irregular intervals and with varying

---

[72] *Ibid.*, note 1. This tendency culminated in the decree of February 22, 1813, which suppressed the Supreme Tribunal of the Inquisition and renewed the jurisdiction of bishops and vicars over cases involving the faith, as had been the practice before the Inquisition was instituted. All property belonging to the Inquisition reverted to the crown. Soon after the restoration of Ferdinand VII the Inquisition was revived, against the will of that monarch, it is said, but it was again abolished by the decrees of March 9, 1820, and July 1 1835.

As a result of the suppression of the Tribunal of the Inquisition on March 9, 1820, and the transfer of its authority over matters of faith to the vicars and bishops, Escriche says that "in the exercise of their jurisdiction some of these prelates exceeded their authority and established in their respective dioceses *juntas de fé*, which turned out to be in reality inquisitorial tribunals with practically the same authority which former tribunals had exercised. They inflicted corporal and spiritual punishments and guarded in their ministry the most inviolable secrecy." As soon as reports of this unexpected assumption of authority came to the notice of the government, Ferdinand hastened to order the suppression of these self-constituted tribunals, without immediate success, however. Escriche tells us that they continued their excesses for some time, "depriving accused persons of the means of defense, keeping from them the names of persons testifying against them," flagrantly disregarding the dispositions of the brief of Pius VII, dated October 5, 1829, in prohibition of exactly these abuses. On February 6, 1830, a *cédula* was expedited which authorized appeals in cases of this nature until three conforming decisions were rendered. The decree of July 1, 1835, abolished these tribunals, ordering the prelates to exercise jurisdiction with appeal to the Department of Grace and Justice (Escriche, *Diccionario*, I, 773).

[73] The author has treated this subject in a separate monograph entitled "The origin of the friar lands question in the Philippines," in *The American political science review*, X, 463–480.

degrees of success, to make the orders prove titles to lands
in the same manner that was required of other corporations and
individuals.[74] The audiencia, as a tribunal, and the individual
magistrates as special commissioners, participated judicially in
the examination of these titles and in the correction of the
abuses which were discovered. The *oidores,* when serving as
special magistrates for the verification of these titles, officiated
in a double capacity. By the very nature of the services
rendered they were judges. They were also agents of the royal
patron and as such they represented the person of the king,
ascertaining whether the royal rights had been usurped or
infringed upon.

Closely similar to the jurisdiction of the audiencia as a
court of final resort in the testing of the titles to lands occupied by religious orders was that which it exercised in the
matter of ecclesiastical visitation. This was a question of a
more thoroughly religious character which did not concern the
civil government as intimately as did the matter of friar lands.
In general, it may be said that the audiencia was utilized by
both sides in the various disputes which arose in connection
with ecclesiastical visitation. During the ecclesiastical administrations of Archbishops Salazar, Serrano, Poblete, Camacho,
Pardo and Justa y Rufina, practically until the end of the
eighteenth century, this question was continually agitated.
These archbishops attempted to visit and inspect the curacies

---

[74] The friar lands litigation began in 1687 and continued until 1751.
The efforts of the government met with considerable opposition. The
oidores who were charged with the inspection of the titles to these
lands frequently abandoned their commissions and recommended that
the friars be left alone. However, in the year last mentioned, the
opposition of the Franciscans, the last of the resisting orders, was
overcome (Correspondence regarding friar lands exists in A. I., 68–4–12
and 68–6–26). See also the Camacho Controversy, Blair and Robertson,
XLII, 25–116; Montero y Vidal, *Historia general,* I, 385, *et seq.;* Concepción, *Historia general,* VIII, 192–206; *Philippine Census,* I, 342–
343· *Sobre una reseña histórica* by the Dominicans of Manila, 65–89).

which were held by friars in lieu of secular priests.[75]   The archbishops relied on the audiencia for assistance in the enforcement of their claims and the friars sought its protection as a court of justice to shield them from the visitation of the prelate.   As in the matter of the friar lands, so in this question, the audiencia acted both as a tribunal of justice and as an agent and champion of the royal patronage.   Indeed, the laws of the Indies established the audiencia as a tribunal and as a compelling authority for the enforcement of ecclesiastical visitation.[76]   The archbishop was directed to appeal to the audiencia or vicepatron for assistance in the subjection of offending curates,[77] but he was forbidden to visit the regulars in their convents,[78] which, of course, did not prevent his visiting them when in charge of curacies.   On the other hand, the audiencia was forbidden to entertain appeals on the ground of *fuerza* from regulars who objected to the visitation of the prelates.[79]

Local conditions in the Philippines did much toward determining the character of the support rendered by the audiencia both to the archbishops and to the friars.   During the later months of the Pardo controversy, when the audiencia had been demoralized by the triumph of the archbishop and the visitor, Valdivia, the decision of the tribunal had but little weight and the prelate did as he wished in regard to the matter of visitation.   In Camacho's time, when the friars were on

---

[75] "In America [and in the Philippines] the monks were given a somewhat unusual position.   According to the canon law they were not able to hold beneficed curacies, but the extent of the American field, and the limited number of the clergy available to occupy it, induced Leo X, Adrian VI, Paul III, Clement VIII, and Pius V to permit them to become parish priests.   Under this order a very large number of these parishes in America in the first century were occupied by friars.   But in the middle of the eighteenth century, this privilege was withdrawn, leaving them only two friars in a conventual province" (Moses, *South America on the eve of emancipation*, 138-139).

[76] See Cunningham, "The question of ecclesiastical visitation in the Philippines," in *The Pacific Ocean in history*, 223-237.

[77] *Recopilación*, 1-15-28.

[78] *Ibid.*, 29.

[79] *Ibid.*, 31.

the point of leaving the Islands rather than submit to visitation, the audiencia and the governor wisely counseled moderation and completely abandoned the obstinate prelate. During Anda's term of office the question was again taken up, but the effort to enforce the principle was abandoned because the government could not find seculars, either Spanish or native, to take the place of the friars who threatened to leave the Islands if visitation were insisted upon. The magistrates likewise rendered invaluable service in imparting legal advice to the vicepatron, friars and others interested. They also kept the court informed as to what was actually transpiring in the colony. It may be seen, therefore, that the audiencia participated in two important ways in the enforcement of episcopal visitation. It was primarily a court; it acted as agent of the royal patron. In these capacities the influence of the tribunal was greatest. It also exercised functions of an advisory character in aiding the authorities concerned to ascertain their rights according to the existing law.[80]

In summarizing the results of the investigation with which this chapter has been concerned, it may be said that the audiencia constituted a court of appeal in ecclesiastical cases wherein the services of an impartial, non-ecclesiastical tribunal were required, or wherein the defense of the royal jurisdiction against the aggression of the churchmen was involved. In defending the civil government from ecclesiastical usurpation the audiencia acted in defense of the royal patronage. Nevertheless, in the cases noted, namely, in settling disputes between orders, between the secular church and the orders, between either of these and the civil government, in entertaining

---

[80] Valuable materials, for the most part original, on the visitation controversy may be found in Blair and Robertson, XXIV, 247; XXIX, 191; XLII, 25–116; XX, 87; XXI, 32–78; XXXVII, 193–200. See also A. I., 69–1–29, 68–4–16, 106–4–21, 105–2–9, 106–4–31. Montero y Vidal (*Historia general*, I, 86–87, 295, 398; II, 134–138, 257 *et seq.*) presents a good secondary account of the subject.

recursos de fuerza, in restraining the interdict, and the abuses of the Inquisition, the audiencia acted by judicial process as a tribunal of justice, and not in the capacity of an administrative committee or an executive agent, as in the cases which have been heretofore described.

BIBLIOGRAPHY

LIST OF PRINTED WORKS CITED

ALCEDO, ANTONIO DE
Diccionario geográfico-histórico de las Indias Occidentales ó América. 5 vols. Madrid, 1786–1789.

ALTAMIRA Y CREVEA, RAFAEL
Historia de España y de la civilización española. 3d ed, 4 vols. Barcelona, 1913.

ÁLVAREZ DE ABREU, ANTONIO
Extracto historial. Madrid, 1736.

ANTEQUERA, JOSÉ MARÍA
Historia de la legislación española, desde los tiempos más remotos hasta nuestros dias. 2d ed., Madrid, 1884.

ARTIGAS, MANUEL
El servicio de aduanas en Filipinas. Madrid, 1895.

BANCROFT, HUBERT HOWE
History of Central America. 3 vols. San Francisco, 1882–1887.
History of Mexico. 6 vols. San Francisco, 1883–1888.

BARROWS, DAVID P.
A history of the Philippines. Indianapolis, 1905.
"The governor-general of the Philippines under Spain and the United States," in The Pacific Ocean in history (Stephens and Bolton, editors), 238–265. New York, 1917.

BELEÑA, EUSEBIO BENTURA
Recopilación sumaria de todos los autos acordados de la real audiencia y sala del crimen de esta Nueva España. 2 vols. Mexico, 1787.

BLACKMAR, FRANK W.
Spanish institutions of the Southwest. Baltimore, 1891.

BLAIR, EMMA HELEN, AND ROBERTSON, JAMES ALEXANDER (editors)
The Philippine Islands, 1493–1898. 55 vols. Cleveland, 1903–1909.

BLUMENTRITT, FERDINAND
Consideraciones acerca de la actual situación política de Filipinas. Barcelona, 1889.

BOLTON, HERBERT EUGENE
Guide to materials for the history of the United States in the principal archives of Mexico. Washington, 1913.
Texas in the middle eighteenth century; studies in Spanish colonial history and administration. Berkeley, 1915.

BOURNE, EDWARD GAYLORD
  Discovery, conquest, and early history of the Philippines. Cleveland, 1907.
  Spain in America, 1450–1580. New York, 1906.
  "The Philippine 'situado' from the treasury of New Spain," in *The American historical review*, X, 459–461.

BUZETA, MANUEL, and BRAVE, FELIPE
  Diccionario geográfico, estadístico, histórico de las islas Filipinas. 2 vols. Madrid, 1850–1851.

CÁNOVAS DEL CASTILLO, MÁXIMO
  Noticias históricas, geográficas, estadísticas, administrativas y militares de las islas Filipinas. Madrid, 1859.

CASTRO, AGUSTÍN MARIÁ DE
  Reseña sobre la guerra de los Ingleses. Manila, 1765.

CAVADA Y MÉNDEZ DE VIGO, AGUSTÍN DE LA
  Historia, geografía, geología y estadística de Filipinas. 2 vols. Manila, 1876.

CHAPMAN, CHARLES E.
  The founding of Spanish California; the northwestward expansion of New Spain, 1687–1783. New York, 1916.

CHIRINO, PEDRO
  Relación de las islas Filipinas í de lo qve en ellas an trabajado los padres de la Compañia de Iesus. Rome, 1604.

Colección de Autos acordados de la real audiencia [y] chancillería de Filipinas. 5 vols. Manila, 1861–1866.

Colección de documentos inéditos para la historia de España. 113 vols. Madrid, 1842–1912.

Colección de documentos inéditos relativos al descubrimiento, conquista y colonización de las posesiones españolas en América y Oceanía, sacados, en su mayor parte, del Real Archivo de Indias. 42 vols. Madrid, 1864–1886.

Colección de documentos inéditos relativos al descubrimiento, conquista y crganización de las antiguas posesiones españolas de ultramar. Segunda serie. 13 vols. Madrid, 1886–1887.

Colección de las leyes, decretos, y declaraciones de las cortes y los reales decretos, órdenes, etc., desde 1837 hasta Diciembre, 1845. 13 vols. Madrid, 1845. Continued from 1846 as the *Colección legislativa de España.*

Colección del real decreto de 27 de Febrero de 1767 para la ejecución del extrañamiento de los regulares de la Compañia. Madrid, 1767

Colección legislativa de España. 180 vols. Madrid, 1810–1898.

COLÍN, FRANCISCO
Labor evangélica, ministérios apostólicos de los obreros de la Compañía de Iesus, fundación y progresos de su provincia en las islas Filipinas. Nueva edición . . . por el P. Pablo Pastels. Barcelona, 1900–1902. [First ed. Madrid, 1663.]

CÓMYN, TOMÁS DE
Estado de las islas Filipinas. Madrid, 1820.

CONCEPCIÓN, JUAN DE LA
Historia general de Philipinas. 14 vols. Manila, 1788–1792.

COROLÉU É INGLADA, JOSÉ
América, historia de su colonización, dominación é independencia. 4 vols. Barcelona, 1896.

CRAIG, AUSTIN
The former Philippines through foreign eyes. Manila, 1916.

CRAIG, AUSTIN, AND BENÍTEZ, CONRADO
Philippine progress prior to 1898. Manila, 1916.

CRÉTINEAU–JOLY, JACQUES
Clemente XIV y los Jesuitas, ó sea la historia de la destrucción de los Jesuitas. Madrid, 1848.
Histoire religieuse politique et littéraire de la Compagnie de Jésus. 5 vols. Paris, 1859.

CUNNINGHAM, CHARLES HENRY
"Origin of the friar lands question in the Philippines," in *The American political science review,* X, 463–480.
"The ecclesiastical influence in the Philippines," in *The American journal of theology,* XXII, 161–186.
"The inquisition in the Philippines," in *The Catholic historical review,* III, 417–445.
"The institutional background of Spanish-American history," in *The Hispanic American review,* I, 24–39.
"The question of ecclesiastical visitation in the Philippines," in *The Pacific Ocean in history* (Stephens and Bolton, editors), 223–237. New York, 1917.
"The residencia in the Spanish colonies," in *The Southwestern historical quarterly,* XXI, 253–278.

DANVILA Y COLLADO, MANUEL
El poder civil en España. 6 vols. Madrid, 1885–1886.
Historia del reinado de Carlos III. 6 vols. Madrid, 1893.
Significación que tuvieron en el gobierno de América la casa de contratación de Sevilla y el consejo supremo de Indias. Madrid, 1892.

448   *Bibliography*

Decretos creando y organizando el cuerpo de administración civil de Filipinas. Madrid, 1870.

Decretos de la Reina Doña Isabel II, . . . desde 1834 hasta Diciembre de 1836. 2 vols. Madrid, 1835–1837.

Decretos del rey Don Fernando VII . . . desde el 4 de Mayo de 1814, hasta fin de Diciembre de 1831 . . . y . . . desde 1832, hasta fin de Diciembre de 1833. 18 vols. Madrid, 1818–1834.

DELGADO, JUAN
> *Historia general sacro-profana, política y natural de las islas del Poniente, llamadas Filipinas.* Manila, 1892.

DESDEVISES DU DEZERT, GASTÓN
> *L'Espagne de l'ancien règime.* 3 vols. 1897–1904.
> "Vice-rois et capitaines gènèraux des Indes espagnoles a la fin du XVIII e siècle," in the *Revue historique,* CXXV, 223–264; CXXVI, 14–60, 225–270.

DÍAZ, CASIMIRO
> *Conquistas de las islas Filipinas.* Valladolid, 1890 [First ed. 1718.]

ELLIOTT, CHARLES BURKE
> *The Philippines; to the end of the military regime; to the end of the commission government.* 2 vols. Indianapolis, 1916, 1917.

ESCRICHE, JOAQUÍN
> *Diccionario razonado de legislación y jurisprudencia.* 3d ed., 2 vols. Madrid, 1847.
> *Estadística de las causas criminales, negocios civiles y expedientes de gobierno despachados por la audiencia de Manila durante el año de 1876.* Manila, 1877.
> *Estadística general de los negocios terminados y pendientes de despacho en la real audiencia de Filipinas en fin de año de 1867.* Manila, 1869.
> *Estadística judicial de negocios despachados por la real audiencia de Cebú en 1886.* Cebú, 1887.
> *Suplemento al diccionario razonado de legislación y jurisprudencia.* Madrid and Santiago, 1851.

FABIE, ANTONIO MARÍA
> *Ensayo histórico de la legislación española.* Madrid, 1896.

FERNÁNDEZ MARTÍN, MANUEL DE
> *Compilación legislativa del gobierno y administracion civil en ultramar.* 15 vols. Madrid, 1888–1898.

FERRANDO, JUAN
> *Historia de dos PP. Dominicos en las islas Filipinas.* Madrid, 1870–1872.

FONSECA, FABIÁN, AND URRUTIA, CARLOS DE
Historia general de la real hacienda. 6 vols. Mexico, 1845–1853.

FORD, WORTHINGTON CHAUNCEY
"Public records in our dependencies," in American Historical Association, *Annual report, 1904,* 131–147. Washington, 1905.

FOREMAN, JOHN
The Philippine Islands. London, 1906.

GACETA DE MANILA, LA
Publicación oficial, diaria, en la que aparecían todos los decretos, reales órdenes y demás disposiciones dictadas por las autoridades en las cuestiones de gobierno, fomento, hacienda, estado, gracia, y justicia, administración . . . *Fué creada en substitución del Boletín Oficial por real orden de 18 de Mayo de 1860 y publicó su último número el 12 de Agosto de 1898.* Manila, 1860–1898.

GARCIA ICAZBALCETA, JOAQUÍN
Don Fray Juan de Zumárraga. Mexico, 1881.

GÓMEZ ZAMORA, MATIAS
Regio patronato, español é indiano. Madrid, 1897.

GOVANTES, FELIPE MARÍA DE
Compendio de la historia de Filipinas. Manila, 1877.
Vida de Don Simón de Anda y Salazar. Manila, 1862.

GRAU Y MONFALCÓN, JUAN
Memorial informatorio al rey . . . *por la* . . . *ciudad de Manila sobre las pretensiones de aquella ciudad, é islas, y sus vecinos, y moradores, y comercio con la Nueva España.* Madrid, 1637.
Justificación de la conservación, y comercio de las islas Filipinas. Madrid, 1640.

GRIFFIN, GEORGE BUTLER
"A brief bibliographical sketch of the Recopilación de Indias," in Historical Society of Southern California, *Publications, 1887.* San Francisco, 1888.

HACKETT, CHARLES WILSON
"Delimitation of political jurisdictions in Spanish North America to 1535," in *The Hispanic American historical review,* I, 40–69.

HARTZENBUSCH, EUGENIO
Apuntes para un catálogo de periódicos Madrileños. Madrid, 1894.

HELPS, ARTHUR
The Spanish conquest in America. 4 vols. New York, 1900–1904. M. Oppenheim, ed. [First ed., London, 1855–61.]

HERNÁEZ, FRANCISCO JAVIER
  *Colección de bulas, breves y otros documentos relativos á la Iglc-
  sia de América y Filipinas.* 2 vols. Bruselas, 1879.
  *Histoire de la persecution de deux saints evêques par les Jesuites, . . .
  l'un Dom Bernardin de Cardenas, evêque du Paraguay dans l'Amer-
  ique meridionale, l'autre Dom Philippe Pardo, archêveque de
  l'Eglise de Manila, metropolitaine des isles Philippines dans les
  Indies Orientales.* Manila, 1691.

HUMBOLDT, ALEXANDER VON
  Political essay on the kingdom of New Spain. 4 vols. London,
  1811.
  Instrucción que los virreyes de Nueva España dejaron á sus sucesores.
  2 vols. Mexico, 1873.

JAGOR, FEODOR
  Viages por Filipinas traducidas del alemán por S. Vidal y Solar.
  Madrid, 1875.

JUAN DE LA CONCEPCIÓN
  See Concepción.

LAFUENTE, MODESTO
  Historia general de España. 25 vols. Barcelona, 1889–1890.

LANNOY, CHARLES DE
  L'expansion coloniale du Portugal jusqu' au début du XIXe siècle,
  in Lannoy and Vander Linden, *Histoire de l'expansion coloniale
  des peuples européens: Portugal et Espagne.* Bruxelles, Paris,
  1907.

LA PÉROUSE, JEAN FRANCOIS DE GALAUP
  Voyage de La Pérouse autour du monde. Paris, 1797.

LEA, HENRY CHARLES
  A history of the inquisition in Spain. 4 vols. New York, 1906–
  1907.
  The inquisition in the Spanish dependencies. New York, 1908.

LEGENTIL DE LA GALAISIÈRE, GUILLAUME JOSEPH HYACINTHE JEAN
  BAPTISTE
  *Voyage dans les mers de l'Inde, fait par ordre du roi, à l'occasion du
  passage de Vénus, sur le disque de soleil, le 6 juin 1761, & le 3
  du même mois 1769.* 2 vols. Paris, 1779–1781.

LEROY, JAMES A.
  The Americans in the Philippines. 2 vols. Boston and New York,
  1914.
  "The Philippine 'situado' from the treasury of New Spain," in
  The American historical review, X, 929–932; XI, 722–723.

Review: Blair and Robertson (editors), *The Philippine Islands, 1493–1898*, in *The American historical review*, XI, 681–687; XII, 143–145; 912–915.

LEROY-BEAULIEU, PAUL
De la colonization chez les peuples modernes. 2 vols. Paris, 1902.

LOWERY, WOODBURY
The Spanish settlements within the present limits of the United States, 1513–1561. New York, 1901.

MALCOLM, GEORGE A.
The government of the Philippine Islands, its development and fundamentals. Rochester, 1916.

MALLAT DE BASSILAU, JEAN
Les Philippines; histoire, géographie, moeurs, agriculture, industrie et commerce des colonies espagnoles dans l'Oceanie. 2 vols. Paris, 1846.

MARICHALAR, A., and MANRIQUE, CAYETANO
Historia de la legislación y recitaciones del derecho civil de España. 9 vols. Madrid, 1861–1872.

MARTÍNEZ ALCUBILLA, MARCELO
Diccionario de la administracion española, peninsular y ultramarina. 12 vols. Madrid, 1868.

MARTÍNEZ DE ZÚÑIGA, JOAQUÍN
An historical view of the Philippine Islands: exhibiting their discovery, population, language, government, manners, customs, productions and commerce. Translated by John Mayer. London, 1814.
Estadismo de las islas Filipinas, ó mis viajes por este país. . . . . *Publica esta obra por primera vez extensamente anotada W. E. Retana.* 2 vols. Madrid, 1893.
Historia de las islas Filipinas. 2 vols. Sampaloc, 1803.

MAS, SINIBALDO DE
Informe sobre el estado de las islas Filipinas en 1842. Madrid, 1843.

MAURTUA, VICTOR N.
Antecedentes de la Recopilación de Indias. Madrid, 1906.

MEDINA, JOSÈ TORIBIO
Bibliografía española de las islas Filipinas (1523–1810). Santiago de Chile, 1897–1898.
Historia del tribunal del Santo Oficio de la inquisición en Chile. 2 vols. Santiago de Chile, 1890.

MENDÍZABAL, FRANCISCO
Investigaciones acerca del origen, historia y organización de la real chancillería de Valladolid, su jurisdicción y competencia, in *Revista de archivos, bibliotecas y museos,* tercera época, XXX, (1914), 62–72; 243–264, 437–452. Madrid, 1914.

MENDIETA, GERÓNIMO DE
Historia eclesiástica Indiana. Mexico, 1870.

MONTEMAYOR Y CÓRDOBA, JUAN FRANCISCO
Sumarios de las cédulas, ordenes y provisiones reales . . . para la Nueva España y otras partes. Mexico, 1678.

MONTERO Y VIDAL, JOSÉ
El archipiélago Filipino y las islas Marianas, Carolinas, y Palaos; su historia, geografía y estadística. Madrid, 1886.
Historia general de Filipinas desde el descubrimiento de dichas islas hasta nuestros dias. 3 vols. Madrid, 1887–1895.

MORGA, ANTONIO DE
Sucesos de las islas Filipinas. Obra publicada en Méjico el año de 1609, nuevamente sacada á luz y anotada por José Rizal. Paris, 1890. [First ed., Mexico, 1609. English translation by Henry Stanley, London, 1868.]

MOSES, BERNARD
South America on the eve of emancipation. New York, 1908.
The establishment of Spanish rule in America. New York, 1898.
The Spanish dependencies in South America. 2 vols. London, 1914.

MURILLO VELARDE, PEDRO
Historia de la provincia de Philipinas de la Compañia de Jesus. Manila, 1749.

NAVARRETE, MARTÍN FERNÁNDEZ DE
Colección de los viages y descubrimiehtos que hicieron por mar los Españoles desde fines del siglo xv. 5 vols. Madrid, 1825–1837.

New laws of the Indies for the good treatment and preservation of the Indians (1542–1543). London, 1893.

Ordenanza general formada de orden de Su Majestad para el gobierno é instrucción de intendentes subdelegados y demás empleados de Indias. Madrid, 1803.

Ordenanzas para el régimen y gobierno de la real Audiencia de Manila con el reglamento para su secretaría, aprobadas las primeras por real decreto . . . Manila, 1868.

PARDO DE TAVERA, TRINIDAD HIPÓLITO
Biblioteca Filipina. Washington, 1903.
Reseña histórica de Filipinas desde su descubrimiento hasta 1903.
Manila, 1906.
"The judiciary of the Philippine Islands," in *Census of the Philippine Islands,* I, 389–410. Washington, 1905.
"The power of the monastic orders," in *Census of the Philippine Islands,* I, 340–346. Washington, 1905.

PARRÁS, PEDRO JOSEPH
Gobierno de los regulares de la América. 2 vols. Madrid, 1783.

PASTELS, PABLO
See Colín, Francisco.
Misión de la compañia de Jesús de Filipinas en el siglo XIX.
3 vols. Barcelona, 1917,

PÉREZ Y LÓPEZ, ANTONIO XAVIER
Teatro de la legislación de España é Indias. 28 vols. Madrid, 1791–1798.

PONS, FRANCISCO RAYMOND JOSEPH DE
A voyage to the eastern part of Tierra Firma, or the Spanish Main, in South America, during the years 1801, 1802, 1803 and 1804.
Tr. [from the French] by an American gentleman. New York, 1806. [First ed., Paris, 1806.]

PRESCOTT, WILLIAM H.
History of the conquest of Mexico. Philadelphia, 1890.

PRIESTLEY, HERBERT I.
José de Gálvez: visitor-general of New Spain, 1765–1771. Berkeley, 1916.

PUGA, VASCO DE
Provisiones, cédulas, instrucciónes de su magestad ·de esta Nueva España (1525–1563). 2 vols. Mexico, 1878–1879. [First ed., Mexico, 1563.]

Real ordenanza de 13 de Octubre para el restablicimiento é instrucción de intendentes de provincias y exércitos. Madrid, 1749.

Real ordenanza para el establicimiento é instrucción de intendentes de exército y provincia en el virreinato de Buenos Ayres. Madrid, 1782.

Real ordenanza para el establicimiento y instrucción de intendentes de exército y provincia en el reino de la Nueva España. Madrid, 1786.

Reales ordenanzas formadas por el superior gobierno y real acuerdo de estas islas en 26 de Febrero de 1768. Para el buen gobierno de los

gobernadores, corregidores y alcaldes mayores de sus provincias.
Manila, 1834.

Recopilación de leyes de los reinos de las Indias. 5th ed., 2 vols.
Madrid, 1841. [1st ed., 4 vols., Madrid, 1681; 2d ed., 4 vols., Madrid,
1754; 3d ed., 4 vols., Madrid, 1774; 4th ed., 3 vols., Madrid, 1791.]

RETANA, WENCESLÁO EMELIO
Catálogo abreviado de la biblioteca Filipina. Madrid, 1898.

RICAFORT, MARIANO
*Reglamento para establecer la comisión de policía, ordenada con
acuerdo de la real audiencia de las islas Filipinas.* Sampáloc,
1826.

ROBERTSON, JAMES ALEXANDER
Bibliography of the Philippine Islands. Cleveland, 1908.
"Catholicism in the Philippines," in *The Catholic historical review,*
III, 375–391.
"Legaspi and Philippine colonization," in American Historical Asso-
ciation, *Annual report, 1907,* I, 143–156. Washington, 1908.
"Notes on the archives of the Philippines," in American Historical
Association, *Annual report, 1910.* 423–425. Washington, 1912.
"The social structure of, and idea of law among, early Philippine
peoples; and a recently-discovered pre-hispanic criminal code of
the Philippine Islands," in *The Pacific Ocean in history* (Steph-
ens and Bolton, editors), 160–191. New York, 1917.

ROBERTSON, WILLIAM
The history of the discovery and settlement of America. New
York, 1858. [First ed., London, 1777.]

RODRÍGUEZ BÉRRIZ, MIGUEL
Diccionario de la administración de Filipinas. 17 vols. Manila,
1887.

RODRÍGUEZ SAN PEDRO, JOAQUÍN
*Legislación ultramarina, publicada con la colaboración de Chorot,
Pierre, y Gonzales Junguitú.* 16 vols. Madrid, 1865–1869.

ROSCHER, WILHELM GEORG FRIEDRICH
The Spanish colonial system. E. G. Bourne, ed. New York, 1904.

SALAZAR, DOMINGO DE
*Carta relación de las cosas de la China y de los Chinos del Parián
de Manila, enviada al rey Felipe II desde Manila el 24 de Junio
de 1590.* Madrid, 1897.

SALAZAR, VICENTE DE
Historia de la provincia de santissimo rosario de Philipinas.
Manila, 1742.

SAN AGUSTÍN, GASPAR DE
Conquistas de las islas Filipinas. Madrid, 1698.

SAN ANTONIO, JUAN FRANCISCO DE
Chrónicas de la apostólica provincia de San Gregorio de religiosos descalzos de N. S. P. S. Francisco en las islas Philipinas, China, Japón. 3 vols. Manila, 1738–1744.

SANTA CRUZ, BALTASAR DE
Tomo segundo de la historia de la provincia de Santo Rosario de Filipinas. Zaragoza, 1693.

SCHMIDT, GUSTAVUS
The civil law of Spain and Mexico. New Orleans, 1851.

SCHURZ, WILLIAM LYTLE
"The Chinese in the Philippines," in *The Pacific Ocean in history* (Stephens and Bolton, editors), 214–222. New York, 1917.
"The Manila galleon and California," in *The Southwestern historical quarterly,* XXI, 107–126.

SHEPHERD, WILLIAM R.
Guide to the materials for the history of the United States in Spanish archives. Washington, 1907.

SMITH, DONALD EUGENE
The viceroy of New Spain. Berkeley, 1913.

Sobre una reseña histórica de Filipinas. Colección de artículos que han visto la luz pública . . . en refutación de los calumniosos erores que el Doctor T. H. Pardo de Tavera ha escrito contra las beneméritas ordenes religiosas de Filipinas en su reseña histórica, impresa en Manila. Manila, 1906.

SOLÓRZANO PEREIRA, JUAN DE
Política Indiana. Madrid, 1776. [First ed., Madrid, 1647.]

Superior decreto sobre las funciones que debe llenar el Sr. Intendente de Manila tocante al tesoro agricultural é industrial del reino. Manila, 1829.

STEPHENS, H. M., AND BOLTON, H. E. (editors)
The Pacific Ocean in history. New York, 1917.

ULLOA, ANTONIO DE, and JUAN Y SANTACILLA, JORGE
Noticias secretas de América. Londres, 1826. [Abridged and translated into English, Boston, 1851.]

UNITED STATES, LIBRARY OF CONGRESS
Bibliography of the Philippine Islands: a list of books with references to periodicals on the Philippine Islands in the Library of Congress. Washington, 1903.

VANDER LINDEN, HERMAN
L'expansion coloniale de l'Espagne jusqu'au début du XIXe siècle,
in Lannoy and Vander Linden, *Histoire de l'expansion coloniale
des peuples européens: Portugal et Espagne.* Bruxelles, Paris,
1907.

VEITIA LINAJE, JOSEPH DE
Norte de la contratación de las Indias Occidentales. Seville, 1672.

VINDEL, PEDRO
*Biblioteca oriental . . . relativas á Filipinas, Japón, China y otras
partes de Asia y Oceania.* Madrid, 1911.

WORCESTER, DEAN CONANT
The Philippines, past and present. 2 vols. New York, 1914.

ZAMORA Y CORONADO, JOSÉ MARÍA
Apéndice al registro de legislación ultramarina. Havana, 1835.
*Biblioteca de legislación ultramarina en forma de diccionario alfa-
bético.* 7 vols. Madrid, 1844–1849.

ZÚÑIGA
See Martínez de Zúñiga, Joaquin.

MANUSCRIPT MATERIALS FROM THE ARCHIVE OF THE INDIES[1]

I. *Audiencia de Filipinas.*
(a) *Ramo Secular.*
1584–1700: Consultas originales correspondientes de esta Audiencia.
67–6–3.[2]

---

[1] This legajo list was obtained from the index of the collection of
manuscripts in the section known as *Audiencia de Filipinas,* of the
Archive of the Indies in Seville. The aim is only to present *legajos*
which contain material on the audiencia. A more complete list covering all the Philippine material in this depository may be found in
Blair and Robertson, LIII.

[2] The above system of reference to documents in the Archive of the
Indies is used universally, and it has been employed consistently in
this treatise. The manuscripts are wrapped and tied in bundles
(*legajos*), which, in turn, are to be found in large cases (*estantes*),
and the shelves (*cajones*) of the cases are numbered. The meaning of
the above reference therefore is *Estante 68, Cajón 6, Legajo 3,* indicating that *legajo* number 3 is to be found on Shelf 6 of Case 68 of the
Archive. A *legajo* contains in the neighborhood of 2,000 pages of
hand-written manuscript. The documents may be originals, certified
copies or ordinary drafts or duplicates. They are supposed to be
grouped according to subject-matter, and usually the materials in a
given *cajón* deal with a phase of the same question. *Legajos* in a
given *cajón* and manuscripts in a given *legajo*, roughly speaking, are

1568–1808: Registros de oficios y partes: reales ordenes dirigidas á las autoridades y particulares de la audiencia. 105–2–11 to 18. 8 legajos.

1594–1698: Decretos originales correspondientes á dicha audiencia. 67–6–4.

1600–1700: Peticiones y memoriales sueltos decretados por el Consejo. 67–6–5.

1567–1699: Cartas y expedientes del Gobr. de Filipinas vistos en el Consejo. 67–6–6 to 17. 12 legajos.

1583–1699: Cartas y expedientes del presidente y oidores de esta audiencia vistos en el Consejo. 67–6–18 to 26. 7 legajos.

1564–1699: Cartas y expedientes de los oficiales reales de Filipinas vistos en el Consejo. 67–6–29 to 33. 5 legajos.

1565–1650: Cartas y expedientes de personas seculares de dicha audiencia. 67–6–34 to 42. 9 legajos.

1629–1791: Reales cédulas, mercedes y informes sobre encomiendas. 105–2–24.

1651–1699: Cartas y expedientes de personas seculares de esta audiencia. 68–1–1 to 2. 2 legajos.

1616–1700: Confirmaciones de encomiendas de Indios. 68–1–5 to 16. 12 legajos.

1572–1691: Autos y otros papeles del Gobernador de Filipinas Don Juan de Silva contra los oficiales reales sobre use excesivo de sus oficios. 68–1–21.

1670: Expediente formado de los procedimientos de Don Francisco Samaniego Tuesta, Oidor de la Audiencia de Manila. 68–1–23.

1615–1837: Materias gubernativas. 105–3–12.

1608–1762: Cartas y expedientes del presidente y oidores de aquella audiencia. 68–4–12 to 35. 24 legajos.

1622–1825: Reales cédulas, nombramientos y informes acerca del presidente, oidores y subalternos de la audiencia. 106–2–15.

1651–1850: Duplicados de gobernadores de Filipinas. 105–4–7 to 24; 105–5–1 to 24; 105–6–1 to 24; 105–7–1 to 24; 106–1–1 to 27; 106–2–1 to 14. 111 legajos.

1670–1831. Inventario de cédulas y consultas. 105–2–5.

1671–1756: Indices de la correspondencia del gobor., auda., oficiales reales y sugetos particulares del distrito de aquella real audiencia. 68–2–30.

---

arranged chronologically, though in many cases they have lost their original order owing to careless handling. This description is sufficient to identify any document to which this classification is applied, as these numbers are not duplicated, though often the documents are, and copies of the same manuscript may be found in different *cajones*.

1675–1765: Cartas y expedientes del gobernador de Filipinas. 68–3–4 to 33 and 68–4–1 to 11. 40 legajos.

1684–1744: Expediente sobre la expulsión de los Sangleyes. 68–5–16.

1685–1688: Testimonios de autos obrados en Acapulco, Méjico y Filipinas, en razón de descubrir los bienes del gobernador de Manila, Don Juan de Vargas Hurtado y su cuñado Don Francisco Guerrero Ardila. 68–1–24.

1687–1690: Testimonios de autos sobre la rebelión, conversión y expulsión de los Sangleyes de China. 68–1–25.

1699–1760: Cartas y expedientes del Virrey de Nueva España que tratan de asuntos de Filipinas. 68–3–1 to 3. 3 legajos.

1703–1850: Duplicados del presidente y oidores de la Audiencia de Filipinas. 106–2–17 to 25; 106–3–1 to 28; 106–4–1 to 21. 58 legajos.

1711–1722: Expte. sobre la restitución de las plazas de oidores de la Audiencia de Manila á Don Gregorio Manuel de Villa y Don José Antonio Pabón; y lo resuelto contra Don José Torralba, oidor de la misma audiencia. 68–5–30 to 31. 2 legajos.

1715–1727: Expte. sobre los procedimientos del Gobr. Don Fernando Bustillo Bustamante y sobre la muerte violenta que sufrió dicho gobernador y su hijo. 68–6–1 to 5. 5 legajos.

1718–1784: Expte. sobre competencia entre el gobernador y audiencia sobre remisión a España bajo partida de registro de Don Diego Martínez de Araque, regente de la misma y otros ministros. 106–5–1 to 3. 3 legajos.

1728–1829: Remisiones al consejo, cámara y ministros. 105–3–10 to 11. 2 legajos.

1729–1748: Gobiernos de los capitanes generales, Marqués de Torre Campo, Don Fernández Valdés Tamón, Don Gaspar de la Torre, é interino del Obispo de Nueva Segovia. 105–3–25.

1740: Duplicados de la causa criminal y prisión de Don Cristobal Pérez de Arroyo, fiscal de aquella audiencia, remitido por el gobernador. 106–4–23 to 28. 6 legajos.

1746–1767: Gobierno del capitán-general, Marqués de Obando. 105–3–26.

1752–1762: Gobiernos de los capitanes-generales, Don Pedro Manuel de Arandía y Don José de Crispo. 105–4–1.

1753: Correspondencia del Gobernador Marqués de Obando, dando noticias del estado de aquellas Islas. 105–4–2.

1755–1789: Expediente sobre expulsión de los Sangleyes ó Chinos Católicos por delitos de infidelidad y otros durante la ocupación de la plaza por los Ingleses. 107–2–27 to 30. 4 legajos.

1759–1821: Correspondencia con gobernadores. 105–4–3 to 4. 2 legajos.

1762–1766: Expediente de la reclamación hecha por Inglaterra de dos miliones de pesos capitulados en la toma de la plaza de Manila. 107–3–1 to 2. 2 legajos.

1765–1824: Informes sobre materias gubernativas. 105–3–13 to 14. 2 legajos.

1769–1780: Gobierno del Capitán-General Don Simón de Anda. 105–4–5.

1776–1787: Gobierno de los Capitanes-Generales Don José Vazco y Vargas y Don Felipe Veringuer de Marquina. 105–4–6.

1691–1819: Informe sobre el ramo de tributos y renumeración de Indios. 108–1–9.

1682: Materias de real hacienda. 107–3–12.

1733–1824: Materias gubernativas de la real hacienda. 107–3–11.

1751–1833: Expte. sobre bienes de difuntos. 107–3–9.

1755–1830: Cuentas de tributos, contribución directa y ramo á cargo de los corregidores y alcaldes mayores. 108–1–10 to 13. 4 legajos.

1759–1833: Cuentas de real hacienda. 107–7–25 to 32; 108–1–1 to 8. 16 legajos.

1762–1765: Expte. relativo al sitio y toma de Manila por los Ingleses. 107–3–3 to 6. 4 legajos.

1773–1821: Expedientes de provisiones de empleos de real hacienda. 107–3–13 to 14. 2 legajos.

1783: Expte. sobre avalúo de la alcaicería de San Fernando, manejo, ejercicio y facultades de su castellano y lo actuado contra Don Fernando de Mier y Noriega que fué el primero. 107–3–8.

1787–1849: Duplicados de superintendentes é intendentes de ejército y real hacienda. 107–5–15 to 31; 107–6–1 to 31; 107–7–1 to 21. 69 legajos.

1784–1787: Expediente sobre establicimiento de intendencias y subintendencias. 107–5–14.

1794: Expte. de Don Frco. Fernández Cendero, Alcalde Mayor y Capitán de Guerra de la provincia de Ilocos, sobre su residencia pendiente de informe de la audiencia. 106–5–4.

(b) *Ramo Eclesiástico.*

1579–1697: Cartas y expedientes del Arzobispo de Manila. 68–1–32 and 33. 2 legajos.

1569–1700: Cartas y expedientes de los misioneros de Filipinas. 68–1–37 to 41. 5 legajos.

1570–1696: Cartas y expedientes de personas eclesiásticas de Filipinas. 68–1–42 to 44. 3 legajos.

1586–1700: Cartas y expedientes del cabildo eclesiástico de Filipinas. 68–1–35 to 36. 2 legajos.

1597–1698: Cartas y expedientes de los obispos sufraganeos de Manila, á saber, Nueva Segovia, Nueva Cáceres, Santissimo Nombre de Jesús o Cebú. 68–1–34.

1626–1795: Reales cédulas y informes sobre diezmos. 108–5–24.

1681–1689: Testimonios de autos respectivos al Arzobispo de Manila y otros. 68–2–1 to 2. 2 legajos.

1692: Expte. sobre la extrañeza y prisión del Arzobispo de Manila Don Fray Felipe Pardo y discordias ocuridas entre las religiones de Santo Domingo y la Compañia de Jesus. 68–2–4 to 5. 2 legajos.

1702–1832: Consultas de materias y provisiones eclesiásticas. 108–5–21 to 22. 2 legajos.

1726–1815: Reales cédulas y informes sobre medias anatas y mesadas eclesiásticas. 108–5–19.

1751: El Gobernador Marqués de Obando da cuenta con testimonio de los informes que se han podido adquirir sobre el número de religiosos que hay en aquellas islas y de los que necesitan para la reducción de los indios gentiles. 108–6–27 to 28. 2 legajos.

1760: Expte. del Obispo de Cebú, gobernador interino de aquellas Yslas y el Arzobispo de Manila sobre en cual de los dos había de recaer el mando de ellas. 108–6–29.

1762: Expte. sobre embargo de bienes de Don Santiago de Orendaín y su mujer Doña María Dominga Arráez, vecinos de Manila, por deudas al ramo de bulas de la Cruzada y otros excesos. 108–7–18 to 19. 2 legajos.

1769: Pliegos remitidos al Consejo por el arzobispo para S. S. sobre el estado de curato y fundamentos de los regulares para eximirse de la jurisdicción del diocesano. 108–6–5 to 6. 2 legajos.

1772: Expte. sobre la remoción de los religiosos de S. Agustín de las doctrinas de la Provincia de Pampanga, secularización de curatos de aquellas Yslas y sujeción de las religiones al real patronato y visita de los ordinarios. 108–6–31 to 35. 5 legajos.

1777: Expte. sobre competencia entre el Arzobispo de Manila, Obispo Sufragano de Nueva Cáceres, vice-patrono real y fiscal de la real audiencia, por disposición al presbítero Don Vicente Ygnacio de Arroyo del curato de Santa Cruz. 108–6–36.

1778: Expte. sobre aprobación de las ordenanzas de la Casa de Misericordia de Manila é el permiso concedido para que esta pueda remitir sus cuentas sin intervención de la real audiencia. 106–5–8.

1778: Expte. de la real audiencia sobre el espolio del Arzobispo Don Manuel Antonio Rojo y demandas introducidas contra él. 108–7–1 to 2. 2 legajos.

1780: Cuatro exptes. unidos sobre pago de diezmo por los religiones y naturales de aquellas Yslas, sin embargo de no estar en practica . . . 108–7–3.

II. *Secretaría de Nueva España.*

(a) *Ramo Secular y Eclesiástico.*

1630–1759: Consultas y decretos originales. 68–2–8 to 12. 5 legajos.

1671–1756: Índices de la correspondencia del gobernador, audiencia, oficiales reales y sugetos particulares del distrito de aquella audiencia. 68–2–31.

(b) *Ramo Secular.*

1724: Expte. sobre el registro del galeón de Filipinas nombrado el Santo Cristo de Burgos que hizo viage el año 1723 desde el puerto de Cavite al de Acapulco. 68–6–11.

1728–1732: Expte. de la Hermandad de la Misericordia de Manila sobre amplificación de sus facultades y privilegios. 68–6–16.

1735–1741: Expte. sobre los 162,992 pesos que se sacaron del comercio. 68–6–23.

1739–1746: Testimonio de autos originados sobre la visita y composición de tierras encargadas al Oidor Don Pedro Calderón, del Consejo de S. M. 68–6–26.

1740–1744: Expte. sobre la prisión y causa criminal seguida contra Don Cristobal Pérez de Arroyo, fiscal de la Audiencia de Manila. 68–6–28 to 31. 4 legajos.

1741–1751: Exptes. y autos sobre la sublevación de los pueblos tagalos y otros por vejaciones recibidas de los religiosos de Santo Domingo y San Agustín, pacificados por el Oidor Pedro Calderón. 68–6–40 to 44. 5 legajos.

1743: Testimonio de autos de la visita que hizo el Oidor Don José Ygnacio de Arzadún, remitidos por la Audiencia de Manila. 68–3–32 to 35. 4 legajos.

1743–1753: Exptes. sobre la presa que hicieron los Ingleses del navío Covadonga y libertad de los oficiales que mandaba . . . 68–6–38 to 39. 2 legajos.

1745–1755:· Exptes. del subdelegado Don Pedro Calderón de la Barca sobre tierras. 68–6–45.

1752–1755: Expte. sobre las altercaciones sufridas por el comercio de Filipinas á causa de las novedades introducidas por el Gobernador Marqués de Obando. 68–6–50–51. 2 legajos.

1756–1758: Expte. sobre los excesos cometidos por el Gobernador Don Pedro Manuel de Arandía. 68–6–53.

1644–1760: Provisiones de plazas togados de la Audiencia de Manila. 69–1–1.

1654–1745: Testimonios de autos que se hallaron sin cartas de remisión entre los papeles del distrito de la Audiencia de Manila. 69–1–13 to 17. 5 legajos.

462   *Bibliography*

(c) *Ramo Eclesiástico.*

1660–1761: Cartas y expedientes de personas eclesiásticas del distrito de aquella audiencia. 69–1–24 to 29. 6 legajos.

1604–1696: Expedientes sobre la visita de los religiosos por los ordinarios. 69–1–30 to 32. 3 legajos.

1691–1696: Exptes. sobre que en las vacantes del arzobispado de Manila, gobierne el cabildo eclesiástico. 69–1–34.

1698–1704: Expediente sobre la resistencia hecha por las religiones á presentar sus títulos de las tierras y estancias. 69–1–37.

1702–1761: Cartas y expedientes del Arzobispo de Manila. 69–1–18 to 20. 3 legajos.

1704–1719: Expte. sobre causa formada á Fray Bartólome Marrón, de la Orden de Predicadores, por un manifiesto esto que imprimió y publicó sobre varios puntos de real patronato. 69–1–38.

1710–1730: Expte. sobre corregir las ordenanzas del Colegio Seminario de San Felipe, etc. 69–1–40.

1730–1740: Tres testimonios de autos pertenecientes á un expediente . . . del cabildo eclesiástico de Manila, sobre organización de boletas. 69–2–1.

1737–1746: Expte. sobre erección de un seminario para la educación de religiosos misioneros de la Orden de San Agustín. 69–2–3.

INDEX*

Acapulco, 67 *note* 42, 76–77, 77 *note* 57, 174.

Acuerdo, 23, 91, 91 *note* 37, 126, 129 *note* 27, 147, 162, 164, 189, 190, 195–196, 199, 200, 208, 210, 211, 213–220, 225, 240ff., 252–254, 269, 287, 293, 299, 301, 302, 315, 367, 375, 376, 387, 390, 400, 403, 427, 435; development of, in judicial matters, 214–215, in governmental and administrative matters, 215, in ecclesiastical matters, 367; *autos acordados*, 215–216; influence of, in reform measures (Constitution of 1812, government of the intendancy, etc.), 217; administrative action independent of governor, 217–218, evil effects of, 218; loss of power, 219–220.

Acuerdo de hacienda, 24, 52, 60.

Acuña, *see* Bravo de Acuña.

Ad interim, administration, 304–361; laws authorizing, 305, 310–314; history of, in South America, 305–308, in New Spain, 308–312, in Philippines, 312–314, 316–338; laws regarding in the *Recopilación*, 314–316; failure of the audiencia, 337–338, 358–359, 361; failure of the church, 359–360; plan of succession, 356-358. *See also* Audiencia of Manila; Lima; Mexico; Peru.

Adelantado, 11 *note* 6, 162 *note* 3.

Administración, Consejo de, 220, 220 *note* 80.

Agriculture in the Philippines, committee of audiencia charged with encouragement of, 186.

Aguilar y Ponce de León, Rafael, governor, 142ff., 142 *note* 60, 300, 396 *note* 85.

Albay, 382.

Alcabala, 44, 44 *note* 19, 162.

Alcalde, 9, 10 *note* 3, 11 *note* 6; judges with criminal jurisdiction in Lima and Mexico, 18.

Alcalde del crimen, 16 *note* 20, 86, 86 *note* 11, 88, 203; authorized to try cases of strangers, 114.

Alcalde del Parián, 248, 248 *note* 45, 250.

Alcalde mayor, 53ff., 100, 116, 135, 157, 196, 218, 282, 287, 300, 309 *note* 12, 346–347, 381, 396 *note* 85, 417; qualifications, powers, duties, 11, 26–30, 218; in the Philippines, 33; supervision over *encomenderos*, 53; conduct toward Indians, 53, 212; jurisdiction, 86, 116; *residencia*, 129, 148–149, 152–155; administration of estates, 174; method of appointment, 200, 201, 202; charged with trial of Indian cases, 212; regulations of *acuerdo* concerning, 215; supervision of collection of ecclesiastical tithes, 392 *note* 72.

Alcalde ordinario, jurisdiction, 26, 30, 71, 86, 116, 207, 237, 248; in the Philippines, 33–34; *residencia*, 129.

*Univ. Calif. Publ. Hist., vol. 9.

Index

Index

Index

Jesuits, in Philippines, 68, 266, 268, 271 note 13, 272, 276, 278 note 28, 241, 280, 354, 386, 388–389, note 66, 395, 418ff., 426.

Juan, Jorge, authority on Spanish colonization, 130 note 28.

Judges, see *alcalde, corregidor, juez de, oidor, residencia,* etc.

Juez conservador, 166 and note 16, 380 note 41.

Juez letrado, 13.

Juez de difuntos, 170ff., 172–173, 264.

Junta de guerra, 22 note 32, 113–114, 114 note 79, 232, 233, 234.

Junta ordinaria de la real hacienda, 162, 162 note 6.

Junta superior de la real hacienda, 162 note 7.

Justice, administration of, before establishment of audiencia, 40; in provinces, 26–31, 32; under audiencia, 49, 56ff., 71–74, 79, 80, 83–120, 137–138, 153–154, 196–197, 210 and note 54, 218 note 78, 227, 234ff., 255ff., 259–303, 307–309, 310, 315, 317, 362, 382, 401, 410ff., 442, 444. *See also* Audiencia, judicial functions, military jurisdiction; Audiencia, president of; Chinese; Governor (captaingeneral); *Guerra, auditor de, junta de,* etc.

King, officials appointed by, 200; final pardoning power, 210.

King's Fifth, see *Quinto.*

Ladrones (Marianas Islands), 127, 144; galleons instructed to stop at, 222.

Lanza, 165 note 11.

La Plata, audiencia of, 17, 20, 21 note 32.

Laudín, Fray Alonso, 414.

Lavezares, Guido de, 37.

Laws of the Indies, see *Recopilación de leyes de las Indias.*

Leandro de Viana, Francisco, *fiscal,* 15 note 18, 182, 217, 300, 345 note 85, 354, 407.

Legaspi, Gerónimo de, governor, 37, 326, 326 note 48.

Le Gentil de la Galaisière, Joseph Hyacinthe, 195, 381.

Legislation, see *Acuerdo.*

León, Manuel de, governor, 333, 434ff., 434 note 64.

Letrado, 13, 74, 238.

Leyte, *encomiendas* in, 110.

Lieutenant-governor, 316, 317.

Lima, audiencia of, 18–21, 86, 117 note 88; assumption of government by (*ad interim* rule), 305–306.

Lino de Espeleta, Miguel de, bishop and governor, 139 note 54, 341–342, 341 note 73; *espolio,* 404 note 104.

Lizárraga, Conde de, governor, 128, 335.

Loarca, Miguél de, *encomendero,* 35 note 4.

Louisiana, under audiencia of Santo Domingo, 19.

López de Legaspi, Miguel de, governor, 37, 260 note 1.

Luzón, 35 note 4, 243, 248, 310.

Macao, rival to Manila, 62.

Madras, 172 note 31, 206.

Maestre de campo, 231, 336, 338, 369 note 7.

Maldonado, see Rivera Maldonado.

Malines, Law of, 92–93, 94, 95, 106, 107, 108.

Manila, captured by British, 343, 344, 349.

Marianas Islands, 127, 144, 222.

Marique de Lara, Sabiniano, 330.

Marina, auditor de, appointment, jurisdiction, duties, 233.

Marquina, *see* Beringuer de Marquina.

Index

Index